Deep in Our Hearts

Constance Curry

Joan C. Browning

Dorothy Dawson Burlage

Penny Patch

Theresa Del Pozzo

Sue Thrasher

Elaine DeLott Baker

Emmie Schrader Adams

Casey Hayden

Deep in Our Hearts

NINE WHITE WOMEN IN THE FREEDOM MOVEMENT

The University of Georgia Press ATHENS & LONDON

© 2000 by the University of Georgia Press
Athens, Georgia 30602
All rights reserved
Designed by Erin Kirk New
Set in 10 on 14 Electra by G&S Typesetters
Printed and bound by Maple-Vail Book Manufacturing Group
The paper in this book meets the guidelines for
permanence and durability of the Committee on
Production Guidelines for Book Longevity of the
Council on Library Resources.

Printed in the United States of America
04 03 02 01 00 C 5 4 3 2 1

Library of Congress Cataloging-in-Publication Data

Deep in our hearts : nine white women in the Freedom
Movement / Constance Curry . . . [et al.].
  p. cm.
 Includes index.
 ISBN 0-8203-2266-0 (alk. paper)
 1. Women civil rights workers—United States—Biography.
 2. White women—United States—Biography.
 3. Afro-Americans—Civil rights—History—
 20th century. 4. Civil rights movements
 —United States—History—20th century.
 5. United States—Race relations. 6. Southern States—
 Race relations. I. Curry, Constance.

E185.98.A1 D44 2000
323'.092'273—dc21   00-034334

British Library Cataloging-in-Publication Data available

Contents

Foreword

BARBARA RANSBY

Deep in Our Hearts is a powerful collection of nine essays that takes us into the lives of a group of young white women who came of age in the era of the civil rights movement, participated actively and passionately in that movement, and were, in many ways, transformed by it.

Although each of the writers has some connection to the Student Non-violent Coordinating Committee (SNCC), which was formed in 1960, beyond that their stories are quite distinct. The diversity of their voices belies any simple one-dimensional profile of whites in the movement. They are not all upper-class students from elite East Coast schools, as the participants in Freedom Summer are sometimes portrayed. Nor are they "red diaper" babies of communists and radicals. Rather, they are from diverse backgrounds — Irish, Jewish, Italian, and southern — and they experienced both the pains of poverty and the comforts of middle-class lifestyles. They come from families that openly treated blacks as subordinates, and from families that strove for social justice and instilled that value in their daughters. It is an eclectic group, and the richness of the collection lies in both its diversity and the common vision that the authors ultimately came to share.

These first-person accounts by white women activists represent a critical voice, yet one that has not been often heard. Following the last days of the Student Nonviolent Coordinating Committee and the emergence of the Black

Power phase of the Freedom Movement, many white participants were reluctant to outline their own interpretations of and emotions about the movement. This book breaks that silence. We hear in these nine voices memories of "dazzling clarity" and profound confusion, idealism, and even disillusionment.

The stories told here involve personal tales of fear and courage, familial rejection and familial support, romance and loneliness, and fear and isolation, all juxtaposed against an enormous sense of purpose. Overall, these stories defy another stereotype about white movement activists in the 1960s: that they either burned out, sold out, or tuned out. These women had periodic setbacks, disappointments, and even moments of despair, to be sure, but some thirty years later what comes through most strongly is a profound sense of pride and continued commitment to the values they embraced as young women in their late teens and early twenties. Most of them, moreover, have continued to live out those values in one way or another.

The map of these nine lives also highlights the networks, intersections, and overlaps between different sectors and wings of the civil rights movement. These women, as a group, were loosely connected to a wide variety of organizations and campaigns: the SNCC, YWCA, Southern Regional Council, American Friends Service Committee, Council of Federated Organizations, U.S. National Student Association, Southern Conference Educational Fund, and Southern Student Organizing Committee. Their stories reveal the intricate ties between multiple left and liberal organizations engaged in civil rights and civil liberties work in this period.

The collective history presented in this anthology is a tremendously important and timely contribution to our understanding of race, gender, class, and social change as these apply to the civil rights movement. But what exactly do we learn by viewing the movement through the lens of these nine white women? What are the lessons we can extract from these stories, as we struggle to understand the past and reenvision the future? In a sense, this collection is a narrative addendum to the work of scholars like David Roediger, Richard Delgado, and Noel Ignatiev, who have encouraged us to interrogate the historical and cultural meaning of whiteness, and particularly the social construction of white identities and white supremacist thought. Today, the popular and academic discourse about race is not simply one that examines black identity and consciousness; rather, it includes other peoples of color and whites as well. Similarly, feminist scholars and activists have begun to analyze and critique gender identity not only in terms of women's lives and histories but also through an examination of masculinity. What is important and different about this collection, however, is that, while much work on white racial consciousness has focused on how racism has shaped and impacted white racial and class identity, the voices of these nine activists illustrate the ways in which white racial identities were, at a particular moment and place in time, profoundly informed by a set of explicitly antiracist politics.

The dominant culture of the white South did not intend to produce a Connie Curry, a Joan Browning, a Dorothy Dawson Burlage, a Sue Thrasher, or a Casey Hayden. Indeed, these young white women created an identity for themselves in the Jim Crow South of the 1960s that was in many ways antithetical to the status quo. It was transgressive and in many ways dangerous. These historical actors not only betrayed the dominant script in terms of who and what they were encouraged to be, but they actively constructed a different identity and a different mission for their lives. Their energies and sacrifices, in the context of a larger movement, not only helped to reshape the face of American race relations, but also enriched the legacy of a minority white antiracist tradition.

Under the leadership and guidance of black activist and veteran organizer Ella Baker, SNCC, in particular, became a cultural and political experiment in which racial, class, and, to a lesser extent, gender hierarchies were turned on their heads. In a social context that cast blacks in a servile role and demanded unmitigated deference to white authority, a small cadre of young white activists chose to play a largely supportive role in a black-led movement that rejected that arrangement entirely, celebrating instead the wisdom and leadership of those at the very bottom of the social, economic, and racial hierarchy in America. It was not Ph.D.s and legal experts who were the heroes and heroines of SNCC and its sister organizations, but ordinary black southerners like Mona Miles, Victoria Gray, Amzie Moore, and Mae Bertha Carter. And in a social and political milieu that distrusted any white person who dared to treat a black person as a human being, let alone an equal, this handful of antiracist whites became "race traitors" in the best sense of the word. They embraced African American men and women as leaders, mentors, friends, and family.

Their choices were not easy ones. Connie Curry tells of being evicted for having a black SNCC activist to her apartment. Casey Hayden essentially put her life on hold to work full time for the movement, living in black neighborhoods and openly defying segregation on a daily basis in a society where such violations could be deadly. And Penny Patch recalls being chased by a white mob and shot at in Panola County, Mississippi. But in these and other recollections of the women represented here, there are few regrets.

When we incorporate these women's stories into the history of the American South and the nation in the mid–twentieth century, simplistic notions of racial profiles are shattered. We can no longer construct a South made up entirely of working-class "rednecks" or middle-class southern belles. Instead a much more hopeful vision emerges as we watch one small minority of white activists build bridges, cross borders, forge new identities, and envision new possibilities for the future.

While these compelling narratives illustrate the power of human agency and indicate some of the variables in the drama that was the 1960s, still these nine women were not wholly self-made and the 1960s was not the start of the story. Their accounts remind us of a longer and larger tradition of white antiracist activism and an older generation of white antiracist southerners — racial renegades, we might call them. In addition to finding inspiration in black elders like Ella Baker, Septima Clark, and Fannie Lou Hamer, white antiracists of the 1960s were also the progeny of people like Miles Horton of Highlander Folk School; Lillian Smith, a progressive white southern writer and activist; Anne Braden of the Southern Conference Educational Fund; and Howard Zinn, a leftist white historian who began his career at historically black Spelman College. Both Zinn and Braden continue their progressive activism to this day.

Deep in Our Hearts gives us another lens through which to view the politics of race and gender in the civil rights movement. It also probes the themes of growth, discovery, friendship, and courage, and it is a priceless pedagogical tool. Invariably, when I teach a course on the black Freedom Movement and show footage of violent attacks on predominantly black protesters, one of my white students will come to me after class and express remorse and shame over what "his or her people" have done to "my people." I usually reassure them that politics are determined in our heads and our hearts, not our genes and our lineage. Fortunately, my white students can choose to embrace and carry on the tradition of Curry, Browning, Hayden, Thrasher, Patch, Del Pozzo, Adams, Burlage, and Baker, rather than helplessly apologize for the likes of those pro-segregationists who defended white supremacy and underwrote Black oppression. The real gift of these stories is a more optimistic legacy for a new generation of blacks and whites as they navigate the ever-volatile path of racial relations into the twenty-first century and, hopefully, take up the challenge that 1960s activists did of trying to make the world a better and more humane place.

Preface

These are our stories of the costly times we wouldn't have missed for the world, and of the people and places and events that filled them. We speak to several questions: Why us? Why did we, of all the white women growing up in our hometowns, cross the color line in the days of segregation and join the Southern Freedom Movement of the sixties? How did we find our way? What happened to us there? How did we leave, and what did we take with us? And, especially, what was it like?

We are answering these questions. We are telling our stories: The sordid details of segregation. The muddy country roads and the tiny rural churches. The handmade picket signs that fell apart in the rain, the ink running down our arms. The nighttime road trips under blankets on the floor so the cops wouldn't see a white girl in the car. The tattered copy of *The Golden Notebook* passed around among us, and our own germinal writing about gender. That cold, bare room where we counted freedom ballots. The segregated court-rooms and dismal jail cells. The white Baptist preacher's story about a feather. Mama Dolly's farm. The Batesville okra coop. The intensity of our daily work. The internal politics. Our friendships. Our loves. Our strategies. The danger. The camaraderie and the laughs. The losses.

During the spring of 1960, seventy thousand young people, almost entirely from African-American colleges, universities, and high schools across the South, participated in civil disobedience against segregation. Out of that wild and spontaneous activity arose an organization, the Student Nonviolent Co-ordinating Committee. SNCC mushroomed, growing from an unstaffed, un-funded committee of local sit-in leaders to a cadre of organizers, sometimes called the "shock troops" of the movement. On ten dollars a week these folks moved into local communities, living with local people, organizing around public accommodations and voting rights, running citizenship schools and mass meetings. Staff grew to twenty and then to one hundred and twenty, working in the toughest counties of the Black Belt South, harassed, arrested, beaten, unprotected and unpublicized, intent on cracking the caste system that had been in place for hundreds of years.

The young men and women of SNCC provided inspiration and opportunity for our involvement in the civil rights movement. We joined them in struggle. One of us was expelled from college for going to a black church, and another was the first white woman in a rural SNCC voter registration project. One of us paid SNCC's phone bill in the early days out of foundation money given for more conservative purposes, and others organized white southern students in support of the Freedom Movement. Some of us were there at the beginning, sitting in with our friends, and on the Freedom Ride to Albany, Georgia. We were also there later, canvassing for voter registration and facing the violence it incurred; challenging the seating of the lily-white Mississippi Democrats at the national Democratic convention; sitting through endless staff meetings, the air thick with cigarette smoke. All of us experienced the joy of lifting our voices to sing freedom songs, and the fellowship and hope of an interracial movement for justice and equality.

We are all very different: southern and northern; rural and urban; state uni-versity and Ivy League; middle class, working class, and poor. We were moved to our radical activities in various ways: by Marxism, Christian existentialism, and immigrant folk wisdom; by our grandmothers and the Constitution; by Thoreau and Dumas; by living on a kibbutz; by African freedom fighters; and by a Deep South upbringing. When we began our work on this book, some of us were uncomfortable writing as part of an all-white or all-female group. Oth-ers didn't feel they fit in the group, that their experiences were too different. Still others felt that their stories were not important enough to appear in print. We moved forward, however, by examining what has been written by others about our lives and times, arriving at the clear perception that no one could tell our stories but we ourselves.

We speak in varied styles, tones, and voices, and each of us speaks only for herself. But we all speak concretely and intimately. We are coming from our hearts. We have tried, in telling our stories, to be true to the best of what we learned in the movement: to be brave and kind and radical and honest.

Our book is about girls growing up in a revolutionary time and place. It is about love and politics and the transcendence of racial barriers. We offer this work to enrich the chronicle of a social movement that forever changed the country and our lives. It was our privilege to have been there.

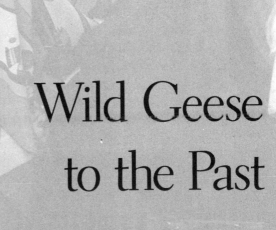

Wild Geese
to the Past

CONSTANCE CURRY

I have been acutely aware of my Irish roots as far back as memory allows. My sister Eileen and I knew early on that our mother and father had been born in Belfast, Northern Ireland, of Protestant heritage, had come to the United States in the 1920s, had married and settled in Paterson, New Jersey, where Daddy worked in the textile business as a silk dyer and where Eileen and I were born — though our family continued to move around until finally settling in Greensboro, North Carolina, in 1943. There were just the four of us — no relatives. I remember singing "Over the river and through the woods to grandmother's house we go," feeling sad and not knowing why. Every Christmas, Eileen and I received by mail either linen handkerchiefs or whimsical colored pictures of dogs or cats with small rectangular calendars attached at the bottom. These were gifts from our Grandmother Curry, Daddy's mother in Belfast. We heard Daddy speak of Uncle Bob, his older brother, or Aunt Winnie, his sister, also in Belfast, and I remember Daddy getting newsletters in the mail from Uncle George, his younger brother, a missionary in Africa. I also see Daddy in 1940, sitting at the dining room table, crying, letter in hand telling him his father had died. (Daddy had not been able to get back to Ireland since his departure in 1925, although he later visited several times before his own death.)

In the fourth grade I cut out shamrocks, colored them green, and pinned them all over my brown coat to wear to school on Saint Patrick's Day. Later in

college I wrote a paper titled "Sinn Fein and the Easter Rebellion." The opening sentence tells of the Easter Rising of 1916 against England, "condemned
as a bloodstained failure which came to be regarded as a signal success." The
paper closes with the lines, "The sacrifice of the leaders of the rebellion had
set Ireland's soul free again. They had said 'Our blood will rebaptize and revi-
talize our land' and the prophecy was fulfilled." I read William Butler Yeats
and other Irish poets and embraced the words from "The Rebel" by Irish revolutionary Padraic Pearse:

> And I say to my people's masters:
> Beware, Beware of the thing that is coming.
> Beware of the risen people,
> Who shall take what ye would not give.

I have often thought that these lines could have come straight from the Freedom Movement of the 1960s. It is clear to me that the Irish struggle got planted
deep in my heart and soul at an early age, and that its lessons and music and
poetry were easily transferred to the southern freedom struggle.

In 1996, Eileen and I decided to take a trip to New Jersey to "reclaim the past."
Since my mother, Constance Hazleton Richmond Curry, had died in 1957, at
the age of fifty-five, and my father, Ernest Curry, had died in 1971, at the age
of seventy-two, this "reclaiming" of our early years was difficult. On the trip,
one mission was to find the grave of our brother. Growing up, I think I was
vaguely aware that my parents' firstborn, James Curry, had died in infancy;
certainly I recall a photograph of a baby dressed in white, lying in a coffin.
Eileen and I wonder now why our parents spoke so little about him in our
presence. We were not even sure of his name, and had no idea of his date of
birth or death. But we found him. He was sixteen days old when he died. The
cause of death on his death certificate reads "traumation of head and neck
during birth causing convulsions." He is buried in an unmarked grave in
Cedar Lawn Cemetery in Paterson. Standing beside that tiny plot of grass
brought sadness as thick as the June heat.

As we women get older, we seem to walk in our mother's shoes more and
more, and I am keenly aware now of the tragedy and pain that stalked Hazle
Curry. Mother was the oldest of three daughters and was only fourteen when

she lost her own mother to cancer. Her two younger sisters were taken to live with relatives. She stayed in their homeplace in Belfast and took care of her father, who was an alcoholic. She was smart and well read, and some now-yellowed certificates show various schools in Belfast from which she graduated. She was working as a stenographer when she met my father at a Boy Scout dance, and was considered by some "fast" because she smoked and went to dances a lot.

My father sailed from Belfast to New York in 1925. Mother followed him the next year. They were married in Brooklyn and then struggled to make a life in the rough, tough textile town of Paterson. After one trip back to Ireland in 1932, Mother never again saw any of her own or of Daddy's family. Eileen says that she now believes Mother may have been chronically depressed, but I only recall a pervading sadness.

Mother was never sick. She was a great cook, seamstress, cat lover, card player, antique collector, reader of books, and most of all she loved my father deeply, which was not difficult to do. Her favorite flower was the lily of the valley and her favorite hymn was "The Old Rugged Cross." I am grateful now to my mother for her legacy to me — her lessons of independence and non-conformity — but when I was growing up her resistance to acting like "other mothers" bothered me. She refused to go to church regularly because she considered most people who went to church every Sunday "hypocrites, who wouldn't give a crust of bread to someone at their back door." She brooked no pretense from her daughters or our friends. She once told a girlfriend of mine that she should be ashamed for refusing to date a boy who didn't have a car and planned to take her to the movies on the bus. She didn't care about country clubs or what part of town you were from. And to the amazement of the few women friends she did have, she paid Social Security benefits for Sadie Belle Thompson, the black woman who came to iron and help clean once a week. This was unheard of in Greensboro in the 1950s. When Eileen and I were unsure about something, Mother would quote Shakespeare, always the same lines: "This above all, to thine own self be true, and it must follow as the night the day, thou canst not then be false to any man."

At times I feel sad about my lack of understanding of Mother back then and of my obvious favoritism toward my outgoing and popular father. Daddy was extremely handsome, very funny, hardworking, and devoted to his family. He could fix anything, from electrical and plumbing problems to broken dolls and necklaces. I used to think he could read my mind. People always told me that I was the "spitting image" of my father, and I was mystified for many young years by that phrase. Mother often told me that I would never find a man like my father, and I sometimes marvel at how prophetic that has been for both Eileen and me, who have not married. All in all we were a close-knit, rather simple family of four, with backyard badminton and croquet, a big brick cookout place, and a basement with ping pong and a jukebox that played for free "I'll Walk the Line" by Johnny Cash. Our friends were always welcome. Ice cream from Guilford Dairy on certain weekend nights, one-week vacations at Myrtle Beach, and a long line of wonderful cats and kittens were among our simple pleasures.

We moved six times in my early years, following the burgeoning textile industry until, in 1943, seventeen years after his immigration, lasting employment for my father came with Burlington Mills in North Carolina. All of that moving around was a lot for a child's early years, leading to fleeting rather than patterned memories. This, plus being the daughter of Irish immigrants, may have left me feeling different and sometimes wondering just where I "fit in." My family was living in Greensboro when I left for college. My parents are buried there, Eileen still lives there, and I consider it home, I guess.

During our 1996 trip to Paterson Eileen and I went to find the house on Pearl Street where we were born, but it was gone. Eileen tells me that there used to be black families on the block and that we had played with them. I don't remember that, but I do remember Ernest Green and another black student in my first-grade class in Hawthorne, New Jersey. These early associations partially insulated me from the white racial prejudice that pervaded the South when we moved there in the 1940s. The scourge of "being different" ourselves was clear then, because for a long time we were designated "yankees," and probably Republicans. At that time most white southerners were "dyed-in-the-wool" Democrats, and preservation of segregation and the southern way of life was their platform. I remember Eileen telling us that a boy at school had said that his father wouldn't vote for Jesus Christ for president, if he were running as a Republican.

My parents were not political liberals and never preached to us about racial equality or social injustices, but they were essentially kind and fair-minded people, probably happy to be in the United States. They were not obsessed with race or class issues, and they let Eileen and me form our own opinions about the world around us. And no matter where we were living, we somehow hooked up with whatever church was closest to our house: Lutheran in Paterson, Quaker in Poughkeepsie, New York, and finally Presbyterian in Greensboro, the church of Daddy's upbringing in Ireland. Eileen and I went to church with him and to Sunday school most of our young lives. I believed what I learned at Sunday school, vacation Bible school, and church camp. In regular school, the Declaration of Independence, the Constitution, and the Bill of Rights loomed large for me — noble and inspiring documents on which my country rested.

I remember first "speaking out" about race when I was in the fourth grade in Greensboro. We were going down the cafeteria lunch line, and a tall boy named Douglas referred to one of the women servers as a "nigger." I told him he shouldn't do that, that the woman was just as good as his mother. Later on during play period, he knocked me down and I fell into a puddle. I had on a new brown and yellow raincoat, and the mud spattered on the yellow.

Probably the most enlightening and broadening experience of my teenage life was attending the United States National Student Association (USNSA) congress in Bloomington, Indiana. It was the summer of 1952, and I had just finished my freshman year at Agnes Scott College, a small Presbyterian women's college in Decatur, Georgia. I must admit that my entry into this NSA world was not entirely from noble motives.

During the fall quarter of my freshman year a handsome, blond young man named Pete Dunlap came over from Georgia Tech to see if any Agnes Scott students were interested in working on a news service to exchange information and ideas about college and university life. It was to be called the International News Center (INC) and would include sharing information with students in other countries. Those interested would go to Georgia Tech for regular meetings to discuss the plans and program. "Great way to meet interesting men," I thought. I had not had much fun at the fraternity parties where we "Scotties" were piled into buses to meet the rushees at Georgia Tech and Emory University, nearby men's colleges.

As it turned out, the INC meetings were interesting — as were the men — and I found out that the INC was sponsored by the USNSA, which was founded in 1947 as an association of student governments in U.S. colleges and universities. The preamble of the NSA constitution stated a primary goal of guaranteeing "to all people, because of their inherent dignity as individuals, equal rights and possibilities for primary, secondary, and higher education, regardless of sex, race, religion, political belief, or economic circumstances." The association's main activity each year was the National Student Congress, held each summer for ten days in August on a midwest campus.

In the spring of my freshman year, Pete Dunlap asked if anyone at our INC meeting was interested in representing our group at the national NSA congress to be held in Bloomington. I immediately raised my hand. I later discovered that Agnes Scott student government had joined NSA early on and was one of the few white member schools in the Deep South. I remember some vague talk about NSA being a "commie front," especially because of its early pro-integration and academic freedom resolutions, but I thought to myself, who cares? My first congress was a gathering of five hundred student leaders — fascinating young people. And the men — oh brave new world! They were so smart, they talked fast, they were funny, and they cared. Such passion in the debates on universal military training, the eighteen-year-old vote, nuclear disarmament, and other issues. I can still recall their names and remember wondering how I could have so many instant crushes in one ten-day period. My euphoria was certainly enhanced by these guys' flattering attention to an eighteen-year-old woman from the South. They delighted in my southern accent, and were somewhat surprised to find my interest in the issues as passionate as theirs.

The structure of NSA called for regional groupings of member college student governments. The regions, chaired by students elected at the national congress, were to carry on NSA activities and hold related conferences during the academic year. In August of 1953 I was elected chair of the Great Southern Region, which stretched eastward from Texas through Arkansas, Oklahoma, Louisiana, Mississippi, Alabama, Florida, and Georgia. It was geographically the largest region in NSA but had the fewest member schools. Suspect to many white southern colleges since its inception, NSA lost some members, including Emory and Georgia Tech, after the 1954 Supreme Court decision declaring the "separate but equal" concept unconstitutional. NSA remained militant in its stand for integration, and it became necessary to lump our few members in the Deep South into this one huge region. I believe that Agnes Scott was the only white southern member school in the region for some time, while More-house, Clark, Arkansas AM&N, and several black colleges in Louisiana re-mained faithful members. Undaunted by the challenge, I was thrilled to be chair of the region and remember clearly laboring into the night in the base-ment of "Main," our central campus building. My "office," provided by the dean's office at my insistence, was a janitor's closet, lit by a bulb that hung on a cord from the ceiling, and it held two cardboard file boxes, a small table, and a chair.

By late fall 1953 I had been able to organize a regional meeting. Segregation was still the law, and the Luckie Street YMCA in downtown Atlanta was the only place that would run the risk of giving us a room for an integrated meeting. I believe the moment when the consequences of racial segregation first hit me personally was lunch hour at that Saturday meeting. It was against the law for blacks and whites to eat together, so the YMCA could not permit a lunch gath-ering. When noon came, the black delegates, some of whom were my friends from the national congresses, walked down the steps of the Y and headed to-ward Auburn Avenue to the black restaurants. The rest of us walked down the steps and headed in the other direction. I realized then that segregation took away *my* personal freedom as surely as if I were bound by invisible chains.

In February 1996 I was reminded of that Atlanta meeting. I was in New York on a book signing tour and had lunch with Babatunde Olatunji, whom I had not seen in forty-two years. Baba is an internationally known musician and drummer. When I first met him, he was an exchange student from Nigeria, at Morehouse College in Atlanta. He had been elected student body president of Morehouse—an unusual feat for a foreign student at that time. Baba was part of the group who walked the other way for lunch. Later that year, we both attended the 1953 NSA congress at Ohio State. Back in Atlanta, we had some "undercover" meetings with our few interested colleagues. We had strong feel-ings for each other, but after graduation went our separate ways. We never forgot each other, though, and that night in New York, after our lunch to-gether, I cried over the memories evoked by the reunion—our clear-eyed be-liefs and optimism that we could change anything.

Another good thing about being NSA regional chairman was that I served on the national executive committee. That involved going to a meeting right after Christmas, which in the winter of 1954 was held at the University of Chicago.

Aside from being colder than I have ever been, I remember sitting in the student union having coffee and talking with several men on the committee. This absolutely stunning, long-haired woman without makeup, dressed completely in black, walked by our table, and we all turned to watch her. I asked the men what it was that made her so alluring, and they replied that she looked "so, so, well . . . mysterious." When I got back to Agnes Scott in January, I entered *my* mysterious stage. I didn't curl my hair, I wore no lipstick, I attempted to waft when I walked, and I donned my one black sweater every day. But the main thing was, I didn't talk much; I just looked into the distance. Within a few days it became clear that my behavior wasn't having the desired effect. I gave it up when several good friends told me that I needed to go to the infirmary.

For years nothing could stop me from making it to the NSA congresses. In the summer of 1954, after an emergency appendectomy in Paris, I flew directly to the NSA congress at the University of Wisconsin. I had been on the Experiment in International Living, was about to fly to Ireland to visit my relatives for the first time, and ended up at the American Hospital in Paris. In his usual supportive style, my father met my plane in New York, got me through customs in a hurry, warned me about adhesion, and put me on the plane to Madison. I don't think my mother and father every really understood what this "NSA" was. They just knew I loved the meetings and all the activities, and that was enough.

Unable to cut the cord, during my Fulbright year in France I represented NSA at an international meeting in Alsace-Lorraine in 1955. In the summer of 1956 I came back to the NSA congress as translator for the French student delegation.

That fall I went to New York, to Columbia University Graduate School. In March 1957 I was meeting Daddy at the Eastside Airline Terminal and looking forward to some time with him during a business visit. We were startled by the voice page at the terminal for us to call home. We called and reached Eileen. Mother had died that afternoon of a coronary occlusion, in, of all places, the movie theater. She was only fifty-five, and I was only twenty-four. It has just been in the past few years that I have been able to fully realize what "only twenty-four" meant. As I have listened to my friends talk about their mothers dying after long lives, I have been struck by how young I was when I lost mine and how ill equipped I was to mother myself. I have also realized that with no other role models and little practice in being "grown up" myself, in the sixties I was often thrust into a mothering role as an "adult" advisor to the Student Nonviolent Coordinating Committee (SNCC) and as the NSA seminar director. After Mother's death I left Columbia and went back to Greensboro to be with Daddy and Eileen. But we were from the "stiff upper lip—carry on" line, and five months later I was back in New York.

I had stayed in touch with NSA while at Columbia, and it was through old connections that I got my job as field secretary for the Collegiate Council for the United Nations (CCUN) in the fall of 1957. Allard K. Lowenstein had been president of NSA in 1950–51, but he returned for most of the national congresses, and we were friends. He was close to Eleanor Roosevelt, who had helped found the American Association for the United Nations (AAUN), and she had asked him to help recruit colleges for the youth branch of the association. Al served for several years, then called me one day in Greensboro in the late summer of 1957 and asked me to come to New York for an interview to succeed him as CCUN national field secretary.

For my interview, Eileen, who had been a New York fashion model, fitted me out in a very stylish gray dress with small black checks, red leather pumps, an elegant red leather purse, and soft-toned gray earrings. I will never forget the comment of the AAUN executive director who interviewed me: "With a chin like yours, you are bound to do a good job." This was the first time I realized that my very determined chin, often likened to a lurgan spade (a tool used in Ireland for digging up peat) and long a source of some pain on my part, could be an asset. I served for the next two years and traveled the forty-eight states, recruiting colleges to join the CCUN, organizing model United Nations meetings, and trying to combat the prejudice and anti-UN feeling that pervaded some parts of the country. In Texas, large billboards read, "GET THE U.S. OUT OF THE U.N." or "IMPEACH EARL WARREN," a Supreme Court justice considered by some to be too far to the left. A vivid memory of this period is of Eleanor Roosevelt walking down the hall to her AAUN office in New York. She would walk right past our college branch office, and I can remember the uncontrollable urge to stand up—in fact, I did on several occasions. I was included in one Christmas party where Eleanor Roosevelt read portions of Dickens's "A Christmas Carol."

My travels in the field took me to campuses in thirty-six states, including many all-black institutions. I have a clear memory, after an afternoon meeting, of a Friday-night dance at Arkansas AM&N, a black university in Pine Bluff. I stood — the only white person to be seen — talking to a history professor, watching the lights and the dancing couples, listening to the music, and wondering if anyone would ask me to dance. The thought "What am I doing here?" passed fleetingly through my head. But by 1960, both my CCUN work with students and my experiences with NSA had paved the way for me to continue working in the civil rights movement. I was used to being the only or one of few white women in the room.

During my CCUN years, I was aware of the work that NSA was doing in the South. Ray Farabee, from the University of Texas, had been elected NSA president in 1957—the first from the Deep South. He strongly believed that many southern white college students were different from their parents and that with exposure to another set of values and encouragement from like-minded people they could be rallied to launch the tides of social change. He also believed that black students were as isolated and fearful of integration as many whites. He wanted to bring young people of both races together for a period of study about the South and what had led to its contradictory and oppressive social and political structures. Ray assembled a star-studded regional advisory committee of southern professors, ministers, activists, newspaper editors, and civil rights leaders, and submitted a proposal to the Marshall Field Foundation in New York. In 1958 the foundation gave a grant of $10,000 to fund the first Southern Student Human Relations Seminar. The idea was to choose eighteen students from black and white southern colleges and bring them in early August to a three-week intensive study of human relations with a curriculum on all phases of the South, including its history, religion, economics, and culture. Experts in each subject area were brought in to lecture, and the participants were assigned books to read and papers to write. A seminar director and a consultant were there for the entire period. At the end of the seminar, the students stayed on for the NSA congress, which brought exposure to even broader ideas and association with students from other parts of the country and the rest of the world. If nothing else, participants learned about the insularity of the "closed society" they inhabited, and they felt a little less isolated in their desire to change that segregated world. After the second seminar in 1959, NSA convinced Field that the idea was working, that the seeds of change were indeed bearing fruit; they asked for a grant not only to fund a third seminar for 1960 but also to start a full-time program based in Atlanta. In December 1959, Field funded for one year the NSA Southern Student Human Relations Project, now known as the Southern Project. I came back south as its first director.

I am often asked how I "got involved" in the civil rights movement, and it's a difficult question to answer. When it comes to 1960, however, I have a specific response: it was a matter of being in the right place at the right time. In December 1959 I found an apartment on Adair Avenue, and Donna McGinty, my college roommate, moved in with me and became the assistant at the project. With the help of the Southern Regional Council, one of the first agencies working for racial equality, I moved into a small office at 41 Exchange Place, S.E. The building housed other "human relations" agencies, a fact that often prompted us to joke about "one bomb destroying half the Atlanta support of the movement."

My first job was to convene the initial meeting of the extraordinary Southern Advisory Committee that I had inherited from previous years of NSA work in the South — comprising representatives from the National Council of Churches, the Anti-Defamation League, American Friends Service Committee, Southern Regional Council, Southeastern Regional NAACP, Community Church of Chapel Hill, University of Louisville, UNC Woman's College, Loyola University of New Orleans, Morehouse College, Atlanta University, and the editor of the Atlanta paper. The listing shows the quality of leadership and diversity of agencies working with NSA from 1956 on, to establish a different framework for students living in a segregated society.

Don Hoffman, NSA president, and Curtis Gans, national affairs vice-president, were also at the meeting. Although new NSA officers were elected each year at the national congress, I received unswerving support from all of the administrations during my four years with the Southern Project.

That first advisory group suggested that we continue with the annual summer seminars and organize smaller integrated workshops and conferences across the South, while establishing a network of like-minded students and faculty. Advisory Committee members put me in touch with all of their contacts from the past seminars' work. With broad goals and lots of encouragement, I was ready to go.

Everything changed within five weeks. On February 1, 1960, I was in Greensboro to visit my sister Eileen and pick up some furniture and clothes. The sit-in movement started—right as I was driving down one of the city's main streets. The news announcer on the car radio reported with some wonderment that four students from the Negro A&T College had just been arrested for refusing to leave lunch counter stools at the downtown Woolworth's store. I had never heard of such a thing—although my neighbor remained convinced until the day she died that I had started the sit-in. I was the only person she knew who was involved in "interracial things," I was in town, and, as she told me, "I can put two and two together."

The sit-in movement spread like wildfire during the spring of 1960, and my office, supported by the Southern Regional Council's network, began to report on what was happening. By March 1, we had put out a newsletter listing the places where demonstrations were occurring, how many arrests were being made, and what help was needed. NSA in Philadelphia quickly passed this information on to a national student network, and the chain reaction of northern student support and demonstrations led to many of our breakthroughs. Several variety-store chains desegregated their lunch counters partly because of national picket lines and demonstrations.

By Easter, more than seventy thousand mostly black southern college students were involved in demonstrations. Students in the United States seized the chance to participate in direct action to bring about social change. It was an exciting time, and the direction of my project soon changed drastically. I don't think I ever even wondered if the Field Foundation would mind this new approach as I set about actually witnessing demonstrations and sit-ins and marches and then reporting to groups who wanted to help or to the media. Maxwell Hahn, the director of the Field Foundation, never questioned me, not in the beginning months, or later when we were actually paying SNCC phone and other bills. Julian Bond, reminding me that he had a key to our small office, used to come in at all hours of the night to use my mimeograph machine to run off press releases, fund-raising letters, and SNCC's newsletter, "The Student Voice."

Ella Baker and I went together to the organizational meeting of the Student Nonviolent Coordinating Committee at Shaw University in Raleigh, North Carolina, during Easter weekend 1960. Details of the conference—where I stayed, where we ate—remain vague. What I see now is like a view through a kaleidoscope imaging young black college students getting up and speaking passionately and eloquently of what had taken place already in their towns or on their campuses and what they were planning to do in this new fight for freedom. And of course I remember Reverend James Lawson and his call for nonviolence to be the credo of the movement, seeing and hearing Dr. Martin Luther King Jr. for the first time, and being inspired by Ella Baker's now-famous speech about the fight and the struggle being for "more than a hamburger."

This meeting gave birth to the student group that was going to follow the call of James Lawson and the Nashville movement for nonviolence as "a way of life"—the SNCC. Marion Barry, from Nashville, was elected the first chair, but the Atlanta delegation won the contest over where the organization's office should be located. The Raleigh meeting was the first time that I stood in a circle, joined hands, and sang "We Shall Overcome." For me, that song always elicits tears, no matter the lapse of time or the occasion of the singing. Following the Raleigh conference, student representatives from the most active colleges met in Atlanta, and the SNCC executive committee chose Ella Baker and me as adult advisors. I was only a few years older than the students, certainly not well schooled in social revolutions, but I was out of college, had a job, and could use the Field grant money to help the fledgling movement. The majority of the campus representatives to the early executive committee meetings were black men, and I became close friends with many of them. Since we are asked so often about sexual relations between white women and black men, I need to say here that I was approached by two in those early days. I said no. One asked if it was because he was black, and I said no. That was the end of it—with no jeopardy to friendships that continue to this day.

Delegates to the May meeting and students at other black colleges began forming their response to the sit-ins and the burgeoning movement. In Atlanta, students from the six black universities and colleges there formed the Atlanta Committee on Appeal for Human Rights. Their first move was to publish a full-page ad in the *Atlanta Journal and Constitution*. The ad was an eloquent expression of the changes needed in Atlanta, which went far beyond the freedom to eat at a lunch counter. Georgia's governor, Ernest Vandiver, was sure that the piece had been written in Moscow, if not Peking. In fact, the money to pay for that ad came from Lillian Smith, a white southerner and author who lived in the north Georgia mountains and was a longtime believer in integration.

In early summer 1960 Ella Baker asked if Jane Stembridge could stay at the apartment on Adair Avenue with Donna and me. Jane, born in Georgia and the daughter of a Southern Baptist minister, was a white seminary student from Union Theological Seminary in New York. She had met Ella at the Raleigh Easter Conference, and Ella asked her to come to Atlanta as SNCC's first executive secretary. Jane, pixie and poet, was wide-eyed and full of Christian existentialism and faith in the movement. She, Ella, and I would sit in the tiny office that housed SNCC at 197½ Auburn Avenue and, as I remember, laugh a lot. The first check that SNCC received that summer to support our work was for $100, from Eleanor Roosevelt. The second check was from Reverend Will Campbell, given in memory of country singer Patsy Cline, who had died that June. I did not realize until much later that it was three women—Ella, Jane, and I—albeit behind the scenes, who helped build SNCC in its early days.

A few months later another roommate moved into our apartment. Bonnie Kilstein was a student from New York University who had come to Atlanta for the summer to work for the Episcopal Society for Cultural and Racial Unity. On August 29, 1960, the *Augusta Courier*, a widely circulated segregationist weekly, reported the following under the headline "Bonnie Kilstein Leads the Attack on Segregation at Episcopal Cathedral": "Miss Kilstein is a 25-year old blonde . . . she has the habit of dating Negro men and she took communion at the Cathedral of St. Philip with one of her Negro boyfriends. This Bonnie Kilstein is reported to subscribe to the doctrine that the Negro is 'the Divine Image carved in ebony.'"

While the whirlwind of sit-ins and demonstrations and SNCC meetings absorbed our 1960 spring and early summer, Donna and I worked hard on the Third Southern Student Human Relations Seminars, to be held over three weeks in August at the University of Minnesota, just before the NSA National Congress. We recruited participants by sending letters to the small band of faithful on campuses in the South or by my making personal contacts while traveling. In March, with the violence of the Nashville sit-ins dogging my consciousness, I went to the University of Texas to meet Sandra Cason, nicknamed Casey. Casey, a member of the Christian Faith and Life Community and active in the YWCA, had been recommended as a seminar participant. We walked to the Night Hawk Cafe near campus, and I told her what I had witnessed as the sit-in movement swept the South. By that time, Casey had become involved herself in direct action. We soon found ourselves crying together into our hamburgers and milk shakes. She came to the seminar, has remained one of my best friends over these forty years, and has been the propelling force behind this book.

That spring of 1960, through SNCC, I had come to know Chuck McDew, a sit-in leader at South Carolina State, a black college in Orangeburg. He came to that first seminar, along with an outspoken, irreverent, brilliant young man, Bill Caldwell from Loyola University in New Orleans, and representatives from thirteen other southern campuses. Reverend Will Campbell, from my advisory committee, had agreed to be the consultant for the seminar and helped me select the group who came to Minnesota on August 3. I remember talking with Will about whether it was more important to have students who were just realizing the need for change in race relations or students like Chuck, who had actually demonstrated and been arrested. We never set a policy and ended up with a group of students at various stages of knowledge and commitment.

The students at that first seminar were in an emotional maelstrom. Valerie, a white woman from Texas Christian University, fell in love with Chuck McDew. (This happened at all of the seminars, and for most students it was the first time to be part of or witness to an interracial relationship). Henrietta, from black Fisk University, came from a privileged background and had spent some time abroad. While one seminar lecturer talked about the cruelty of the cotton sharecropping system and its perpetuation of racism, Henrietta burst into tears and began to frantically rub her hands together — "hands," she told us, "that had never even touched a cotton plant." One participant from North Carolina State, it seemed to me, spent much of his time warily wondering what he was doing there in the first place, and wild Bill Caldwell exhorted the group to "act" when they returned to their colleges.

The closing of the seminars was always hard. The intensity of the three weeks bound us all together and changed us irrevocably. On that last day in Minnesota, knowing that we were all going back to a separated life, Will Campbell told us good-bye with an offering that was later published in a magazine as "The Display of a Feather." I wish I could print the whole piece here, because it is eloquent and speaks in a timeless manner of the relations among human beings. Essentially he tells of a primitive savage returning from battle who stooped over and picked something up. "It was red and brown and yellow and green. It was pretty — it wasn't worth a thing. He took it back to his cave and kept it because it spoke to his deepest feelings. But soon he knew that its beauty spoke forth only if he shared it with his fellows. With this feather, civilization began and human relations began." Will told us that human relations still relied on the display of a feather, the effort to say there is some other way; that things didn't have to be as they were; that the times were out of joint. It was a matter of aesthetics, having to do with that which is true, which is pure, lovely, gracious — and with justice and love. Will then said each participant would be playing a different role in the struggle, for there was no one way. "As to *how* you involve yourself in the crisis, I have no parting words of advice . . . that role you must now go forth and find. In this moment of farewell, I say that your heart will not rest till it finds rest in personal involvement. And so, good-bye."

That 1960 seminar is especially memorable, perhaps because it was my first one, but also because that year was so pivotal for the movement. During the national congress following the seminar, Casey was on a panel at a plenary session. The night before, representatives of the Student Nonviolent Coordinating Committee had told the congress the meaning of the sit-ins and civil disobedience and had asked for NSA's support. The panel had been hastily assembled to meet demands by white southern students to answer the SNCC presentation, and I, responding to NSA officers' request for advice, recommended that Casey be on it. The five hundred mostly white delegates from colleges and universities across the country were dumbstruck when Casey took the microphone. The headline of the *Minneapolis Tribune* article covering the event was "White Coed Backs Sit-ins, Gets Ovation." The opening paragraph read: "A beautiful University of Texas coed with honey blond hair and a southern voice so soft it would not startle a boll weevil made a statement of ethical principles on the Negro sit-in movement Thursday." Part of her speech was quoted:

> I cannot speak for the sit-ins or for white southerners. I consider this problem to be an ethical one for which there can be only a personal decision. On this question, I hope we do not lose its essential simplicity because of its complexities. The simplicity is this: when an individual human being has been denied by the attitudes of his community the exercise of his rights as a human being, has he the right to peaceably protest? The answer to this simple question can only be yes.

To this day, I can close my eyes and recall Casey, fresh from the South, where the jails had been packed with young demonstrators, saying to a packed auditorium, "When Thoreau was jailed for refusing to pay taxes to a government which supported slavery, Emerson went to visit him. 'Henry David,' said Emerson, 'what are you doing in there?' Thoreau looked at him and replied, 'Ralph Waldo, what are you doing out there?'" My scalp tingles as I hear again the thunder of the standing ovation and see all the eyes filled with tears. There is no question that this was a personal turning point for many of the white delegates and probably a decisive moment in the history of NSA's civil rights activism. Although I was not aware of it at the time, Casey and I, two southern women, through my suggestion of her and her participation on the panel, helped solidify NSA support for civil disobedience and the Freedom Movement.

The other three panelists, white southern men, spoke against the sit-ins as "being violations of the law, involving private property and legal rights of businessmen." Following the panel, the congress, by a great majority, passed a resolution endorsing the sit-ins and promising support for the movement on the national and local campus levels.

In December of that year, seminar participant Valerie Brown, then editor of a campus publication at Texas Christian University, sent me a copy of their fall issue. It carried a reprint of a letter from Chuck McDew written to Valerie in October, on brown paper towels, from the Orangeburg jail:

> Hi Val, . . . Please excuse my stationery. I was arrested over an hour ago along with three other students. We sat down at the S. H. Kress & Co. lunch counter

and asked to be served. . . . I can hear singing outside. They are singing "We Shall Overcome" and it sounds so wonderful that I kind of want to cry. Dot, the girl in the next cell, can see them and there are nearly four hundred students outside . . . all singing. Now they are singing the "Star Spangled Banner" and I feel a kind of bitter sick feeling deep inside. I know that singing as well as we who are in here believe that "we shall overcome and the truth will make us free" and I'm trying so very, very hard to believe too that this is the "home of the brave and the free." I keep asking myself just how brave are the people who put me here? . . . Oh, God why must it be this way? Why can't we be a world of blind men. Then we would all be free and equal. Or would a group of blind bigots start discriminating on the basis of tone quality. Would all people with high voices have to live in filthy ghettos and be second class citizens?

Would the children of high-voiced people have to fight mobs to get into school. Would their braille tablets say that they aren't as good as the low-voiced and that they smell bad, have V.D. and live from day to day with one dream in their dark world — to sleep with a low-voiced woman? Oh, sickness, oh hate. Go and leave the hearts of man. Let me be me, Charles Frederick McDew, man, student, lover of life. I don't want to be that nigger with no personality, no being, just a dark blob. I want to be me with my color that I love, with my eyes, my body, my dreams and aspirations. I'd better close now. It has been a very trying day and we have trial in the morning. Pray for us, Val; pray for us all.

Chuck, or as the fellows in this cell call me, 24771

When I came back from the seminar and NSA congress in late August, I found that my belongings had been moved, lock, stock, and barrel, to another apartment. Bonnie, it turned out, had invited Ed King, a black SNCC worker, to our upstairs apartment, and the landlady had seen them going in the door. She had then called immediately and given us notice to be "out by sunset" that same day. Donna and Jane found another apartment; Bonnie left Atlanta. It was a strange feeling to go from the airport to the totally different place where Jane and Donna were living. That same summer, my red and white Karmann Ghia, my first car and pride and joy, was spray-painted with blue KKK signs and circles, we received threatening phone calls, and a friend of Donna's told us that we were under surveillance by the Georgia Bureau of Investigation. In an issue of the *Augusta Courier*, the NSA Southern Project address and phone number were listed under "Atlanta Mixing Organizations," and Donna and I were specifically cited as two white women working for "mixing the races." I don't remember ever being afraid during this period — only angry at the stupidity of the harassment. In retrospect, I believe my lack of fear is indicative of the heartfelt faith among our small band that we were engaged in a right and just struggle.

The Southern Project sponsored three more summer seminars, and participants continued to go back and "find their place in the struggle." Bob Zellner, from Alabama, became the first white person on the SNCC field staff. Joe Louis Smith was expelled from Southern University in Baton Rouge for his civil rights activities. Miles Lovelace, at Ole Miss, wrote an article on the shame of the riots there in 1962. Joan Browning, third seminar, was jailed in Albany after the freedom ride from Atlanta. They, along with the sixty-odd other southern students, black and white, who came to the four seminars between 1960 and 1964 heard Will Campbell's same farewell and challenge. Will named us "The Order of the Variegated Feather."

Building on the seminar contacts and the work that the students did when they returned to their campuses, I traveled a lot — trying to stay in touch with them as well as putting them in touch with a growing circle of young people who were tired of living in a segregated world. Meanwhile, still carried by the 1960 NSA pledge to support the movement, national officers of the organization pushed for involvement in voter registration. This was part of a broader effort to engage movement workers in citizenship education, and foundation money was given to support the Voter Education Project, based in Atlanta. In the winter of 1962, NSA hired Dorothy Dawson (now Dorothy Burlage) to join the project as assistant director. Dorothy planned and held a voter registration training program in Raleigh in the summer of 1962, which helped lay the groundwork for SNCC's future work. In 1963 the Southern Project helped pay travel expenses for black student leaders to attend a Civil Rights Leadership Conference in Nashville. Later on, I was at the meeting that led to the formation of the Southern Student Organizing Committee, an organization of southern white students working in white communities. There I met and became friends with Sue Thrasher.

During the months after its founding, SNCC continued to gather momentum and to define and redefine its goals. On October 15, 1960, we sponsored a conference on "Nonviolence and the Achievement of Desegregation."

The speaker at the closing rally was Lillian Smith. She was described in the program as "Author of *Strange Fruit, Killers of the Dream, One Hour,* and countless articles concerning the South — its fears, its needs, its hopes. She comes to us with her deep concern for her native south and all of its people. She comes with a great history of lonely stands, courageous words, and unending fights for the integrity and dignity of every human being."

Jane Stembridge and Lillian Smith by then had become friends. Later that fall Jane and I, together with Donna and her brother, Miles McGinty, a student at Emory, rode up to Smith's house on Old Screamer Mountain in Clayton, Georgia. I was in seventh heaven, having read her novel *Strange Fruit*, a complex tale of a black woman and a white man in love in a small Georgia town, several years earlier. She was ill with cancer by then, and you could feel her yearning to have been part of a "movement" where people believed in and marched and sang for freedom.

For much of my four years with NSA and SNCC, life and work merge together in a stream of vivid memories. I attended our never-ending SNCC meetings, which were usually held in the back room of B. B. Beamon's Restaurant (now gone) on Atlanta's Auburn Avenue. Volumes have been recorded on the politics, strategy, successes, and failures of SNCC. Our issues became more complicated as students dropped out of college and began to live in and organize communities. Then in 1960 Bob Moses came down from New York to work in the movement. Jane and Ella asked him to go to Mississippi to talk to some of Ella's NAACP contacts. His letters reinforced the intransigence of white supremacist forces, and the enormity of our struggle began to sink in. As our executive committee meetings expanded to include full-time staff members, we sometimes pondered very personal questions, such as what SNCC's responsibility was if anything (like a radio) was stolen from a home hosting a SNCC staffer in Albany. Did we have enough money to pay for a young woman pregnant by a SNCC worker to fly to Mexico for an abortion? What was our policy on people who simply turned up and said they wanted to work with SNCC? And always the discussion on whether we believed in nonviolence as a tactic or as a way of life. I think we split down the middle on this one. And I remember the small things as well, like the after-midnight meetings when Bob Moses and I would order hot fudge sundaes to keep us going.

Through all those years, I remember my deep friendship with Ella Baker — many years older but my peer as an "advisor." In the fall of 1960, Ella and I staged a two-person sit-in at the YWCA cafeteria on Edgewood Avenue. I am not sure if it was officially segregated, but I had never seen black people eating there. We quietly went through the line and then sat and ate our lunch with no further ado. By then we were working in the same building, and in the evening I would take her home in my Karmann Ghia — Ella holding on to her hat until we reached the Waluhaje, her apartment building, where we would relax, she with a glass of bourbon, I with a glass of scotch, and mutually partake of lamb chops. Ella seemed quite satisfied with her life as a single woman, and I was always mystified by her attempts to matchmake and her advice to me to find a boyfriend.

Later in our SNCC meetings we talked about whether to pursue the "fill the jails" tactic, as we did in Rock Hill, South Carolina — our first attempt. I went to Rock Hill with Ella to observe and report on the demonstrations. My most vivid memory is of Ruby Doris Smith, a SNCC representative from Atlanta, as we sat in the living room of a local minister's house in the very early morning. We were ready to go downtown, but we had to wait for Ruby Doris's hair curlers to set. She sat with us and dared anyone to budge.

While the Southern Project Advisory Committee fully supported my involvement in the movement, my place on the SNCC executive committee, and really almost everything I did, they were clear that my role did not include direct action, being arrested, or going to jail — which suited me fine. In other words, they held me to the original idea of the project's being a vehicle for southern white and black students to communicate, but they understood my support for SNCC and how important it was to observe and report to the outside world on SNCC demonstrations, arrests, and trials. I treasure the acceptance of my role by my friends in the movement in a time when "putting your body on the line" was often the test of your commitment.

Years later, Julian Bond wrote a friend describing my work: "Connie was a bridge between the overwhelming number of black sit-in students and white students who were predisposed to join with us. And she got us into the NSA network. It was an invaluable resource for recruiting money and political support [and] provided the basis later for Friends of SNCC groups on college campuses. She publicized the sit-in movement within the NSA network, interpreted it, and created an audience for us that might not have been there."

One occasion when I was an observer/reporter remains especially clear in my memory. Paine College, in Augusta, Georgia, was established by the United Methodist Church and the Christian Methodist Episcopal Church in the early 1900s. In 1930 the college started an annual statewide Christian confer- ence — one of the earliest attempts at an integrated meeting for students. Over the years, a few faithful white and black campus ministers silently and secretly took students to spend that weekend at Paine. By mid-April 1961, the students who came to the conference were seeing a new interpretation of their duty as Christians. Reverend James Lawson, still one of the strongest leaders in non- violent training for direct action, was there, and by Saturday of the weekend conference an integrated group of students was ready to sit in at the H. L. Green store in downtown Augusta.

Silas Norman (later with SNCC) was chair and William Didley was vice-chair of the ongoing movement at Paine. They had been demonstrating since early April, using structured methods, with people designated as security (the larger men), monitors, and observers. They had been notifying the Augusta police thirty minutes before the demonstrations. On this Saturday afternoon, for some reason, the student security was not in place as the interracial group of sixty students from the conference walked toward the store. William Didley was one of the black leaders at the front of the group. Suddenly a man from Bennettsville, South Carolina, emerged from the gathering white mob, pulled a knife, and stabbed Didley close to the heart. Didley was quickly put into a car and taken back to campus and then to the hospital.

Inside the store, Silas Norman, who was in charge of the demonstration, told the white students to get out and head for a safe place. They dashed into a store nearby and, men and women alike, huddled in a dressing room in the women's ready-to-wear department.

As one of the designated observers, I had been walking on the sidewalk outside the store as the group of marchers quietly approached. The stabbing had taken place right in front of me, and I think I went into a brief state of shock. I remember wandering on down the street looking into store windows, trying to assimilate what I had just witnessed. The police finally arrived, after the violence.

Joan Browning, then a student at Georgia State College for Women, was also at the Paine conference and the Saturday demonstration. She and I drove to Augusta later to testify at the hearing. Although the students' lawyer tried to prove that William Didley had been targeted as one of the Paine leaders, his assailant was released. The charges pressed against William, for carrying a concealed weapon (not true) and inciting to riot, were dropped, and he was released on his own recognizance.

I left NSA and the SNCC executive committee in the spring of 1964. It was time to move on. I was thirty-one by then, SNCC had shifted its focus away from campuses toward community organizing, and many of the "old guard" that I knew best were leaving. But my next eleven years of work (1964–75) as southern field representative for the American Friends Service Committee (AFSC) allowed me to stay in the natural flow of the movement, involved in grassroots implementation of rights under the 1964 Civil Rights Act and the 1965 Voting Rights Act. The AFSC, a Quaker service organization headquartered in Philadelphia, already had a long history of race-relations work in the South in fair housing, employment, and school desegregation.

My first assignment, in May 1964—working under the relentless energy of my black supervisor, Jean Fairfax—was to go to Mississippi, where Jackson, Biloxi, and Leake Counties were under court order to desegregate their schools the following fall. I was to work with six white women from Jackson, from diverse backgrounds but bound together in a statewide organization they had formed called Mississippians for Public Education (MPE). My job was to share with them the AFSC's experience in peaceful school desegregation in other southern communities. Of prime concern was their desire to prevent "another Little Rock" (1957) or New Orleans (1962), since memories of the violence in those two cities, not to mention the riots at Ole Miss in 1963, were still fresh in their minds. I stayed with one of the women, Winifred Green, who often traveled with me in Mississippi and later went to work with the AFSC.

Under the shadow of threats in the Mississippi legislature to close the public schools rather than integrate, MPE took the stand that uninterrupted public education was essential for the children of Mississippi. We also preached that violence was harmful to the economy and that Mississippi could avoid costly outcomes. Meanwhile, Jean Fairfax was recruiting black first-graders to enroll in the previously all-white schools in the three districts under court order. Whatever the forces that combined to keep potential violence at bay, black children entered the white schools without incident in all three districts in September 1964.

Memories of that summer include the smothering fear that engulfed the white community and my own sense of isolation. I was usually introduced to potential MPE members as Winifred's visiting college roommate, so afraid were we of me being tarred as an "outside agitator," particularly one from a suspect "leftist" group like the American Friends Service Committee. During one meeting in a Jackson home I hid in a closet because a potential member knew who I really was. On the few occasions I went home to Atlanta, when I crossed the state line I would holler, "I am Constance Curry, Free at last, Free at last."

During the 1960s, the Mississippi State Sovereignty Commission, an agency financed by the state, spied and reported on the activities of civil rights workers. One of their reports on my work with MPE characterized me as a "blonde atheist who talks about Communism all the time and who was seen in night clubs with Sammy Falls, Winifred's husband at the time." The report neglects to say that Winifred was there as well. I was taken aback when I read my description, because none of it was true, except maybe the "blonde" bit. My faith, though not always within an institutional-church framework, has been abiding and simple. I remember my hesitancy in singing the verse of "We Shall Overcome" that says "God is on our side." I knew our cause was moral and just, but I wasn't sure that the God I envisioned "took sides."

Summer 1964 was also Freedom Summer, when a thousand black and white volunteers from out of the state "descended" on Mississippi to work on voter registration, community organization, and citizenship schools. Mickey Schwerner, James Chaney, and Andrew Goodman, three movement workers, were murdered several weeks after I came to Mississippi, and I sneaked away to nearby black Tougaloo College to mourn them with Casey and Jane Stembridge and other friends from the movement who were living on campus. While I became friends with some of the white women working in Jackson, I missed being with the SNCC workers. By midsummer I felt at times so isolated that I convinced Winifred we needed a cat—always a solace for me. We went to the Jackson equivalent of an animal shelter and brought home a tiny brownish kitten. He began to cry in the middle of the night and was dead the next morning—of internal parasites.

One August afternoon, Winifred and I spent two hours at a picnic table in a public park along the Natchez Trace talking with a middle-aged white woman. She lived with her husband in a small town near the Trace and had read in the papers about efforts to save the schools. She had secretly sent in a small contribution and arranged by phone to meet Winifred and me. She was sad and scared. I later described our conversation to the AFSC:

> She talked most of the time and it was really just an outpouring of the things she has felt, from Medgar Evers' death to Barry Goldwater as a presidential candidate, on the racism of a Jackson Baptist minister to the removal of Camera Three from television programming. As we started to leave, she apologized for keeping us so long but said that she "hadn't had anyone to talk to in ten years." She cried, telling us of caring about public schools and of hearing about MPE but being afraid to speak to anyone about such matters, much less having us come to her home.

The Civil Rights Act of 1964 was passed that July, and a few hours after the announcement Jean Fairfax, winning our complete admiration, marched into the Sun and Sand Restaurant in downtown Jackson, and was served. Under Title VI of the act, school districts were mandated to formulate a school desegregation plan if they were to continue receiving federal funds. Many districts came up with "freedom of choice" plans, which in practice put the full burden on the shoulders of black parents, who exercised that choice and enrolled their children in previously all white schools. The AFSC and other agencies quickly became aware of the harassment, intimidation, and often violence suffered by black families who did enroll their children or even made known their intent to do so.

The NAACP Legal Defense and Educational Fund, along with the AFSC, quickly formed a school desegregation task force to encourage enrollment of black children and to document the difficulties they faced. I left Mississippi in the fall of 1964 and went back to Atlanta to coordinate the task force. The majority of our task force community workers were black. In 1965 alone, our efforts helped register about four thousand black children in previously all-white schools in seven southern states.

Our task force network not only encouraged families to exercise their rights but also investigated and documented local compliance with the federal law. The AFSC then reported to various federal agencies, urging them to enforce the law and not to leave the initiative to black families, who often faced retribution. During the years of the task force we met a host of courageous parents, driven and determined to procure a better education and life for their children, no matter what the cost.

Some of the school districts were still under court order, including Perry, a small community in Houston County in south central Georgia. The district had been ordered to open the first grade to all children, and the enrollment deadline was in mid-August. Two stories remain vivid. Winifred Green and I had been visiting homes in the black community with the help of a local black woman, Mrs. Cora Lee Durham, who had enrolled her own first-grader, joined us in telling other mothers what their rights were under the court order and outlining the advantages at the white elementary school.

One afternoon about dusk, Winifred and I took a left turn out of the black community onto the street that divided blacks from whites and were immediately pulled over by a car with a flashing blue light. The Perry policeman said we had gone through a stop sign and we would have to come to the station. My knees shook as all the worst images from movies, TV, novels, and reality itself kicked in. Winifred and I were very brash by then, though, and, once at the station, we told the officer that we were staying at the New Perry Hotel, that we had to call John Doar at the Justice Department by seven that evening to report on how things were going, that we had talked with the mayor of Perry that very day about our activities, and that we were leaving in the morning. We probably didn't need to say all that. Suddenly, the policeman looked out the window, and, following his gaze, we saw hundreds of black people standing quietly in the parking lot in front of the station. Mrs. Durham had seen, or been told, what had happened, and she had rallied the group to come and just stand there in the twilight. We were released and returned to the New Perry, ate lots of the best pie I have ever eaten, and left the next day.

On our way to Perry earlier in the week, we had stopped in Warner Robins, also in Houston County, but an easier situation because of the nearby air force base. We had found that a military presence in a southern town gave some support to desegregation efforts and that the black community often felt a little more secure. We went to visit Mrs. Kathleen Bynum, a leader in the black community. She lived in a mobile home and greeted us gracefully and warmly. She was wearing a black leisure suit and lots of jewelry. As we discussed the situation in Warner Robins, Mrs. Bynum offered us some French bourbon. We told her we had never had any but would love to try some. As we sat there sipping out of elegant cut-glass goblets, I noticed that my stomach was getting pleasurably warmer with each sip and that my body was sweating on what was already a sweltering afternoon. All of a sudden, school desegregation was seeming such an easy thing! We were lucky we reached Perry safely, after that. We later discovered, too, that the "French bourbon" was actually white lightning, or moonshine, a homemade corn-based whiskey that usually runs one hundred proof or more! The next morning we somehow struggled through the door-to-door canvassing, burping gusts of alcohol that probably could have been ignited in the ninety-eight-degree heat.

Heat is a pervading memory of the summers in the Deep South states when we worked on school desegregation for September openings. The enrollment deadlines were always in August, and the reports of harassment and intimidation reached us just as the "dog days" settled in. The heat in southwest Georgia or Mississippi or Alabama is like the tropics: You are wet all over all the time because of the humidity. You can barely breathe. You move slowly and your brain feels wet and foggy. You are "spitting cotton" thirsty. One time Winifred and I each chugged three ice-cold bottles of Coke one after another when we got to our motel in Moultrie, Georgia. And the bugs! When working in the rural areas, the rhythmic waving of your hand in front of your sweaty face becomes reflex to scatter the gnats and flies.

One August Saturday in 1965, Winifred and I drove to Alamo, a tiny town in Wheeler County, southeast Georgia. We needed to talk with the Reverend Gorham, a black minister who had enrolled his daughter in the white elementary school but, after threats and harassment, had withdrawn the application. We found his house and heard the whole story. As we left to drive on to the next town on our schedule, we noticed a car following us. It was the county sheriff, and he finally pulled us over right at the town square. He was another stereotype from sixties TV and Hollywood movies about the South: big, red-faced, burly, and threatening. And the square itself seemed to be a movie set for any and every small southern town: the courthouse in the center of the square, the Confederate soldier in front, and the little stores on the facing streets—a dry goods, a five-and-dime, a drug store, a few cafes, the bank, maybe a lawyer's office.

"What were y'all doing at that nigger Gorham's house?" We both got out of Winifred's green VW bug and told the sheriff that we were part of a task force reporting on southern school desegregation. By this time, we noticed, the word was out: a small crowd was gathering. I was more scared than I had been even in the Perry incident. Again there was the heat, but there was also something—a combination of William Faulkner and Tennessee Williams—in the scene and the people who surrounded us. They were mostly men, including the owner of the dry goods store, who also happened to be the mayor. What incensed them the most was that Winifred was from Mississippi. In their eyes, this lovely, blonde white woman was a traitor—indeed, their worst nightmare. The sheriff pointed to a strapping nineteen-year-old, barefoot and wearing only denim overalls. "See Benjie over there? He just got out of the mental institution, and of all the things he hates, nigger-lovers is first." The mayor then came up and said that the sheriff and several patrol cars were going to escort us to the line of neighboring Telfair County but that he could not guarantee our safety from then on and we were to never set foot in their county again. I then told them that we worked for John Doar and the Justice Department, that they knew our every move and were waiting for our evening report. The sheriff expressed zero interest.

We got in the car and headed out of town. What worried us most was that the end of the little procession included about five pickup trucks with the perennial gun racks in the back window, the guns in them. Winifred did not help when she told me to get down in the seat if one of the trucks started to pass because that could mean they were going to shoot into the car!

At the county line everyone behind us stopped, and we high-tailed it to the closest motel in McRae and called Jean Fairfax in Philadelphia—who in turn really did call John Doar to report the incident. Winifred and I drank some scotch and finally went to bed exhausted.

When Stokely Carmichael, chairman of SNCC, issued his call for Black Power in 1966, I was neither surprised nor alarmed. I understood the new emphasis on Black Power within some ranks of the movement; dashed dreams, broken heads, and loss of faith can demand a new strategy. I had lost touch with Casey and Jane and my other white friends who had been part of the controversy and divisions within SNCC. I had continued to live in a white community in Atlanta, and I remained close to my black AFSC co-workers. Certainly the black families I continued to visit, offering them support for their plodding struggle to gain rights, never changed their attitude toward us white workers.

I also remember that Barbara Moffett, white director of the AFSC Community Relations Division in Philadelphia, my supervisor and good friend, had joined the Meredith March and had heard Stokely's question "What do you want?" and the roaring response "Black Power." She, too, understood and felt neither frightened nor threatened. Another AFSC representative on the march reported what Stokely had said to him: "The Negro in Mississippi working for three dollars a day is no better off than his slave great-grandfather, so he has nothing to lose and everything to gain. He must be made to feel his own power. It is a simple fact that this is something a white man can't give him. We are not racists. We are not anti-white. We are not violent, but we know the Negro must speak for himself."

In 1966, along with the work of the school desegregation task force, I became the administrator for the AFSC Family Aid Fund. The fund, supported for ten years by grants from the Ford Foundation, had been established to help southern families or individuals who were harassed, or worse, in their attempts to exercise their civil rights. The program probably helped a hundred families involved in school desegregation or voter registration across the South. In the early 1970s, as cases of individual harassment decreased, the need for economic development in the black community was becoming increasingly crucial. We concentrated our efforts on Lowndes County, Alabama, where Lowndes Wood Products became an income-producing company owned and operated by the black community. In Greene County, Alabama, we worked with the Reverend Tom Gilmore and William Branch in their voter registration efforts, and in 1967 Winifred Green and I took vacation time to work for their election as the first black sheriff and judge. In 1968 I was the AFSC liaison to the planning of the Poor People's Campaign, Dr. Martin Luther King's effort to direct national attention to economic injustices as well as racial inequality. I was with him at a meeting the day before he went to Memphis, where he was killed.

The Family Aid Fund continued to make loans and grants to individuals and to community groups until 1975, when Ford terminated funding to the AFSC. Cases of individual harassment had decreased, and the Foundation, along with the AFSC, realized that we could not meet the vast needs for community and economic development. The South had changed from the turbulent days of the sixties, and the national AFSC could no longer justify the position for a "hands-on" southern field representative. The regional AFSC office stayed in business, however, and support for integrated and quality education continued as a major commitment.

For about six months I collected unemployment. I also spent quite a bit of time at my beach cottage on Hunting Island, South Carolina, where I walked on the beach, played the three country-music songs I knew on my guitar, and wondered about my future as a civil rights worker who had never "specialized." Many of my movement friends were into housing or fair employment or educational equality, but I was characterized as a "civil rights generalist." Luckily, an old Southern Christian Leadership Conference friend and poker buddy called me to come home for an interview with Atlanta mayor Maynard Jackson. He was looking for a woman to direct his newly established Atlanta Bureau of Human Services, and he was interviewing white candidates so his appointments would reflect his belief in an integrated staff.

When the federally funded Model Cities Program closed out, Mayor Jackson had realized the city could not summarily terminate programs that directly helped the mostly black inner-city population. Hence the Bureau of Human Services was created, and the staff of the old Model Cities Program became the bureau staff. Julian Bond and John Lewis gave me glowing recommendations, and in the fall of 1975 I was appointed to the position of director, with an all-black staff of forty. Politically, I was to their left. I encouraged day-care workers, for example, to sit in in order to get their checks from a city grant on schedule. I rejoiced with a neighborhood after their mass appearance at a City Council meeting brought reassurances that they would get the funds for their promised service center.

The adjustment from civil rights activist/organizer to government bureaucrat was not easy for me, and I could not have done it if the goals of the Jackson administration had not projected enormous improvements for a city rife with problems. Atlanta, which had long prided itself as "too busy to hate," had a hard time translating that image into acceptance of its first black mayor and his commitment to change. Sweeping reforms in minority participation in city contracts, as well as widespread programs in child care and employment for a staggering number of families below the poverty level, rocked the long-standing white power structure. At the same time, the lack of low-income housing, creeping problems of homelessness, and the city council's ambivalence over its responsibility for human services meant a constant struggle for program approval and financial resources for my bureau.

Once during those years, a longtime close friend and co-worker, an African-American woman about my age, illustrated unforgettably for me the true meaning of being color blind. She is a seamstress, and we were talking about what kind of material to get for her to make some white slacks for me. I had mentioned that I didn't like it when you could see through the fabric the line where your underpants left off and your skin started. My friend said, "Well, just get you some black underpants and you won't be able to see that line." She had forgotten that I was white.

Andrew Young succeeded Maynard Jackson as mayor, and I served for two more terms. From 1981 to 1984 I attended the Woodrow Wilson College of Law at night, and then passed the Georgia Bar. I went to law school just because I wanted to—I never intended to practice. In fact, my first act as an attorney (and one of the very few at that) was to write a letter on my new personalized stationery to the Atlanta Humane Society, protesting the wrongful death of a cat.

In May 1990 I resigned from city government to spend a year at the Carter Woodson Civil Rights Institute at the University of Virginia and to begin a rewarding phase of my life—as a writer. In 1988 I had attended an Atlanta conference on women in the civil rights movement and was reunited with Mae Bertha Carter, one of the women I knew from my Mississippi AFSC work. We had been in close touch from 1966 until 1975 and then had no contact for thirteen years. Spotting each other at Ebenezer Baptist Church, we ran through the pews to hug. Mrs. Carter told me that all eight of her children who desegregated the Drew schools in 1965 had graduated and gone on to college, and seven of them had graduated from the University of Mississippi. About this same time, the AFSC was gathering material for its seventy-fifth anniversary celebration and encouraged me to revisit Mississippi and interview

Mrs. Carter and her now-grown children. The hours spent talking in her living room and driving around with her on the back roads of the Delta inspired me to write up the Carter story; the result, *Silver Rights*, was published in 1995.

In December 1996 I received a call from Aaron Henry, another of my heroes from the sixties — one of the leaders of the Mississippi Freedom Democratic Party and head of the Mississippi NAACP for over thirty years. He had read *Silver Rights* and wanted me to write his story, stressing that I knew how to write about the "ordinary people" who had changed the South and that young folks should know that you don't need to be famous to make things better.

Going back to Mississippi, reliving those earlier times with the Carters and Aaron Henry, and then telling my own story for this book have caused the floodgates to be lifted. The remembering has jelled into an awareness — viscerally deep my whole life — that I have no true "sense of place." That awareness took form when I went to a conference of southern writers a few years ago. All of the speakers talked about their sense of place and how their books are rooted in the call and recall of early years with parents and grandparents — a house, a farm, a school — and patterns. "Sense of place" is also strong in the chapters of my co-writers on this project, particularly the southern women. If this sense has to do with feeling at home, or secure, or belonging, then mine lies in the Beloved Community and Freedom Movement of the early sixties, with our vision of a truly integrated society. Can one have a "sense of place" in a vision or movement rather than in a special geographical spot on the earth? When I articulated this question to a friend, he said, "Hmm, there's something biblical about that. The early Christians were called the 'People of the Way.' They weren't rooted in a certain space, and 'way' referred to a way of living."

The other difference I have observed about my life is that, other than my mother, who died early on, I have had no real women role models. Thus, instead of being guided into the civil rights movement by a strong-willed woman, as some of my co-writers were, I just sort of barreled my way into a place where my heart felt right. On the other hand, I have been lucky in that my "way of living" has meant working for forty years in jobs and with people whose goals and values were close to those of the early Freedom Movement. I am grateful for the continuity that has provided for me. Today, in addition to writing, I devote my time to fighting for drastic change in the criminal justice system. With the staggering number of young black men already incarcerated and the increasing number of black women going to jail, the struggle is, for me, the cutting edge of the civil rights movement of our day.

My years have also been filled with an unfaltering circle of friends, including women from forty-odd years ago at Agnes Scott; a family that expanded with my father's two remarriages and added a half sister, three stepbrothers, in-laws, and nieces and nephews. I did not marry, and I have no children.

I was sustained through the whole of the sixties by a relationship with a man with whom I shared completely my passion for the movement. He had commitments elsewhere that left me free to conduct my life independently, as I preferred. Sadly, that affair had to end. Nowadays, they say women who choose unavailable men are afraid of intimacy. I don't know about that. There is an intimacy born of shared struggle, dedication, excitement, compassion, sorrow, and danger that is matched by no other. The fire of that love fueled my work for racial justice and gave me a safe place for all of my passions. It also gave me time to learn how to lead a life as a single woman, with freedom to follow my basic, unorthodox beliefs. I have stayed in Atlanta for thirty-nine years, saved enough money to buy a house fourteen years ago, and, following another passion, have traveled extensively, including visits to Russia, China, Cuba, Chile, and fifteen trips to Ireland.

I have had a long string of crushes, flings, and trysts and an even longer time of celibacy. I carry little sense of sacrifice or regret for the choices I have made freely along the way. Enhanced loneliness may come with growing older, but I am gratified to be around long enough to tell the stories — to shine the light on some heroes from the Freedom Movement. In writing about the Carter family and Aaron Henry, I came to realize that it is indeed the telling of the stories that is important — the passing on of the legacy. Perhaps lessons of hope and courage can make the future way a little brighter, a little clearer. As I continue to write about people and times that require memory to fly backward, lines from Thomas Kinsella, a contemporary Irish poet, inspire me:

Ended and done with never ceases,
Constantly the heart releases
Wild geese to the past.

Shiloh Witness

JOAN C. BROWNING

"**W**hich Side Are You On?" was *the* question every southerner in my lifetime had to answer about race. This is the story of how I, a white, rural, southern woman, came to my answer, of where that answer led me in the turbulent days of the 1960s, and of how the answer has affected all my life.

In the Freedom Movement story, I am supposed to be the enemy, screaming ugly epithets at young black children who are braving my wrath to enter "white" schools. You might therefore expect that, as a freedom fighter, I had to reject all of my upbringing. I did not. As I understand my journey, I was searching for restoration of my membership in a loving family and community, membership that comforted me in early life and even yet remains an elusive goal. For me, the Freedom Movement of the early sixties was the "Beloved Community." It was an expansion of my early life.

Mine is largely a spiritual journey, symbolized by the biblical places important to the Hebrew children's search for home, Shiloh and Mount Zion. Shiloh means peace. Mt. Zion was the heavenly city of God. Both sides of my family, in isolated country places in Georgia, armed with their Christian faith, sought peace in a place where God dwelled with them. So did black Christians in Albany, Georgia. My Freedom Movement journey takes me from Daddy's all-white Shiloh Methodist Church in south Georgia and Mother's Mt. Zion Baptist Church in west Georgia to Albany's all-black Shiloh and Mt. Zion Baptist Churches, where I was welcomed as a Freedom Rider. That journey seemed natural to me. Early in my movement days, I did not believe I was taking sides. I thought I was merely witnessing to a universal belief.

At Shiloh, Wheeler County, Georgia, in the shadow of the Methodist church, I was born into a loving family and community, my first beloved community. Since leaving home and venturing into the larger world, my spiritual journey has been the search for my place as an individual within a community, a place where I can answer the question posed in Micah 6:8: "What does the Lord require of you?" Micah's answer, and mine: "What does the Lord require of you but to do justice, and to love kindness [mercy], and to walk humbly with your God?"

My world was small. When I was four years old we moved about six miles from Shiloh to a sparsely settled part of Telfair County, where I grew up. Then my boundaries expanded in several increments of about a hundred miles each. I attended Georgia State College for Women (now Georgia College and State University) in Milledgeville. Then I moved to Atlanta. Atlanta was my home for thirteen years, although during that time I lived eight months in Boston and a year in West Virginia. I left Atlanta in the 1970s to move first to a farm in Georgia's mountains and then to West Virginia.

My speaking part in Freedom Movement histories consists of one line, uttered on Tuesday, December 19, 1961; it was recorded by Howard Zinn in *SNCC: The New Abolitionists*:

> Shiloh Baptist Church was packed that first night after the prisoners came out of jail. People stood up and sang Freedom Songs. In front, leading the singing, holding hands, was a line of SNCC workers, among them several who would later become known throughout the nation as the Freedom Singers: Bernice Johnson and Rutha Harris of Albany, Bertha Gober, and Cordell Reagon. In the middle of the meeting, Joan Browning, the young white girl who had been arrested with the original riders from Atlanta, walked down the aisle to the microphone. She had just been released from jail, and was out of breath. She spoke briefly in her soft southern accent: "First time I've ever been in jail. It's a funny mixed up feeling to hate being in a dirty place—but to be glad you're there for a good reason. . . . We hope you'll keep going."

That evening is etched into my memory. Shiloh Baptist Church in Albany, Georgia, was packed with people sitting on the floor and standing along the walls, and those unable to get into the church were crowded near the door. Finally, after days of solitary imprisonment, huddling in my coat and filthy army blankets, always chilled in the dingy, unheated white women's jail cell, I was in a warm room. But most important, after days of isolation, I was within the Beloved Community. Weak from my hunger strike, almost blinded by the bright lights after days of neither light nor dark, I remember feeling that I was where I was supposed to be, perfectly at home in Albany's black Shiloh Baptist Church, amid hundreds of black citizens of Albany, Student Nonviolent Coordinating Committee (SNCC) volunteers, and newspaper reporters. All the white people I knew who were involved with SNCC came to Albany: Casey Hayden, Bob Zellner, Connie Curry. My race did not seem a problem here. For me, the Freedom Movement was the all-inclusive true church, and the church was the logical center of the movement.

How did I arrive in Albany? My story begins at Shiloh Methodist Church in Wheeler County almost two decades earlier.

South was home. I was born in sweltering July heat in 1942 in the shed room enclosing part of the front porch of my family's rented house in Shiloh. I have always loved knowing that I was born at home, with my maternal grandmother, Mama Red, and Aunt Frankie and Aunt Ruth there with Mother. I was welcomed into the world by strong, loving women. The most influential was Mother, whom we honored by calling her "Mother" instead of nicknames such as "Mom," "Mommie," or "Mama."

Shiloh was not a town, not even a crossroads. It was a wide spot in an isolated rural road, consisting of one store, one church, a school, and four or five homes. Shiloh community had been home to my father's people, the Brownings and the Maddoxes, for several generations. As far as I have been able to learn, its entire population was white. I was the second child and first daughter in a family that would grow to five sons and three daughters. I remember feeling contented in my early childhood. Our family life may have contained difficulties, but I was blissfully ignorant of any unhappiness. Mine was a small but safe world with loving family and neighbors.

Our home at Shiloh has always occupied a special place in my imagination. As an adult, I visited the house several times, even after it was used to store hay, until it was bulldozed to make way for a farm pond. My older brother,

Wayne, shared my affection for that home. My few memories there are peaceful, true to the biblical message of "Shiloh."

I remember Wayne holding me on top of a huge land turtle as it slowly strolled across the yard. We brought our turtle into the house — probably with the help of our grandfather, because we don't know how the two of us could have lifted such a large animal. Our gentle mother helped us make the turtle, which we called a "gopher," a better home in the fenced chicken yard. We both wailed with sorrow when our pet turtle dug its way out and continued on about its business.

Mother's family lived in northwest Georgia. Her grandfather had built and preached at Mt. Zion Baptist Church and her grandmother was called a hillbilly teacher. My maternal grandmother, Mama Red, was a strong and independent woman. As a very young widow with two children, she married my grandfather, and when he died young of Bright's disease, she was once again a widow, now with four more children. I never knew my grandfather. Mama Red raised her six children alone but married again when she was seventy years old.

Mother finished all eleven grades offered in her school and went with her sisters Ginny and Frankie to Macon, Georgia, to work in a cotton mill. There she met Daddy, who was a fixer or mechanic in the cotton mill. When they married, they lived with Daddy's sister, my Aunt Ruth, and his brother-in-law, my Uncle Merritt Livingston, on a rented farm in Telfair County. When I was four, almost five, Mother and Daddy bought this farm with a New Deal loan. It was only six miles away, but because it was across Alligator Creek and Little Ocmulgee River we now lived in Telfair County.

That Telfair County house, too, occupies a special place in my memories. It was a splendid log house that had been covered over with planed board siding. It also had four rooms, though they were much larger than the Shiloh house's. The shed room was all across the back of the house, adding a kitchen and dining room. An unfinished attic offered storage, as well as mystery and opportunity for mischief. The front porch was probably as large as our entire first home. My younger sister, Joyce, and I shared a room. To this day, the aroma of cedar reminds me of the bed, chest of drawers, and dresser that Mother had custom built by a local furniture maker for my sister and me.

We grew up with the family lore that Mother and Daddy had paid $5,500 for 55 acres. When the farm was sold in 1961, it was advertised in the *Telfair Enterprise* as having 58 acres of "A-1 Southern Soil," 33 acres in cultivation, with 10 acres of cotton allotment and 1.27 acres tobacco allotment. These were small allotments. Five acres was the minimum profitable tobacco allotment. The auction advertisement said that it had "good fence up — that will hold any livestock" and "ideal pond site." Our farm had a half mile of highway frontage on U.S. Route 341. We were eight miles from both McRae and Lumber City. Neither served as a "home town." Our sense of community was much closer to home, less than two miles in each direction.

We all thought we were well off. When I was eight years old, ours was the first house for miles around to get electricity; the first with a telephone; the only one near us with encyclopedias and bookcases of *Reader's Digest* condensed fiction and farm journals. We had the community's first rubber-tired farm wagon, the first tractor, the best milk cows, the finest farm. After Daddy began commuting to Brunswick to build houses, we also had cash money. Wayne, Joyce, and I remember being proud of our farm, proud of how well we worked, and proud of our successful crops.

My brothers Wayne and Bobby, sister Joyce, and aunts Helen, Ruth, and Frankie all agree that none of us knew until much later that the government would classify us as poor. When I later spoke of my family, bemused friend and hostile foe alike called me "poor white" and sometimes tacked on "trash." My words failed to communicate my truth about our place in the world, so I stopped talking about my childhood. If we were poor, we did not know it.

We were farmers. Truck farmers, we said, although truck crops such as watermelons, cantaloupes, and other melons and vegetables shared the fifty acres we owned and the fields we rented with corn, cotton, tobacco, sugar cane, and sometimes peanuts. The allotment system limited the acreage each farmer could plant in the cash crops of cotton, tobacco, and peanuts. Allotments were meted out by the federal Agricultural Soil and Conservation Service (ASCS) through a system of local county committees that had power to control a farm's cash crop acreage and thus to help or destroy a farm family. Daddy unsuccessfully offered himself for election to the Telfair County ASCS committee for several years.

We often rented neighbors' tobacco allotments. Our family garden was several acres. The only livestock we kept was for our own table, usually the offspring of our milk cows, hogs we raised from piglets, and chickens. We ate very little beef, but our chinked-log smokehouse was stocked with sausage, ham, and bacon. Wayne's and Mother's occasional forays into the fields and streams produced rabbit, squirrel, and fish. Mother always kept at least two hundred laying hens, sometimes more, and she sold eggs to McRae grocery stores. Our few rows of sugar cane produced gallons of syrup. This family farm used mostly family labor to support us all.

Our sense of pride as successful farmers was reinforced by the fact that in Telfair County in the 1950s farmers were the foundation of the local economy. Even people who were not farmers were aware that whatever they did for a living depended on farmers' successes. So not only was my family successful within the sphere of local agriculture, but we also knew that our farming provided the economic basis for doctors, lawyers, merchants, and schoolteachers. We owned our land, a proud symbol of wealth and independence. Even when times got hard, there was a pride and comfort in knowing that we owned the wall our backs were up against. Even now, armed with sophisticated sociological and economic criteria, I cannot see that we were poor, and certainly we were not trash, though we were clearly white and a very large family on a small farm. Measures that value only material terms miss the degree of security that our small family-operated farm provided.

For spiritual as well as economic reasons, we worked at being better farmers. We tried consciously to be good stewards of the land. The stewardship message was preached from the pulpit of our church and in *Progressive Farmer* publications. Besides terracing fields to prevent soil erosion, we rotated crops so that the old single-crop agriculture system did not deplete our soil. We planted velvet beans and peanuts in the corn and let pigs root in the fields after the fall crops were harvested. We planted lupine for soil improvement. Wayne and I, as well as Mother and Daddy, read books, Agriculture Department tracts, Extension Service pamphlets, and brochures from feed and fertilizer companies. Mother often ordered packets of seeds for Wayne and me to experiment with. Wayne and I even performed some of our own crop improvement experiments.

Money was not the sole criterion for success, as it has become today. We proudly produced much of what we needed, especially food. Mother was a skilled seamstress. She selected flour and chicken feed in sacks with desirable fabrics, which she fashioned into custom-made dresses, blouses, skirts, shirts, curtains, and even doll clothes. She did not need store-bought patterns, because she could duplicate any dress from pictures I would show her in *McCall's* or other magazines. I was proud and style-confident in Mother's tailored clothes, which I considered superior to ready-to-wear garments from stores. When I was in high school, she bought fabric to make dresses for me. Our store-bought clothes consisted of socks and shoes, underwear (always white), and when I was older, bathing suits and the world's most beautiful pink strapless prom dress. One of the hardest adaptations for me when I left home was figuring out which store-bought clothes could possibly replace Mother's "feedsack fashions."

I think one of the most important things that molded my life was the fact that I was born between my brother, Wayne, two years older, and sister, Joyce, two years younger. Between them, I was anchored securely in my place in my family. Wayne was my first friend and, until Joyce and I were older, my best friend. Although we have been estranged most of our adult lives, Wayne was, after Mother, the second most important person in my early life. As for Joyce, from the time she was born she and I shared a room, a bed, a wardrobe, fantasies, and daydreams. When she had trouble falling asleep at night, I made up stories about marvelous adventures we would have and about space exploration. Many of my wild imaginings, such as space flight food supplied from toothpaste-type tubes, have been realized. Joyce, too, was my best friend. Later, we added brother Danny, and we four were the "older kids." Three younger brothers, Bobby, Jimmy and Bruce, and a sister were the "boys and Polly," or the young 'uns.

I learned to read at home when I was about four years old while watching Mother help Wayne with homework. By first grade, I was tested at third-grade level in math and reading. Two sisters taught our two-room school. Each grade formed one row of seats, with four grades in one room, three in another. During my six years there, peak enrollment for the two rooms was fifty-two pupils. A recent conversation with the principal, Mrs. Mary Lee Nunn, confirmed my recollection that we were so isolated that when the measles hit, all except two students were sick at the same time. Even she had measles along with us, leaving only her sister, Mrs. Eloise Boswell, and two students in the entire school for more than a week.

Towns Junior High School was always racially segregated until it closed in the mid-1950s. Because every family I knew in our area except one was white, it also stands in my memory as a community school. The teachers were family friends. We knew everybody. School was an extension of family and community, a totally safe place. I do not remember a single incident in which my family and my school were in conflict. The same values, the same commitment to the protection and rearing of children, persisted in both places. I was a good student. I was considered "so smart" that they had me skip seventh grade, going directly from sixth grade at Towns to eighth grade at Lumber City High School. I graduated from high school at sixteen. While I was proud at the time of being promoted early, it caused me to be the youngest in my group in high school, college, and throughout my early years in the Freedom Movement.

In my memory, 1953 dawned as a typical year in rural south Georgia. The rhythms of life on a small truck farm were all in place. The mild winter, with its short daylight, slowly receded, there were intriguing subjects to learn in school, and evenings were spent doing homework or reading alone or aloud with my large family around the comfort of a flickering, subdued fireplace. Spring came early, as it does in that part of the country, and farm life again dictated my family's activities. In early March Daddy hitched two mules to plow the rich loam, Piedmont clay mixed with coastal gray sand. Clods of earth tossed upward quickly crumbled, leaving a soft, even surface.

We were busy planting tobacco one April Saturday. Joyce was in the house, baby-sitting Jimmy and the baby brother that Mother had given me the honor of naming Bruce Randolph. When we looked up from the tobacco rows, the house had tall columns of flames coming from the kitchen. There was a huge black hole in the roof. I had never seen a house ablaze. The image haunted my dreams for years.

Neighbors gathered as we arrived, breathless, at the flame-engulfed house. All my family were in the yard, except Bruce, who was still in his crib. Daddy jumped through an open window into the burning house, plucked Bruce by feel from the now smoke-filled crib, and threw him into waiting hands in the yard. I can still see the entire front wall collapse, barely missing Daddy as he leapt off the porch.

The forest service lookout tower had reported the fire, and a forest service truck futilely sprayed its one tank of water onto the nearby buildings—the chicken house, the smokehouse, our rabbit hutch. Even these were consumed in the fire's anger.

Before the last embers of our log house had cooled, Aunt Ruth and Uncle Merritt had taken us to their small home. Neighbors trekked in, offering to take one or two members of our large family for temporary shelter. Aunt Ruth said no. She told me that she told them, "No, sir. We're keeping them with their mother and daddy." I shall always be grateful to Aunt Ruth for keeping us together as a family. Each evening, she took the mattresses off her beds and spread them on the floor. There was no room to walk, but by crowding together, we all slept. For the weeks we stayed at her home, she cooked and washed all day while Mother and Daddy worked at finding us a place to live.

The community stepped forward to help. Unasked, neighbors brought spare clothing and furniture, some brand new, much from their own supplies. Uncle Merritt took time from his own work to go from door to door, friend to business associate, in Telfair and Wheeler Counties. He collected enough money for us to rent the vacant house nearest our farm. In north Georgia, Mother's family solicited money, clothing, and household furnishings for us.

The message imprinted on my mind was that one does not wait to be invited to help in the face of tragedy. The community and family response to the fire was proof that individuals could rise to help their neighbors. I truly lived within the comforting arms of a Beloved Community.

After that fateful day my family's life was forever changed. Before the year was out, Mother's life was endangered by her eighth pregnancy; our youngest sister, Polly, was born prematurely; Daddy, in utter frustration, hit the red mule on its hip with a hammer and was repaid when the equally frustrated mule kicked him in the jaw; we moved to a tenant house where frogs bred in the shallow well; most of us got boils; and because it did not rain, nothing grew.

Those droughts of 1953 and 1954 are the backdrop for years in which I acquired my interpretation of the world and my role in it. Looking back, I link virtually every major decision made in my adult life to the changes that year. Years later, when I read of ancient Greeks who suddenly understood that the earth beneath their feet was not firmly resting on the back of a giant tortoise but was simply floating in space, I viscerally understood. I knew what it felt like to have the solid earth beneath my feet shift.

My eleventh birthday that summer of 1953 was not a time for celebration. In that year I went from protected child to adult without benefit of adolescent years of transition. As the oldest daughter, I became the assistant mother. I saw motherhood as arduous physical and mental effort, endless demands, and little time, energy, or resources for one's own life. I knew I wanted to be a mother — someday. After many adventures in the wide world, I would return and marry Jimmy Pittman, the young man I had chosen (without his knowledge!) for my future husband. We would have nine sons to staff our own private baseball team. Such are the dreams of an isolated rural girl. School, which had always been one of my favorite places, became my refuge. I could read and learn about ideas, people, and places far removed from the drudgery of unending tasks.

Before the drought of 1953, I felt secure. The gradual erosion of my parents' marriage was invisible to me, or perhaps it only began that summer. My awareness of Daddy's radical personality change dates to that year. I now understand much more about how that year might have been more than he could endure, and about how having his jaws wired shut for six months and pain medication and possible brain damage affected him. But at the time, and until years after his death in 1982, all I knew was that my daddy was replaced by a miserable wretch. He began commuting about a hundred miles away to Brunswick, to build houses. The rest of my time at home, five years, he left before daybreak on Monday and returned after dark on Friday. Mother managed the farm.

Just as I became an assistant mother, Wayne, at the age of thirteen, became a substitute father by assuming burdens far beyond a child's ability to carry. I looked to him for security in a world that no longer seemed safe or predictable.

Millions of southern farmers shared the tragedies of that drought-stricken year, and a compassionate extended community weathered those heart-wrenching events in my family with us. My family and community ordeals and the responses people had to them prepared me for the Freedom Movement's concept of the Beloved Community.

Another life-transforming event in that terrible year was, I thought, mine alone. After our home burned, we were living in a house with only a shallow water well without pump or indoor plumbing, so we often bathed in nearby Sugar Creek. On a hot July afternoon, after we had worked in the fields all day, probably chopping cotton, Daddy took all us to the creek for a splash and a bath.

Sugar Creek is very narrow, and in most places very shallow. Joyce remembers that I was adventurous and hardheaded and that I wandered away to explore the creek.

The leaves formed a carpet on the creekbed. I can still remember the feel of the soft, slightly slimy leaf mold on the bottoms of my bare feet. Unfortunately, leaves do not form a firm foundation. Soon, I was bobbing up and down, under water and then out. I was drowning. I was dying. I remember thinking, "Oh, so this is what dying is like. It isn't so bad." There was nothing to fear—it was entirely calm, painless, peaceful. While these tranquil thoughts flashed through my head, I was flailing away at the water.

In very slow motion, everything around me seemed clear. On one out-of-water bob, I saw Joyce still protecting our younger brothers in the shallow water near the creek bank, all of them frantically waving and yelling. I was sorry for their distress. I remember feeling a sense of serenity, of peace, even as I was frantically clutching at Wayne, who was desperately trying to rescue me. Instead, we both kept going underwater and then emerging again. I saw Daddy rushing toward us. Daddy yanked us out of the water.

My next recollection was of excruciating pain. I was lying on my stomach over a log, and enormous pressure was being exerted on my lower back. Daddy was forcing Sugar Creek out of my lungs. It burned.

Recent conversations with Joyce and Wayne added new information and dimension to this experience. Importantly, I did not know until January 1996 that Wayne almost drowned trying to save me, and that Daddy rescued both of us. I also learned that both Joyce and Wayne remember my long "beautiful blonde" hair floating on the top of the water, and how terrified they were of losing me. Even now, after our three-decade-long estrangement, which began with my civil rights involvement, both remember that afternoon with deep emotion. They clearly loved me very much and were devastated at the thought that I might die.

The date is imprinted in my sister's memory in part because it is also the birthday of our youngest sister, Polly: July 6, 1953. In this, Mother's last pregnancy, both she and baby Polly had been at risk. Polly was born prematurely, delivered by emergency cesarean section. We had all been anxious about both Mother and baby. Daddy had returned from McRae Hospital, probably after a part day of farm work, and now had the responsibility for getting us bathed and fed. Although I never talked with him about it, I can now imagine the horror of his having faced the possible death of a wife, an unborn child, and a daughter and son all in the same hot summer afternoon.

My near-death experience came into perspective for me very quickly. Wayne and I had joined our Scotland Methodist church during an earlier revival, when I was about ten years old. Joining the church meant, among other things, that one always had an adult available to talk things over with. Soon after nearly drowning, I had a long private conversation with the Methodist minister. We spoke of life, of death, of the before-here and the hereafter. We reviewed the story of creation and of God's loving relationship with mankind from the Garden of Eden to today, a story that gives me ownership of all of Jewish history and theology as well of Christianity. With his guidance, I was able to place the plagues that had afflicted my family into a perspective that made them seem transitory and tolerable. At eleven, I was learning that present chaos was a small chapter in a longer-term perspective that included my previous security and my future in another life after death. The peace with which I bobbed up and down, the calm reassurance from the minister, and something newly formed in my consciousness left me from that time until now unafraid of my own death and able to tolerate chaos and failure.

The two big intellectual experiences of my high school years were discovering Shakespeare and having Sputnik blast into space. The year between my junior and senior years at Lumber City High School, I read the complete works of Shakespeare. Imagine finding Hamlet and King Lear and Romeo and Juliet and all those obscure but melodious sonnets all in one summer! I hid out in the chinaberry tree behind the chicken house and read aloud, undeterred by my ignorance of the pronunciation or meaning of strange words, or of the concepts or history behind the stories. I was enchanted by the music and poetry and the passion.

But it was Sputnik that challenged me most. I memorized weights and trajectories and payloads and what the little satellite was supposed to accomplish. I bravely agreed to argue the first affirmative on our debate team when the topic was the unpopular "Resolved: That the Russian system of education is preferable to that of the United States." I really wanted to be involved in the space program.

I believe the lessons I learned at church, first at Shiloh Methodist Church and then at Scotland Methodist Church. These two rural congregations were few in number, probably no more than a dozen families each. Scotland Methodist shared a minister with three other churches. He visited us one Sunday each month, but we had a vigorous Sunday school. Our preachers emphasized the Methodism tradition that compelled individual responsibility for other people, strongly stressing individual as well as congregational duties for foreign and local missionary work. The minister during my teenage years was a short, chubby, jolly fellow who simply loved life. He came to our home after church for Sunday dinner and an afternoon of visiting almost every month. He loved Mother's fried chicken, which was our Sunday meal year round. When the drive-in theater opened, leaving many church people aghast at such a sinful presence in our pastoral community, he loaded us older Sunday school kids in his car and took us to the movie there.

Methodism as practiced at Shiloh and Scotland, Georgia, and in my home was an exuberant, joyful, life-affirming faith. The choir and congregation sang intensely personal hymns. In song I learned that "Jesus loves me, this I know, for the Bible tells me so" and that "Jesus loves the little children, all the children of the world; red and yellow, black and white, they are precious in His sight; Jesus loves the little children of the world." A banner from the church's founding proclaimed, "God Is Love." In sermons and song, Scotland Methodist Church prepared me for the congregational singing and intense emotionalism of Freedom Movement mass meetings.

The God we worshiped loved His Creation, loved every one of us, even when we were not good. I did not think that God created a hell to punish me for sin. I thought that when I was bad, He, like my Mother, just cried.

My schools, church, friends, neighbors — except for one family who lived at the very edge of the school attendance district — and all social institutions were all white. Segregation simply was an unquestioned way of life. I do not recall growing up with overt racist messages, but I learned that the same soil that nurtured me also produced two of the most powerful and notorious racist politicians in Georgia's history. Governor Eugene Talmadge's farm was only four miles from ours. He was, to us, a neighboring farmer. As a child, Governor and U.S. Senator Herman E. Talmadge swam in the same Sugar Creek in which I almost drowned. We knew Eugene's widow and Herman's mother, "Miz Mitt," as we called Mattie Thurmond Talmadge, a South Carolina native and cousin to Strom Thurmond.

Growing up, I do not recall a single incident, or report of an incident, or even rumor or gossip about an incident, involving racial animosity. Racial segregation in the Telfair County of my youth was rigid and unchallenged, yet I was not aware that segregation was violently enforced. Perhaps racism was in the air and those, like me, who did not pay close attention somehow just didn't "get it."

Since I had such scant direct experience with black people — really, little direct experience with anyone outside our small community — much of what I knew about them came from reading the county newspaper, the *Telfair Enterprise*, which came to our home weekly; the weekly *Lumber City Log*; and the daily *Macon Telegraph*. Reading the newspaper cover to cover and discussing it over supper or during long evenings was a regular activity. I read the *Log* and the *Enterprise* every week and read most of the *Telegraph*. These showed an interest in the school achievements and deaths of black people, as well as an evenhandedness of administration of justice regardless of race. Without any personal contact with black people, without knowing whether their lives were fully reported in the newspapers, I could only assume that the sagas of their lives were covered in a similar manner as my family and our neighbors.

The *Telfair Enterprise* honored native son Herman Talmadge and printed his attacks on the Supreme Court school desegregation decision and on integration. Other state and regional racist politicians received approving coverage as well. In the 1955–62 period, when I would have been reading the *Enterprise* avidly, it seemed to use the word "nigger" only when quoting an identified speaker. In its general coverage, black people were referred to as Negroes or colored. Black students were commended for admission to colleges, the Negro farm club members were commended for success in a corn-growing competition, and some black deaths (though surely not all) received obituaries. The fund drives of black churches were publicized, along with lists and amounts contributed by white benefactors. The bookmobile stops were announced in advance and were listed as being open to either by white and colored patrons.

I never thought of my family or myself in terms of racial attitudes until after the Freedom Movement forced people to openly take sides. Even then, I knew that Mother was not prejudiced against any of God's children, although Daddy came to speak badly of everyone, including his own children. When I recently asked Wayne and Joyce what we called the few black people with whom we had contact, they agreed that we did not use the word "nigger." As they reminded me, we just called them by their first names. If forced to refer to the race, we said colored people or we said "Nigra," but nobody in my house could say "Negro."

My personal contact with black people came in our family's cotton patch. Tobacco and cotton were our primary cash crops, and both were labor-intensive. The flue-cured tobacco we grew had to be harvested on a weekly basis, one leaf at a time. We usually exchanged labor with another white family to harvest tobacco.

Cotton picking, however, called for that very rare event on our farm: paid farm labor. We picked cotton all day, side by side—hired black men and women from McRae or Helena and everyone in the family who was old enough to pull a cotton sack. At noon, we sat under shade trees, black mothers and fathers on blankets or quilts with their children, we on our blankets. Mother brought slabs of store-bought bologna, which to this day I associate with working in tobacco and cotton fields. She brought store white bread, which we believed to be inferior but necessary on cotton-picking days. Mother (and later, when he could drive, Wayne) brought tubs of iced-down Royal Crown Cola, Nehi, and Coca-Cola. We ate clustered in family groups, in the shade. The groups were near enough to banter, to converse in normal voices. All of us saved our strength for the long afternoon ahead, however; picking cotton, in temperatures often above one hundred degrees, was far more important than socializing or horsing around.

Cotton picking meant that one had a large sack slung over one shoulder by a strap. The picker dragged this sack and stooped over cotton stalks, pulling lint from hard wooden bolls. As bolls opened, they formed sharp points, so at the end of a day the skin around the fingernails would show hundreds of tiny punctures. Some of the adults carried very long sacks, choosing to drag heavy loads to save the time lost by going to empty smaller sacks. Each of us emptied the cotton from our sacks onto separate large sheets that were made from four croker or burlap sacks sewn together. When the sheet was full enough, opposite corners were tied and knotted.

At the end of the day, the sheets were weighed on portable hanging scales mounted on a long, debarked pole. One end of the pole might rest on the tailgate of the truck, or on a man's shoulder. The scale's hook, about midway the length of the pole, was slipped under the knots in the sheet. Another man — Granddaddy, Wayne, or one of the black cotton pickers — would lift the other end of the pole, suspending the sheet off the ground. The sheet full of cotton swung freely. With the cotton picker looking on, Mother or Wayne or Granddaddy moved the hanging weights down the balance beam's arms until the weight was determined. We all gathered around the scales in eager anticipation. Everybody wanted the maximum weight. Mother and Daddy wanted the highest yield to take to the gin; I wanted the pride of being a good cotton picker; and the hired workers were paid by the pound, so weight determined their pay for the day's labor. Each family had a scrap of paper on which Mother wrote their weights.

Wayne and Joyce and I all remember attempting to pick a hundred pounds of cotton in one day. A hundred pounds in one day was a rite of passage into adulthood. At seven, Joyce was so sad at being left out of cotton picking that she wheedled her way into the cotton patch with her own miniature cotton sack. Wayne thought that if he picked the rows between a proficient black husband and wife and stayed right alongside them all day long, picking two rows at a time the way they did, he would pick a hundred pounds. His best record was eighty pounds, after which he quit picking cotton and found other useful chores. That summer of 1953 when I turned eleven, I picked my first hundred pounds of cotton in one day. It was a day of triumph, a sign of growing up. Later when I took high school typing, we learned to pace our fingers by listening to recordings with rhythms for different typing speeds. I remember progressing from ten words a minute through twenty, thirty, forty, fifty, and sixty. My ambition during typing, however, was not to be a good typist but to keep my fingers quick and nimble so I could pick more cotton. By the time I was sixteen, I was picking over two hundred pounds a day.

A few weeks later, when we could not afford to hire hands to help us gather the late-opening bolls, I missed the camaraderie of the black cotton pickers. As much as I loved being with my family, I also enjoyed having other people around, new people. In summer, our only contacts with people outside our family came in our fields and in church.

I was a senior in high school the first time segregation affected me personally. That fall, 1958, in response to "recent world developments"—Sputnik—the Georgia State Chamber of Commerce began the Student-Teacher Achievement Recognition, or STAR, program to honor the state's best students. STAR selected the high school student in each school, county, region, and finally the state who scored highest on the College Board Scholastic Aptitude Test (SAT). I was tickled to be the area's first STAR student, since I've always liked to win. My pride turned to anger, however, when I read in the *Telfair Enterprise* that the Chamber of Commerce did not allow the black students in the segregated school to compete. I felt cheated of the chance to compete against all the county's students and have a chance to prove myself the legitimate STAR student. Now I would never know if I were the best student or not.

My math and verbal SAT scores were almost identical. Somehow I had learned more math and science than the limited high school curriculum taught. The high school course most likely to lead to the space program was physics, so I decided I wanted to be a physicist. The only avenue I knew for studying physics was to attend Georgia Institute of Technology, but because of gender segregation Georgia Tech at that time was a men's school—white, of course. Since the door to outer space was closed, I would have to find another science-based challenge. Since I could not be an astronaut, I decided to become a doctor like Dr. Duncan McRae. Our family physician, he had interned as a marine in World War II. He was wonderfully skilled but had no patience for malingering. He led our county's New Group, which sought to wrest power from the Talmadge-backed Courthouse Group of Democrats. Mother's work with the New Group is one source of my social conscience.

My parents did not have money to pay for college, and allowing me to go also meant that the family would lose my labor on the farm. Wayne had married and moved to Macon. Now, without either Wayne or me, Mother would have to change the way she farmed. I sometimes still feel guilty because I know that I could have been a great help to my family if I had stayed home instead of going off to college. Joyce remembers feeling that I abandoned her. And of course, that's exactly what I did.

In June 1959, two weeks after high school graduation, I enrolled at Georgia State College for Women (GSCW) in Milledgeville. Mother paid the first summer's fees: $257. Scholarships and work study would have to take care of college expenses thereafter. I planned to finish a pre-med B.S. in three years by attending summer school as well as three regular quarters. By accelerating through college and medical school, I thought I could be earning money in about six years. Then I could help my brothers and sisters go to college.

After a world in which I knew everybody and their kin, as well as their family history, Milledgeville with its twelve thousand people seemed to me to be a huge city. Its rhythms were less protective, more cosmopolitan, than anyplace I had ever been. College—classes, laboratories, the library—was exciting. It was harder to make good grades than at Towns Junior High or Lumber City High School, and so I studied even harder. Several nights a week I was the last student to leave the library, and then left only because it was closing.

College was full of possibilities, and I was confident that I could master whatever I wanted. I ran for class president, barely losing in a good-natured but intense competition with my roommate. I was a reporter on the college newspaper. My freshman-year campus job, serving sixteen other students at linen-covered tables in the dining hall, was made bearable with the help of my "big sister," Jo Dunahoo. Her two tables were near mine, and she pinch-hit for me when my laboratory classes caused me to be late.

Racial integration of higher education was the dominant public policy issue in Georgia at that time. Georgia's state university segregation was successfully challenged in 1960–61. Governor Ernest Vandiver was elected on the pledge that during his administration no black student—"no, not one"—would attend the same school as a white student. The state legislature was threatening to close the entire state university system rather than admit Charlayne Hunter and Hamilton Holmes to the University of Georgia. In the spring of 1960, the legislature appointed a Milledgeville native, John Sibley, to hold hearings around the state to gather citizen input and accept petitions on whether people preferred to close the schools to avoid racial desegregation or keep them open. I followed in Jo Dunahoo's footsteps and signed, then recruited signatures on a petition drive for the Sibley Commission. We were asking that the free public schools not be closed to avoid integration. I remember that we garnered about 450 of the 650 student signatures, although the *Colonnade* reported that only 375 students signed the petition. Although we were directly opposing the white supremacists' political establishment, dominated still by the Talmadgites, I do not remember feeling that we were doing anything radical or dangerous.

After an initial infatuation with paved streets and paved sidewalks, I missed my family. I missed my rural home of small places and small groups. The thousand-member whites-only Milledgeville Methodist Church was so large that the college-age Sunday school class had many times more people than my rural church in its entirety. I marveled that they even used the same Methodist hymnal and order of worship. The choir performed for the congregation. Even the few hymns sung by the congregation were unemotional, stiff, and formal.

I was homesick for the natural environment that had nurtured me and the warmth of my family and neighbors. Wanting to combine the best of urban intellectual life with a more idyllic, more primitive, contact with "nature," in my second fall on campus I discovered the overgrown miniforest of a retired professor of art. Here I found nooks in the undergrowth where I could sit, watch birds and clouds, read, and breathe free. I read Thoreau's *Walden Pond* here and, since they always seem to be printed in the same volume, his essay protesting slavery, *On the Duty of Civil Disobedience.* My wilderness connected my imagination and my internal sense of truth again to the mysteries and wonders of nature.

On my trips to this urban wilderness retreat, I met Reverend Mincey, a young black minister. His parsonage and church, Wesley Chapel African Methodist Episcopal, were just across the street from the college and my retreat. He would often be raking leaves or doing other outside chores and would wave and speak cordially to me, talking about weather and my reading. One afternoon, he asked me which major league baseball team claimed me as a fan. I didn't know, but accepted his invitation to watch a baseball game in his home, with his wife and young children. Our friendship developed slowly as the leaves blazed in autumn glory. In my home further south, trees didn't put on such a show of color. I was as astonished by fall leaves as I would later be with my first experience with snow. My friendly conversations with the minister were often about trees and leaves and weather.

During the fall of 1960 I attended his church occasionally. I still sometimes attended Milledgeville Methodist Church and was active in the Wesley Foundation programs. In addition, Dr. Isabelle "Izzie" Rogers, the campus YWCA director, led discussion groups over pancake breakfasts, which I participated in. Izzie brought small groups of us to the "Y" apartment to meet Flannery O'Connor, a local celebrity, whose peacocks impressed me more than the horrible people in her stories.

I was now a sophomore, and my campus job was as a student assistant in the science building. I was immersed in botany and physics, histology and chemistry. In extracurricular activities, although I was not at the pinnacle of campus leadership, I was a "somebody." I worked on the student newspaper, held offices in science clubs, and was elected worship chairman of the Wesley Foundation. My grades were respectable for someone who had leapfrogged from a tiny school into advance placement math and English. I won the freshman chemistry prize. I related well to faculty and other students. If the state kept the college open and the college kept providing scholarships and work study, there was every reason to believe I could finish my degree in three years.

That year I found a new friend, Faye Powell, who had the other room in my Sanford Hall dormitory suite. Faye was a junior, a Milledgeville native, a Methodist, and president of the Wesley Foundation. Main Street Methodist Church was her childhood home church. By now, however, I had grown to dislike the cold and formal Main Street Methodist so intensely that, for the first time in my life, I sometimes avoided Sunday worship. I tried the Episcopal church, which was interesting, and the Catholic church, where the service was conducted in Latin and Spanish, languages I did not understand. Some Sundays, I just stayed in my room.

During the late fall, Faye began accompanying me to Wesley Chapel A.M.E. Church. We were warmly welcomed by Reverend Mincey and by his congregation. Early in the winter quarter, Reverend Mincey asked the two of us to present a program to his Youth League. Early that Sunday morning, GSCW's president, Dr. Robert E. Lee, telephoned us in the dorm. He said he had received a threat of violence if we presented the program and asked us not to do it. We agreed that Reverend Mincey should make the decision, as it was his church and congregation that had been threatened. Faye phoned the minister, who agreed that we should postpone our presentation.

In February and March 1961 we became engaged in discussions with the president, the dean, and Faye's major advisor, Dr. Frances Hicks of the psychology department, about our attendance at the black church. The college administration essentially ordered us to stop attending the church while they reviewed the situation. We were ordered to President Lee's office to discuss our irregular and, in his opinion, dangerous activities. He closed the door to his office and, with a theatrical flourish, pulled a copy of the *Augusta Courier* from his bottom desk drawer. The *Courier* was published, and much of it written, by rabid racist politician Roy Harris, a Talmadge confidant and Governor Ernest Vandiver's appointee to the state university system's Board of Regents. This paper, printed in black and red ink, was famous for publishing the names of everybody connected with the protesting of segregation. Dr. Lee seemed intimidated by — even terrified of — Roy Harris.

I felt that Faye and I were facing serious decisions in an increasingly hostile place. We were already in deep trouble with GSCW for attending the black Methodist church. I needed more information to understand why attending a Methodist church caused anonymous threats of violence and Dr. Lee's fears. When we learned of Paine College's annual Christian student seminar, "The Christian Student and the University," in Augusta, it seemed a godsend. We decided to attend. Since all absences from campus had to be approved by parents and the college, we submitted routine requests to go to Augusta. Dean Barbara Chandler refused to approve our request to attend the racially integrated Paine Conference even though our parents had given us blanket approval. We circumvented her opposition by claiming to make a home visit to Faye's parents in Gray, about twenty miles away. We boarded a bus, rode from Milledgeville westward to Gray, got off, then got on an east-bound bus that took us back through Milledgeville and on to Augusta.

The Paine College Student Christian Conference introduced me to the Freedom Movement. I learned that Paine students had organized the Paine College Steering Committee and begun staging sit-ins on April 9, 1960. When I arrived in Augusta a year later, they were skilled and experienced. The conference speakers, Rev. James M. Lawson Jr. and Dr. Louis Glover, gave me the spiritual and political basis for antiracist protest. With the Paine College students, Reverend Lawson and Dr. Glover taught me how to behave as a nonviolent Christian witness against racism. They echoed and expanded lessons I had learned from childhood, showing me how to be a Shiloh witness that God is love.

My first demonstration, "Operation X," picketing downtown stores, took place that Saturday afternoon. This was disciplined protest, with rules for picketing: remove conference badges; no dangerous weapons such as nail files, pencils, or pins; don't talk to reporters; leave if asked by a policeman in uniform or showing a badge; have no spokesperson; avoid talking. We were protesting not only lunch counters but employment—water fountains, shoe stores, dressing rooms, rest rooms. We were thirteen picketers, including Reverend Lawson. We started at 4:10 and ended at 5:15 P.M.

We returned to the Paine College campus, and from there once again went to downtown Augusta, where we staged a carefully planned and disciplined sit-in at the H. L. Green variety store. Two white Mercer University students, Cecil Hudson and John Weatherly, and Connie Curry were also at the 1960 Paine Conference. Four whites—John and Cecil, Faye and I—sat on stools at the lunch counter surrounding Paine College Steering Committee leader Sylvia Rice, a black student who was an area commander. Connie paced across the street, trying to be invisible as she served as the observer. Black Paine College students walked a picket line outside the store to alert potential shoppers that we were conducting a protest. Inside the store, black Paine students were joined by black Laney High School students, whose role was to mill around and pretend to be considering purchases. They were really there to be a critical mass of friends on hand.

Green's was just around the corner from a store that served as a hangout for the Ku Klux Klan and White Citizens Council. A knot of hostile white men quickly gathered. One, later called a "blowhard" by the judge, paced behind our backs, muttering threats to Cecil that they would "get" him. The Paine College area commander told us it was time to go. As he escorted us from the store, a white man raised a knife that Cecil thought was meant for him. Bill Didley, co-chair of the Steering Committee and another area commander, leapt up to intercept the knife and was brutally stabbed just under his heart. Either Bill or Silas Norman, another Paine College student, ordered the white protesters—John, Cecil, Faye, and me—to run. We ran into the Lerner Shop a few doors down and cowered together behind racks of women's clothing and in the ladies dressing rooms until the white mob had dispersed.

Bill Didley, the young black man, was patted down by a policeman while he lay bleeding on the sidewalk, and given a ticket for "carrying a concealed weapon." Three young black men appeared quickly and took him in their car to a black doctor who treated his wounds. Didley joined us back at Paine for the postdemonstration debriefing, but began to bleed again and had to be hospitalized.

The next morning, I attended my first "mass meeting" at Tabernacle Baptist Church in Augusta. Cecil was asked to say a few words for us white students, and he was eloquent. I felt as welcome and loved as if I were in my home church at the end of a revival meeting.

Connie, Faye, Cecil, John, and I returned to Augusta to be witnesses at Didley's court date. Connie's role during the picketing and the sit-in was that of the observer, so her court testimony was crucial. In a cynical application of justice, Didley was charged, on the basis of the policeman's patting him down, with carrying a concealed weapon, the knife protruding from his ribs.

At the 1961 Paine College Conference, Faye and I met Connie Curry and learned about Connie's National Student Association's Southern Student Human Relations Project and her Southern Student seminar. John Weatherly and Casey Hayden had participated in the 1960 seminar. Faye attended the second one a few months after our Paine College Conference, along with Bob Zellner, who would become my fellow Albany Freedom Rider. Southern white antiracists inhabited a small world then. Connie traveled through the South, finding and encouraging the handful of us and introducing us to our black counterparts and to the Freedom Movement.

Faye and I had unknowingly aroused white segregationists' worst nightmares. I thought that by attending black Wesley A.M.E. Church and a Student Christian Conference at Colored Methodist Episcopal church's Paine College I was exploring new dimensions of my own Christianity. In fact, however, by placing ourselves in racially integrated settings we were perceived as actively rejecting segregation's protection from miscegenation. The way I saw things, our white skin allowed us to show racial solidarity on the Augusta picket line and lunch counter sit-in. Most important, it gave me an opportunity to practice what I believed.

In a recent evaluation of our participation, Bill Didley said that it was significant that we were the first whites, other than several Paine faculty members, who had demonstrated in Augusta. He thinks that our being southern white students from southern colleges helped raise the consciousness of people in Augusta, added to the Freedom Movement's credibility, and led some white people to be sympathetic to the students' cause. He believes that university regent Roy Harris, together with the rest of the higher education network, knew that we were picketing and sitting in in Augusta, and that each of us was known by name and school.

Fate could have chosen no more ironic place for my first demonstrations than Roy Harris's home. I suspect that Harris expressed to Dr. Lee outraged displeasure with two GSCW girls demonstrating with Paine College Steering Committee activists in his town, and even worse, during the Master's golf tournament. Even if Harris did not make direct contact with Dr. Lee, the aura of his intimidation was pervasive in Georgia's political and higher education domains. Harris was the most powerful and the most feared man in Georgia politics. He was the kingmaker in every Georgia governor's election from Eugene Talmadge's first gubernatorial campaign in 1932, demanding racial bigotry in return for eagerly sought approval, which he last bestowed on the successful 1970 candidate for governor, James Earl Carter of Plains, Georgia. Harris organized the Georgia White Citizens Council (WCC) and was president of the South-wide WCC. In 1957, he traveled with Georgia's governor Marvin Griffin to Little Rock to foment violent resistance to Central High School's desegregation. A skilled propagandist, he used the Georgia Education Commission, Georgia's version of the Mississippi Sovereignty Commission, as well as his *Augusta Courier* and his position as head of the Georgia Democratic Party Executive Committee, to promote racial segregation. He usually controlled the governor's office, and he dictated higher education policy from his position on the state Board of Regents. He was ruthless.

After Faye and I returned to our campus, I remember with a sting of outrage GSCW dean Chandler's heavy-handed threats about my campus job and scholarships. She questioned whether I had been truthful about financial need on my scholarship applications because of the shiny new bicycle, my father's only gift to me after I was sixteen, that I rode around campus. Dean Chandler would not believe that I had not asked for the bicycle and that I did not have the influence with Daddy to ask for money instead. She encouraged me to leave college and enlist in a women's branch of the military.

I was told that I was not welcome back at GSCW, that if I tried to return I would be expelled and my permanent record would be blemished, and that I would not receive any further financial assistance. If I kept quiet the remainder of the quarter and left voluntarily, nothing on my record would prohibit my transfer to another college. I went quietly.

I visited the black Methodist church not because it was black but because the minister and I had struck up a cordiality that was reminiscent in style to my rural roots. I went there to worship, not to break some racial barrier. Certainly I had no notion that attending church would lead to my expulsion from college. I did not know that society had built those limits into my own freedom. If asked today to choose between attending that church and completing my education, I am not sure which choice I would make. But at the time, I thought that I was making a choice of a church community, not the end of my stay at GSCW.

I stumbled innocently, unaware, across southern racism's dividing line. In the rural isolation of my home, I did not know that there was a taboo against black and white Methodists worshiping God together. In the end, my search for the warmth and friendliness of a small community meant ostracism from the very thing I sought. As I crossed that racial line, it seemed that an invisible but powerful force snatched my white-world passport. The personal history I was writing made me an outcast in white southern society, while my white skin sometimes separated me from black people. I became, at once, irrevocably, racially homeless.

I don't think anyone except Mother knew why I left Milledgeville. In Georgia, in 1961, if you didn't fit anywhere else, you could always go to Atlanta. So with $25 and a one-way Greyhound bus ticket given to me by Mother, I landed in Atlanta at the age of eighteen, with one quarter of my junior year in college completed. I believe this was the first time in my life that I was really frightened. All other bad spots in my life had been shared with my family or my community or, in leaving college, at least with Faye. Now I felt alone, cast out from that supportive world and unprepared to make it on my own.

I was not totally alone, though. Mother had arranged for me to stay at least a few days in Uncle Charlie and Aunt Ruth's home in southwest Atlanta. Faye also gave me the phone numbers of her friends Phil Cole and Becky.

In five days, I had a job at Emory University Library and a spare room in Becky's apartment for the summer. By the end of the summer, Phil had dropped out of Georgia Tech to join the army and I moved into his $30-per-month, three-room, furnished apartment. It was a fourth-floor walk-up at 240 Ponce de Leon Avenue, apartment no. 25, a genteel slum, but to me it was paradise. After living in a crowded home and dormitory, I found no. 25 to be huge. In a world I was navigating without understanding, I now had a refuge that was all mine.

When Georgia State College for Women forced me to leave, they accused me of belonging to or working for several organizations, none of which I had even heard of. Now settled in my own apartment, with a job, relishing full participation in St. Mark's Methodist Church and its college-age group, I wanted to find out what these organizations were. I was dating Bill Humphries, a student at Georgia Tech who also worshiped at St. Mark's. I told Bill, "You know, I was accused of working for all these organizations in Atlanta, and that's why I had to leave college. So do you know about these organizations?" He didn't, but he and I did some research, and we then systematically made the tour: Urban League, Southern Regional Council, NAACP; I don't think we found the ACLU or maybe it didn't have an office then. We made appointments and visited these groups' offices, where they gave us generous amounts of time. We asked questions: What are you about? What do you do? My ultimate quest was to find the connection between these organizations and my untimely departure from college. It was instructive, and I am glad I did it, because it was the first time I had ever seen large numbers of black professionals. Of course, I already knew Connie Curry, and I visited her United States National Student Association office. She introduced me to Ella Baker and Casey Hayden, who worked for the YWCA in Connie's office building.

And then, whether through Connie, Ella and Casey, or on our own, I don't remember, Bill and I found the Student Nonviolent Coordinating Committee. My first SNCC contact was with Jim Forman, Executive Secretary. Julian Bond was there as well. He was a writer, and I thought writers were mysterious, creative, magical people. Norma Collins was Office Manager. I was drawn to SNCC's few dingy, poorly lit, upstairs rooms on Auburn Avenue. I remember dilapidated desks and chairs, with lots of commotion, always lots of people mimeographing. I felt lucky to do whatever Jim, Julian, or Norma asked me to do. Julian Bond wrote press releases, and I folded them and put them in envelopes, feeling I had been entrusted with a very special task. Mostly, I turned the crank on a ditto machine or typed stencils. All that typing practice that I thought was good training only for cotton picking was now being used for the movement. There was a sense of urgency about everything that happened in the office, and Jim, Norma, and Julian were amazingly tolerant of my inexperience. I wasn't paid. I didn't know anybody was. In the past few years, some movement people have defined hierarchies of involvement, using subsistence payroll stubs from SNCC as the highest level of commitment. Since I was not on the payroll, this definition in a sense devalues my work with SNCC, though I don't look at it that way. I thought that surely this intense effort to overcome racial discrimination would succeed in a few months, and I was proud to participate. Besides, Emory paid me $225 a month, surely more than a SNCC worker earned.

Later, in the Albany jails, my confusion about fighting for civil rights as a volunteer versus as a paid worker intensified. Jim sent me a note written on a paper napkin saying, "You are now a SNCC volunteer worker." Norma sent one saying, "Would you consider working for SNCC." In reply, I said that I had a job, at the Emory University Library, and I needed to get back to it. In my mind, there was a difference between working for pay and working for social justice. For me, working for racial integration was like going to church; it was just something I had to do.

I planned to begin night classes at Georgia State College in January 1962. Meanwhile, I continued working and enjoying Atlanta. I felt absolutely accepted as one of the people who belonged in the SNCC circle. We sometimes ate free at B. B. Beamon's on Auburn Avenue and at Paschal Brothers across town. My volunteer work at the SNCC office was an exciting addition to a full and varied life.

During the fall, Connie Curry and Eliza Paschal of the Greater Atlanta Human Relations Council organized a Student Council on Human Relations. Frank Smith of Morehouse College was elected chairman, and I, vice-chairman. We organized interracial college student get-togethers and projects. In the fall of 1961 and spring of 1962, through the Council on Human Relations and St. Mark's Methodist Church, I worked with the Wesley Memorial Methodist Church in Atlanta in its recreation program for children in the Capitol Heights and Techwood housing developments.

Sometimes people ask when I joined the movement. "Join" is too formal for how the movement happened. People identified a role for themselves and then moved in and out in response to individual inspiration. I tried to be a student and nonviolent and one of the coordinated. That is how I came to be on the Albany Freedom Ride.

Some historians have called the Albany Freedom Ride the "Rosa Parks" incident that incited the Albany Movement to begin massive direct action demonstrations. I don't know. But I was an Albany Freedom Rider.

The U.S. Supreme Court had legalized racial segregation in its 1896 decision *Plessy v. Ferguson*, which said that railroads might require black passengers to sit in separate but equal Jim Crow cars. In December 1960, the Court reversed *Plessy* in *Boynton v. Virginia*. Freedom Rides, tests of compliance with the court's decision, became front-page news in May and June 1961. Television, radio, and newspapers drew images of Greyhound buses afire, with towers of black smoke rising above Anniston, Alabama. Integrated groups of Congress of Racial Equality (CORE) riders from North and South and black and white Nashville SNCC students were bloodied by brutal police-assisted mobs in Birmingham and Montgomery. Freedom Rides proved that southern white men, defying the U.S. Supreme Court, intended to enforce racial segregation in interstate transportation. Long prison sentences in Mississippi's barbaric Parchman Penitentiary met those Freedom Riders who rode as far as Jackson. The Freedom Riders' courage led ultimately to the Interstate Commerce Commission (ICC) ruling that all interstate transportation facilities — buses, airlines, and trains, and the ground facilities that supported them, such as airports, bus stations, and train depots — must integrate and serve all passengers. The ICC ruling went into effect November 1, 1961.

Bill Humphries and I heard that SNCC was planning a Freedom Ride on a train to test the recent ICC ruling. I was one of many SNCC people who had tested ICC compliance at the Atlanta bus terminal facilities. In November others had tested ICC compliance on buses leaving Atlanta for towns throughout the South, but no one had tested trains, the transportation mode involved in *Plessy v. Ferguson*. SNCC field workers in Albany and the Albany Movement invited us to help them by testing that town's train station. Bill and I attended meetings at the SNCC office to learn more about this Albany Freedom Ride.

Jim Forman wanted the ride to be half white and half black people. He had recruited four blacks: Bernard Lee of the Southern Christian Leadership Conference, SNCC's Norma Collins, Atlanta University graduate student Lenora Taitt, and himself.

When Bill and I joined the discussion, four other whites had volunteered to take the ride, three of whom would be part of the group to integrate the demonstration portion of the ride: Bob Zellner, field secretary for SNCC, whose weekly stipend was paid by the Southern Conference Education Fund; Per Laursen, a Danish journalist who was writing a book about America; and Tom Hayden, who I understood was on assignment to write an article about the student movement for *Mademoiselle* magazine. To have eight testers, the ride would need nine participants, because it was standard discipline in integration tests to designate one person to stand apart from the group, an observer safe from arrest. This role of observer was crucial to protect those subject to arrest. The observer often was the only witness, other than arrested demonstrators, who could be relied on to tell the truth in court and to the press. The observer also would not be in jail, and so would be free to contact the SNCC headquarters and others who could mobilize whatever resources were necessary. Importantly, the observer had the responsibility of feeding information to Julian Bond, who would issue press releases and ensure that public attention kept those in jail as safe as possible. Both the designated observer and Julian's public information job were responsible roles. Because Sandra Cason (Casey) Hayden, with her job at the YWCA, could not afford to go to jail, she was the Albany Freedom Ride's designated observer.

Bill desperately wanted to be the fourth white freedom rider, but it was impossible. If he were arrested, his Air Force Reserve Officer Training Corps scholarship would be revoked and he would immediately be drafted and sent to Korea for peacekeeping, or to Vietnam. I wanted to do something in the movement and believed that when I started night school at Georgia State College the next month I would not have time to work full time, go to school, and be in demonstrations. My white skin made the Albany Freedom Ride half white and half black, so I volunteered to go.

Nine of us planned to board the train in Atlanta. We would attempt to sit together in a "white" passenger car all the way to Albany. If we got to Albany, we would go into the "white" waiting room. Then we would meet SNCC field secretaries Charles Sherrod, Cordell Reagon, and Charles Jones, and go to an Albany Movement mass meeting. We would be guests of local people in their homes overnight and take the train back to Atlanta on Monday. Of course, we knew that we could be stopped at any point. We might not be allowed to board the train in Atlanta. We might be taken off at any stop and arrested. We might be beaten and brutalized anywhere along the way. All I told my supervisor at Emory was that I needed to be away from work on Monday and maybe Tuesday.

I was a little apprehensive, I suppose, because I knew that buses had been burned and Freedom Riders had been brutally beaten or thrown in jail. But I trusted Jim Forman and Casey Hayden to know what to do. Jim seemed to be a strong, affectionate, and wise man. I thought that he would look out for me. And Casey, the designated observer, was open and accepting, articulate, posed, and stylish. Seeming to know when I needed a reassuring hug or a squeeze on the shoulder, she inspired absolute confidence in me that she had the savvy, toughness, and caring to do whatever needed to be done. Indeed, I saw in her depth of commitment and generous affection the embodiment of the Beloved Community. Casey and Jim would decide what to do, and all I had to do was stick with the group. I was not blindly naive and trusting. Jim and Casey had earned my confidence.

I followed Casey's instructions and obediently put clean underwear and my toothbrush in my purse. I felt silly and a little risqué with dainties in my purse and hoped that nobody would ever know. Since this was not only a demonstration but also a Sunday, I carefully dressed in my new Sears & Roebuck olive green corduroy suit, with fabric-covered buttons on the jacket, a plaid vest, and an A-line skirt, and brightly shined penny loafers.

On Sunday, December 10, 1961, the nine of us boarded the train in Atlanta. The rude conductor ordered the four black Freedom Riders out of the "white" car, but when they didn't move, he allowed us to sit together.

The train ride to Albany was fun. We cracked jokes and we sang freedom songs. Tom Hayden and Bob Zellner had just come from McComb, Mississippi, and they talked about what they had experienced there. Others told stories from the sit-in movement. Casey Hayden awed me with her anti-establishment wit. I had heard people solemnly preach and lecture about evil, but she was the first person I ever heard make fun of things that I had thought it naughty to laugh at.

The train usually stopped in Macon only long enough to let off and take on passengers. It stopped normally this day, but then did not move. My understanding was that the railroad people were calling train headquarters to see if they should proceed, or what they should do with us.

I got off the train and had a long talk with my friends Faye Powell and her husband-to-be, Cecil Hudson, a Korean War army veteran with whom we had demonstrated in Augusta during the Paine conference. They had come to the station to see us Freedom Riders and to help if we were arrested in Macon. After a delay of about half an hour, I reboarded the train and it proceeded toward Albany.

Our group became very quiet as we neared our destination. When the train pulled into the Albany station, we all got off. Casey Hayden separated from the rest of us. Eight of us walked past the freight station into the "white" waiting room. A few sat on benches, but I didn't. After about five minutes, we all proceeded through the station and into the parking lot. We were met by about fifty cheering black people and a handful of white hecklers. I had been directed to a black taxi cab and was actually seated in the back when I was pulled out to be placed under arrest. Eleven of us were arrested: in addition to myself, the three white men, two black men, and two black women who had boarded the train in Atlanta, plus SNCC field secretary Charles Jones and two Albany State students, Bertha Gober and Wilma Henderson.

I had never dreamed that I would be in jail. I was embarrassed to be there, but also proud because I had acted on my beliefs. The community around me, white and black, male and female, sustained me. Without the comfort I derived from Casey Hayden, Norma Collins, and Lenora Taitt, I could not have endured those frightening and lonely days.

The details of the Albany Freedom Ride are contested historical territory. It is enough for this story to say that I was the only white woman on the Freedom Ride or in the Albany Movement in jail during that week and a half. After a long day and night in the Albany city jail, we were bailed out late Monday afternoon and attended a mass meeting that night. We were out of jail until Thursday morning but remained in Albany for court proceedings. On Monday night, Casey Hayden, her husband, Tom, and I were housed in the home of Jack Singletary, a white Baptist minister who was associated with Koinonia Farm in Americus. Tuesday and Wednesday nights the three of us were housed with the black Slater King family in Albany.

Ironically, being the white girl was fraught with special dangers, for me and everyone around me. On that first day I wrote to Faye from the Albany jail:

> Rumor has it that I am a special mark. The white men feel that they should take steps to save me from myself and these people I'm with. . . . I just heard that I caused a hell of a disturbance. It seems that never in their experiences has a white girl—especially such a quiet, soft-spoken, all-American type—been involved. Jim Forman, Chairman of SNCC, tells me the cops and local whites are amazed. . . . White toughs attempted to follow Tom, Sandra (his wife) and me as we were going to lunch. We returned to the City Hall & our lawyer called a white cab—Negroes & whites are forbidden by law to ride in the same cab. They have a law against fraternization. . . . Last night we played hide-&-seek with cops to get into the white man's car & get to his house. We chased back and through a church. Exciting.

After a mockery of a trial, nine Freedom Riders were returned to the county jail on Thursday. Tom Hayden stayed out of jail on bond, and he and Casey left town to keep other appointments. Again I was the only white woman in the jail, although this time my cell shared a brick wall with the black women's cell. We could talk through our open but barred windows. With Casey gone, Lenora Taitt and Norma Collins joined Jim Forman, Bob Zellner, and Per Laursen in their efforts to keep my spirits up. They wrote notes on scraps of paper, napkins, paper towels. My fellow Freedom Riders stand out in my memories as truly a "circle of trust, a brotherhood of love."

As the Albany Movement exploded around me in my solitary confinement, sending hundreds of black Albanians to jail each day, a network of concerned people hovered nearby. Both Bill and Mother came to the Albany jail. Neither was allowed to see or talk with me, although my jailers made sure that I knew they had been there and had been turned away. Cecil Hudson and Faye Powell phoned attorney C. B. King, who reassured them that I was okay and that there was nothing they could do by coming to Albany. At some point during the week, Connie Curry and Ella Baker were in town, as was Frances Pauley, director of the Georgia Council on Human Relations. Frances was a white woman who became quite important to me in the movement. I stayed in Albany ten days, all but two of them in Albany City or Dougherty County jail.

The Albany Freedom Ride was big news in south Georgia. My name was printed in all the newspapers. My brother Wayne opened his *Macon Telegraph*, saw my name, and disgustedly threw the paper in the trash. When Mother called him and asked him what she should do, he advised leaving me there. All over south Georgia television stations broadcast the Thursday return of the Freedom Riders to jail. From the Dougherty County jail, I wrote to Faye: "Today we were escorted in a line two abreast across the street to here. Lenora Tate [*sic*] and I led the line talking and laughing and especially making remarks to the effect that these guys are nervous as if they expect someone to knife them in the back and that they couldn't quite understand our nonviolence." Later, Mother told me that she had seen a television news broadcast of me taking that walk.

Mother and Daddy were divorced in the previous year, in 1960. Daddy had very little contact with any of us from then on. She remarried in the fall of 1961 and moved back to Wheeler County, to Spring Hill community, about two miles from Shiloh. The immediate consequence of my being in jail was that Mother and her new husband decided that I could not come to their home for Christmas. Christmas without my family was unimaginable. Mother felt that she would not be able to remain in Wheeler County and raise her six small children without harassment if she openly supported me. She didn't disagree that segregation was evil, and she didn't mind that other people's children put themselves in jail and at risk to end it, but she couldn't put her own existence on the line for my beliefs. She made it clear that she still loved me, but that I could not come home. As Wayne said, "We just wrote you out of the family."

Being "written out of my family" has scarred and shaped my life ever since. It was immediately horrible. I did not yet have a fully formed identity apart from my place in my family, so I literally did not know who I was. I searched for a new identity in the new, exciting intellectual climate in which I now found myself. I had come from a fairly isolated world to a place where previous sureties could be challenged. Building on the lessons about duty I had learned in childhood, I took a deeper sense of my need to be a moral agent from the intellectual ferment of the times, a ferment that for me included Thoreau and Gandhi. I enjoyed free run of the Emory University Library and had found the Carnegie Branch of Atlanta Public Library. Georgia Tech's library was in walking distance from my apartment, and it was open twenty-four hours a day. Most exciting of all was the leadership of young people, people my age or not more than a few years older, engaging in Freedom Rides and sit-ins. Young people, mostly southerners, black and white, men and women, were creating this new blend of action and moral beliefs. If they could help create a better world, so could I.

On October 12, 1961, I went to Atlanta University Center to hear the Reverend Martin Luther King Jr. expound his theology of nonviolent resistance in a speech titled "Nonviolence, Civil Disobedience, and the Future of the Negro." White ministers and theologians were reinforcing that message. The co-leaders of my college-age church group, in which we studied major religions of the world, were professors from Candler School of Theology, including Thomas Altizer, the author of *God Is Dead*. The same radical Christian ideals were circulating throughout the South. At Georgia Tech's Wesley Foundation, I heard various visiting speakers. Among them was Rev. Joseph Mathews of the Christian Faith and Life Community in Austin, Texas, a central figure to my co-writers Casey Hayden and Dorothy Burlage, who had lived in the Community; his talk inspired me to subscribe to the Christian Faith and Life's monthly "Letters to Laymen." Increasingly, I found my spiritual exploration turning from organized Christianity to activism and into existentialism and eastern mysticism. I read Dietrich Bonhoeffer and Alan Watts, whom I also heard speak at the Wesley Foundation.

Hope and fear permeated the atmosphere around me and the thoughts in my head. The Freedom Movement's early successes in forging a different kind of force, the power of disciplined nonviolent direct-action protests, had given me hope that a peaceful way of solving social problems might be applied more broadly. The Cuban missile crisis in October 1962, however, tempered that hope. Atlanta was reported to be a prime target for Castro's missiles. I was damned if I would die in those musty civil defense shelters in office building basements, so I had my penny loafers resoled. When the bombs first fell, I planned to start walking north, toward the mountains, and I'd walk until the radiation killed me. I would die standing up, out in God's creation.

I was attracted to the Freedom Movement and to the people in it whose commitment to a just society led them to willingly face death. The movement allowed harmony in myself between ideas and ideals and action. I could be more fully whole in the movement than anywhere else. I also thought the movement promised a new way of bringing reconciliation and peace where there had been anger and lynchings. The Beloved Community might save the planet from nuclear or other environmental destruction. It might save the endangered soul of modern man. It might be the restoration of the apostolic church.

Seeking a fuller understanding of how to define and live a moral life, I committed myself to try to act on my beliefs. My involvement was an expression of my profound belief that each of us is one of an infinite number of actual images of God, and so race is irrelevant. That belief identified me as one of a handful of persons in the South promoting racial integration. In Georgia before 1965, a woman, whether white or black, could not engage in racial integration activity on even the most private level without being the object of public attention.

In 1962 I met Dorothy Dawson, newly arrived in Atlanta as assistant director to Connie Curry's National Student Association project. Dorothy was soon evicted from her apartment for having black guests, and Connie asked if Dorothy could move in with me until she found another place to live. As much as I loved my private three-room kingdom, in the spirit of the times I of course said yes.

My tranquil home became a hectic meeting place for movement people. I never knew who might be there, or how long they would stay. All these people were older than I, and they all seemed to be working full time in the movement. I sometimes wonder how my life might have developed without these older, better-educated, more experienced, and more committed people around me.

During this period, it became increasingly clear that I had been targeted for official surveillance. At the time, I believed that the FBI was observing me. Since I do not have an FBI file, however, I have come to the conclusion that I was being watched by the Georgia Bureau of Investigation and the Georgia Education Commission. Dorothy's and my mail was opened; sometimes it was steamed open carefully and resealed, though sometimes the vandalism was blatant. For several months in 1962 and early 1963, two white men in trench coats stood hours at a time across the street, leaning up against the windows of a shop where one could buy live chickens. At one point, we were so certain that the telephones had been tapped that we borrowed a long ladder from the building superintendent and crawled into the attic crawl space to check; sure enough, something new and shiny had been added to the wires running into my apartment. This surveillance was perhaps a result of the notoriety I'd gained on the Albany Freedom Ride, or from having my home turned into a freedom house visited by black and white friends and Freedom Riders, people older and more radical than I, some of them red diaper radicals from the North.

The same core values that attracted me to the Freedom Movement operated in other arenas of my life. I had entered college as a pre-med major. When I lost scholarships because of my attendance at a black church, I had had to abandon my goal of becoming a doctor, but I still sought scientific experiences. With two years of college-level science and math under my belt, I applied and was accepted for a position as water purification technician for the city of Atlanta, Department of Water Works. When I went to meet my prospective supervisor and fill out personnel papers, he mentioned that it was fortunate that I had applied, since a black man with a master's degree in biology was the most qualified candidate and they did not want to offer the job to a Negro. I turned the job down on principle. This was not a trivial decision. I wanted that job, but only if I were the most qualified applicant; since I apparently wasn't, I wanted it to go to the best applicant, regardless of race — especially regardless of race. (Is there any way to know whether they hired the black man?)

During the spring of 1962, I participated in sit-ins in Atlanta at Woolworth's, at the Trailways and Greyhound bus stations, and at Leb's Restaurant. I accompanied Bob Zellner on a trip to Talladega College in Alabama, where we joined black students protesting segregation at the town bus station.

Dorothy's friend Michael Sayer, from New York City, was a 1962 summer intern on the *Atlanta Journal* and rented the apartment next door to mine. Connie and I tried to show Mike the real South. We took him to the Rio Vista, an "all you can eat" catfish restaurant, and, with Faye and Cecil, to a large KKK rally at Stone Mountain, Georgia. We warned him that if he uttered one

Brooklyn/Harvard syllable, it could be us and not an empty cross burning on the barren rock.

I worked only part time in the summer of 1962, so I used my free time to explore the world. The Disciples of Christ Church gave me a scholarship to attend Fisk University's week-long Race Relations Institute, where I met the Reverend Will Campbell, who is a spiritual mentor for many of my generation. I traveled north for the first time, going by bus to Washington, D.C., where I toured the city. Sputnik again overpowered Shakespeare, as I chose to see the air exhibits in the Smithsonian instead of the Folger Shakespeare Library. In New York City, Mike Sayer's parents graciously showed me around. In Boston I spent a few days with Phil Cole, who was in army intelligence and stationed at Fort Devens. From Boston I flew to Columbus, Ohio, to attend Connie's three-week Southern Student Human Relations Seminar and the NSA congress. Will Campbell was the seminar's advisor.

In the fall of 1962, I helped elect another graduate of one of Connie Curry's seminars, Stuart Strenger, as the first Jewish president of Georgia State College's student government. It was a nasty campaign. Frank Smith left college to work with SNCC in Mississippi, so I assumed the chair of the Greater Atlanta Student Council on Human Relations. And I resigned as book review editor of the Georgia State College *Signal* rather than agree to heavy-handed administration censorship of an editorial I wrote claiming that we were all guilty of the murder of two people during the riot that accompanied James Meredith's enrollment at Ole Miss.

Using Connie Curry's office mimeograph, I mailed a letter to college students in the metro Atlanta area announcing the Greater Atlanta Student Council on Human Relation's fall program. In it I proposed that we engage in "work camp projects, discussion groups, tutoring, research projects, a newsletter, hosting foreign students, recreation projects, a statewide conference on human relations." Hoping to finish my A.B. degree by the end of the school year, I began dreaming about graduate school, in either English or biochemistry. Unfortunately, money was always a problem. Jim Monsonis of Students for a Democratic Society handled a fund to help with "freedom fighting losses." I wrote him: "Briefly, the reason I need money is that my mother was so upset by the Albany business that she refused to co-sign a loan, which had been approved; and since I am a mere 20 years old, my guardian must sign. Whether this constitutes 'freedom fighting' loss you should know better than I."

In that unsung nurturing role played by women in the Freedom Movement, Connie Curry and Ella Baker sought scholarship funds for me, securing $300 from the American Baptist Home Mission Societies. The task of finding such funds was not an easy one; as Connie put it in a letter written on May 9, 1963, to J. C. Herrin, southern area consultant to the Baptist Home Mission Societies, "most groups have not made scholarship money available to white students in the South who have had difficulties because of their participation in the Freedom Movement."

Freedom fighting, supporting myself, trying to finish my baccalaureate degree, and all the unresolved issues of art, religion, and politics were intensely stressful. Connie Curry described me to Herrin: "The strains of too much responsibility and too much sadness at too young an age are already beginning to show."

In 1962 I attended the Fisk University Race Relations Institute, where I met Lynne Strauss, a student at Ohio Wesleyan University. Lynne had stepped into Mary King's leadership position in Ohio Wesleyan's Student Committee on Race Relations (SCORR), a student sit-in support organization, when Mary King moved to Atlanta to take Casey's old job with Ella Baker at the YWCA. That fall, I sent Lynne a submission to her SCORR newsletter with the explanation that

> the "Notes to the North" idea was born of the agonizing loneliness and isolation of the "new" Southerner who is freed of racial or ethnic bigotry and is alone. We are denounced by friends and family as traitors, distrusted by Negroes, and misunderstood by non-Southerners who fail to understand how we can simultaneously reject the "Southern Way of Life" and cling sentimentally to the South and love this corner of the world.

I felt suffocated in the South. Dorothy knew of a job opening as a laboratory technician on a human chromosome research project at the W. E. Fernald State School in Waverly, Massachusetts. With the synchronicity that has blessed me all my life, the director of the laboratory was a Harvard classmate of my GSCW biology professor, Dr. Clyde Keeler. Dr. Keeler's recommendation helped me get the job. It paid $2.50 an hour, $100 a week—good wages for me then. I was somewhat worried when, arriving with very little money, I learned that they would pay me only after a full month. Mother sent me a check for $150 that provided security, but fortunately I didn't need to cash it because I talked the lab into paying me an advance on my wages. For most of the summer, my daily ration of food was two sandwiches of peanut butter and banana or apple, and two glasses of reconstituted powdered milk.

The Fernald laboratory was an interesting mixture of the century's dispossessed peoples—those fleeing Nazi Germany, Eastern Europe, the Russian Revolution, Irish poverty, and Mao's revolution—and a Nova Scotia Presbyterian. These refugees from the world's totalitarian regimes shared a revulsion toward the white South in its violent resistance to racial desegregation. Nonetheless, they overcame their antipathy against white southerners. I quickly became the darling of the laboratory.

I attended a few Friends of SNCC meetings. Peggy Dammond, of the Friends, asked me to speak to a group of high school students because, as she wrote to me, "this is a majority white group and . . . it would be invaluable for you as a white Southerner to talk to them very honestly and deeply."

On the July Sunday before my twenty-first birthday, my traumatized Mother called to tell me that Danny, my sixteen-year-old brother, had been killed in a car wreck. I went to Mother's home for a week. My family's new minister, the Reverend Homer Ledbetter of Spring Hill Baptist Church, tried to help us as a family unite around our love for each other and our loss of Danny. No one spoke of racial politics. Wayne, now married and a father, stayed a short time and then returned to his home and job in Macon.

Again, my faith was being challenged. Before moving to Boston, I had begun to question nonviolence as my way of life. I had written to Dorothy Dawson Burlage saying that I was so frustrated by Bobby Kennedy's failure to send federal help to the movement in Greenwood, Mississippi, that I was tempted to buy all the guns in Atlanta and send them to Greenwood Movement people for their use in self-defense. Danny's death, the first death of someone really close to me, plunged me back into a tenderness for all of life. Any lingering questions about my own preference for nonviolence were laid to rest by President Kennedy's assassination.

On that fateful November day, I was happily immersed in chromosome studies at my electron microscope. My supervisor, Mrs. Hirsch, who had fled

Nazi Germany shortly before the Holocaust, tentatively tapped me on the shoulder and told me the president had been shot in Texas. I joined the other laboratory workers in shocked silence as we stood around a radio. Even though they were fond of me, the death in the South of the local boy made president raised fears and suspicion of all southerners, even me. This death of a national figure, so soon after Danny's death, cemented my commitment to valuing all human life. Nonviolence was definitely a way of life for me, not merely a power tactic.

I tried to find a way to finance the rest of my education. Clark University in Worcester, Massachusetts, had a southern civil rights scholarship, but it was only for black, not for white, students. They said they had never heard of a white southern civil rights activist. I was admitted to Boston University, but the tuition was out of my reach and there was no offer of financial aid.

Homesickness consumed me: not homesickness for my childhood home, which was long gone, but homesickness for the South. When I went scouring Boston's black Roxbury neighborhood for grits, I knew it was time to go home. I moved back to Atlanta on New Year's Eve 1963. Connie was not home, but she had left the keys to her apartment and to her Karmann Ghia, a sports version of a Volkswagen bug with the engine in the rear. I drove the Karmann Ghia all around Atlanta, even in an unusual snowstorm.

Mother called New Year's Day to tell me that she and Wayne had been with Mama Red when she died during the night of December 29, too late to call me in Boston before I left. Now they were all snowbound in west Georgia. The funeral was delayed because the ground was frozen and the family cemetery was up a hill that had become impassable. I desperately wanted to be there, to be with my family and to say good-bye to Mama Red, but Mother ordered me not to try. Even the weather seemed to isolate me further from my family.

I had not yet abandoned all hope of a career in science or medicine, or of using education and work to climb up into the middle class. After re-enrolling as a full-time evening student at Georgia State University, I got a thirty-hour-a-week job at Emory University, this time as a laboratory technician in the medical school's anatomy department. School and work, finding an apartment, and settling back into Atlanta kept me busy.

The SNCC office had moved and changed. Lots of new people were everywhere. Now, staff were doing all the tasks that volunteers used to do. For some of them, I was disturbed to see, nonviolence had become a tactic, not a key to the Beloved Community. Now, instead of the Sunday clothes I wore to demonstrate and to participate in the Freedom Ride, SNCC folks wore the denim I had worn to pick cotton.

I no longer fit perfectly, but I still maintained loose contact with SNCC, doing the useful tasks that fit with my beliefs. I remember volunteering for a project called Books for Equal Education, where I sorted thousands of donated volumes for Summer 1964 Mississippi Project's Freedom School libraries. I attended SNCC meetings and put up SNCC people in my home. I got my landlord to allow about a dozen visiting SNCC people to stay at no cost in a vacant apartment in my building. I still partied with SNCC friends. SNCC and the movement, though, were less central to me.

Meanwhile, I was finding it impossible to balance the demands of school and work. I tried to sustain myself with part-time jobs: in Emory's anatomy department, working under Dr. Geoffrey Bourne at the Yerkes Primate Research Center, as night director of St. Joseph's Hospital's day care center, as a temporary office worker. The day I fainted twice in the library because of malnutrition, I quit college. Once again, I found my Beloved Community among the antiracist organizations headquartered in Atlanta. I began an employment journey through them: the Southern Regional Council, where I clipped newspapers, worked as secretary for the labor education project, and did research for the prison reform project; the American Civil Liberties Union, which worked mostly on one-man-one-vote and capital punishment cases; and the National Urban League's Volunteers in Service to America (VISTA) training project. When the Westinghouse Learning Corporation won the regional VISTA training contact, I advanced to regional training director. I consulted with the regional VISTA office on recruitment. I was now one of those middle-class, well-dressed professionals who had so impressed me when Bill and I first conducted our survey.

I was securely ensconced in this sector of the Beloved Community when SNCC moved into the Black Power phase. From my perspective, Black Power was about cultural richness. I attended parties at Doris Reed's home on Hunter Street where Charles Black patiently taught me to dance the limbo. I had helped to organize the Federation of Southern Cooperatives, a marketing, training, and service organization owned by more than thirty cooperatives that grew out of the Freedom Movement. As marketing specialist, I tried to sell Shell Oil Company on the idea of using brilliantly patterned dashikis made from African produced fabric and sewn by southern cooperatives, black and white, as a premium for Shell's preferred customers. I admired and envied the beauty and simplicity of the natural black hair styles, which perhaps inspired me a few years later to stop torturing my own hair with chemicals. I always wanted to expand my boundaries, and as I experienced the cultural aspects of Black Power, it added new richness to my world.

By early 1968 I had overcome my anger at his actions as attorney general and become a passionate supporter of Robert Kennedy. Connie Curry, our colleague and friend from SNCC John Lewis, and I had attended the Federation of Southern Cooperatives' first annual meeting at Mount Beulah near Jackson, Mississippi. The three of us were in Connie's room in the Jackson Holiday Inn rejoicing as Bobby declared himself a candidate for the Democratic presidential nomination, and when he "met the press" on St. Patrick's Day 1968. Along with Connie and a small band of others, I helped organize, and served as treasurer of, "Georgians for Kennedy." I was devastated when Robert Kennedy was assassinated. Although I half-heartedly leafleted for George McGovern in 1972, I gave up on electoral politics.

One of my most satisfying activities during this time was helping to organize an alternate Georgia State Democratic Party Convention that sent a delegation to the 1968 Democratic Party Convention in Chicago to sit beside the official Georgia delegation led by Governor Lester Maddox. Julian Bond, the leader of our alternate delegation, was nominated for vice president.

I worked as handicraft marketing specialist for West Virginia Institute of Technology for a year in 1969. Back in Atlanta, after a stint with the American Friends Service Committee, I was helping the National Urban League organize a Rural Development Project when I learned that Mother was terminally ill with cancer. I dropped everything and went to live with her the last few months of her life.

When I returned to Atlanta in the summer of 1972, I did a little consulting with antiracist organizations but essentially dropped out of social activism circles. My fear of random street crime motivated me to move far out into Atlanta's suburbs, but I was uncomfortable as the only single person in a family neighborhood. I then moved to a farm in rural, mountainous Union County, Georgia, where I worked the four-to-midnight shift at a Burlington Industries carpet factory; was a substitute teacher at Woody Gap School, whose one hundred students in kindergarten through twelfth grade studied two grades to a room; and tended land. Tired of working so hard with little success, and sick of having tourists watch me tend my acre of tomatoes and fields of potatoes and onions, I moved to West Virginia. Here, I live alone on Fort Hill, a mountain overlooking the Greenbrier River.

As the years passed, my Freedom Movement memories receded. Connie urged me to return to Atlanta in 1990 for the thirtieth reunion of the Atlanta student movement. I went, and was pleased with what fine people we had grown to be. In 1991 Connie was a fellow at the Carter Woodson Institute in nearby Charlottesville, Virginia, where she reintroduced me to Julian Bond. Both were thrilled with my little stationery box of letters and notes from the early 1960s, and both urged me to write about my memories.

Anonymity has been a protective cloak that I shed reluctantly so that future activists might know more about the Freedom Movement and perhaps more successfully apply its lessons to the issues before them. I believe that each individual holds complete ownership of her private life. Accordingly, I have tried to tell the truth about those parts of my life that seem to me to have led me to the Freedom Movement, but I have also tried to respect the privacy rights of others.

My participation in the Freedom Movement was not a special project. It grew naturally out of my beliefs about my role as a Christian in response to social sins. My role was that of "witness" to spiritual values. Casey Hayden's definition of "organizer," coming as she does from the spiritual basis in the Beloved Community, is almost identical to that of my witness. Witnessing is a lifelong enterprise, required by internal values. Success doesn't depend on society's response to the witness. Losing, for a witness, is the failure to stand up for principles.

I was not rebelling against my culture, merely trying to help overcome its most glaring faults. I was genuinely surprised that crossing the color line was a one-way trip, a lesson that had to be repeated many times before I understood it. In an October 3, 1962, letter of protest about censorship to the Georgia State

College *Signal,* I wrote: "Never have I been considered one of the 'beat' rebels against conformity." For me, fighting for an end to segregation was not something confined to picket lines or direct-action demonstrations, but a way of life. I would live as if I could straddle the color line, bringing together whites from one side and blacks from the other.

Being part of the Freedom Movement was a life-changing experience. In participating, I lost my only real opportunity for a higher education, and I was alienated from my church. I experienced a lifelong separation from my large and loving family, and was set apart from the world in ways that affected all my relationships and employment options. For me, and for many other women like me, participation made us outcasts — women without a home.

My experience was not unique or exceptional. Variations of this story could be told by hundreds of movement people — men and women, black and white, young and old — including many who acted in isolation. Perhaps this book, *Deep in Our Hearts,* will bring forth more stories.

In the search for restoration of belonging, for a community in which I could nurture and be nurtured, I have often looked in the wrong places and among the wrong people. Now I live in a place I love, alone in my home but freely moving among various groups I value in my town and state. None of these share my particular history. I have shelved that part of my life that was formative, transformative, that set the course of my future.

I still witness to the values that brought me to the Freedom Movement. Without children of my own, I consider myself a part of the village that it takes to raise everybody's children. I am deeply involved in almost every area of community improvement, especially promoting public education at all levels: community college, public library, the public school system. In all these activities, I am known as someone who believes in racial, gender, economic, and age integration, in tolerance and celebration of diversity, in a Beloved Community large enough for everyone.

In 1994, thirty-five years after I entered my GSCW freshman class, I finally, proudly, completed a Regent's B.A. degree, at West Virginia State College, a historically black state institution. I ended my pursuit of higher education after finishing one-third of a masters in humanities. I still study the Christian Bible, usually with the Old Stone Presbyterian Church. I still fight the same internal battles about whether the institutional church is capable of being the agency for the Christianity in which I believe so deeply.

I write here because those who use the movement as a model for current social justice efforts need to know that the movement was not something imported in the briefcases of a few "leaders" but was an ongoing, living process involving thousands of people. Although most of those people were black, some were white. Many were women. Most were southerners. As for me, I remain all three. In every place I go, I still try to stand as a witness to the eternal principle that all are created valuable and equal. In this sense, I am still engaged in the Freedom Movement.

Truths of the Heart

DOROTHY DAWSON BURLAGE

I was born in San Antonio and shaped by a family that had lived in the Deep South since 1742. It is painful to write about my growing-up years, for doing so brings back memories of the insidious world of racial segregation. Looking back, I can see that it was my deep and loving childhood connection to black people in my extended household and seeing how they were mistreated by the tradition of Jim Crow that led me to commit my life to getting rid of segregation.

Our roots in this country, and especially in the South, were deep. It was important to my mother that the family had come over on the Mayflower and had the credentials for the Daughters of the American Revolution, the Daughters of the Confederacy, and the Daughters of the Republic of Texas. My forebears, some of whom came from Georgia and Alabama to Texas in the early 1800s, had been teachers, preachers, farmers, doctors, and businessmen, some rich, some poor, and others somewhere in the middle.

My father, a geologist, was from northern Louisiana, and my mother was from East Texas, both from the Black Belt and the Bible Belt, both Protestants. My father's features — auburn hair and blue eyes — reflected his English and Scotch-Irish background. He loved to read and travel and to sing ballads and gospel songs in a lovely Irish tenor voice. My mother was a pretty hazel-eyed brunette, known for her charm and wit. Both were avid readers, especially of history. Both had bachelor's degrees from the University of Texas; my father also had a master's degree in geology.

We lived in a Tudor-style house, stone with brown trim and tile roof, in an upper-middle-class neighborhood, with a yard large enough for the neighborhood football games that I was allowed to play in until my mother thought I was too old. We were close enough to the country to find an occasional rattlesnake in the yard, which I or someone else in the family would shoot. Though black people, as well as white, did a lot of work for my family, my parents themselves were also hardworking, joining in the care of the yard, car, laundry, meals, "putting up" the fruits and vegetables, and sewing and scrubbing, working late into the evening and beginning again at dawn.

Despite the significant roles that black people played in my family, I was taught, like most southern white children, the tradition of racial segregation and how to keep black people at a distance, in a lesser status. They were family, but not family. I learned to be polite and respectful to all my elders, regardless of color. But while I was to speak to white adults as "Mr." or "Mrs.," I was taught to address black men and women by their first names. Only white people were "ladies" and "gentlemen." Blacks were "colored men" and "colored women" or "Negroes." Although I learned their last names when I got older, I use only first names here in order to protect their privacy.

The first black person I can remember was Hiawatha, so named, I was told, because he was part Native American. Hiawatha was tall, dignified in his bearing, and always perfectly, almost elegantly dressed. He lived in the servant's room attached to the garage behind our house and had worked for my parents since before I was born. He helped take care of my older brother, who grew up to look like Robert Redford and be a successful businessman. When I was born, Hiawatha was "let go" because it was not thought safe or proper for a man to be in the house alone with a small girl—even more so for a black man with a white girl. He went to work for another family, friends of ours, who had only a boy. Fortunately, he was often hired to help at my home as I was growing up, and I would also see him at our friends' house. His kindness toward children was legendary, as was his way of providing companionship even while he was working. I was jealous that the boys were allowed to have closer contact with him than I was, since no physical contact was allowed between black men and white girls, but white boys did not have the same restrictions. I resented my brother's being allowed to sit on Hiawatha's shoulders and rough-house with him when I could not.

Hiawatha carried considerable moral authority and adult power with the children he watched, teaching us right from wrong, how to settle arguments, and the rules of fairness. I heard the parents in our social circle talk about how much they appreciated his role in raising their children and in helping manage social events. While picking up and delivering children, helping with parties, and running errands, he was in and out of the homes of many white people in San Antonio, but only through the back door. I was too young to understand the ironies involved in his being given so much authority and responsibility even as he was denied the most basic of rights and courtesies.

Ernest was another important black person in my childhood. He was trim and muscular and always dressed in a freshly ironed shirt and a felt hat with a brim he had hand shaped to shade him from the hot Texas sun. He worked in the yard, helped with the house and the car, fed the hunting dogs, and generally kept things going. He was a significant person not only for me, but also for my parents and grandparents, who regarded him as playing a special role in our family. My mother told me that when I was a child and my father was on his deathbed, he called for Ernest and asked him to watch over the family after he died. Ernest worked for our family for more than forty years altogether, until in his seventies he moved to Waco, where his children lived, several hours away. Even after he had moved, Ernest continued to drive back every few weeks to take care of things.

Ernest was patient with my childish interferences. I was allowed to take his jelly glass filled with iced tea to him from the kitchen. He would stop working for a few minutes and lean on his rake or hoe, pushing back his sweat-stained hat to wipe away the perspiration dripping down his forehead with his handkerchief. Then I would ask him the kinds of questions kids ask grown-ups. I knew he would always give me honest answers, although if I asked taboo questions about segregation, such as why he couldn't drink from the same water fountains as white people, he might offer an evasive "I don't know, chile." He was a source of common sense, wisdom, and comfort. When my grandmother died, because of her loyalty to him and in appreciation of his loyalty to our family, she left Ernest about twice as much money as she left to her grandchildren. Nonetheless, both Ernest and Hiawatha ate on the back stoop and had their own separate dishes and utensils, and when driving in the car, they always had to sit separate from my family, in the back seat.

Georgia and Lola Mae, two sisters who worked for my grandmother for more than thirty years, were also part of my extended household. I saw them almost daily. I had affection for them and often sought their company and advice, but was also careful in their presence because they enforced my mother's and grandmother's rules. They usually dressed in black or navy, following my grandmother's standards for proper decorum. Unlike Ernest and Hiawatha, they ate in the kitchen. Although privy to many of our personal matters, they were quiet and reserved, and never disturbed my family's privacy.

The legal reality of Jim Crow was very much apparent whenever we left the house. Southern white children learned early that black people were treated differently in public and private. Before I could read, I could recognize "White Only" and "Colored" signs for water fountains and restrooms. Mother would give me a disapproving look if I started to make a mistake. Stores had front doors for us and back doors for blacks. Hospitals and schools were segregated. I would ask for explanations for these rules, but my mother usually told me, especially if I asked in public, that it was just the way it was, don't talk about it. Sometimes at home later I would get a lengthy explanation about the southern way of life.

My family conformed to the Jim Crow laws, but they were adamantly opposed to the Ku Klux Klan and to any form of violence toward black people. In spite of the segregation that was the pattern in Texas, my family had a very strong Christian belief in being responsible and charitable toward one's fellow man, including black people. An example of the ideals they taught was contained in a telegram I received from my grandmother on one of my early birthdays, in which she exhorted me "to climb to the mountaintop in your values and service to humanity."

My grandmother told me that my great-grandfather, who had fought in the War between the States, purchased land for the black family that worked for him each time he purchased land for himself: every time he bought five acres for his own family, he bought and gave one acre to the black family. He built a church and provided schooling for the black families in the area. My great-grandmother was described as being the nurse and doctor not only for her family, but also for the neighbors, both black and white. I was taught by example and instruction to be socially responsible but only later understood the unfortunate aspects of their paternalism.

My maternal grandparents lived in San Antonio while I was growing up, but they considered their real home to be a very small town in East Texas, where they had been born and raised. East Texas, with its cotton crops, magnolia trees, and swamps, is much more a part of the Deep South than is San Antonio. We spent extended periods at those several hundred acres bought by my great-grandfather in the mid-1800s as the country place for extensive visiting, congregating, and family reunions.

JennieVee and Ed were black people who worked for my family in East Texas. I was allowed to go with Ed on adventures, but only if my brother was with us, at which time Ed had absolute authority to make us behave. Ed taught me how to shoot alligators ("Aim for his eye") and how to avoid rattlesnakes and copperheads. He would also reprimand me if I showed bad manners or misbehaved.

Ed and my grandmother would sit on the front porch in the evenings. She would rock back and forth in her chair, while Ed would sit at the far edge of the porch, with his chair facing away at an angle from her and almost with his back to her, so that no one could ever mistake that they might be facing each other. In this way, they were able to talk for hours—about the family and its history, the oppressive heat, the crops, the county gossip, and the mosquitoes—without ever violating the southern white rule that blacks and whites should not appear to be in the same class or relating as equals. From my child's point of view, I remember thinking how friendly they were and how much they enjoyed each other's company in spite of all those rules. Sometimes my brother and I would stop chasing lightning bugs and sit on the porch and listen while the grown-ups told stories about when our forebears fought in the Civil War and how the Yankees stole and burned our property and wanted to change our southern way of life.

I dutifully absorbed all the lessons of tradition and law about how to behave in a segregated world. At the same time, from an early age I was saddened by the barriers that kept me from being close to the black people who worked for my family. I always felt uncomfortable with the discrimination against them. These relationships continued to be an unconscious but powerful determining influence on me during the years I was growing up. I was grateful for their kindness, inspired by their strength and dignity, felt deeply attached to them, and thus felt even more keenly the injustice of our being separated because of color. These were the compelling truths that ultimately overcame the tradition of segregation for me. In the end, the truths of my heart were stronger than segregationist ideology. Segregation became my enemy.

In the early years of my life, we lived in Jackson, Mississippi, while my father explored for oil all over the state. With Jackson as our home base, we traveled the country roads of Mississippi, the swamps of Louisiana, and the everglades of Florida in a Chevrolet sedan, my parents in the front seat and my brother and I in the back. Often I could see the waves of heat rising from the road. We carried a thermos of water, a picnic basket of bread and peanut butter, the good flat silver, a linen tablecloth under Mother's seat—she was always a lady, even under the most difficult circumstances—a pickax, a microscope, binoculars, a spare tire, and a couple of suitcases in the trunk.

As we drove down the roads of the Deep South, day after day, month after month, I sat in the back playing with my doll. The only other activity was looking out the window, where I saw black and sometimes white people chopping and picking cotton. They looked hot and tired, strained from bending over all day long, with the handkerchiefs tied around their heads providing little relief from the beating sun. I saw the "shotgun houses," so called because all the rooms were in a straight line in a row, like one box after another, so that if a bullet were shot through the front door, it would go straight through every room. I saw the dilapidated shanties, perhaps with a hand-wringer washing machine on the front porch or a broken-down car in the front yard. I saw outhouses and the painted white stones outlining barren yards. The South still bore the ravages of the Great Depression, and my parents always expressed compassion for the people who were suffering financially. I winced when we passed chain gangs working on the side of the road. Later, I would reflect upon the causes of the suffering I had seen uncritically as a child. Twenty years later, I traveled those same roads in Mississippi, but instead of waiting while my father negotiated drilling rights with plantation owners, I was setting up meetings of black and white students to talk about ending segregation.

By the time I began elementary school, my family had returned to San Antonio. In 1946, when I was eight years old, my father developed heart trouble. He was sick for several months and died that same year, a terribly traumatic experience for me, a devastating loss that significantly shaped the way I would see the world. Not only did I lose a father, but I lost a friend who had taught me history and geography, music, an appreciation of nature, and shared his eagerness and curiosity about life. His death left my mother a widow at age thirty-four with two young children to raise. We had social standing but limited financial means, and my mother had to go to work. I saw her strain as a widow and a single parent, overworked and worried about money. I began to view things differently than other children in my social circle, especially with regard to financial and social vulnerability.

From elementary through high school, I regularly attended church and Sunday School, where we studied the Bible. Segregation's supporters argued that the Bible mandated White Supremacy, and passages in the Old Testament were interpreted to justify it. Southern preachers cited, for example, the story in Genesis about Noah placing a curse on Canaan, the son of Ham (who was described as black), saying that he would be the lowest of slaves to his brothers and a servant to all others. Another much-quoted piece of scripture was from the book of Joshua, which stated that the descendants of Canaan were "hewers of wood and carriers of water." That was interpreted to mean that blacks should be manual laborers working for white people. One platitude spoken from the pulpit was "race mixing is against nature."

Such sermons became more urgent when President Truman desegregated the military in 1948 and again in 1954 when *Brown v. Board of Education* began the desegregation of schools. Most southern white children heard discussions of these events in their homes, their schools, and their churches, and from politicians and evangelical preachers on the radio.

Various mechanisms in southern culture limited dissension and prevented exposure to different viewpoints. A common rule of social etiquette was that race, religion, and politics were never to be discussed "in public" by a "lady." Texas schools sometimes banned controversial books. Because my parents had a well-stocked library and encouraged my reading, they gave me the tools to question the accepted mores. I remember especially reading about Darwin's theory of evolution and studying anthropology books that taught me different ways to understand racial issues. I began to realize that misinformation maintained prejudice and that open discussion was needed to deal with issues of segregation.

During junior high and high school I seemed on the surface to be much like the other girls and was even considered a student leader. My closet was filled with the requisite long dance dresses and crinoline petticoats, but I was inwardly preoccupied with issues of social justice and the moral teachings of the church. I kept struggling with the contradictions between the messages I heard about segregation and the ones I heard in church about love and brotherhood, justice and righteousness.

I became aware of the discrimination against the few Mexican Americans who attended my high school and wrote essays about it for the school newspaper. My criticisms of prejudice shocked some of my fellow students. I had learned from my school textbooks that the Constitution and Bill of Rights were written to protect all citizens. However, I was learning from experience that the opportunities afforded to the majority were denied to minorities and that black children were unfairly segregated into separate schools.

The major influence on my thinking about social issues during those years was my boyfriend, John Worsham, who was my good friend from the fourth grade on. I had been trained to believe that it was more important to be polite than to be right, but John, with his extraordinary southern charm, usually could figure out how to do both at the same time. For me, any small challenge to the Jim Crow system was a monumental undertaking. I went with John, with much trepidation, to interracial meetings at the George Washington Carver Center, where there were discussions about desegregation. It was my first excursion to the forbidden black side of town. I felt as if I were doing something both daring and defiant—and of course did not tell my family or friends. We also decided to ignore the Jim Crow rule by sitting in the "Colored Balcony" of the movie theater. Undoubtedly it was I who bolted before we could get caught, fearing that I would get in trouble with my mother. I also felt angry that I had to behave in such a sneaky fashion because of a law that was unfair. I was learning that my own freedom was limited by segregation as well.

In 1955 I went to Mary Baldwin College, a private women's school in Virginia. In those days, some Texas girls, myself included, were sent off to such colleges for a year or two, partly for the educational opportunities and partly to be "finished." I traveled by train, a two-day trip with an overnight in the Pullman car, carrying trunks full of clothes and shoe boxes filled with peanut butter sandwiches and fried chicken. My family was at the train station to say good-bye. Believing that Virginia was all too close to the North, my mother's parting words, spoken only somewhat facetiously, were "Don't you dare marry a Yankee while you're up there."

At college, when most of my fellow college students were arguing for "States Rights" and "Separate but Equal," I wrote a paper challenging school segregation that caused a stir among the students. I also attended an interracial regional meeting of the National Student Association (NSA) that year. I felt like a traitor.

In the fall of 1956, I transferred to the University of Texas (UT) in Austin, a liberal oasis in the state. It was expected that I, like other college girls, would find a mate and settle down in Texas, but during my years at UT I became an activist about segregation, a development that initiated a transformation in my identity as a southern woman. I had been raised with the expectation that I would be a southern lady—well mannered, never involved in political discussion or controversy, with all opinions and personal matters kept private, and dependent on men. I was not to be "forward" or even speak very loud. I could be strong, but only as long as it was not apparent. The fact that my mother had a job was of course inconsistent with her southern model, and in that sense she displayed an alternative to what she taught me. As I got older and felt morally compelled to speak out about civil rights, my outspokenness conflicted with my training to be a southern lady, creating an internal struggle that began in college and continued during my years in the movement.

I had begun my student life at UT by pledging a sorority, but that became a problem when I became friends with Robb Burlage (whom I married in 1963) and other student leaders who participated in NSA activities through the UT student government. Association with NSA, because of its stand on racial integration, was virtually forbidden by the sorority. Also, I later found out that sororities had "white only" clauses in their rules for membership. I quit sorority life because of those policies, a decision that shocked my sorority sisters and violated the stereotype of the southern lady.

At the university, many influences and mentors, mostly religious, helped me clarify my ideas and encouraged me to be more outspoken. The YWCA, an interracial, ecumenical Christian organization, was a major force in the

struggle for racial justice. It was the gathering place for intellectuals and activists, and an alternative to sorority life for me. I joined in 1956, and for the first
time I felt a clear and strong connection between religion and social justice.
The YWCA was the first interracial organization in which I was intensely active,
providing an opportunity to work closely with black students and participate
in discussions about racial issues.

I also attended lectures at the Christian Faith and Life Community, known
simply as "the Community," an interracial off-campus residence, privately
owned and not affiliated directly with the university. It had one dorm for
women and one down the street for men. I remember hearing that because it
was desegregated, a cross had been burned in the front yard, and there had
been death threats by mail and telephone. It was at the YWCA and the Community that I was inspired by thoughtful, outspoken women leaders—Anne
Appenzellar and Mildred Hudgins. Another mentor was Rosalie Oakes, originally from Virginia, who was on the staff of the Y. She later went to South
Africa to work against apartheid, but sent back letters encouraging me to work
against segregation in the south.

Many of my friends who were active in the Y lived at the Community; they
suggested that I move there. On the day I moved in, my life took a dramatic
and an irreversible turn, when all the contradictions of my southern upbringing and my emerging social consciousness came together during a ten-minute
car ride. I got in my pink and gray Chevrolet Belaire to drive from the Community's women's dorm to the men's, where the lectures were held. I offered a
ride to a white student who then saw two black students coming out of the
building, so he offered them a ride as well. One of the black men got in the
front seat of the car. In a split second, I felt my world turn upside down. For
the first time in my life, I experienced being in a situation of apparent social
intimacy with a black man—not just in a meeting or a class, but in my
mother's car, breaking my mother's rules and violating nineteen years of her
training. Although I felt physically sick with fear that I had crossed the color
line and worried about possible retribution for breaking this southern tradition, the very intensity of my reaction taught me how deep had been my so-
cialization into the racist system and how irrational it was to have such a reaction. I did not want white children to be raised the way I had been. From
that moment on, I was even more determined to fight segregation.

There were many experiences during my university years that encouraged my political growth. The Community provided an opportunity to meet and talk in depth with black students from UT and from Huston Tillotson, a neighboring black college. I got to know Sandra Cason (nicknamed Casey, later to marry Tom Hayden, and a co-author of this book) through the Y and the Community, where she was my roommate.

I chaired the UT Great Issues Committee, working closely with the president of the university, Harry Hunt Ransom, to bring prominent speakers from elsewhere in the country. I felt too shy and inexperienced for the task of selecting, contacting, and then introducing people such as W. H. Auden and Wernher von Braun to packed auditoriums, but I managed to do the job. Meeting such remarkable people expanded my worldview.

I had other secular liberal influences at the university as well—professors educated at northern schools as well as some Texas-born and -bred professors who taught about populism and civil liberties. I also became friendly with the editors and writers for the liberal newspapers, such as Ronnie Dugger of the *Texas Observer* and Robb Burlage of the *Daily Texan*.

A catalyzing event for me at UT involved the policy regarding black and white participation in student theater and musical productions. In the spring of 1957, contrary to accepted practice, Barbara Smith, a black student, was chosen to play a leading role opposite a white male lead. Some members of the Texas legislature were upset and put pressure on the university. She was removed from the production, and in response, professors and students mobilized to defend her right to appear. At stake was not only segregation, but academic freedom. My conscience compelled me to support her rights, so I helped with petitions and joined the protest in front of Hogg Auditorium. I thought that Smith had been treated unfairly and that it was right to protest, but in those years the "public display" of such opinions was not behavior considered appropriate for a lady and so it was not at all easy for me to do. Most of what I remember about the experience is my fear, which was palpable. Usually my commitment to the cause of fighting segregation would be stronger than my southern lady persona and I could act on behalf of principle—but not always. The upbringing of southern white women with my class background was more repressive than most of us can comprehend these many years later.

My decision to live in a desegregated residence was embarrassing to my mother, so she did not tell my grandmother that my dorm was interracial. My grandmother had the address and, without any forewarning, drove to Austin from San Antonio to see for herself where I was living, bringing Lola Mae, the black woman who worked for her, along for the trip. As they drove up, the sight of black students coming out of the dorm made it clear that I was living in an interracial residence. I cannot remember who was the most shocked and distressed by that encounter— my grandmother, Lola Mae, or I. I do remember that my grandmother stiffened her back and squared her jaw and that she communicated her intense disapproval when her blue eyes turned cold as steel. Lola, who was typically reserved and quiet around my grandmother, though they had known each other for years, did not say a word, but looked shocked and worried. I think my grandmother finally said something like, "Lord have mercy!" Within minutes she drove off, leaving me feeling like a leper, rejected by the matriarch of the family. The incident was never discussed, and race and politics remained painful topics in my family.

This split over beliefs about segregation was the beginning of a twenty-five-year period in which I would see little of my family. The rift was extremely painful for me, but I was adamant in my belief that the South must change. My beliefs were not based on a missionary spirit of "saving" blacks, but on my conviction that segregation was a toxic presence in the South for all of us.

I worked with others to desegregate both the university and the public facilities close to the university in 1958–59 with efforts such as the "Steer Here" campaign to desegregate restaurants, an attempt to desegregate the theater, and the Fellowship of Sitters—nicknamed "Fellowship of Sippers" by Robb because their goal was to ensure that anyone, regardless of color, would be allowed to sip a cup of coffee. Over the Christmas holidays, I attended the national YWCA conference at the University of Illinois, where race relations was a major topic of discussion and where I could actually eat in interracial groups on and off campus. I had come a long way since my childhood when I had pestered my mother about why Ernest had to eat on the back stoop.

At UT, I was still accepted as a student leader in spite of my political stance on segregation. I received many honors—Most Outstanding Student, Bluebonnet Belle, member of Mortar Board, and others. I received support from other students who came from homes more liberal than mine and from northern students. In 1959, the year I graduated, I was chosen to be an exchange student to the Soviet Union for the summer. My refresher course for the trip focused on American freedom, democracy, and human rights, the same civic lessons I had been taught in school. However, when I had to debate Russian students on the trip, I was flustered and speechless because there was no way to justify that black people did not have the right to freedom of assembly, to vote, or to attend the same schools as whites. I came home further disillusioned about the hypocrisy in the United States. At the same time, my experience in the U.S.S.R. led me to an extreme dislike of Communism as practiced there. Whatever its avowed idealism, the reality was that it was totalitarian and oppressive.

I returned in the fall of 1959 to Austin, where I shared an apartment with Casey. I was a graduate student at UT and continued my friendships with liberal political leaders around town. I gave speeches about my Soviet trip, discussing the contradictions of representing a country that boasted about its freedom and democracy but denied these freedoms to its black citizens.

While in Austin, I was asked to take a position as program director of the YWCA at the University of Illinois. I decided to accept the offer as a way to continue my involvement with the Y and its social justice programs, and I moved to Champaign-Urbana in January 1960. There I spent my time organizing speaking programs, workshops, and action projects around racial issues. I also used the Y as an organizational base to provide support for the southern movement, working with the Congress of Racial Equality (CORE) staff to picket Woolworth's. In addition, I worked with the students involved in NSA—whom I would see again at the NSA congress later that year—on resolutions regarding segregation.

Though my framework for challenging segregation was becoming secular as well as religious, I still felt that my Christian background was the major source of my social ethics. I was considering a career with the YWCA working in social justice programs and had lengthy discussions with YWCA staff and UT President Ransom, with whom I was still in touch, who urged me to go to Harvard Divinity School. Many of my kin thought Harvard was atheist and liberal and argued against my going. It was never easy for me to go against my family's values or wishes, but over their protests I applied, was accepted, and was soon on a train north to Boston.

When I got there, I searched for a way to continue my efforts in civil rights. I thought the northern church, more liberal than southern churches, should be leading the way on moral issues of segregation and civil rights. I did not find that to be true at Harvard Divinity School. Disappointed, I gradually became estranged from the institutional church. Though I stayed in school for a year and a half, I began looking for other affiliations.

One of my professors, Thomas Pettigrew, invited me to go with him to a Quaker meetinghouse to hear Dion Diamond speak about his experience in the Freedom Rides. Dion invited the audience, "Close your eyes and let me take you on this trip. . . ." Then, in the dramatic style of a southern preacher, he told about white people bombing the buses in Anniston, Alabama, and riders getting on new buses rolling on to Jackson, Mississippi. There were state troopers on each side of the state line and helicopters with the National Guard overhead to provide protection from white mobs. Dion reported that upon arrival in Jackson, the Freedom Riders were arrested and taken to a penal farm at Parchman, put on death row, and tortured with cattle prods. I walked out of that meeting feeling deep shame about my southern white background.

Outraged by the violence in the South and determined to uphold the struggle, I started talking to my fellow students about forming a northern group to support southern activists. I organized a civil rights group, which took off like wildfire with the help of Harvard undergraduates and theology students, and also thanks to the Student Christian Movement network of religious leaders, campus ministries, and by YM-YMCAs. As the leader of this loose organization, I mobilized students to picket the Trailways bus station in downtown Boston and support the bus boycott of Trailways being sponsored by CORE. We also began working with local fair housing committees and settlement houses.

In October 1961 I went to Texas to attend Casey and Tom Hayden's wedding. There, I saw Alan Haber, Students for a Democratic Society (SDS) president and executive secretary, whom I had known since the NSA congress of 1960, when I joined SDS. Al told me about the voter registration work of the Student Nonviolent Coordinating Committee (SNCC) in the South, and I decided to shift my efforts to helping them. Back in Boston, I got in touch with James Forman, executive secretary of SNCC, to discuss how to initiate fundraising in Boston. One idea was to create and sell SNCC buttons. Though I was working my way through school as a typist and did not have much money, I put up a little over one hundred dollars to make the first batch. Initially, the buttons had green and white hands shaking, replicating the logo of the SNCC stationery. My recollection is that when we needed more, the printer was out of green ink and that was how we switched to black and white buttons — the way they would remain for many years. After receiving a check from us for $178, Julian Bond of SNCC wrote a thank you letter saying that the SNCC workers in Terrell and Lee Counties in Georgia had been forced to chop cotton and pick squash to raise money for their civil rights work. By December we were able to send about $3,000, which at the time seemed an astronomical amount.

As our group got bigger, we moved some of the work out of my apartment and into the basement of Harvard Epworth Methodist Church, where they let us use the mimeograph machine to get out mailings to the local chapters as events unfolded in the South. That basement continued to be used for movement activity and later became the office where the Friends of SNCC recruited volunteers for Mississippi Freedom Summer.

That October, in New Haven, the New England Northern Student Movement (NSM) was formed, with Peter Countryman as chairman. Some of our Boston group went to that meeting, and afterward Peter asked to come to Boston to discuss merging our two groups. Peter's primary focus at the time was inner-city tutoring. We were one of the earliest fundraising projects in the country to raise money for SNCC, and he wanted NSM to join our effort. I was reluctant to affiliate with an organization that seemed to be more focused on the North than the South, but at an all-night meeting I finally agreed because I could see the logic of developing a college-based civil rights network for the entire New England area. Mike Sayer, a Harvard student, came up with our new name, the Boston Metropolitan Area Northern Student Movement Coordinating Committee, or Boston NSM, and I continued to be the chairperson. By then, we had groups organized on sixteen campuses in the Boston area. The New England NSM adopted our Boston organizational model for college chapters and the use of SNCC buttons for fundraising.

I invited Chuck McDew, chairman of SNCC, to come up during the first week of December to speak about the southern movement. Chuck mesmerized the audiences with his stories of being jailed in the sit-ins in Orangeburg, South Carolina, and in the massive arrests in McComb, Mississippi. I stayed out of class all that week to take Chuck to speak at local colleges. I was no longer interested in graduate school and was eager to get back to the South.

At about that time, Casey tried to arrange for me to work with her and Ella Baker at the YWCA project in Atlanta. The Y did not have enough money to put me on staff, but in the fall of 1961 Paul Potter, vice-president of the National Student Association and a leader in SDS, invited me to work for the NSA Southern Student Human Relations Project in Atlanta, directed by Connie Curry. I consulted with my professor, the political philosopher and theologian Reinhold Niebuhr, who had been supportive of my work in civil rights, about whether to drop out of Harvard. He told me to go with his blessing and also encouraged me to use his name in the cause of justice whenever I could, an offer that I later delivered to SNCC. I left Harvard for Atlanta in the winter of 1961–62.

In Atlanta, I became involved in the movement full time and lost my ties to organized religion. The Protestant church's influence faded as the Freedom Movement became more relevant to addressing the ethical issues that concerned me. I was at home with the ideals of the Southern Freedom Movement, with its religious tradition and its commitment to nonviolence and creating a Beloved Community. The movement became my new spiritual home.

At the time, I wished that my mother would support my decision to work full time in the Southern Freedom Movement and understand that I was acting on the moral values that she and our church had taught me. I was deeply hurt by her lack of understanding and approval. In retrospect, I can understand her reaction better than I could then. At the time, I thought she objected primarily to my views on civil rights. I can now appreciate, however, that, even more, she was concerned about the potentially disastrous social and financial consequences my choice might bring. As a widow raising two small children, she was completely focused on creating a secure future for my brother and me by helping us get through college and into stable work and family situations. My activism threatened to undo all her labors of love. She tried to cope with each of my new ventures — moving into desegregated housing at UT, traveling to Russia, going north to Harvard, and having liberal friends; these changes were difficult for her, especially the ones that challenged her Deep South upbringing. My activities embarrassed her, and she kept them secret from many family members and friends. She tried to be tolerant and supportive, but when I went to Atlanta she disinherited me, removing me from her will. After that, we lost touch for months at a time. It was terribly sad for me. Many years later, to her credit, her courage and caring overcame her disappointments and we were reconciled.

For the next nine years, the political work that had been part-time for me since college became full-time. In the south, I was home again, able to share my idealism about an integrated society with other southerners. My work in the movement involved organizations with acronyms—SNCC, NSA, SDS, NSM, SSOC, SCLC, YWCA, and others. My political identity shifted from moderate to liberal to radical. I moved frequently in and out of cheap apartments, slept on people's sofas, and had various roommates and short- and long-term visitors. I was constantly producing or reading and lugging around boxes of papers, notes, mailing lists, position papers, pamphlets, and leaflets—all without benefit of computers or copying machines. I organized and attended meetings and conferences, traveling by bus, train, plane, and broken-down cars, and engaged in discussions, debates, strategy sessions, and demonstrations—sit-ins, stand-ins, kneel-ins, and marches. It gave me overwhelming joy to live in a time when my life seemed to make a difference and I could share my idealism and commitment with some of the best and brightest young people in the country. This network of friends and co-workers became my family.

The movement brought out the best in people by appealing to that part of us that wants to do right and believes that, with good works, social justice will prevail. For that moment in history, we believed we could create a world in which skin color and class differences would not determine how we relate to one another and in which we could build a less hierarchical society. And by some miracle, it seemed that people of all ages, colors, genders, and class backgrounds shared that view. It was an extraordinary and exhilarating time to be alive.

Atlanta, however, with its segregated housing, stores, and public facilities, presented immediate problems. I moved into a small frame rental house on McLendon Avenue on the white side of town, a few blocks from Casey and Tom. Although I worked for the NSA Southern Project, I continued my volunteer efforts to support SNCC, located on Auburn Avenue. I gave my Boston mailing lists to Julian Bond of SNCC to be used as fundraising contacts. I was happy to help out with running the mimeograph machine and stuffing envelopes and was inspired by participating in SNCC meetings and conferences. I helped get northern support during crises and did use Reinhold Niebuhr's name to send telegrams to the Justice Department when SNCC people were arrested or jailed. As one of the first prominent white national figures to publicly back SNCC, Niebuhr influenced religious, labor, and other liberal leaders to support SNCC as well.

One night in Atlanta I invited several SNCC people to a party, but because the party was interracial, three policemen came knocking on my door. An officer explained that neighbors were forming a mob and advised that everyone disperse while the police were there to prevent violence. Since we had been singing freedom songs, I told the officer that we were having a prayer meeting but agreed that everyone would leave. The next morning, I was evicted. I was taken in by Joan Browning, a young woman from Georgia, who was gracious enough to let me share her apartment on Ponce de Leon for the next year or so. Soon after I moved in, events made us suspicious that someone was tampering with our mail and telephone. Friends, family, and neighbors had told me since my trip to the Soviet Union in 1959 that my activities were being tracked, so this was not a new experience for me. It was always nerve-wracking, though, to wonder if my conversations and activities were being monitored. Our apartment became a place where activists came to visit, party, eat, or stay whenever they needed a place.

Although I was considered an anomaly by most of the southern white world, I continued to see myself as a personally conservative young woman who happened to believe strongly in civil rights. When I first arrived in Atlanta, I bought an ironing board at the Goodwill on Ponce de Leon. It was the old-fashioned variety made of wood, on sale for $1.50, with a big hole in it that I patched with cardboard. I kept my clothes ironed and usually wore pumps and pearls. I remember, for example, that I dressed in my Sunday best, wearing white gloves, the first time I visited the Mennonite House on Houston Street, where Vincent and Rosemarie Harding, its directors, along with volunteers, served the movement and the community. Invited often for meals, I shared in many discussions at their round dining room table about theology, the church, and the segregated South.

My job at the Southern Project was to develop educational programs for black and white students in southern towns and campuses, as well as to plan and direct a voter registration program. I worked in the office with Connie Curry at 41 Exchange Place, the same building in which Casey and Ella Baker had the YWCA office. Our work was similar, making it convenient for us to collaborate. Though paid by the Y, Ella was the mentor for SNCC. She remains a legend in the movement.

Ella was petite, but she was a commanding woman who always stood tall. She dressed in tailored suits and often wore a hat. Her elocution and delivery, undoubtedly learned in church, made her a compelling speaker. She looked people straight in the eye. For the next several years, she provided me with steady support and a clear sense of direction in the movement. My relationship with Ella marked the reshaping of my relationships with black people, allowing the kind of open communication I had always wanted but not been able to have as a child.

How to address black men and women was a matter of no small importance. For white people to address black people by their first names, without permission, was one of the more degrading practices of the Old South. Thus I was careful to address black people, especially ones who were older than myself, as Mr., Mrs., or Miss. When I met Ella Baker, I called her "Miss Baker," but soon after we met I slipped and called her "Ella." I immediately apologized, but she was quick to respond, saying, "It's okay. People know when it's right to call me Ella." And so it was from then on.

Because it was illegal in southern towns to have interracial gatherings, our meetings were usually held on black campuses or, if at a white campus, in the buildings of organizations with religious affiliations such as the YWCA or campus ministries. The complexities of travel to and from these meetings, such as the ones at Tougaloo College in Mississippi, reveal how deep racial barriers were and how dangerous it was to cross them. In Jackson, Mississippi, for example, I would take a white cab to the edge of the white side of town, then get out and change to a black cab for the black side of town. The interracial conference at Dillard University (all black then) in New Orleans was more tolerant of racial and ethnic differences, possibly because the city was a major harbor and melting pot. Chuck McDew and I took a long drive from Atlanta to Jackson, McComb, and Holly Springs, Mississippi, with James Forman and other male SNCC staff, during which I hid under blankets on the floor of the car whenever we might be visible to white people. I flew to Birmingham with Wiley Branton, a highly respected black lawyer and director of the Voter Education Project, but when we got off the plane we had to ride in separate cabs from the airport to the Sixteenth Street Baptist Church (later bombed) for a mass meeting with Martin Luther King Jr., Dick Gregory, and SNCC staff as speakers.

Sometimes I deliberately broke the taboos, though I was careful not to take excessive risks. One time I went to a restaurant in the white working-class outskirts of Atlanta, the Pickrick, owned by Lester Maddox, known at the time as a fervent segregationist. I was in an interracial group with Cordell Reagon (black) and Bob Zellner (white). We had agreed that we would sit down and leave, if asked, without protest. We were seated, but were quickly chased out by women battering us with their pocketbooks, a man wielding an ax handle, and Lester Maddox yelling, "Get out of here!" Bob said he saw Maddox brandishing a gun, but I was already running to the car by then. We all made it to safety.

The presence of a white woman with black men was inflammatory for most southern white people. This issue, as well as questions of women's roles, came up clearly in a discussion raised by Anne Braden of the Southern Conference Educational Fund (SCEF), a southern civil rights organization, in early 1963. Anne had arranged with SNCC to fund one staff person to try to reach the white community on the issue of civil rights. Bob Zellner from Alabama held that position initially. When Bob talked of leaving SNCC, Anne suggested me for the job, then paying the wage of $40 per week. Anne wrote to say that Chuck McDew, chairman of SNCC, supported me for the position. She added that Bob thought the person "had to be a man — in fact, he seemed horrified that I would suggest otherwise. I didn't argue with him, but just told him that when he got ready to fight for the rights of the whole human race to let me know." Anne also quoted Jim Forman as saying that he "saw no reason why it should not be a woman. He did say though that if they put two people on the job, a white and a Negro, he supposed (since they'd probably be traveling together and considering the realities of the South) that they should be the same sex." As it turned out, the discussion was irrelevant because Bob decided to stay.

It never occurred to me to be upset by Bob's comments; at the time, I had little awareness of women's issues. When Bob and I discussed it later, he said that he had the same view of women's roles that I did, but also that he was concerned about my safety. Anne's feminist viewpoint about including the whole human race was an eye-opener for me. She was far ahead of her time in recognizing women's issues, before the women's movement began and at a time when many of us did not think about discrimination against women. But now there was a confusing contradiction for me: I was doing more than I had been raised to think that I, as a southern white woman could do; on the other hand, I had not paid enough attention to the complexities of why women were sometimes viewed as not being able to handle certain tasks.

While based in Atlanta and working with students across the South, I was also developing the NSA Voter Registration Project. The project had three goals: "registering Negro voters, strengthening Negro political involvement, and providing an educational experience for the participants." It presented a new challenge in the movement because it was one of the first interracial voter registration efforts and one of the first attempts to bring northern students to the South. Foundation money was given by the nonprofit Voter Education Project, so there could be no direct action against segregated facilities.

Ella Baker and Connie Curry were involved in planning the project. Bob Moses of SNCC suggested that we work in Mississippi, where he was already doing voter registration. I met with the administration of Tougaloo College in Jackson and Rust College in Holly Springs to discuss the possibility of locating the project at one of those campuses, but the NSA Southern Project board, which would have legal responsibility, thought it was too dangerous. We considered having a group of only men go to Mississippi, but even though I had limited appreciation of women's issues at the time, I thought it was important to have women as well as men participate in the project. Ella suggested that I contact the Raleigh Citizens Association (RCA) in North Carolina. She had worked with this umbrella organization of black civic and church groups in April 1960 to set up the first conference of sit-in students at her alma mater, Shaw University, when SNCC was created. The RCA eagerly welcomed the Voter Registration Project. St. Augustine's, a black college, offered housing on its graceful campus of antebellum-style buildings, not in the best of repair, but shaded by beautiful large oaks and magnolias.

Although I was only twenty-four years old, barely older than most of the project participants, I was the director. It never occurred to me that I could not do the job because I was a woman. I recruited applications through the networks of NSA, SNCC, SDS, the YWCA, and the American Friends Service Committee. The fifteen young people, mostly college students, that I chose were about half black and half white, half southern and half northern, and half men and half women. I included Jane Stembridge, SNCC's first executive secretary; McComb, Mississippi, SNCC activist Bobby Talbert; and Sharon Jeffrey, one of SDS's founders. Most people who were chosen had experience in civil rights activities, and several had spent considerable time in jail for demonstrations against segregation. Our group had people from every social class, from elite private universities and underfunded black southern colleges.

I spent many long hours with members of the RCA, including John Winters and Dr. Grady Davis, to develop a voter registration strategy. We made maps of the targeted areas, lists of people in each area who could help, churches to promote the campaign, and mechanisms for keeping records. Most of the plan was in place before the project began, but it did need to be adjusted later when we were actually in the field. Working closely with the RCA and with students from St. Augustine's and Shaw University helped us avoid being rendered ineffective as outsiders, do-gooders, or naive young people, though we were all of the above. We would live and work on the black side of town and use only facilities open to all of us, which in effect meant only black facilities. On the few occasions that we traveled out of Raleigh, blacks and whites rode in separate cars to minimize the risk, and we anticipated where we could find restrooms available to all of us along the way. We also were prepared in how to respond with nonviolence if attacked, and we hid money and phone numbers in our clothes in case of emergency.

Our interracial men's and women's teams canvassed daily from door to door, encouraging people to register to vote. Men and women did the same work, including clerical tasks. We held block meetings and spoke in churches. The RCA circulated handbills appealing to churchgoers that said, "It is your Christian duty to vote!" We had to overcome resistance because many people feared losing their jobs if they registered. Many people worried about passing the literacy test. Others feared that they might be pressured to pay higher taxes or back taxes if they registered.

We registered more than 1,600 black voters during that summer, thereby significantly strengthening black electoral power. Local and national leaders applauded the project for its success. SNCC's Reggie Robinson sent a positive report about the project to James Forman, SNCC's Executive Secretary. We had shown that it was possible to have an interracial group of northern and southern women and men work effectively in voter registration in the South. However, unlike the Mississippi Freedom Summer two years later, the Raleigh project was in a "safer" part of the South, it involved fewer staff, and it was focused on one small town. Being so few, we did not overwhelm community people by sheer numbers.

We strengthened black political involvement primarily by registering so many new voters, but also because the RCA and our project mobilized the community in the process. However, it was clear to me that we were only short-term foot soldiers in what was a long-term struggle for meaningful political participation. Working and living in the community provided the participants' greatest educational experience. More formally, I invited speakers, conducted workshops, showed documentary movies, and set up a civil rights library. Many people, black and white, from all over the United States, Europe, and Africa, came to visit the project. Several SNCC staff, including Chuck McDew, Reggie Robinson, and Bob Zellner, spent time with us and provided inspiration and advice. They also helped us by speaking at mass meetings.

The RCA asked me to set up a tutoring program for the students who would be the first to desegregate the Raleigh public schools by going to a previously all-white school in the fall. Our program had many of the characteristics of the SCLC citizenship schools and the later SNCC Freedom Schools: we tutored in traditional subjects like English and math, but we also sought to build the self-confidence and political awareness of the twenty-five junior high students who faced the new school situation. We encouraged them to discuss their opinions on political issues. They defined "freedom," for example, as "a new world," "hope," and "to be able to live where I want without being harassed." One student said, "Freedom helps us to understand each other. Understanding is important. If we could understand each other, we could all live in peace."

Managing the project that summer of 1962 was not easy or glamorous. I worried about how living interracially for the summer might expose us to violence. I remember picking up the participants at the bus station and at the train depot. They came neatly dressed, looking fresh and eager to remedy social injustices. Anticipating the work we would be undertaking, I remembered an expression of my grandmother's as I thought to myself, "The Lord willing and the creek don't rise, we will all get through this safely." I directed the actual work, and also had to settle arguments about who was going to drive or about who stayed out too late or played radios too loud. I tried to use the organizational style I had learned in the YWCA—nonhierarchical and democratic—but it was not the most efficient way to get the job done. Although I tried to be assertive in the director role to resolve problems and make things work, often I was diverted by having to deal with interpersonal issues. I had to learn on the job, and I made mistakes. Whenever I got stuck and could not figure out what to do, I was able to turn to Ella and Connie in Atlanta, Jane and Sharon in Raleigh, or one of the visiting SNCC people. Except for these friendships, it was a lonely summer for me, as I put my personal relationships on hold in order to devote myself to the public role of directing the project.

The conflicts among our group tended not to be racial, but often reflected the difference between northerners and southerners. Northerners generally had more experience in administration, committee work, research, writing, and recordkeeping and could be intimidating to the less sophisticated southerners, whose slow-moving style tended to make them more effective at meeting strangers and convincing them to register.

Romantic relationships, some interracial, led to a certain amount of conflict. Competition for the same person caused arguments that on occasion were articulated along racial lines. One night I was really scared that someone might get hurt when two women were interested in the same man, and one pulled a knife on the other. After helping them resolve their dispute peacefully, I felt more like a housemother than a civil rights worker.

We went on a few trips together, always as interracial groups, usually with frightening incidents. On the way to a conference at nearby Duke University in Durham, for example, we tried to eat in the recently desegregated bus station restaurant. As soon as we sat down, some rough-looking white men started making threatening remarks about "race-mixing" and uttered racial epithets. Following our policy of avoiding racial confrontations, I signaled our group to leave. The men chased us out of the building and threw rocks at us. After that, all I can remember is jumping in Jane's orange VW bug and Jane flooring the gas pedal, her body rigid with tension, as we raced away. Looking back, I saw the other car in our group and then the men in a pickup following us. The truck followed us for several miles before finally giving up the pursuit.

Most of the white students said the project was their first experience as a minority in a black-majority situation. One young white woman said that Raleigh was a greater culture shock for her than her experience in Africa. The whites learned that because they associated openly with blacks, their "rights" could disappear — the right, when in an interracial group, to use a public restroom, for example, or to eat a restaurant meal. They learned that their lives might be threatened by white people. One white woman said this experience sensitized her to the difficulties black people faced in carrying the burden of desegregating the schools and public facilities. Several said they had learned for the first time just how vicious racism could be.

It was the first experience in an interracial group for several black students, who said they were very positive about it. One black student from the Deep South wrote, "The students worked hand in hand, like sisters and brothers, where nothing mattered — race, creed, or color: everybody was as one."

When the project was over, some participants stayed in Raleigh to work on desegregating the public facilities. They had a "swim-in" at the public swimming pool, a sit-in at the Howard Johnson's, and tried to desegregate the bleachers at the ballpark. Two project members were arrested and chose jail without bail. Newspaper reports said that several hundred people picketed to protest their arrest, and Raleigh civil rights leaders credited the voter registration project with helping mobilize their community.

Other participants went back to their campuses and towns to continue movement work. Sharon Jeffrey returned to Ann Arbor and continued her tutoring in a black community center as well as her SDS activities. Bobby Talbert went back to Mississippi and worked for SNCC. Within his first couple of weeks back home he was beaten while trying to integrate the state fair. He wrote me about being dismissed from his all-black college, "because the Dean said I was a bad influence on the school because I am in Civil Rights. So he said it would be better if I pack up and leave."

The North Carolina black newspaper, the *Carolinian*, ran an article based on a lengthy interview with me in August 1962. The reporter asked me to explain why a white woman from Texas would be in Raleigh working on black voter registration. I talked about my concern with racial equality and that I and other white southerners could not really be free until the South was rid of racial segregation. The article described me as "an unassuming, soft-spoken real American Freedom Fighter," and noted the contradiction between my political activism and personal conservatism.

In the spring of 1962, soon after I arrived in Atlanta, I developed a long-term relationship with movement people in Monroe, North Carolina, which continued during and after the Raleigh project. Although I made friendships throughout the South when I was in the movement, Monroe held a special importance for me because of an extraordinary woman named Azalea Johnson, who was a leader there. She explained about the movement in Monroe, where the goal was political liberation, not just racial integration, and where they believed in armed self-defense against marauding Klansmen when the judicial system did not protect them.

North Carolina is a border state, with Raleigh, the capital, in the Piedmont, the hilly, industrial, urban, and developed part of the state. Monroe, in contrast, is more similar to the Deep South geographically, politically, and economically. Reputed at that time to be a stronghold of the Ku Klux Klan, Monroe was just a few miles from Rock Hill, South Carolina, where there had been sit-ins and freedom rides involving violent attacks on civil rights workers.

Monroe became important in the history of the civil rights movement because it was the first place where blacks, under the leadership of Robert Williams in the 1950s, began to publicly put forth the ideas of "armed self-defense." Williams argued in *Negroes with Guns* (1962), "It has always been an accepted right of Americans, as the history of our Western states proves, that where the law is unable, or unwilling, to enforce order, the citizens can, and must, act in self-defense against lawless violence. I believe this right holds for black Americans as well as whites." Williams was very controversial because of his position, and he had been asked to step down as head of the NAACP in Monroe.

James Forman had spent a few weeks in Monroe in 1961 before he became executive secretary of SNCC. While there, Forman got involved in direct action to desegregate facilities and was beaten badly on his head while surrounded by a mob of hundreds of screaming whites, after which he was arrested and jailed. In *The Making of Black Revolutionaries* (1985, rev. 1999), Forman labels that experience the "moment of death." He also described the oppression in Monroe by the Ku Klux Klan and the resistance of the local black population under the leadership of Williams. Monroe became regarded as a place where blacks were armed and promoted the equivalent of "black power."

I knew nothing about Robert Williams, his political ideas, or the history of Monroe when I accepted an invitation from Septima Clark to speak at the Southern Christian Leadership Conference (SCLC) voter education training program. It was held in late April 1962, in Dorchester, a small rural town two miles from Midway and nine miles from Hinesville, in southeast Georgia. Dorchester was so small that if you needed to use a telephone, you had to go to Midway. People came from all over the South to this SCLC program for training in how to pass the voting tests in the various states.

The plan was for me to drive to Dorchester with the Reverend Andrew Young and Dorothy Cotton of the SCLC staff and to stay for a week. We rode down Highway 29, a country road, in Dorothy's brown Pontiac sedan, with Andy at the wheel and Dorothy, a couple of other SCLC staff persons, and me in the car. Driving past cotton fields, trying to ignore the heat, we saw a small ramshackle shanty on fire, about a hundred yards off the road. Two very small black children, maybe too young to walk, sat petrified on the front porch as the flames crept closer to them. Andy stopped the car, got out, and ran to help. He snatched the children off the porch in time so that they were not burned. Soon the parents came in from the fields and found their children saved, but watched as their house burned down.

Meanwhile, I had to sit frozen in the car. I didn't say anything and neither did anyone else because we all knew the realities in the rural South: if I got out, it could draw the attention of white passersby to our interracial group. My white skin could endanger us all. All it would take was one crazy white person driving by in a pickup truck. I can still remember my frustration and rage, knowing that segregation rendered me not only unable to help, but also potentially harmful to the very people I cared about.

When we reached Dorchester, the training center was a simple two-story building, with dorms for men and women. One meal was particularly noteworthy, with a menu that read, "nonviolent tomato juice cocktail, equality baked ham, recruit early fresh peas, passive resistant macaroni pie, registered candied yams, literacy garden salad, freedom fighting hot rolls, citizenship cake, and democratic tea."

There I was assigned a room with Ethyl A. (Azalea) Johnson of Monroe, North Carolina. Azalea, a close ally of the notorious Robert Williams, introduced me to a different view of nonviolence and thereby furthered my intellectual and political growth. She was a large, solid black woman, dressed in a plain print housedress. I don't remember how many years of schooling she'd had, but I remember that she told me she worked at a cleaners.

In our first meeting, after a couple of polite exchanges, she asked me what I thought of Mao Tse-tung. Revealing my ignorance, I asked, "Who's he?" Thus began several years of political discussion and friendship. She forever disabused me of the notion that formal schooling was the only way to become an educated person. Azalea, born in a little town in the Deep South, would read the writings of Mao and other political theorists at night, trying to understand how to deal with racism. She was a rare combination of devout Christian and radical firebrand. She told me what had happened to black people in Monroe: being physically attacked by white people, harassed by the Klan, unfairly arrested, held in jail, and not able to get protection or justice through the legal system. From her I learned about freedom struggles in third world countries. We had lengthy conversations about nonviolence as a belief and as a tactic. It was from Azalea that I first heard the term "Afro-American" and learned that the major goal of her group was the liberation of black people, not integration with white people. Even if we sometimes disagreed, our relationship mattered more than the ideological issues.

Azalea and I kept in touch after we left Dorchester, and when I went to Raleigh for the summer we made plans for the members of our project to visit Monroe. Monroe was about two and one-half hours south of Raleigh, down Routes 1 and 74. Azalea carefully planned the safest route to her house on Boyte Street, mailing me a map in advance to show the back roads and side streets into Newtown, the black part of Monroe. She said that I should drive in only at night under cover of darkness and that she would have her neighbors alerted, with shades drawn and men watching. I went the first time with only a couple of other people to minimize the risk of traveling in an interracial group. We had blankets to cover us if needed.

I was shocked when I arrived at Azalea's house and she told me that the men had guns, even if only as a precaution. I believed in a nonviolent movement and thus was jolted by being around men with pistols. Despite the guns, it turned out to be an uneventful visit, lasting only a few hours. We had brought sandwiches; she had made iced tea in the morning, giving it time to soak up the sugar. We talked about what was happening around the South. I reported on Raleigh, she on recent events in Monroe. She gave us copies of the column she had been writing, "Did You Know?" for a newsletter, the *Crusader*. We met her son, Raymond, a good-looking twenty-year-old who was a premedical student at North Carolina College. After meeting us, he decided to take the summer off and go back to Raleigh to work with us on voter registration. He subsequently became involved with one of the white women in our project, whom Azalea liked. She always inquired enthusiastically about the couple. And so we visited back and forth all through the summer.

On one trip, we drove in after dark, by moonlight. We were not there long when we heard gunfire. Then the phone rang and when Azalea answered, a man, claiming to be a Klansman, threatened to kill us. We immediately high-tailed it out of Monroe and got back to Raleigh that night.

In late August, my work in Raleigh finished, I returned to Atlanta. A few days later, I was sitting in the YWCA office with Ella Baker working on a conference, when the phone rang. It was Azalea, her voice breaking through the tears, to tell me that Raymond had drowned in a swimming accident while attending a voter education program in South Carolina. Rumors were circulating that white men in a nearby shrimp boat had seen him going under but made no effort to help him. Azalea asked me to come up to Monroe, but warned me that the situation was tense. When I told Jane Stembridge, she felt it was too dangerous for me to go alone. Ella, on hearing the story, said she wanted to come with me. It was just like her to be there for movement people, to attend to their personal pain, and to offer her support—no questions, no hesitation.

I sent an announcement to all the people who had worked in the Raleigh project to let them know about Raymond's death. Telegrams, letters, and flowers poured in. By the time Ella and I got to Monroe, the funeral was over, but friends were still bringing salads and cakes. We stayed in Azalea's small white frame home a couple of nights. Ella and I shared Raymond's room. Again

Azalea mentioned that men with guns were protecting us. They sometimes retired to the front yard when the living room was too crowded or to get some air. Azalea, Ella, and I sat around the kitchen table when everyone had gone home, sipping a little Jim Beam and picking at leftovers, and talked late into the night. Ella, in her long white cotton robe, her head as always held high, was like an angel in the room. The epitome of emotional strength, she also had a rare talent for finding the right words in times of tragedy. Azalea was devastated by the loss of the son for whom she'd had such high hopes. A few months later she decided to move north to Philadelphia, and we stayed in touch for the next several years.

Although Azalea espoused an early version of black power, she welcomed white support for the Monroe Defense Committee, a local civil rights organization. Azalea invited white people not only to raise money for legal defense, but also to come to Monroe and participate in civil rights work. Her ideas forced me to think about what was truly important to people in the South. Azalea had her eyes on the economic and political prizes, not just on racial integration.

My experience in Monroe also made me think seriously about the questions of nonviolence and self-defense. After all, I came from Texas, where pistol-packing people believed fervently in the right of self-defense and were adamant about the right to own weapons. I had owned hunting rifles and shotguns myself, hunted when I was young, and used guns to protect myself from snakes. I appreciated Robert Williams's analogy to the West, where people, both black and white, kept guns for hunting and to defend themselves. But it was new for me to hear black people publicly talking about weapons and declaring that they would defend themselves against lawless attacks by white people. I spoke to Ella at length about the issues of Gandhian nonviolence and armed self-defense. For myself I was still committed to nonviolence but certainly could understand and sympathize with people wanting to use arms to protect themselves if the law would not.

Azalea told me she wanted the South to change without more violence, even as she related stories about incidents of armed conflict between Monroe blacks and white Klansmen. Timothy Tyson, a professor in the department of Afro-American studies at the University of Wisconsin, has done extensive research on the nature and extent of armed self-defense in Monroe and writes about it in his book *Radio Free Dixie: Robert F. Williams and the Roots of Black Power* (1999). He argues that armed self-defense was much more extensive in the South, including Monroe, than is generally known. And as for looking to third world countries for leadership and ideology, Azalea made clear that she did so because she was disillusioned about making the American democratic system fair for black people. I would remember the frustration of the people in Monroe when the riots later broke out across the country.

I continued working for the Southern Student Human Relations Project out of Atlanta until the summer of 1963 and then left to go to Washington, D.C., where I shared a house with Robb Burlage and Todd Gitlin, SDS president. While they focused on SDS projects, I worked with Bill Higgs, a lawyer from Mississippi. He was drafting civil rights legislation, and I lobbied congressmen dressed in my best Sunday clothes and emphasizing my slow southern drawl. We were there for the March on Washington. Then, in the fall, Robb and I moved to Nashville. Robb was on leave from Harvard, where he was a graduate student in economics, to do research on the Tennessee Valley Authority. In December 1963, we were married.

Before leaving Raleigh, I had been interviewed for a newspaper article and been asked about my plans for the future, including marriage. The reporter wrote, "Miss Dawson said she hoped to be able to continue to work in the South and carry on her crusade for a free, better America. She says she does not rule out future marriage, but she does not plan to allow that to affect the task which lies so close to her heart."

In fact, for a couple of months after I got married I was unable to keep on course with my political work. I'd had a steady compass directing me forward before marriage, but after the wedding the needle started flipping around uncontrollably. I lost my footing in political work, not because of Robb, but because I became confused. I had learned in my southern upbringing that marriage was not just a way to legalize a loving relationship, but a job description — to be a helpmate to my husband. That meant going where he wanted to go, supporting his work, and deferring to his needs. My perception was that southern women were like certain gemstones: polished to be pleasing in appearance, but not brilliant. Women, particularly those with my kind of background, were socialized for this role from the time we were young. It was all too easy for me to move into the background.

In Nashville, Robb's income as an intern was meager and I did not yet have a job, so we lived in a tiny two-room apartment over a garage on 18th Avenue South, close to Vanderbilt University. The stove was from an earlier era, and the oven was unusable. Like many poorer buildings in the South, this one had no insulation under the roof, so the pipes froze in the winter and the roof radiated heat like a furnace the rest of the year. We had squirrels that tap-danced, chased each other, and rolled pecans and acorns on our corrugated tin roof. In that apartment, with the ironing board brought with me from Atlanta, I ironed Robb's long-sleeved, button-down Oxford cloth shirts as the perspiration poured off me. Then I would stop and read Simone de Beauvoir, and then iron again; then read Betty Friedan, then iron some more. Back and forth, Anaïs Nin and the ironing board; Doris Lessing and back to the ironing board. Somehow being a "married lady" and a political activist were not mixing well. Occasionally I would stop and write to Casey, saying something was wrong with all this. She and I corresponded frequently during this period, sharing our thoughts about the role of women in the movement.

My marriage and struggle for an identity in that framework forced me to address the tangle of gender, racial, and class issues in the South, especially as they influenced my own life. Somehow I had always intuitively understood that there was a connection between the segregation of blacks and the creation of suffocating roles for white women. The positions of blacks and of white women were part of the same myth about the Old South. It was Lillian Smith's *Killers of the Dream* (1949, rev. 1963) that clarified for me the function of women's roles in maintaining segregation. I found it easier to see the problems of how women were socialized, particularly those of us brought up with the southern lady myth, than to change my attitudes and behavior. Fortunately, I had strong women around me such as Ella Baker, Septima Clark, Casey Hayden, and Mary King with whom I discussed women's issues.

Not only was I confused because I could not figure out my conflicting roles of wife and activist, but I was married to a "movement heavy"—the designation for men who were considered important leaders in the movement. Robb was a major figure both in SDS and also in the Southern Student Organizing Committee (SSOC). This, as well as his brilliance, made it even more tempting to defer to him. He was, in fact, an unpretentious and undemanding man who was always supportive of me and other people.

In addition to the issues of gender and race, I needed to sort through Robb's and my different styles of work. There tended to be a difference in work styles between those of us engaged in southern organizing and those working with SDS. It was during my years with Robb that I had my most intense and frequent involvement in SDS. Many SDS men excelled at sophisticated theoretical analyses. My skills as an organizer were different, involving listening to, enabling, and empowering others. These attributes seemed better suited to southern organizing and did not fit well with the intellectual approach of SDS. My skills were well adapted to what I had been doing on campuses and in communities. There was not much opportunity for conflict with SDS men because we tended to work in different arenas—me with racial issues in the South and they in antiwar activities or furthering economic social change. SDS men such as Todd Gitlin, Al Haber, Bob Ross, and Dick Flacks became lifelong friends.

Robb and I constantly discussed politics, which helped us function as a team. We had worked together at the University of Texas on civil rights issues, been together at the early development of SDS, worked on the Port Huron statement (the major SDS position paper), written position papers on the South for SDS, and often worked together in the southern movement. But all this political collaboration did not provide us with any experience in combining marriage and political work. Sometimes we juggled them well, sometimes not.

I think it was a letter from Jane Stembridge, in early February 1964, that finally got me into action again. She wrote me about the murder of a black man, Lewis Allen, age fifty-five, in Liberty, Mississippi, his head filled with buckshot and his body found under a truck. She also wrote that movement people in Atlanta were worried that the House Un-American Activities Committee was going to investigate civil rights workers and that they were being red-baited. I knew then it was time to get back into political work.

Since early 1962, Robb, Casey, and I had been talking about creating new ways to reach white students. We had discussed the possibility of developing a southern arm of SDS, though the culture of SDS was not very comfortable for many southern white students. It was meeting Sue Thrasher, Archie Allen, Ed Hamlett, and David Kotelchuck that gave us the opportunity to fulfill this dream.

The Southern Student Organizing Committee was formally launched at a meeting in April 1964. Robb wrote a position paper for it on his old black Smith Corona portable typewriter, entitled "We'll Take Our Stand." In it he said, "We, as young Southerners, hereby pledge to take our stand now together, here to work for a new order, a new south, a place which embodies our ideals." The organization was interracial, but the focus was on challenging white southerners to shed racial prejudice.

I did a lot of cooking for the SSOC people and offered our home for people to get together or to stay when they needed a place, functioning as a support person for southern activists and a bridge for people from different organizations, especially SSOC, SNCC, and SDS. Many political activities originated in our apartment, and we held innumerable meetings there, surrounded by piles of movement pamphlets and literature. Our place was a crossroads where people met, talked, and shared ideas, contacts, and strategies. The movement grew because of such personal connections and relationships, often encouraged and developed by women.

As I regained my sense of myself as an independent political person, I became more directly involved in political work again. I worked with Myles Horton, director of Highlander Folk School in Monteagle, Tennessee, going to workshops and helping with his organizing efforts. Highlander, like many other organizations — and individuals — in the South that defended civil rights, had been red-baited relentlessly. Its buildings had even been burned. Particularly after the 1954 Supreme Court decision, red-baiting had become a common segregationist scare tactic, and it found fertile soil because of the Cold War.

Robb and Highlander introduced me to Appalachia. We began traveling to the mountains, trying to make connections on campuses for SSOC and with community groups for SDS. We helped organize a conference in Hazard, Kentucky, in conjunction with the Hazard Roving Pickets (a movement of coal miners), the National Committee for Full Employment, and SDS.

On one occasion, I remember driving to meet Florence Reece, the wife of a miner, who wrote the song "Which Side Are You On?" Originally written

for the labor movement, the song had been brought to the civil rights movement at Highlander. I was beginning to appreciate how little I had learned in
school about the contributions of many white southerners such as Reece, who
had stood up bravely on social issues. I had never been taught about the abolitionists, the antilynching movement, or the labor movement. On the way
home from the meeting with Reece, as we drove through the mountains, with
Robb at the wheel and Sue Thrasher, Ed Hamlett, and me as passengers, the
car stalled in a blizzard. To relieve the tension while Robb tried to get the
motor started again, we began singing the old Baptist and Methodist hymns
we had grown up on — Robb, who had sung backup with Elvis Presley in the
honky-tonks of Texas, Sue and Ed with their church choir–trained voices, and
I, for whom the old hymns were still bedrock. Then we prayed, "Oh Lord, oh
dear Jesus, please deliver us." All of a sudden, the car started, and we got home
safely that night.

In 1965, Robb and I moved to Washington, D.C., so that he could work with
the Institute for Policy Studies (IPS), a liberal think tank, on issues of health
care policy. I worked as an organizer in southeast Washington, the area across
the Anacostia River, through 1968. The area included Anacostia, Congress
Heights, Garfield, Stanton, and other sections, but we usually referred to it
simply as Southeast or Anacostia for short. Frederick Douglass had a home in
this part of town in the late 1800s. It was reputed to have an active White
Citizens Council. When I went to work there, the area was a mixture of races
and classes but contained more than half of Washington's public housing. It
was considered an isolated and forgotten part of Washington, so much so that,
according to Zora Martin, a local leader, residents filed a class action suit to
obtain equitable public services for the area.

I was invited to join a group of organizers known as the "Target Team" of
the Southeast Neighborhood House, an old, established settlement house with
an interracial staff and board of directors that was receiving funding from the
antipoverty program. The team included John Kinard, who had worked in
Africa with Operation Crossroads and had a strong sense of black identity and
black institutions, and Pharnal Longus, who had trained at Howard University
in social work and was frustrated by how the welfare system disempowered its
recipients. There were six other men on the team, one of whom was white. I

was the only woman on the team. Also in the area, though not on the team, were extraordinary women organizers, such as Theresa Jones and Mary Kidd.

We began our organizing efforts in one small area, at the suggestion of John, hoping over time to build a strong grassroots community-wide movement. We set up an office in the basement of a building in the most run-down housing project, Barry Farms. It was plagued by rats and roaches, poor transportation, high rates of unemployment and welfare, restless high school dropouts, and few social services. However, I always felt safe working alone there.

We talked with community people one on one or in small groups, helping them find their own power, define their own issues and goals, and develop their own strategies. Strong leaders quickly emerged. They learned to handle interviews with the press and negotiate in meetings with public officials. Our plan was to work ourselves out of a job with one group, then start with others and repeat the process.

The teenagers organized first, calling themselves "Rebels With A Cause." These kids, many of whom had never been in downtown Washington and could not even recognize the dome of the U.S. capitol, became a strong force for change in the neighborhood. They negotiated new traffic lights for the area as well as more recreational facilities, an athletic program, and a neighborhood youth program. Over time, they developed and directed their own alternative school for high school dropouts. They demanded and received funding for these programs from the federal antipoverty program, which then tried to replicate the Rebels' model in other cities.

Soon the women in Barry Farms formed their own organization, the "Band of Angels." They began with a clean-up campaign, then, after many angry and well-publicized meetings with public housing authorities, they got a pest extermination program and received a commitment of about $1 million for renovations. They also got the Highway Department to pave the streets and demanded a decision-making role in the administration of the housing project, thereby establishing a model that was copied elsewhere in the city and the country. Next, they won reforms and policy changes in the Welfare Department. They consulted with other groups in Washington and eventually became major players in the National Welfare Rights Organization and the National Tenant Organization.

With public housing in such capable and successful hands, our team then moved on to problems of private housing, beginning with the Parkchester Apartments, where we organized a tenant council to deal with violations of the housing code. One night, as I was leaving a tenant meeting on the second floor, I fell down the unlighted, broken-down stairway that lacked a handrail. My foot was broken. Pharnal called an ambulance to take me to the hospital, where I had surgery. The next day, the angry tenants organized a rent strike to demand repairs. They won the rent strike and went on to make the complex into cooperative housing, owned by the tenants.

Community people were overcoming their fear of public authorities, their sense of alienation and apathy, and the fragmentation of their community. They were feeling pride and self-confidence. They knew that their power came from shared responsibility and action. The press covered the community developments regularly, sometimes daily. And the area was looking better.

The Rebels, Angels, and other community groups we organized worked with other citizen groups on citywide campaigns. Marion Barry, head of the SNCC Washington office, directed a bus boycott in protest of an increase in bus fares. (Marion had been the first chairman of SNCC.) We mobilized the boycott and provided alternate means of transportation. In March 1966, Nation's Business ran an article complaining about our "war" on business and printed a photograph of me explaining to volunteer drivers a map of bus routes. The boycott reduced bus usage by 85 percent, and the rate increase was stopped. Later, we cooperated in a citywide effort for Home Rule to gain local government for Washington.

One of my roles was to connect the Anacostia movement with other community organizers. When SDS held a conference on welfare reform, and when the Citizens Crusade Against Poverty sponsored a national conference, I arranged for the Band of Angels and the Rebels to participate. Their experiences and success made them among the most articulate people at those conferences. They were highly respected for their accomplishments. We also created seminars so the Anacostia residents could explain the problems of poverty, marginal employment, and housing to academics, researchers, and public policy analysts.

Our work attracted many SNCC workers, including Ralph Featherstone.

Ralph had been working on food cooperatives with SNCC in Mississippi in 1965, and he came to meet with us about possible food co-ops in Washington. His idea never really took off, possibly because people were already too busy with other issues. I appreciated his thoughtful, serious style and his ideas about economic problems. Working with Ralph helped keep me connected to the Southern Freedom Movement.

Stokely Carmichael also came to Anacostia, where a large crowd gathered for his speech on Black Power. His message was consistent with what local people were doing: taking control of their lives and institutions. The concept of Black Power was prevalent in the country during the several years that I was working in southeast Washington, but it was not discussed often in meetings; instead, community people wanted to talk about how to solve specific local problems. Our organizing approach, to focus on particular social issues, meant that our movement was primarily black, but any white people who wanted to participate were welcome.

Riots, looting, and mayhem erupted throughout Washington after the assassination of Martin Luther King Jr. in April 1968. The community organizations in Southeast provided a network of help and support even in that crisis. I was asked to drive a car marked as an emergency vehicle. I delivered food, drove people to medical facilities, and located lawyers. During the riots, without the identification as an emergency worker, I might have been attacked as a white person who did not belong in the black neighborhood. Lots of people in Southeast did know me, but not everyone, so it was a potentially dangerous situation. I was often afraid because I could not be sure where or when violence might erupt, but I tried just to do what had to be done and not think too much about the danger. Fortunately, I was not hurt.

In Southeast, the work required a shift in focus from desegregation to the issues of jobs, housing, welfare, and schools—the same issues Azalea Johnson had taught me about years before. Although we had many extraordinary successes and I believed strongly in what I was doing, I saw for the first time the enormity and difficulty of resolving these fundamental social problems. I also recognized that these issues were ones of class as well as race. The world seemed much more complicated than when I had first become an activist in college, fighting segregation.

During these years between 1965 and 1968, when many of my friends left the movement, I was blessed to work with this effective interracial team. I was also able, during that period, to maintain my connections with many movement friends because so many SNCC, SSOC, and SDS people were living in or traveling through Washington. And significantly, the work in Anacostia gave me the opportunity to define further my own identity as an autonomous woman, capable of doing serious political work on my own, independent of my marriage.

In 1965, women whom I knew through SDS and IPS began discussing women's issues and invited me to participate. Though I attended some of their meetings, I did not become active in the women's movement at that time, for several reasons. For one thing, I was working around the clock in Anacostia and was focused on issues of race and class, feeling that those problems, often about survival, sometimes life and death, were more urgent. For another, I was satisfied with the role I was playing there as an equal member of a team, so had no immediate discontent to inspire me to join the women's movement. Since first becoming an activist, I had, for the most part, been able to do the work I wanted to in the movement, sometimes as a member and sometimes as a leader and/or founder of organizations. Also, as a southern woman, my issues seemed different from those of the northern SDS women I knew in Washington. Coming from liberal or left-wing families where they were encouraged to be political, they resented the limitations they felt in SDS. I usually felt, in contrast, that I needed to struggle with myself against the limitations of my Old South upbringing, and even then, most of the southern white women in the movement with whom I was friends were from homes that were more liberal than mine and in which it was more acceptable for them to be politically outspoken. I did become serious about women's issues when I went to graduate school a couple of years later.

The organizing effort in Anacostia, where I worked days, evenings, and weekends, absorbed most of my energy during those years. Robb was deeply invested in his work at IPS and was still involved with SDS on a daily basis. While we were supportive of each other's work, we were going in separate directions, and we eventually separated and were later divorced. That pattern was not unusual for "movement marriages." We sometimes understood how to create a supportive environment in our work lives, but many of us did not know how to have fulfilling, responsible personal lives at the same time, especially during such a chaotic and intense period of history. The breakup of the marriage was difficult for me, not only because Robb had been my life partner but also because he had been my main tie to my roots in Texas.

Four years was a long time to do movement work in the same place. The transience of movement people reflected the fact that we were often improvising the movement as we went along and that our ideas and our organizations were always changing. Being in the black community so much of my post-college life, moving so often, adjusting to so many new organizations and work settings, had left me with a confused sense of myself that complicated my personal relationships.

By 1968, the members of the Target Team felt that the local people were able to operate without us and we decided to disband. Robb and I had separated, and I took a job with the Model Cities Program in Philadelphia, working in housing and urban development. I lived in a black neighborhood and worked in the black community, but the government job was not a good one for me. I was a stranger to the North. I was uncomfortable in a bureaucracy, especially with its top-down approach to community development and social change. Unfortunately, I also began to lose touch with my movement friends, who had scattered. I needed to find another direction.

Around 1969 I called Ella Baker, who had guided me wisely for so many years. Now living in an apartment in Harlem, she invited me to visit. She buzzed me in and I walked down a long hall to the back of her apartment, where she was sitting snapping beans and drinking a gin and tonic with lime. Offering me one, she reported with pleasure that she had bought the limes on sale. Both hospitable and practical, as always! She was surrounded by piles of papers — letters, reports, newspapers: the stuff of her political work. Her welcome was as warm as ever. I felt at home again and safe to be talking with her about my life. I do not remember all of what we shared — a little about her family, a little about my personal life, what she was up to in New York, how our movement friends were doing, what was happening politically in the country, where I had been and what I might do next. We talked about Black Power, what had happened in SNCC, and the role of white people in the struggle. As usual, Ella was positive, looking for ways to move forward. She talked with enthusiasm about my going to graduate school and "making something of yourself," sounding like my mother.

Ella and I also talked about whether I should go back to my maiden name when my divorce became final. At the time, the choice of last name was an issue being discussed in the women's movement; many women were keeping their maiden names when they got married or reverting to them afterward. I asked Ella what she thought. She told me, "Oh, I would not bother to change back to your maiden name. It would just cost you money to go to court and anyway you're still going to be the same person." So I am still called Dorothy Burlage. There was no way for me to know it at the time, but it was the last meeting I would ever have with Ella before she died. She had been the major influence in my life for the previous eight years.

Emotionally and symbolically, it was Ralph Featherstone's death in a car bombing in 1970 that most dramatically signaled for me the end of the movement as I had known it. When I saw the announcement in the paper, I wanted to honor him by attending the memorial service. I rode the train alone to Washington, tears trickling down my face, lost in memories of movement tragedies, of the many good people who had been beaten, jailed, harassed, or killed. Arriving at the funeral home, I first went into the wrong room, where someone else was laid out, lying stiffly on the table. I searched for the right room, trying to remain unobtrusive in the darkened halls and rooms. I did not see anyone else who was white. I felt unsure and uncomfortable. My instincts told me I should not be there, and I left. That experience marked my personal feeling of loss of the movement I had known.

It had been fourteen years since my conscience pushed me into the struggle for social justice. I had begun my work with high hopes and a deep, heartfelt belief in the nonviolent movement. Now it appeared that many of my movement friends — my tribe — had scattered in a kind of diaspora. I had lived many places and worked with many organizations. I had made many friends, only to lose track of them with my many moves. I had crossed the color line and burned many bridges behind me. And there I was: not a typical southerner, not a northerner, not an academic, not a liberal, not a leftist, not a hippie, not a feminist. I wasn't black, but I didn't feel very white. I did not fit anywhere. I couldn't go back, but I didn't know how to go forward.

In 1970, following Ella's advice, I applied to graduate school and was admitted to a doctoral program in clinical psychology at Harvard. I had been away from theology for almost ten years, had no more interest in it, and wanted to understand more about human behavior. I received scholarships, grants, and awards and got teaching jobs to pay for school. I also did research for several years at Harvard Medical School. I received a Woodrow Wilson Fellowship in Women's Studies for my work on women and families. When I finished my Ph.D., I interned at Children's Hospital in Boston.

As a graduate student, I still had the same passion for social justice that I had felt in the Freedom Movement, but it took a new direction when I began my work as a child psychologist. My efforts in this arena over the last thirty years, to which I brought similar commitment and fervor, can only be mentioned briefly here because they are from a different chapter of my life. I finally began to take a serious interest in women's issues because I was studying child development and wanted to understand the family as the framework for child-rearing. I did research on women's roles, especially on the effects of economic conditions on parenting. In 1972 I was invited to give the Lentz Lecture at Harvard, which I did on "Women and Sexuality." The following spring I wrote a contribution to an anthology entitled *Sexist Religion and Women in the Church.* During that period, I also organized a group of psychologists to develop a nonprofit center for women, the Women's Counseling and Resource Center, which still exists more than twenty-five years later. I found space for the center in the same church basement where I had begun fundraising for SNCC eleven years before.

Now I work with children as a child psychologist both in private practice and at the Harvard University Health Services. My work with children is similar to my work in the movement: my task is to help remove obstacles so that people can be the best they can be, develop to their greatest potential, and engage in mutually respectful relationships. I try to use concepts in my work that I learned in the movement: how power works in relationships, how change comes about, how people grow and develop, and how they get courage in the face of adversity. I try to listen to what people really care about and try to remain true to the guiding principles of honesty and integrity, compassion and hope. I remain committed to the struggle against racism, but now I also advocate for the rights of children, believing that to be another way to create a better society.

Over the years, I began to be reconciled with my past and to put the various pieces of my life together. I had grown up and received my real education in the movement. It helped me learn to follow my own vision, have a political voice, and develop leadership skills. And it helped me abandon some of my restrictive southern upbringing in personal relationships.

I attended SNCC, SDS, and SSOC reunions, where I was overjoyed to see old movement friends. I traveled to Texas and was able to see Hiawatha and Ernest, Lola and Georgia, before they passed on, and I felt the same warmth and kindness with them that I had experienced as a child.

Thankfully, I became closer to my family as well. My brother remained steadfast over the years, regardless of what he thought about my politics. I was able to spend more time with my mother and grandmother for a few years before they died, regretting only that I had missed so many years with them. Once, on a visit, my mother and I went to a restaurant and were seated next to a black family. I held my breath waiting for her reaction, but she seemed not to notice. Her behavior had changed, and apparently her attitudes as well. I knew that legally, at least, the South was finally desegregated. Most of my extended family still do not know what I had done in those movement years. If they learn as a result of this book, some may be shocked, some horrified, and some tolerant or even pleased.

It had been a very bumpy road for me out of the segregated South. I had stumbled many times along the way, and I still have bruises, yet I am immensely grateful for the opportunity to be in the movement, what felt like a holy war for justice. I feel, and felt at the time, that I had no choice but to do what I did, both for my own self-respect and to honor what I believed in. Otherwise, I would have suffocated in the mentality of the Old South. I regret that we were not able to eliminate racism, but I believe that our values will endure and that a new momentum will come from those of another generation who will find their own light of freedom, learning from our successes and our mistakes.

Postscript: A few weeks before this chapter was to go to press, I found boxes with my movement papers and correspondence that had been put in storage almost thirty years ago and which I will now give to an archive. Reading some documents, I noticed that most things were exactly as I remembered. However, it is clear from writing my story that there is the actual history of what happened and then there is the past that resides in my memory, which is selective and sometimes may be mistaken. I have told the story as honestly as I can and believe that if there are inaccuracies or omissions, what I have written reflects the truths of my heart.

Sweet Tea at Shoney's

PENNY PATCH

M̲y mother was eight months pregnant when the FBI knocked on her door in November 1943 and asked why she and my father were exchanging telegrams consisting of lists of names. My father, stationed in Moscow in the foreign service, had telegraphed Natasha, Kalinka, and Pasha. My mother, living with her parents in New York City, had telegraphed back: Prudence, Helen, Grace, and finally, Penelope. If I turned out to be a boy there was no question that I was to be named Isaac Patch V, but my parents were addressing the possibility that I might be a girl. A number of telegrams passed back and forth as they tried to decide what to name me. World War II was in progress, and the FBI, suspecting that my parents were communicating in code, had arrived to investigate. This was to be my first, but not my last, contact with the FBI.

My mother's family, which included descendants of the Mayflower as well as more recent immigrants from Germany, was a middle-class family from New York City. They were politically to the left, musical and intellectual, never financially comfortable, struggling at times to sustain a genteel life in Manhattan. My father grew up in wealth and privilege in Gloucester, Massachusetts, the son of a successful banker. As in my mother's family, family members, including the women, were active in politics and civic life. The difference was that my father's family was decidedly Republican.

My father joined the navy in 1941 serving on a tanker in the Pacific. In 1942 he injured his back falling down the hatch while carrying a load of ammunition. That ended his navy career. His next step was to prepare for a diplomatic career, and he met my mother when they both enrolled in the same Russian language graduate program at Harvard University. Reflecting the attitudes of the times, on the first day of class the professor announced that inevitably the two women in the class would drop out. At the end of the term, my mother came in first, the other young woman second.

My father's politics and social attitudes were drifting leftward, a process that continued over many years thanks to his wife's and later his children's influence. An oft-told family story about the early days of my parents' relationship is that my mother, a deeply nonviolent woman, hit my father with a flyswatter while arguing with him about labor unions. My mother had strong beliefs in political and ethical matters, and we all knew it.

I come, then, from a family that was intensely political and active in civic life. National and international issues were part of our family discussions. We were raised to feel that we had a responsibility to contribute to making positive change in the world, and that it was in our power to do so. Some of these attitudes are related to class and privilege, and some have to do with my parents' character.

My father took a foreign service position in Moscow in April 1943. He did not return to the United States until October 1945. My mother had planned to follow him to Russia, but in the end was not allowed to because of the war and because she was pregnant with me. I spent the first two years of my life with my mother and her parents in an apartment on East 16th Street in New York City.

My father's next posting was to China. In March 1946, my father, my mother, and I departed the United States by ship sailing for Dairen, Manchuria, a port city on the northeastern coast. I was two and a half years old. My father had been offered a job running the tiny consulate in Dairen, and my mother had said he couldn't go unless she and I went too. So, ignoring warnings from the State Department about the dangers of taking such a young child to the ends of the earth, we set off together.

It was then that I entered a world that had experienced World War II directly. I have a picture of my mother and me standing on a street in Manila in the Philippines surrounded by rubble. Wherever I lived during my childhood there was rubble — in Dairen, in Czechoslovakia, and eventually in Germany. Rubble-strewn streets and collapsed buildings, then a part of my waking life, are still a part of my dream life.

We stayed in Dairen for two and a half years, much of the time cut off from communication with the rest of the world, dependent for social life and support upon a small group of refugees and expatriates from around the globe. This was 1947 and 1948. The Japanese occupation had ended; Mao Tse-tung's people had taken over locally, although Soviet troops occupying Dairen exercised significant supervisory authority over them. We were the only Americans in the city. My parents, with a small Chinese staff, ran the tiny consulate office. Local Chinese people worked for us as cook and houseboy (yes, houseboy), and a woman whom I called "Amah" was my nurse.

Other Chinese, never sure which way the political and ideological winds were going to blow, were afraid to associate with us. Later, when we no longer lived in China, I overheard my parents discussing how my Amah and the young men who worked for us had probably been shot after we left. I sat quietly in the back seat of the car thinking, If this could happen to Amah and her family, could it happen to us too?

In Manchuria, people of many nationalities came in and out of our house. Some were Jewish refugees from Nazi-occupied Europe who had boarded any boat available and ended up in China. My father worked to get them papers so that they could eventually emigrate to other countries, or perhaps even return home. There were Russian, Chinese, and even German guests in our house. The Germans, all wives and children of Nazi diplomats and Nazi businessmen who had spent the war years living and working in Manchuria, were stranded in Dairen. In 1945, at the end of the war, their husbands had been interned in Siberia by the Russians, leaving the women and children in China.

One of these German women helped to organize the nursery school I attended. We had Maryknoll nuns as teachers, and my schoolmates included several German children, Austrian-Jewish refugee children, some Russian children, and some Chinese children. My nursery school friends also gathered at my birthday parties. I have pictures of one such party, evidence that my earliest friends included Jewish refugee children and the children of Nazis.

Later, when I asked my father how he could send me to school with the children of Nazis, he said, "They were just women and children." He said that there were so few foreigners and it was such a crazy time that everyone banded together.

In 1948 we returned briefly to the United States until my father was sent to work in Prague, Czechoslovakia. I attended kindergarten in Prague, where we lived for nine months before my father was expelled abruptly from the country, accused of being an American spy. We were given twenty-four hours to leave, and I was taken to my friend Eva's house that night to say good-bye. I remember walking on the dark path leading up to her door, and the lighted room inside, where I stood opposite Eva holding my mother's hand. I didn't understand anything except that everyone around me was upset, our house was suddenly full of big boxes, and I was leaving my friends.

By now I had two siblings: my sister Eliza, born in our house in Dairen with the assistance of a Russian doctor and a midwife, and my sister Nabby, born in Massachusetts during our brief sojourn in the States. We drove over the border from Czechoslovakia into Germany in our red jeepster: two adults, three children, and two cats, our belongings piled around us.

Was my father an American spy? What he has always said, and what I believe, is that he was caught in one of those situations during the Cold War when the United States expelled somebody and the Communists expelled someone in return. In addition, my father has always been a gregarious person with excellent communication skills. Throughout his relatively brief diplomatic career, he got himself into hot water by talking to anyone willing to engage in conversation. While in Moscow during World War II, he and a friend hopped trains out into the countryside, walked onto collective farms, talked with people, and got into trouble with the authorities, Russian and American.

My father, who could speak Russian, was offered a State Department job in Frankfurt, Germany, interviewing Soviet defectors. I lived for a total of six years in Germany, interrupted by one year spent in Gloucester, Massachusetts. My brothers Ike and Nick were born in U.S. army hospitals in Germany during these years. My parents, who believed in exposing their children to the culture they were living in, sent us to German schools. They have told me that they had doubts about living in Germany after the war, not knowing if they could live side by side with people who had committed such horrors. Yet they too, like me, adjusted to life there and made friends, German friends.

One sunny day in 1952 my parents took me to Dachau, the concentration camp just outside of the city of Munich, where we now lived. I was nine years old. I remember standing in a line of people facing a row of ovens. In my memory I see whitewashed brick. I am horrified and I am scared. It must have been a few days later, as I sat with my friend Ingrid and her parents after school in their kitchen drinking coffee heavily diluted with milk, that I suddenly blurted out, "How could you let the murder of the Jews happen? How could you not do anything?" No one said a word. We continued to sip our coffee in total silence, and I never got an answer. I never mentioned the subject again to Ingrid. I learned rapidly that there were some questions I should not ask if I wanted to be welcomed into the homes of my friends.

The father of my best friend, Elizabeth, had served on the Russian front and spent three years in a Russian POW camp. He had never been a Nazi party member. Another friend's father, a kind and friendly man, had been a "brown shirt," a party member. Another man who came in and out of our house, I learned, had worked for Goebbels as an art historian. This is where conscious memory begins of my lifelong effort to resolve something that for me is unresolvable: How could Germans do what they did? How could people who inhabited my childhood, who were kind to me and made me feel at home, have perpetrated the Holocaust, or let it happen? And how was I going to be able to keep on loving these people? By the time I was ten or eleven, the question of German responsibility for the Holocaust was a conscious and urgent issue.

The Holocaust was certainly not talked about in the German school I attended, the school that I came to as a member of the American occupying forces, never sure initially who liked me because I was me and who was being nice to me because of my privileged status as an occupying American. In time, I became quite secure and comfortable there, felt appreciated for myself, cared for, and nurtured.

In 1956, when I was thirteen, we left Germany and came "home." The next year I entered the Dalton School in New York as a high school freshman. Dalton was socially and politically progressive, and it was also, I found out, eighty-five percent Jewish. I did well in school and, after a while, made a few close friends. But I did not talk much about my past in Germany. I knew that

I would lose friends if I admitted to loving Germans. I was very vulnerable by then to my driving need for friends and community, having lost both so frequently. Again I kept silent.

The question for me now is how did my unusual childhood, in which I moved frequently between cultures, contribute to my involvement in the black Freedom Movement? After all, I had little contact with black people during my childhood or high school years. I remember a black woman who was a colleague of my father's in Germany. Her name was Louise, and I, with my parents, attended her wedding to Leo, a Russian émigré. At the time, I overheard remarks that their life together would be difficult, but I had no idea why this should be the case. There were few black students in my high school in New York City. Peg Dammond, a light-brown-skinned young woman in the class above me, was one. It never occurred to me that she was particularly different. In fact, I am sure I thought I was far more out of place than she.

I did not have much experience with African American people and their culture. And I myself had never suffered serious deprivation or oppression. On the other hand, most white middle-class young women were far more sheltered than I from the knowledge that such hardship existed. I had been overwhelmed at a young age by my knowledge of the Holocaust and strongly influenced by my powerful childhood connections to both Jewish refugees and German perpetrators and bystanders. Once I became aware that the evil of segregation existed, I did not want to be one of those people who did nothing. Finally, the dislocations of my early life, which culminated in my reluctant return to the United States, left me an alienated teenager in a culture that was not mine. I was an outsider. I was searching for a community, and I was ready for the Freedom Movement when it came.

In September 1961 I entered Swarthmore College in Pennsylvania, a college grounded in Quaker principles, and quickly joined SPAC, the Swarthmore Political Action Committee. Influenced by my parents' politics, I was a liberal Democrat and a Kennedy supporter.

One night I heard Mimi Feingold, a white Swarthmore student, speak about her experiences taking part in the Freedom Rides. Mimi was a small woman and she looked tiny at the podium on the stage of that large auditorium. Such a very young woman, only two years older than I was, and look what she had done. I was awestruck. The next step for me, into activism, just seemed to happen, as if the decision had already unconsciously been made and all I had to do was seize the opportunities as they came along.

My first involvement in organized protest later that fall was to take part in a test case involving the integration of a roller skating rink in Chester, Pennsylvania, which had designated black nights and white nights. This was illegal under state law, but the owners had been getting away with it for years. On a white night, several young black people from the local National Association for the Advancement of Colored People (NAACP) youth group were turned away with the excuse that the rink was full to capacity. Five minutes later, another white Swarthmore student and I walked up to the ticket booth, bought tickets, and were admitted. Our admission was used to prove that the rink functioned on a segregated basis. I don't remember how the case was resolved, but a couple of times we were admitted and went roller skating in integrated groups on white nights. Some angry whites in the rink tripped and kicked members of our integrated group. It was scary, but I remember being buoyed by a very strong sense that what we were doing was right.

In January 1962 I began to participate in sit-ins along the Eastern Shore of Maryland. Black students from traditionally all black colleges in the Washington-Baltimore-Philadelphia area who were organizing sit-ins in segregated restaurants invited students from mostly white colleges in the area to join them. And we went by the busload, on the weekends, from Swarthmore, Haverford, and Bryn Mawr. I was arrested for the first time on St. Patrick's Day 1962 while on a march from Baltimore to Washington, charged with trespassing on private property. The march was part of an attempt to draw attention to the plight of Student Nonviolent Coordinating Committee (SNCC) field secretaries Chuck McDew, Bob Zellner, and Dion Diamond, who were imprisoned in Louisiana on charges of criminal anarchy. I was arrested several times that spring. I would drive back to school at the beginning of the week after overnight stays in jail, then return to the demonstrations the next weekend.

The force of the movement was electrifying. I can remember the headiness of those days, the sense that we were doing something important, and we were doing it together, black and white. And I experienced for the first time the music of the movement. The music was so beautiful. Everyone sang, and the songs bound us together and made us strong. I had my first experience with a white mob while picketing outside a restaurant on the Maryland Eastern Shore that refused to serve us. A large crowd of white men and women gathered around us screaming, waving baseball bats, throwing things as we tried to walk our peaceful circle. I was scared, but I also drew enormous strength from the people in that picket line with me, and from the songs we sang. There was terror in the work—but such joy and passion as well. I remember dancing to the twist one night in Maryland, high as could be. No alcohol, at least not for me, but I was just flying. We all were.

Needless to say, my school work suffered. I also became impatient with the academic discussions that went on at our liberal Quaker college about the rights and wrongs of civil disobedience. For me, there was nothing to debate. People were suffering and change needed to happen now. It was time for action. When the already legendary SNCC workers Reggie Robinson and Dion Diamond turned up at our demonstrations recruiting students to work on southern voter registration and direct action projects for the summer, I immediately volunteered. Mostly, of course, they were looking for black students. They seemed pretty doubtful when I asked them if there was anything I could do. They offered the Atlanta SNCC office as a possibility, but hedged even on that. They did, however, take my name, and in May I got a phone call. SNCC had decided to take white students, women as well as men, to work on an integrated project in southwest Georgia for the summer. Charles Sherrod, working as a SNCC organizer in southwest Georgia since October 1961, had a vision of an integrated field project that would live the values of an interracial society. As Sherrod outlined his plan, he intended to take integrated teams of student volunteers into the rural counties around Albany, Georgia, to work with and develop local black leaders and to encourage voter registration. The idea of white superiority lay at the root of segregation, and to break down this image in black and white minds he proposed to offer another: that of black and white working together side by side.

Other SNCC folk thought Sherrod was mad to attempt such a project, but in SNCC at that time there were only twenty-two staff people, and if you wanted to do something you tried to get a consensus. And the consensus usually was that if you wanted to do it, you could. So SNCC approved Sherrod's southwest Georgia project.

In June 1962, at the age of eighteen, I joined SNCC and went to southwest Georgia. I was to be the first white woman working in a SNCC field project in the Deep South.

I flew to Atlanta from New York with Peg Dammond, my former Dalton schoolmate, who had also become involved with the Civil Rights Movement, and Kathleen Conwell, another young black woman taking part in the summer's project. We were met at the airport in Atlanta by SNCC people and were taken to an apartment to spend the night. The apartment belonged to Jim Monsonis, a white SNCC staff member, and was in a white neighborhood. We were an integrated group, eight or nine of us by that time. The three women got the one bed in the back room; the men slept on chairs, the sofa, and the floor. Around midnight we went to bed, we women in our pajamas, one of us with her hair in rollers. Suddenly we heard a loud knock. It was the police. An upstairs neighbor had complained about the racial mix of the group. When we three women wandered sleepily into the living room, Bill Hansen, a white SNCC organizer, pushed us back into the bedroom, whispering, "Get on some clothes, get on some clothes." We got dressed in a hurry, went back out and showed our IDs, and after some muttering and grumbling the police left. The next morning we left for Albany, 170 miles south of Atlanta, traveling in one of the old and unreliable automobiles that SNCC people drove.

In Albany, we were taken in by Goldie and Bo Jackson, a local couple very active in the already existing Albany Movement, of which Goldie was secretary. We went to their home, a tiny white house on a dirt road, surrounded by other small houses on dirt roads with no streetlights. For the next two or three weeks as many as nine of us stayed at Goldie and Bo's while they and the experienced SNCC staff oriented us to the work ahead. From Sherrod and the others we learned about the history and people of the Albany Movement. And Sherrod gave us John Dollard's *Caste and Class in a Southern Town* to read.

In 1962 Albany was a fast-growing commercial center for south Georgia and a thoroughly segregated small city of fifty-six thousand, of whom 40 percent were black. Until SNCC field secretaries Charles Sherrod and Cordell Reagon came to town in October 1961, Albany had experienced little protest activity. The exception was the presentation of a petition, early in 1961, by a group of adult black leaders to the city commissioners, requesting the desegregation of certain city facilities.

Sherrod and Reagon were soon joined by Charles Jones, another black SNCC organizer, and the three set up a voter registration office in a rundown little building in the center of the black community of Albany. Black high school and college students were the first to be attracted to the equally youthful SNCC workers, but by the end of November the local black ministerial alliance, SNCC, the NAACP, and other black organizations had formed a coalition that became known as the Albany Movement. On November 22, 1961, several students from all-black Albany State College, testing the enforcement of the recent Interstate Commerce Commission (ICC) ruling prohibiting segregation in public facilities, tried to use the restaurant in the Trailways bus terminal and were arrested. On December 10 an integrated SNCC group of nine—among whom were my co-authors Joan Browning and Casey Hayden—rode the train from Atlanta to Albany sitting together in the white car. They too were arrested after being ordered out of the white waiting room of the train station. The subsequent mobilization of large numbers of the black population into an ongoing protest effort, as well as the involvement of Dr. Martin Luther King Jr. in these efforts, is well documented elsewhere.

That summer in Albany a number of high school and college students from the community worked in the movement full time. Local adults, on the other hand, were more likely to be employed—unless they had lost their jobs due to movement involvement—and would more often participate in the evenings. I began to help write, type, and distribute leaflets for mass meetings. Margaret Sanders, a sixteen-year-old high school student, and I canvassed house to house in the black community, urging people to come to meetings and to register to vote. I remember that sometimes people greeted us with great friendliness, other times with few words and obvious fear. I remember the heat, and that I often had a headache.

We went to the nightly meetings, introduced ourselves, and were welcomed into the protest community. The mass meetings in the Mount Zion Baptist Church were exhilarating—hundreds of people crowded into the church, people hanging out the windows, the steaming heat, the church pews filled with women trying to cool themselves with small cardboard fans. Speakers explained the status of negotiations, and preached to the crowd as we prepared to march downtown into the police lines. Above all, I remember the music: "Ain't Gonna Let Nobody Turn Me Round," a song that was particularly Albany's own; Bernice Johnson Reagon singing "Over My Head I See Freedom in the Air"; and the song I always think of as Charles Sherrod's, one so embedded in my heart that I have sung it to carry me through many difficult times these past thirty years, "Oh Freedom Oh Freedom Oh Freedom over Me, and Before I'll Be a Slave I'll Be Buried in My Grave and Go Home to My Lord and Be Free." And of course, "We Shall Overcome."

My awareness of myself as one of very few white people in a crowd of black people rapidly diminished. Did I notice in the beginning? Probably so. But within a few weeks conscious awareness faded, and the sensation for me was of melting into the crowd. If I looked at my arm I would see I was white, but if I looked at other people, which is more often what I was doing, then I would see people just like me. Or rather, what happened is that I came to feel that I looked just like them. This was, of course, an illusion, and at times a dangerous one, both emotionally for me and physically for other people. I was white, and other people were black. Although I often forgot it, many black people certainly did not. And when in the course of our work we moved out from the relative safety of the black community into the areas controlled by white people, the white southerners we encountered did not forget either.

I am sure this experience was common to other whites in the movement. And of course, the warm welcome we whites received from the black movement community contributed greatly to our lack of discomfort. Perhaps for me, though, this state of color blindness was easier to reach than for others, white and black, because of my multiracial and multicultural childhood experiences. The truth is that I was more comfortable than I had been since leaving Germany at the age of thirteen.

One day, on Jim Forman's initiative, we cleaned Slater King's house. We mopped and waxed the floors, and we washed the windows. Slater and his wife, Marion, were members of a prominent local movement family, and had housed, fed, and supported us and our work for months. Late in the afternoon, Mrs. King, who was seven months pregnant, returned from visiting imprisoned students in Camilla, Georgia. She had been beaten to the ground and kicked by two policemen. Shortly afterward, she lost her baby. The entire black community shared the pain and anger of the King family.

After several weeks some of our group moved out into the surrounding rural areas—Lee County and Terrell County (known as "Terrible Terrell" because of its long history of brutality against black people). I remained in town longer than any of the others because I was a white woman and my presence in the countryside increased the danger for everybody. These were the facts: being a white female afforded me a degree of protection from murderous assault by whites because of the white South's cultural history of placing white women on a pedestal. Black people, especially black men, on the other hand, were at even greater risk when white women were present in the black community because nothing triggered white male rage as much as seeing what they perceived as evidence of interracial friendship and interracial sex. All of this was new to me, coming as I did from my liberal northern family, and I was shocked as I began to understand the implications of my presence. Looking back, I think it took a long time for me to really "get" it.

In July, though, I joined Peg Dammond and Kathy Conwell in Lee County. Situated just north of Albany, Lee was old plantation country. Black people made up over 60 percent of the population, but only a handful of them had ever been registered to vote. Black people for the most part lived on white folks' land as sharecroppers or worked on it as day laborers. A very few owned small farms.

We lived on the farm of one of the few black landowners, sixty-five-year-old Mrs. Dolly Raines. Born and raised in Lee County, she was known to everyone as "Mama Dolly." She was a practical nurse and midwife, and estimated that she had delivered more than a thousand babies, black and white. After we came to stay with her, she received numerous threatening phone calls. White people whose medical emergency calls she had answered in the middle of the night turned on her when she became active in the movement. Mama Dolly was my first connection to the world of maternal-child health; little did I know that many years later I too would become a rural midwife.

Whenever we had a functioning automobile, we spent our time going house to house in this rural community talking about the right to vote and encouraging people to meet with us in a small church or to accompany us to the larger meetings in Albany. Our training for this work had been minimal. We simply learned on the job. The first time we knocked on someone's door we might not even mention registering to vote. Instead we would talk about the children, the weather—just make contact. Of course, everyone knew who we were and why we were there. Later on we would go back and mention voter registration; then we would go back again and talk a little more, try to persuade them to come to a meeting. People were afraid. Simply attending a meeting could lead to the loss of a job or a home or to physical violence. We visited many people ten or fifteen times before they could be persuaded to attend a meeting. Black staff members also went out into the cotton fields on plantations to talk with workers there, to pass out leaflets, and simply to get to know people. White staff members usually could not do this; we would be far too obvious out in the "boss man's" field.

What follows is an excerpt from one of the daily reports I wrote for the SNCC office in Atlanta:

July 24, 1962—James Mays took us canvassing this afternoon. Our first stop was Mrs. Adams' house. Mrs. Adams is with us all the way. . . . She will also help us teach people to read and write. Our plan is to get some of the other teachers in the area, particularly those fired, teaching the citizenship schools. . . . Ed Wright, an extremely talkative gentleman, is already a registered voter and said we could use his church for meetings. He apparently has been quite outspoken in the past and is even willing to send his children to the white school this fall as are several other people. . . . We also now have names to contact in Leesburg, a small town with 500–600 Negroes; this will be the hardest nut to crack we are told. Friday night we hope to have a strategy meeting with some of the potential leaders. . . .

July 25, 1962—The Mays brothers picked us up at about 6 P.M. and drove us to the Terrell "mass" meeting. Attendance had diminished since last week's visit by the sheriff, but the spirit was strong in those that were there. . . . The law came to our meeting again—in the form of Z. T. Mathews and between ten and fifteen armed men. This time we had the reinforcement of three reporters, from the *Atlanta Constitution* and also the *New York Times*. Their presence decreased Z. T.'s confidence greatly, and he did nothing but talk—about the necessity for preserving the peace, about the general contentment of the colored people in Terrell, and about the outside agitators from Massachusetts, Ohio and Virginia.

Sheriff and co. stayed for the entire meeting—people not only prayed but sang freedom songs, three or four local people spoke, and by the end of the meeting we were quite effectively ignoring our visitors. When the sheriff asked for names, most refused to give them. . . .

On July 26, 1962, the *New York Times* printed Claude Sitton's article about this meeting on its front page, which resulted in life-saving publicity and a modicum of federal attention to our work in rural southwest Georgia. I remember the group of armed white men standing at the back of the church, one of them slapping his long flashlight against his hand. I remember the palpable fear in the tiny wooden church that night as we carried on our meeting. I remember the flashlight beam that came out of the darkness and lit up my face as I climbed into a car after the meeting. I don't remember that they had let the air out of one of our tires, or that cursing white men in cars circled us as we changed it and followed us afterward until we reached the relative safety of the black community in Albany, but Claude Sitton reported these things.

On August 3, 1962, my father, emerging from a subway station in New York on his way home from work, was confronted with a newspaper headline in the *New York World Telegram* that read: "White Girl in Mire of Hate." This article told the story of a July 27 encounter I and other voter registration workers had with the authorities and local white citizens in the small town of Smithville, Georgia. I was the only white person in the car with several black women. We were stopped by police, ticketed for supposedly running a stop sign, and taken to a tiny square stucco building just next to the railroad tracks. This was the jail. Then all the law enforcement people disappeared and ten or twelve young white men appeared at the door. They singled me out for their threats. If I ever came back, they said, they were going to throw me in the swamp. They said they'd fix me up a little first, before they threw me in. A little later we were released, with threats of jail and fines if we ever came back to town. This kind of intimidation was not unusual, not all that different from what routinely happened. Nevertheless, it was terrifying. We reported the threat to the attorney general's office and to the press, as we did all such events. My SNCC report says that on July 31 we drove back into Smithville to canvass and to find a church to use for meetings. We had no trouble with either the law or the white population and returned home safely.

After this there was more publicity in northern newspapers about my involvement in the movement. In addition, my parents had connections: they were personally acquainted with politicians and journalists; and if they didn't know them personally, they knew how to reach them. They used these connections to create public attention about SNCC and the work we were doing. Over time, as more young white people went south to work in the movement, more white middle-class parents used whatever influence they had to publicize the work of the movement. I hated the publicity because it was embarrassing. It was clearly happening because I was white, middle-class, and a woman to boot. And it reflected the greater value placed on my life, and the lives of other white civil rights workers, than on the lives of black people. At the same time, this public attention often led to more federal intervention, and may have saved my life and the lives of others in the movement, black and white.

As a result of the publicity, my parents received hate mail—lots of it. At one time my mother had a file full of obscene and threatening letters directed at my family and me. My parents consistently supported me, despite their anxiety about my safety. An August 3, 1962, *New York World Telegram* article quotes my mother: "We've always been interested in social problems, said Mrs. Patch, but she's gone a step beyond us."

Later in August, I was transferred back to Albany. Mrs. Raines had asked me to leave her farm because threats to her life and threats to others in the black community were escalating. I remember having mixed feelings about the move. It bothered me that I had been sent back to work in the office, not allowed to stay with the others in the rural counties. I felt left out. It was all part of my education about the limits my whiteness placed on my usefulness, and I was struggling hard to grasp that if I wanted to do this work, I was going to have to subordinate my personal needs. On the positive side, there was a lot of action in Albany and it was intoxicating to be back in the middle of it. Sometimes I spent my days walking the streets of Albany, canvassing house to house. I also wrote more reports and spent more time in the office than some of my peers because I was a white woman and I could do this work without creating unacceptable levels of danger for the black community. In general, we women, black and white alike, did more office work than the men. But black women, who did not have the same constraints as white women, consistently did organizing work outside the office on equal footing with the men.

Later that year, I wrote a report to Wiley Branton, director of the Voter Education Project in Atlanta, which helped to fund the voter registration piece of our work.

Here are excerpts from my report:

December 8, 1962

Dear Mr. Branton. . . .

It is now five o'clock in the morning and the cocks are crowing. You know, southwest Georgia is very, very beautiful. It just needs a little bit of fixing.

We moved into southwest Georgia as an integrated group in June 1962. I do not think that all of us were aware of the magnitude of this move or its full implications. . . . To be fair, perhaps I should only speak for myself. Sometimes I feel extremely ignorant of how deeply embedded the system of segregation is in both the black and white man. . . .

One day this summer while canvassing in Smithville (Lee County) we met a woman of about 45, a medical doctor. She lives in a large farmhouse, part of what used to be a farm. A farm bought by her family right after the Civil War. . . . Listening to Dr. Griffith speak I think all of us were taken back to the days of her ancestors, the former slaves who first settled there. The pictures of her ancestors were hung on the walls — some Negro, some American Indian, some white. She, Dr. Griffith, said: "We must come to flow freely among ourselves." That is it, I think. . . .

We are an integrated group now working in southwest Georgia. . . . Here, for the first time, all southerners are able to see Negroes and whites working side by side as equals and as friends. . . . We are confronting the community with what should be and what will be. We are showing here and now, rather than talking about black and white together, that a dream can be reality, and that words can mean something. There are few things that in my mind are designated as totally, absolutely and completely right. Integration is one of those things. . . . And this is why the integrated group is an essential part of our entire philosophy and mode of action. . . . I come up on a porch and an ancient lady, full of dignity in *her* world, says "yes ma'am" and offers me her chair. An enraged white face shouts curses out of the car window. Jack Chatfield walks up to a house and the lady on the porch shakes visibly. The voter registration team is greeted with fear at the door. "I didn't know colored people could vote." And people ask why we are down here.

That fall of 1962 I did not return to college. I remained in southwest Georgia working for SNCC. Then, several months later, I registered at Swarthmore for the spring semester. Predictably, I didn't finish the semester, and spent far more time on movement support activities and recruitment efforts for SNCC than on my studies. In February 1963, on the third anniversary of the sit-ins in Greensboro when SNCC was all the rage in certain circles in New York, there was a benefit concert to raise money for our work. I walked onto the stage at Carnegie Hall with other SNCC workers to massive applause. I remember standing in the wings with the others waiting to go on and saying to Bob Moses: "You deserve to be up here, but I certainly don't." And Bob said, "Yes you do," and gently pushed me on stage.

The pull of the SNCC community, the movement, and the work was too strong. I went back to Albany, Georgia.

I lived with two families during my time in Albany, first with Mr. and Mrs. Sanders and their children, Mary, Margaret, Jean, Sharon, and Bobby, and later with Mr. and Mrs. Gaines and their daughters, Patricia Ann, Marion, and Peaches. Both families were active in the movement, and they increased the already existing level of danger to themselves by inviting me into their homes to live. Every member of the Gaines family was arrested at different times, including two-year-old Peaches, who was jailed while on a picket line with her mother. Being jailed for the movement was one way to prove your bravery and commitment and was no longer, as it had been, a cause for shame within black families. Rivalries existed between family members as to who would go to jail on a given night. Someone would have to stay out to go to work or tend to the baby. Lots were sometimes drawn. Marion Gaines, age eleven, her fifteen-year-old sister, Pat, and many other young people frequently led the line of marchers into downtown white Albany. Small and lithe, singing and clapping, Marion faced police lines and hostile whites almost with gaiety, the epitome to me of the spirit that produced songs like "Ain't Gonna Let Nobody Turn Me Round." One day Pat Gaines and Margaret Sanders stole the "COLORED" sign from above the water fountain at the Dougherty County courthouse. They eventually gave it to me as a gift. Recently I returned it to the Mount Zion Albany Civil Rights Movement Museum, where it is now on exhibit.

During my time in Albany I was arrested four or five times, sometimes while participating in demonstrations and sometimes while simply walking down the street. The charges commonly included trespassing, disorderly conduct, or parading without a permit. Once, however, I was charged with inciting to riot, which was a felony and carried serious consequences. Of course, there was no riot, unless you counted what the white bystanders were doing. This conviction was eventually dismissed in federal court, as were all the others, allowing me later in my life to answer "no" with truthfulness when asked on job applications if I had ever been convicted of a felony.

Often my jail time was spent in solitude, since even the jails were racially segregated. In the Albany city jail I was placed in the white women's cell down at the very end of a dark, narrow cell block. My black comrades were confined on the opposite side of the cell block. We could hear each other only if we yelled or when we sang. The cell was about six by ten feet, with two metal bunks suspended from each side wall, leaving a corridor about three feet wide down the middle of the cell. In the back between the beds were a toilet and a small sink; in front were iron bars looking out over the corridor, which was lit by a couple of small windows high up in the wall. There was no privacy and when you sat on the toilet there was always the risk that the jailor would choose that moment to wander by. The cell was filthy, as was the toilet. There were bugs. The mattresses stank. The smell that I carry with me in memory, though, is the pervasive smell of disinfectant — Pine-Sol, I think — so they must have cleaned the place occasionally. Next to me were the white men's cells, and some of my most difficult times involved listening to my fellow white male SNCC workers being beaten up by other white inmates. It was in the solitude of this jail cell that I took up smoking cigarettes.

My own experiences in the small cell were reasonably benevolent. My companions, if any, tended to be local prostitutes and drunks, who after an initial period of antagonism generally were more curious than anything else about my association with black people. Sometimes one of the women would mother me and keep me safe from the others. I remember a woman named Ellen, older, with gray scraggly hair, missing a couple of teeth, who was in jail for drunkenness. She kept the aggressive ones from coming too close, standing in front of me, blocking them as I leaned back into the recesses of the lower bunk. "Leave her alone," she said, "she's just a girl."

I still dream about that jail. Feeling claustrophobic, I am invariably squeezing myself through a tiny doorway. Sometimes it is so small that I am crawling on the ground to get through. There are policemen behind me pushing me on. I can't go back. I can't breathe very well and I am close to panic. Once in the cell, I know I can't get out. There is no way I can fit through that doorway again. Then I usually wake up.

During the summer of 1963 I spent eleven days in the Albany city jail on a hunger strike. This time I had company. By now there were other white women working for SNCC in Albany, and several shared the cell with me. I don't remember what the hunger strike was about—perhaps it was simply in protest of our arrest. We refused all food, but drank water. I remember Chief Laurie Pritchett's frequent appearances in front of our cell eating some tasty morsel. I have an especially intense memory of some delicious-looking lemon meringue pie. This man was waging psychological warfare, and he was good at it. When I was bailed out, twenty pounds lighter, I was told by a doctor to eat soup and eggs for a week, but that afternoon I was home taking a bath when Marion Gaines sauntered through eating a peanut butter and jelly sandwich. So I ate one of those. Then I went to a staff meeting and everyone was eating ravioli and I ate that too.

I still have a letter I wrote Judy Richardson, a fellow student at Swarthmore who later became a SNCC worker. Judy was doing civil rights work up north at the time. I have my copy because Judy took the letter to the *New York Times*, where it came to the attention of my father's friend Harrison Salisbury, then editor of the op-ed page. Mr. Salisbury wrote to my father assuring him that the *Times* was on top of the situation in Albany and sent him a copy of my letter. I found it in my mother's files. Here are excerpts:

Dear Judy—

July 12, 1963—Things are hell down here, and the town is about to explode, in a very violent direction. The people are sick and tired of nonviolence and both the Negro and white communities are armed to the teeth. The Klan is supposedly planning a raid tomorrow night and we have demonstrations planned for tomorrow at the segregated swimming pool. There's a whole crowd of guys who are planning to jump the fence into the pool. . . . Reverend Wells, one of our few militant ministers, was arrested Monday night (as was Sherrod) and was dragged into the jail by his genitals. . . . But we can't seem to get the news out—and the police brutality is getting worse and worse. Yes, we need bail money. We need it very badly. . . .

July 14—Well Saturday is over. Success was not great in terms of numbers, but quite a bit as far as impact on the white and black communities is concerned I think. A bunch of guys jumped the fence and went into the swimming pool and swam. This is a great victory (in a manner of speaking). It's a pretty insane and cool idea anyway. The police (for once) were caught by surprise and didn't know what to do. . . .

Less cheerfully, we had a visit this morning from a family whose son was shot and killed last night by a white man, in the presence of a police officer. They know who did the shooting and the man is still walking around free. Oh Judy I'll never forget the face of this man's wife as she was telling the story. She saw it happen. Another man was shot in the back but not killed the day before yesterday. . . . Please write soon—will see you in a month or so.

Hang on.

Love, Penny

I had gone south the summer of 1962 an idealistic, intelligent, but very naive eighteen-year-old. I had very little understanding at the time of the history and dynamics of the situation I had entered. I knew the bare bones. Also, because I was so young, I had few practical skills. Often I did well with people and was able to establish genuine trust. Sometimes I made serious mistakes. I remember greeting a male leader of the Albany Movement with a kiss on the cheek in a public meeting—and afterward being told in no uncertain terms that I was not to make that sort of contact with a black man in public ever again, that I could cost him his life. I learned a lot, very fast, and never knew enough. Because my presence as a white woman in a field project was a first, we had no precedent to guide us. I was an experiment and no one knew precisely what boundaries to set for my activities. In truth, during my movement time I learned to cook, type, and do office work. I also learned to drive a car, listen and persuade, develop strategy, organize people to register to vote and go on demonstrations, act independently if necessary, speak in public, and keep working despite fear and exhaustion.

Charles Sherrod, our project director, set out general rules. We young women were not allowed to wear pants because black people were unaccustomed to women wearing pants, especially blue jeans. We were forbidden to drink, which could cause community disapproval and also lead to arrest. He also told us to confine any sexual activity within the staff and to keep it as discreet as possible. The discipline we maintained was ragged at best, but we tried hard. The black staff had more freedom of movement. There were times when black staff members went to black bars to drink, relax, and have fun while white staff members remained at home or in the office. Much of the time I accepted these restrictions without question. Sometimes I remember feeling isolated and resentful. These were issues that we talked about as a group, usually because Sherrod insisted that we do so.

SNCC conferences gave us the opportunity to all party together. These meetings lasted several days and often took place outside of the Deep South or in relatively secure locations. The first one I attended was in November 1962, at Fisk University in Nashville, Tennessee. In later years, conferences were open only to staff members, but in the early days invitations went out to all supporters. There were about two hundred people at the Fisk University conference. They included representatives from protest groups on southern campuses, SNCC organizing staff, and local people from Mississippi, Georgia, Alabama, Maryland, Arkansas—wherever we had projects. The high point came when Bob Moses, director of SNCC's small Mississippi project, rolled in with a busload of people from Mississippi. The people in the bus represented the movement in the most racist and dangerous state in the union, and our excitement as they arrived was enormous. We talked all day long and into the night. In those days decisions were made by consensus and meetings were long. We sang a lot, and late at night we partied very hard. The stress we normally lived under was enormous. Relationships were intense and as a group we formed close and seemingly unbreakable bonds.

Early in 1964 I went to work in the Jackson, Mississippi, Council of Federated Organizations (COFO) office, this time helping to organize the application process for the Mississippi Summer Project. Hundreds of students, overwhelmingly white, were coming to Mississippi during the summer of 1964, in an effort to focus the attention of the country on conditions in that state. I left New York driving with Ivanhoe Donaldson, a black SNCC worker. It was not unusual for SNCC workers to travel into the South in integrated groups, although it always meant a journey fraught with danger. I often missed large parts of the southern landscape on those trips because I spent so much time lying on the floor of the back seat with a blanket over me. On this trip, in Gastonia, North Carolina, we were not cautious. We were hungry. Hunger always presented a problem when we traveled in interracial or all-black groups, as there were few restaurants that would serve us. For just that reason, black Americans usually packed food in the car when traveling in the South. But this time we had no food, and Ivanhoe, with characteristic recklessness, proposed that we stop at a Howard Johnson's. Howard Johnson's was at the time, of course, largely segregated in the South, despite the ICC ruling, and this was to my mind a chancy way to try and acquire food. I objected: It was too dangerous. No one knew where we were. I thought briefly about whether Ivanhoe would be safer if he went himself and I stayed back to call for help. Next thing I remember, we were marching up to the door of Howard Johnson's, a black man and a white woman, planning to request service. My heart was pounding and I felt slightly nauseous. I opened the glass door and we stepped into the small restaurant. Silence greeted us. We turned right and sat down in a booth next to the window. Ivanhoe asked for service and a waitress came over. I ordered a tuna fish sandwich, Ivanhoe, a piece of pie and a soda. The food came. We ate. The restaurant was sparsely populated — a good thing, I suppose. There was absolute silence as the food was served. I too sat in silence, trying to get the food down as quickly as possible so that we could leave. Were the police being called? Were we going to be hijacked as we left town? Anything was possible. Yet what happened was that the restaurant complied with the ICC and no mob gathered to do us injury. We finished our food, paid, and left town without incident, arriving safely in Atlanta. In truth, we did things like this, black and white together, frequently. It was not that we thought we were immortal, but we were ready to push all the boundaries. And we knew we were right.

In the Jackson COFO office during the winter and spring of 1964, we sorted through hundreds of applications for the Mississippi Summer Project. There was much discussion and difference of opinion as to how many and whom to accept, as there was about the entire concept of the project. We had embarked on this huge effort and there was no turning back, but many people, mostly black, some white, had misgivings. It was at this time that I began to notice the beginnings of antiwhite sentiment in SNCC, for the most part expressed in the context of fears about how such a large influx of white students would affect the movement in Mississippi. I knew these feelings were not directed at me; I had been with the movement for a long time. Like the small group of other white students who had joined SNCC in the early days, I felt entirely welcome. I did not feel that anyone was seriously questioning my right to be there in Jackson, working in the Mississippi Movement. For other white people, particularly those who came in 1964 and after, it was not the same.

I was aware, however, that some of the black women on the Mississippi SNCC staff were not particularly friendly toward me, and I found it difficult to close the distance they maintained. For the most part I experienced no overt hostility, but I felt excluded. I now recognize that some may have been reacting to my romance with a black male staff member. Unfortunately, at the time, I was abysmally ignorant of their feelings. For me it wasn't an issue. For me, black as well as white SNCC men were my comrades, and I saw no reason I should not fall in love with one of them.

In retrospect, if I had known how my sexual relationship with a black man could affect black women, I hope I would have acted with greater sensitivity and discretion. It is, however, unlikely that I would have changed my behavior significantly. We were young, we were living in wartime conditions. We were always afraid; we never knew whether we would see one another again. We were ready, black and white, to break all the taboos. SNCC men were handsome, they were brilliant, they were brave, and I was very much in love.

It occurs to me that as the nearest and safest white women, some of us became vessels into which black women, if they chose to, could pour their accumulated anger — anger they had borne for hundreds of years. I am trying to say, I suppose, that if we hurt each other, it was not my fault, nor theirs. It is slavery and oppression that created the distance between black women and white women, not the fact that white women slept with black men during the Civil Rights Movement.

Our work continued. By early June I felt as if I knew the name and location of every college in the country, as well as the names of hundreds of individual students. Some of the volunteers, in time, I came to know well, others not at all. There were so many. I attended the first orientation session at Oxford, Ohio, with other SNCC staff, and on Saturday, June 20, 1964, I left Oxford on a bus with staff and volunteers heading for Mississippi.

At 4:30 on Sunday afternoon, June 21, I was in the Jackson office when a report came in from Meridian that three of our colleagues, James Chaney, Michael Schwerner, and Andrew Goodman had not arrived back from Philadelphia, Mississippi, where they had gone to investigate a church burning. James Chaney, black, and Mickey Schwerner, white, were CORE workers in Mississippi and longtime colleagues of many of the civil rights workers in the state. I knew them both, although not well. Andrew Goodman, a white Mississippi Summer Project volunteer, had arrived in the state only the day before. I did not know him at all.

We told the young woman handling communications in Meridian to begin calling the jails near Philadelphia. Her name was Louise, and this was her first day on the job at the office in Meridian — a baptism by fire into the Mississippi Summer Project. In the late afternoon, with no word about the three men, we started calling jails from Jackson. We telephoned the FBI and were told by an agent that they couldn't do anything for twenty-four hours. We called the Justice Department and were told they would check on it if they had time, but that we shouldn't worry yet. Later that night the press was informed that three workers were missing.

I remember the next week in flashes. I was always on the phone. I remember that when I slept it was on a desk in a small side room of the office. Around midweek I broke down in tears, whereupon Bob Weil and Bill Light, SNCC staff working on communications, gathered me up with some tenderness and took me back to the Freedom House to rest. During my breakdown I glimpsed Dick Jewitt hunkered down quietly at his typewriter in a back room. Dick was CORE staff and a good friend of Mickey Schwerner's. He had become increasingly silent and remote during these tragic days. I yelled at him, accused him of not caring. Later of course, I understood that his withdrawal did not reflect emotional indifference. We all coped in our own ways. We were not always able to support one another well.

We assumed that they were dead, and we only hoped it had happened fast. At some point a body was found, as a number were during that long search, most of them the bodies of other murdered black men. I remember having to call back and forth between Meridian and Oxford to try to find out if Mickey had been wearing high-top sneakers and what color his socks had been.

When I tried to sleep at the Freedom House I had nightmares and so I stayed at the office round the clock. I carried my own private feeling of responsibility for Andrew Goodman's death, as I had handled his application and accepted him into the project. Months later I dreamed I was standing in a forest on a dark night and Andy's very large dark eyes were looking at me from the branches of a tree.

The bodies of James Chaney, Michael Schwerner, and Andrew Goodman were found in August of that summer, buried beneath an earthen dam in Philadelphia, Mississippi. In 1967 the U.S. Justice Department finally charged their murderers with conspiracy to deprive the three men of their civil rights, and seven of those charged were convicted and sentenced to prison terms of from three to ten years. The state of Mississippi never charged the killers with murder.

Later in the summer I moved to Greenwood, Mississippi, to work in the COFO office there. My family visited me in Greenwood and my mother wrote down her impressions:

> Life in the office — if you leave your work for a few minutes you may find your chair gone, your typewriter disappears, no ashtray. People just pick out a vacant spot and start working. . . . Staff meetings in the morning line up assignments, but by the end of the day some emergency has probably changed many plans. However, much gets done in spite of time out for tracing people, expeditions to collect or distribute cars, time out to bail people out of jail etc. . . . Southerners, and sometimes northerners have criticized the student civil rights workers who have gone to the South, implying that they are somehow communistic, or that they are infiltrated or instigated by communists. I can only say a less communistic group of young people cannot be imagined, or a less communistically organized operation would be hard to find. There are many strong individualists involved, and many different political points of view, but I saw there a truer devotion to real democracy than has perhaps existed in this country since Thomas Jefferson. And the organization itself, instead of being tightly organized, directed from the top, is very loosely put together, depending on individual initiative and self-discipline, and on a few strong individuals who are listened to because they are respected. It is a cause for perpetual wonder that so much constructive work comes out of such seeming utter confusion. The high caliber of the people involved, their integrity and belief in the democratic process seem to me to be the obvious reason for their growing success.

In September 1964 I moved again, this time to the COFO project in Panola County, and spent the next year working in this rural Mississippi county on the edge of the Delta. The county was home to a number of large white-owned plantations, worked by black sharecropping families. Also, a sizable group of small independent black farmers owned land in Panola County's hill country. In 1959 five of these farmers had formed the Panola County Voter's League. In 1964 they got a federal injunction eliminating the most difficult questions on the voter registration test. This test, which contained complex constitutional questions, had historically been used to fail any black people who dared to try to register to vote. White people who took the test passed whether or not they answered the questions correctly. Black people made up 56 percent of the population of the county, and before the injunction fewer than fifty black people had succeeded in registering to vote. COFO came to Panola County in the summer of 1964 to help the already existing Panola County Movement register as many voters as possible before the injunction ran out the following May.

I lived with other civil rights workers on the farm of Robert and Mona Miles. The following are excerpts from a letter I wrote my parents in New Jersey, dated September 22, 1964:

Dear Patches,

I don't believe I've written you a letter in months and I hardly know how to begin. Life in Batesville is quite different from life in Jackson or Greenwood, kind of like the old Lee County days. The county is primarily rural, with lots of little towns in various corners, and I live on a farm with cows, horses, pigs and fresh milk.

The Miles themselves are beautiful people: husband, wife, and two small boys, eight and six, named Kevin and Vernon, plus a couple of grown sons who are away at school. Mr. Miles, along with four other people from Panola County, organized the Panola County Voters' League in 1959 and shortly thereafter filed a suit against the registrar of the county. . . . The Miles family, of course, has had a rough time these last few years, and the house has been shot into, bombed and tear-gassed. Mrs. Miles suffers from a kind of nervous paralysis apparently brought on by the emotional trauma of these last years. . . . The neighbors have now taken it upon themselves to guard the house, all night every night. Vernon, the six year old, has nightmares and can't go to sleep until he has gone out to check if the guards are out there to protect him. (If you should ever come to Batesville don't drive into the Miles' yard at night without blinking your headlights three times, or you'll be met with a shotgun blast.)

As you may have heard, Mrs. Fannie Lou Hamer and Dr. Aaron Henry are running as independents in the election this November. . . . On the basis of that vote, and a Freedom vote which will be held three days prior to the official election in which every Negro over 21 can vote, and the Federal Corrupt Practices Act, we plan to challenge the seating of Stennis and Whitten in the House and Senate in January. Here we go again. . . . So there's a lot of work to do. . . . There are three other staff members working in the county, all of whom I like. . . . The local people are great, so if in one sense it's lonelier and very isolated from everyone else, the pain is much less. . . .

Love, Penny

Primarily I was glad to be far away from the center because, in the aftermath of the Summer Project, the racial climate within SNCC was changing markedly. The pain I refer to in my letter reflected the fact that the antiwhite feelings I had become aware of the previous spring were increasing. I was beginning to feel a growing distance between my black SNCC comrades and me, and I no longer felt as welcome as before in my beloved SNCC community. Unlike some of the newer white staff or summer volunteers, I experienced little overt hostility. People simply withdrew from me. At a SNCC gathering in late 1964 or early 1965, I walked delightedly up to an old friend I had not seen for many months. She stood with a group of friends, head high, sunglasses on. She looked through me, around me, anywhere but at me. She did not acknowledge my presence. Shaking inside, I walked away. We never spoke again until we saw each other thirty years later at a movement reunion.

Only once did I experience a direct attack, when our black male COFO project director locked me out of our office in Batesville while screaming at me that I was a white bitch. I have no memory of what triggered his outburst. I do remember that I stood in the hallway, banging on the door, trying to persuade him to let me in, trying not to make a scene that local people in the building would notice. I walked off finally in despair. Although we did reconcile enough to continue to work together, his profound doubts about my right to participate in his movement remained.

As the months went by, I felt torn whenever I observed hostility directed at white volunteers. I felt that as a white person I had some responsibility to be supportive of them, yet I felt loyalty to my old black comrades. I also was afraid that if I expressed my dismay at their attitudes I would lose my own place in the SNCC community. One thing was clearly changing by the end of 1964: interracial sexual relationships were no longer tolerated—black SNCC folk who took part openly in such relationships were subject to the charge of "backsliding," and those relationships, when they did occur, tended to be hidden from view. Looking back, I am aware that some white volunteers were no doubt guilty of arrogance and insensitivity, but many were not. It seems to me that ultimately it did not matter how anybody, white or black, behaved. The sheer number of white volunteers simply constituted a perceived threat to the integrity of the black movement, or at least to SNCC, a predominantly black organization in which the leadership had always been (and continued to be) black. Our history as black and white Americans overwhelmed us.

Meanwhile, the work continued. We campaigned to elect black representatives to the county Agricultural Stabilization and Conservation Committee, a traditionally all-white body that possessed the power to dole out cotton allotments to both black and white farmers. Elaine Delott worked with Chris Williams, a white SNCC worker, and with local black leaders to organize an okra marketing cooperative. On the night of February 21, 1965, after Malcolm X was assassinated, I found myself at a small rural voter registration meeting in Panola County. I was the only civil rights worker at the meeting, and I remember sitting in a right rear pew toward the back of the small church trying to figure out if it was my place because I was white to say anything or not. Eventually I stood up and gave a small eulogy for Malcolm X. People needed to know who he had been, what he had done, and how he had died. If I didn't talk about it, some of them might never know. My conclusion was, Better me than nobody. I heard some "amens" as I talked about how another leader of the Freedom Movement had been assassinated in New York.

In March 1965, a group of black Panola County high school students decided to make the first local test of the public accommodations section of the 1964 Civil Rights Law. We were afraid for them, but since the young people were determined, we helped them run nonviolent workshops and pick out the largest, most visible restaurants in Batesville, the county seat. The students attempted to sit in at two restaurants on the main square. They were thrown out of both restaurants by white patrons. While driving them home, Roland Nelson, a local movement supporter, was arrested on charges of speeding. As Mr. Nelson was being tried and fined, about twenty students and several civil rights workers demonstrated outside of the courthouse and were all arrested. Heavy fines and high bail were set. The demonstrators refused bail, electing to remain in jail until their trials. For ten days the jail was flooded with parents, friends, and relatives coming into town to bring food, books, blankets, and clothes to the young people. White people also gathered daily near the jail to observe the proceedings.

On the day of the trials a picket line of about one hundred students and civil rights workers (myself included) was thrown around the jail. The tension was enormous. Hundreds of white hoodlums who had poured in from outside of town met us outside the jail. A group of white men attacked civil rights workers and local black people, stomping and beating them. Mr. Miles, leader of the Panola County Movement, fought back. At that point, the sheriff and highway patrol stepped in and told us to get out of town. Chris Williams and I climbed into one car but found ourselves boxed in by the howling mob, with cars in front and in back of us preventing us from moving. Angry whites, male and female, their faces contorted with rage, screamed at us through our windows. They began to rock the car. They were going to roll it. What saved us was that someone pulled away in front of us. I never knew if they were black or white, whether it was intentional or inadvertent. But we were able to escape to relative safety in the black community.

The following night the Miles house was shotgunned as Chris and I sat with the family in the front room watching television. The buckshot splattered the living room walls but missed all of us in the room. Chris pushed me onto the floor. Mr. Miles grabbed his shotgun and dashed outside. The next thing I remember is crawling into the children's bedroom. I pulled Kevin and Vernon onto the floor, cuddling their soft pajama-clad bodies next to me. The next afternoon several rifle shots narrowly missed four of us as we left the Batesville jail after visiting our friends. I was later told that these shots came from a distance of less than seventy-five yards away, so I think they intended to miss.

That spring of 1965 I was very scared, more so with every violent incident. I felt anxious most of the time. I slept even less than usual. I was exhausted. This was nothing new. I think I had been exhausted for quite a while. Most of us were.

And the fact that my SNCC community was disintegrating contributed to my fear and despair. I was losing my black SNCC buddies, my comrades, but also communication and trust within the organization in general were breaking down. There were problems with how resources from the central office in Atlanta were getting distributed to field projects. I was in one of these projects, and we felt very removed from the staff in Atlanta, which is not how it had been previously. I have a letter that I wrote, signed by a number of people working on the Panola County COFO project in March 1965, that was sent to SNCC headquarters. Those who signed this document, three white and two black, were all SNCC staff. The letter demonstrates a frightening level of alienation between our field project and the Atlanta office. Looking back, I wonder how I got so angry with this organization I loved so much. How had it come to this? I am embarrassed by the rage, by the language used. The issues mentioned in the letter seem to me less important than the angry, powerless feelings that were being expressed.

Batesville, Miss
March 19, 1965

To SNCC folk:

There are several things which have been bothering me the last week or so.

First of all—the WATS line reports are kind of frightening. They have all the earmarks of being propaganda sheets, and I am at the point where I feel compelled to try and read between the lines to find out what is happening in Selma, Montgomery, etc. Is this necessary? Would it not be possible to send us information on what is happening without making everything SNCC propaganda.

p.s. This tendency is also seen in the report sent of the latest staff meeting in Atlanta. (It was nothing but horseshit), and other reports, on Selma.

It makes me sick

Second of all—Some of us would like an explanation of SNCC's seemingly contradictory positions on demonstrations in Alabama. First I hear that SNCC is opposed to the demonstrations because we are all tired and local people are tired of getting their heads beat in for nothing . . .

Was this the real reason behind our opposition to demonstrations and the March on Montgomery? Or is it that we were just opposing SCLC's position? *I want to know.*

It sounds to me like you all are fucked up!

However, now SNCC—with Forman in the lead—seems to be leading demonstrations day and night, and fighting with SCLC ostensibly because *they* are opposing demonstrations. What the hell is going on? . . .

Third of all—How many staff people are in Selma and Montgomery, and what are they doing? (I would like more of an explanation please than the one which is usually given, i.e. We are here because SCLC has deserted the people after building up their hopes, and we feel we have a responsibility to stay on with them.) We would like to hear from any number of people on these issues. Would some of you please reply. Thanks.

Penny Patch, Chris Williams, Elaine Delott, Louis Grant, Ed Brown

The letter was mimeographed by the Atlanta SNCC office staff and sent back out to field projects with a note saying: "The following letter was sent in to the Atlanta office this week, addressed to SNCC folk. If you have similar thoughts, or disagreements with this letter (or other things) let us know." I don't know whether this was an effort to embarrass us, or whether it revealed a very SNCC-like commitment to openness and free speech.

Whatever the reality, those were our perceptions. We no longer functioned within a circle of trust. We struggled in staff meetings to create programs, over what to do next. A major issue was whether the organization could continue functioning in its former decentralized fashion or whether it needed to become more highly structured with more centralized decision making. By instinct, I supported the old ways. I never wanted SNCC to become an organization in which someone at the top told people what to do. This approach seemed antithetical to everything I had thought we were about. What little I subscribed to in the way of ideology had to do with believing that all people had the right to make the decisions governing their own lives.

But more than anything else, my private anguish revolved around the separatist feelings that were surfacing among black SNCC people. I had never had a problem with black power as a political concept. I was not afraid of black economic power. These were what our work had always been about. It was the exclusion that hurt so bad.

In April 1965 I sent a letter of resignation to the SNCC office in Atlanta. I didn't keep a copy. It was short, I think, and basically said that SNCC was no longer an organization I felt able to be part of. I remember that I couldn't write a longer letter because it hurt so much to write it at all. I wrote it and mailed it and felt like I had lopped off an arm, a leg, my head. I felt like I was spilling blood everywhere.

I continued to work in Panola County for several months after my resignation. The local movement people remained ever welcoming of my presence. I probably could have continued to work in that community indefinitely, but it became clear to me during the summer that I couldn't survive psychologically without the support of the SNCC community. I had lost my family. In retrospect, I understand that the extent of my anguish was intensified by some of my childhood experiences around loss of community. As a child I had moved frequently, lost people I was profoundly attached to, lost home and community too many times. This time, my resilience exhausted, I made a choice not to stick around longer to try to influence what was happening. I was desolate and full of rage—rage at the system, at the country, at all the white people who opposed change or did nothing. And I was full of rage at my own beloved SNCC community for what felt like a betrayal.

I finally left the South in August 1965, setting out for California with Chris Williams to make a new life. That fall I heard from Mrs. Miles of Batesville, who said that she and her husband had sent Kevin and Vernon, aged nine and seven, to join other local black children in integrating the local white elementary school:

> The boys like school a little better now, especially Vernon. I am a bit surprised because Vernon doesn't seem to be making friends as quickly as Kevin. Kevin's teacher is an elderly woman and a bit prejudiced too. My reason for saying that is because Kevin came home one day angry because the teacher threatened to send him to the principal if he played with the white girls again. Just the same, he has claimed himself a girlfriend. He mentioned it to me and I had to tell him to keep it a secret from everybody for a while. Even the girl should not know about it just yet. . . . The majority of Negro children that ride the school buses have had and some still are having trouble on the buses. The big boys and girls throw paper, pull the girls' hair. When boarding the bus at school they kick the little fellows when passing. Practically all of the parents with children registered in the white school in South Panola have had to move, that is those parents who lived on white property. A Klansman called me and said an accident had been planned for my husband and nigger children. I recognized the voice as someone I had heard on previous occasions. Some calls have told us that we have only about twenty-four hours to get out of town. As of today we are still around.
>
> Hoping to hear from you soon.
>
> With love, Mona Miles

I experienced the loss of African American SNCC people, as well as local movement people, as devastating. For me, the loss was total. It is also striking that we white SNCC people were mostly unable to support one another in the years after the movement. Many of us were struggling to find our places outside of the African American Freedom Movement in a white world we did not feel was ours. We felt tremendously isolated, but even when we were together we did not talk about our history and our feelings. We were, for the most part, silent. In time I numbed myself to the pain and couldn't even feel it, much less articulate it.

From 1965 to 1967 I lived in Berkeley, California. I tried to work in the antiwar movement and I worked briefly in the Cleveland, Ohio, Students for a Democratic Society (SDS) project. I generally felt ragged and lost. I remember that in 1966 Stokely Carmichael came to Berkeley to speak. Old black SNCC friends, who were accompanying Stokely, called and asked whether they could come by to visit. Stokely arrived in town and I sat at home, not wishing to subject myself to his Black Power speech, waiting for my friends to appear. They never did. For three days I did not get out of bed. My despair went way beyond the loss of a couple of friends. I was grieving the loss of my entire community. There I was sobbing in my bed with Stokely across town hollering about Black Power.

After a while I could no longer try to find another way to work in the movement and I left.

In 1967 Chris and I moved to Vermont, married in 1969, and had a son, Seth. With other friends, we purchased land on a remote hillside in northeastern Vermont, the poorest part of the state and the only part where we could afford to buy land. We built a communal house. Neither this marriage nor our communal effort was successful, and Chris and I separated in 1970. In 1973 I was happy to move with my partner (now my husband), David Martin, and Seth into our own little house on another piece of land. In 1977 David and I had a daughter, Elizabeth.

I was living like a hippie, but I was far too political and had an emerging consciousness that was far too feminist to be comfortable in the fairly traditional roles that women and men living in the backwoods in those days fell into. I identified with the women's movement: finally, here was something that was mine. I remember the relief. But when it came down to it, I did not spend much time working in local feminist organizations. All the women were white (particularly in northern Vermont, where I lived), and many were relatively unaware of racism as an issue that affected their lives. Eventually I found exceptions to this rule, especially among lesbian women, who had a keen sense of oppression, their own and other people's. But for years I felt alien. Power and community for me continued to reside in the black world. Racism for me trumped sexism. Even all these years later, although I have always counted myself a serious feminist, it still does. I don't walk into a room, ever, without assessing the racial balance.

I eventually found the next stage of my work in the world, and that was midwifery. During the early 1970s, I began to attend home births in the area's countercultural community. The first time, a friend was having a baby in her home and asked me to come, and then I was invited to another because I had been to one and was therefore more experienced than others in the area — a common story in the home birth movement.

Here I began to use, once again, what I had learned in the Freedom Movement. Our efforts as women to take control of our own birth experiences, remove ourselves whenever possible from the male-dominated, interventionist medical establishment, and reclaim our physical and spiritual power were highly political. We who served as birth attendants and midwives at home births were and still are subject to a set of consequences ranging from intense disapproval on the part of the medical community to criminal prosecution. In those years I constantly drew strength and wisdom from my experiences in the Freedom Movement. I continued to believe that all people, however powerless they might seem, carry within themselves the ability to make great change. This thread runs through all of my efforts to change and transform not only myself but also the many people I have touched in my work in the years since the movement.

From 1970 until 1982 I lived in the backwoods, without electricity or plumbing. We built our house in a hardwood forest, grew food and flowers in our garden, took care of our children, and spent an inordinate amount of time doing the basic household chores required to survive in that environment. During those years in the woods I finally put down roots. I developed a profound connection to our land, and to the natural world in general, a connection that serves as my spiritual base. I would have loved to bring up my children in a more diverse environment, but I did not move. My need to stay in one place, to become rooted, had become the driving force in my life. I eventually realized that the landscape of Vermont reminded me of Bavaria, the southernmost part of Germany, where I had grown up.

In 1982 we moved into the small town of Lyndonville, fifteen miles down the road. Our life was changing. The children wanted to join Little League and go to dance class. David and I wanted to be more in the world. This is the point at which I made a decision to participate again in the institutional and professional culture of our country. I subsequently spent many years working as a public health nurse with the pregnant women and young children of our community. Most of my clients were white, and most were poor. In time I returned to school and became a certified nurse midwife. I also work with an organization called "One by One," whose mission is to facilitate dialogue between the children of Holocaust survivors and the children of Nazi perpetrators and bystanders. Clearly, promoting communication across historical abysses is a theme in my life.

From 1965 until the 1980s I had little contact with my movement past. I kept a thread of connection to a few white SNCC women, notably Emmie Schrader Adams, Casey Hayden, and Theresa Del Pozzo. I missed the first SNCC reunion in 1977 because no one knew where I was. Someone found me, and I attended Miss Ella Baker's birthday celebration in 1978. Finally I was on a SNCC mailing list. But boxes of documents sat in the dust under my bed. I could not bring myself to open them and look. I talked about my history with only a few people — my husband, my children, my father, occasionally with friends — all of whom struggled to understand. And I shielded myself from the full impact of my experience. For years I didn't trust my own perceptions. I wasn't truly sure whether white people had been finally expelled from SNCC. (They were, in 1966). Had black-white relations ever been a serious issue? Did they affect other people as profoundly they did me, or was it simply that I, with my personal history of serious childhood losses, had been deeply wrenched by something that was only a very minor part of the black liberation movement? Had there ever been a Beloved Community?

In the early 1980s, though, there was a shift. The Civil Rights Movement was rediscovered, and SNCC in particular became an object of study. I began to get requests to speak in schools or at community events about my experiences. People asked me for interviews, my children became old enough to ask more questions, and I began to talk about it in therapy.

It wasn't until 1988 at the Trinity College Conference in Hartford, however, that I found real SNCC people, black and white, again. An enormous healing took place for me there. I was overwhelmed when Michael Thelwell said from onstage during the Black Power panel that the expulsion of whites from SNCC was the single most traumatic moment in the life of the organization. My old friend Bob Mants found me and hugged me shortly after I walked in to the conference hall on the first day. After listening to Martha Prescod Norman's compelling speech about SNCC's place in history, I was struck again with a sense of the chasm that exists between black women and white women. When I said so to my old friend Judy, she replied, "Yes, but we can reach across at times." She said, "You will always be my friend. And I will always be your friend." I remember standing in a line with Casey Hayden, Dorothy Burlage, and Faith Holsaert, all white women, as Hollis Watkins led the singing, and feeling proud to be with them. And yet we all, black and white, sang together. On our last night we ate and drank, we laughed and told stories, and we called the names of the missing. On Saturday night at midnight, after it was all over, I went back to our hotel room with my family—I sat on the bed, put my head in my hands, and began to cry. I howled. David and my kids held me as I cried.

In 1994 at the reunion for the Mississippi Summer Project in Jackson, Mac-Arthur Cotton and I went out to lunch. Mac had been a loving and trusted friend during my time in Mississippi. That day we left the Tougaloo College campus in Mac's truck to drive to Shoney's Restaurant. The seat belt didn't work on the passenger side. It had been a long time since I had ridden in a car without a seat belt, but it just seemed to be part of the picture. This sort of risk felt like nothing compared to the emotional risks of once more attending a movement reunion. I was also nervous about venturing outside the safe boundaries of the black community in Jackson, alone with a black man. Is this really okay? Have times and attitudes really changed? I assumed MacArthur must know what he was doing and it must be safe, but I still felt uneasy and confused.

Inside Shoney's there were black and white patrons, and black and white waitresses. No one seemed to give us a second glance. We ordered from the salad bar, and asked for "sweet tea." We talked about our present lives and our families. I told him I had heard he became a Muslim for a time and that he didn't talk to white people. He said yes, that was true, and at the time that was just how it was. He didn't say that apologetically, just as a fact—as if at the time he had not felt he had a choice. He asked me if it had hurt when I heard about it. I told him it hurt very much. We smiled at each other a lot.

I dreamed in August 1994 that I was in a SNCC project office, a small house with dim light, wooden walls, and a dusty floor. A young black man enters. We argue about the photographs I am carrying. I say they were damaged. No, he says. He makes fun of me because he says my hands shook so much I can take only blurry pictures, like it is my fault the pictures are messed up. I get mad and say NO! they were messed up before, and I know it, by the person at the store. I am forceful and sure. The young man is angry and storms out. I race down the stairs after him. I can't see clearly, everything looks dim and fuzzy, but I recognize his back and know it's him. I cry to him, "But you are the one who was really my best friend."

So much is fuzzy, as in the dream. From the present looking back, it is dim, or at least the facts are much dimmer than the feelings. The dream asks who has got the truth. And who has made the truth be blurry—the camera store developer, or me, with my fear? Blessedly, I seem to be clear that it isn't me and my shaky hands. It is not my fault that things didn't come out right, didn't develop well.

Race consciousness always defined the SNCC experience. How could we escape it? We embarked with an immense hopefulness, fighting for freedom and justice, believing that it was possible to change people's lives, including our own, to make fundamental political, economic, and institutional change. Some of us shared a vision of an integrated society. Our hopefulness carried us a long way.

Now, thirty years later, my old wounds have been exposed, the scar tissue is realigning itself in a healthier way. So much is better, so much is healed. For a very long time I felt that white people overvalued what I did, and black people undervalued it. I now feel recognized, my small contribution acknowledged, and I have felt warmth and affection from my former buddies. It is unfortunately also true that we now reflect the greater society we live in more than we used to. After the initial ecstasy of reunion, it becomes clear there is a great deal of distance between us, generated by the reality that we have led separate lives for thirty years, and that for the most part the close relationships that have continued over the intervening years have been segregated ones: black with black and white with white. There are exceptions. There are a few white and black SNCC people who have succeeded in maintaining and developing close interracial friendships with one another since the movement time, but these are small in number. And I am not one of those people.

I understand well that what was between us will never be again, but still, that experience remains at the core of who I am. The fact that some of us had deep friendships that crossed all racial lines is simply a miracle. For short periods of time, in those early years, we leaped over all of the history and all of the minefields between us. For most of thirty years I have been silent about what it was like for me to lose my place in the movement. Certainly I never said anything publicly, except that I understood the political and historical necessity for Black Power and Black Nationalism. I am saying now that this was my experience. No matter what came after, there was a brief time when we were black and white together.

The Feel of a
Blue Note

THERESA DEL POZZO

It was my mother's unhappiness with the oppressive macho culture of the Italian American world that initially propelled me in search of a different life. I grew up in one of those European immigrant neighborhoods that are now romanticized in American nostalgia. My father was a butcher and we lived behind his shop, which was also a neighborhood hangout. He was a handsome and charming character who would philosophize and give advice on all subjects while he cut your veal chops and made sausage. However, he'd leave his charming self behind in the butcher shop whenever he stepped into the refrigerator compartment that had a back door leading into our apartment. At home he was a minor tyrant who, after the first year of marriage, had little interest in family life. His world centered on his men friends — hanging out with them, playing cards, shooting craps. It was a Damon Runyon world, with buddies named Lawyer, Spin, Black Ace, and Studebaker. (All these years I thought this guy was named after the car — and I only recently found out that my folks were saying "Stu de baker," in Italian American patois.) My father went out with the "boys" every night after work, on Sunday afternoon, and on his day off. No wives were welcome. My mother stayed home and cried.

It's still painful to think back on those years and remember my 4'11"-tall mom struggling to maintain her dignity, never giving up her fight for a better life. But this petite twenty-year old never totally acquiesced. There were always acts of defiance and independence. She loves to dance, and in the few

173

years before she had children and still could move about on her own, she would often slip her dancing shoes into her purse, tell my dad she was going to her mother's, and take the train into Manhattan to go dancing at Roseland. Later she became one of the first women in our neighborhood to drive, and she used that mobility to get herself, my brother, and me out of our narrow world. She showed us that there was more to life than Bronxwood Avenue by taking us ice skating or swimming, to Manhattan to see shows at Radio City Music Hall, and on trips to upstate New York for summer vacations. These might seem like pretty ordinary excursions to middle-class Americans, but my brother and I were the only kids in our neighborhood who got to do anything like them. Sometimes we would just drive around the suburbs looking at the large single-family homes with big yards and "dads" in them raking leaves — scenes that clearly belonged to another kind of life.

My mom lived in a world of women. Her mother, sisters, and girlfriends were her constant companions. Her message to me was strong and clear: "There's a better life out there. Don't get trapped into a marriage and kids like I did." She was a product of her times, however, and considered herself to be lucky to have come of age after the advent of the washing machine, which freed her from the drudgery of washing bed sheets, towels, and kids' clothes by hand. When I look back on my life, I feel lucky to have come of age during the climaxing years of the interracial civil rights movement, which made it possible for me to cross over the racial divide and experience the world of black America. And in a way, the contrast between those two "lucky realities" pretty much reflects the difference in our lives and times.

Later, I learned that it is a common pattern for women who are dissatisfied in their marriages to push their daughters to look for a more fulfilling life, and then they are the ones who suffer the most when their daughters do break away. It was sad, but true, that my mother was the person most hurt by my struggle to free myself from her world. She had no way to understand the person I was becoming. She couldn't figure out what she had "done wrong" to end up with a daughter who was so different: a race-mixing, left-wing, commie-sympathizing, antiwar, protesting, soon-to-be hippie.

I realized, watching my brother as he made plans for college, that even though I was a girl (which in my culture was a big-time difference) college could be my "way out" as well, and I took it. I was the only one of my neighborhood friends who signed up for a college preparatory course in high school. I loved the anonymity it gave me, the chance to meet new people from different backgrounds and ambitions. For the first time I found encouragement for my inquisitiveness and intelligence.

What I thought of as my "secret life" began then at age fifteen. At night and on weekends I'd hang out with my neighborhood friends; in school I'd eat lunch with them and meet them in the bathroom for a smoke, but in the classroom, I was on my own. I made friends with other kids who were in the "academic track." They were mainly Jewish and black.

It was the first time I'd known anyone who wasn't Italian, and it was just chance that the girl with whom I became best friends, Isabelle, was a warm and funny Jewish girl, and a "red diaper baby," someone who had been brought up in the tradition of the radical left. My life, in contrast, fell somewhere between *Grease* and *The Godfather*. We'd swap stories about our "outside" friends and families and laugh in amazement at our different worlds. I also developed friendships with several African American girls who were part of a group of students who traveled from Harlem to the Northeast Bronx each day to attend what was considered a "good" high school. They were the best-dressed, most stylish girls I'd ever seen, and all of them were headed for college. They were a striking contrast to the stereotypical images of blacks I'd grown up with.

All this new input coincided with my brother Fred's first year at City College. He was a bright and sensitive boy who hated the Italian macho culture he had refused to join. At college he found stimulation and excitement in the new ideas and culture he was exposed to. He would come home and talk to me about psychology and theater, and he brought home books, records, and magazines I never knew existed. It was in the *Village Voice*, one of the first weekly "alternative newspapers," that I read about the Student Marches for School Integration. It was the first time I'd ever thought about the issues of segregation and civil rights, but it was immediately clear to me what was right, as in righteous. I'd been brought up on an egalitarian folk wisdom that extolled the value of the common man; all I had to do was expand it to include people of color. I've always been someone who takes ideas seriously, and the clear injustice of segregation and disenfranchisement of African Americans spoke for itself, as well as going to the core of the unequivocal moral teachings of the

Catholic Church in which I had been raised. Even though I had been kicked out of catechism classes for asking too many questions, the fundamental positive Catholic values, which later spawned "liberation theology," had made a clear and permanent impression on me.

In high school the excitement of my newly expanding world was fed by my enjoyment of learning and the new people I was meeting. I'd begun to realize how limited my background was and set out to find out more about what I didn't know. In school I found lists of books one was supposed to be familiar with by college age and began to read voraciously. I also started to follow current events in the *New York Times* and the *Village Voice*. It dawned on me that going to college was not only a way out of the Italian American ghetto, but it would also make it possible for me to have a life that could grow out of my own interests and values. In the meantime I felt as though I was marking time, waiting for my future to begin.

During those high school years I led a double life. There was my school self and there was my inherited self. I continued to hang out and party with my neighborhood friends, had boyfriends with nicknames like Guinea and Batman, snuck out at night to go clubbing at local bars, bleached my hair blonde, and plucked my eyebrows till only a quarter inch remained, redrawing the rest each morning before school. My mother thought I looked great—"just like Kim Novak." (She still reminds me forty years later how nice I looked then, as compared, I guess, to ever since!) From the outside I looked like a dizzy, boy-crazed, teenage bleach blonde who had nothing on her mind but "hanging out" and being part of the neighborhood scene. But in my academic classes I didn't have to hide the fact that I was intensely interested in abstract ideas and history. With hindsight I realize that I'd always had tremendous mental energy, but no place for it to go. I had always been stimulated by the learning part of school, loved to read, and was fascinated by information.

It's sad that the more interested I became in school and the outside world, the more tense things became at home. The first time my mother came to a parents' day at high school she was shocked when my home room and history teacher praised me for the same thing that up until then I'd always been criticized for: "asking questions," finally recognized as basic intellectual curiosity. My folks lived in an insular world. They believed that everyone thought as they did because they didn't know anyone who thought differently. Since none of their friends' children were concerned about segregation or nuclear war, why should I be? Their reading was limited to the *Daily News*. The great educator of the working class, TV, was still limited to programs like *Uncle Miltie* (the Public Broadcasting Service, my parents' favorite for the last twenty years, didn't yet exist). I began to seem more and more odd to them. Of course it didn't help matters that the things I was most interested in were social and political issues and that my "new" ideas on social and economic equality sounded like nothing they'd ever heard of, but probably were "communist inspired." This was the late fifties and thanks to McCarthy everyone had heard of that.

I looked for every opportunity to stay away from home. I worked after school, on Saturdays, and full time during the summer at Macy's in Manhattan — an hour subway ride in each direction. Best of all, I figured out a way to graduate from high school six months early and planned to be out of the Bronx by January of my senior year. I'd started thinking about which college to go to in my junior year in high school and was amazed to find out that college recruiters would be coming to my high school to talk about out-of-town colleges. I decided to go along when a black classmate told me she was being excused from science class to hear a representative from Howard University. I didn't understand what was happening when I entered the classroom and found myself to be the only white person in the room. I'd never heard of Howard, nor did I know there were "Negro colleges." I guess my friend was either too surprised by my ignorance or too embarrassed to explain that reality to me. But I took it in stride and just absorbed it as another part of the larger world about which I knew so little.

My schoolmate Isabelle introduced me to two of her friends who were applying to the University of Wisconsin. Once it began to sink in that people really did things like go to out-of-town colleges, I realized that that would be perfect for me. I could get away from home, and it would give me "a place to go to." A few nights later at the dinner table, with typical teenage arrogance, I "informed" my folks that I had decided to go to college in Wisconsin. On cue, just as I had mischievously anticipated, they freaked out. By this time they didn't want me to go to college at all because they were convinced that school and contact with "outsiders" was the cause of their problems with me. They were hoping I might be "saved" if I stayed at home and got a good job as a secretary. Frightened by the possibility of losing me completely, however, my mother offered to pay my expenses if I went to college in New York City and lived at home. My father's response was to laugh derisively and ask, "Who do you think you are, and where do you think you will get the money from"? I was ready for this: I told them I planned to use the money that had been put in savings bonds, in my name, when I was a baby and on special birthdays (a result of being a war baby, when everyone bought savings bonds). If they didn't give me that money for college, the coming summer when I was eighteen, I'd get a lawyer and sue them for it! My mother was right: all that reading was ruining me, and college would only make me worse.

Even before my graduation in January 1960 I found a full-time job as a receptionist in Manhattan. With my newfound freedom from school and financial independence, my tolerance for the constant fighting with my parents had reached its limit. I packed my clothes, took my typewriter, called a taxi, and moved out. The only place I had to go to was my newly married brother's one-room apartment, which obviously could be only a temporary stop. Within days I found an ideal location in bohemian Greenwich Village, on Thirteenth Street between Fifth and Sixth Avenues. The address was sexy, but it wasn't quite the change in lifestyle I'd looked forward to: my new home, the Evangeline House, was a women's dormitory-style hotel run by the Salvation Army. It housed their female officers as well as young women like me with no other place to live. Although I was finally out of the Bronx, I was in limbo for the next months while I worked full time and took night classes at City College, to prove to the University of Wisconsin that I was capable of college-level work (a condition of my acceptance).

In September, when it was finally time to leave for Wisconsin, I was more than ready. I'd found out about a charter flight for New York students and discovered that most of the other New Yorkers were from liberal and leftist backgrounds. Many had chosen that college because it was known as a progressive school with an especially good and radical history department. I, of course, had known nothing about this but had chosen history as my major because for me it held the thrill of unraveling a never-ending intellectual mystery. I just lucked into the perfect place.

I was ecstatic when I got to Madison. I had never been on a college campus before, or anywhere except New York City and the Catskill Mountains. The campus, situated on a rolling hillside that sloped down to a vast lake, looked straight out of a movie. It was early fall, and the trees were full of color. The Student Union, with its activity rooms, glass-enclosed cafeteria, and stone terrace overlooking the lake, was a picturesque meeting place for students. In between classes we would fill the terrace's wrought-iron tables, talking about classes, teachers, books, films, the day's news, social and political events, and especially the latest developments in the dramatic fight for civil rights then emerging in the South. The wait for my new life was over: I felt as if I'd died and gone to heaven.

Some say timing is everything, and for me it certainly was. I had the good luck to be out, into the world, just as America was moving from the banality of *Ozzie and Harriet* to serious debate of the status quo and political agitation. The black southern student movement laid down the final challenge to segregation, and their rebellion against the last legal remnants of slavery compelled thousands of students to take sides. You could stand by and watch young black people like yourself be spat upon, beaten, and dragged off to jail for refusing to be restricted to the Jim Crow seating at the rear of a bus or for sitting at a lunch counter reserved solely for people with white skin or you could "do the right thing" and take action to support the fight for human rights. A movement community in support of the sit-ins, boycotts, picket lines, and Freedom Rides began to develop on almost every college campus. There weren't any membership cards, just people acting together in loosely affiliated groups like CORE, NAACP, SCLC, SNCC, and hundreds of grassroots organizations. If you were there and participating, you were part of the "movement." The social activists of the early sixties were inspired by the gutsy, dramatic, and principled confrontations initiated by the black southern students. Their example was electrifying, and made others realize not only that direct action against social and political evils could make a difference but also that the very act of opposing social injustice was itself liberating.

When I arrived in Wisconsin, I immediately took up a double major — in history and social activism. I joined a campus civil rights group that was picketing Woolworth's in support of the southern sit-ins and worked on a local antidiscriminatory housing effort. With the exception of required courses, my academic studies centered on my interests in social, political, and economic issues and were supplemented by extracurricular speaker programs, debate, and journals like *Studies on the Left,* which was based in Madison. Being at a school that attracted leftist professors and graduate students as well as political exiles from South Africa, Ethiopia, and South America was a stimulating intellectual bonus. I learned as much from discussions in the cafeteria as I did in the classroom.

Another advantage of the University of Wisconsin was that it was one of the few American schools that had an interdisciplinary African Studies program. Although it was primarily for graduate students, I was able to take two full years of African history, African anthropology, and courses on economic development in Third World countries.

During the summers I stayed in Madison and worked full time to earn my tuition, which for out-of-state students was $250 a semester. I did go home at Christmas, but it was like walking on a verbal minefield. My parents were still against my being in college because they were afraid that I was becoming some raving radical. And of course I was. My folks were pretty smart, and I'm sure I was also pretty obnoxious about the way I stated my ideas, as nineteen-year-olds can be. Naturally, I didn't see that at the time, but now I can appreciate how difficult my transformation was for my parents. I never stayed home for long.

During the summer of 1961 I attended the annual convention of the National Student Association, which was being held that year at the University of Wisconsin. For the first time I met student activists from other parts of the country like Casey and Tom Hayden. It was the beginning of my involvement in the informal national network of movement activists. Because Madison was my home base, I was able to facilitate the lobbying effort of the Liberal Studies Caucus by supplying mimeograph machines, meeting places, and housing. The Caucus's main efforts at the convention were directed to support of pro–civil rights and anti–House Un-American Affairs Committee (HUAC) platforms.

There was a lot of opposition to HUAC, a congressional leftover from the 1950s McCarthy era of political witch-hunting. The film *Operation Abolition,* which had been showing at colleges throughout the country, had a big impact on the growing opposition to HUAC because it exposed the committee's red-baiting and smear techniques and ended with footage of the police beating demonstrators who were peacefully picketing the committee hearings.

This was pretty shocking stuff in 1961. These protests against HUAC were part of the first wave of student clashes with the government that took place outside the South.

At this time most northern activists still looked to the southern civil rights and international student movements for inspiration and direction. We could scarcely imagine that in only a few years American student agitation and protest would stop a war or bring down a government. But in fact the national explosion of student involvement and protest that began to erupt in 1963–64 and culminated in the anti–Vietnam War campaign was fueled by the ever-expanding student movement that had begun in the South in the late fifties and early sixties.

Study and protest alone would be an unbalanced life for any college student, and I avoided this pitfall by taking part in an interracial music and dance scene that followed a party circuit on the weekends. My life was integrated, as I partied with the same people I debated and picketed with. However, I became totally distracted and depressed when I suffered a "broken heart" in the winter of 1963 and decided to drop out of school. I felt I needed a change of geography in order to heal. It was an inspired move, for the minute I got on the bus I was fine!

Back in New York, I stayed with my folks and got a clerical job at Columbia University. One day I saw an announcement that Charlie Jones from the Student Nonviolent Coordinating Committee (SNCC) would be speaking at a meeting in Harlem. After work I went to the meeting. This began my association with the Harlem Education Project (HEP), a part of the Northern Student Movement. HEP was led by Carl Anthony, an imaginative black architectural student. It focused on housing issues (especially "pocket parks," which got local groups involved in cleaning up and creating recreational areas or gardens in empty lots), tutoring programs, and, later, the fight against employment discrimination. It was one of the early 1960s efforts to build a northern-based civil rights movement instead of being just a support base for the southern struggle. I began volunteering as a tutor in the evenings and on weekends, but several weeks later I gave up my clerical job and went to work for HEP full time. Once I began spending time in Harlem, it was impossible for me to continue to live with my parents, since they were totally opposed to what I was doing. So I moved out and found an apartment with some Columbia students and each day took the bus from the mostly white Upper West Side to HEP, on 135th Street and Eighth Avenue, in Harlem. A short distance, but worlds apart.

Harlem was a revelation to me. Nothing I knew prepared me for the revolting conditions inside some of those tenement buildings. I felt it was a miracle that the kids we worked with could be anything but deranged when their everyday reality was filled with such desolation. Every day they confronted the stench of unwashed stairs; holes as big as they were in walls through which rats ran freely; apartments without heat or hot water; winos and drug addicts to be climbed over on their way to school.

In 1963 the racial atmosphere in New York City was charged. Black nationalist groups with varying ideologies were flourishing, the most organized and active were the Black Muslims led by Malcolm X. Although Malcolm had begun to receive national attention, he was still very much a local leader. When I heard him speak at a street corner rally there were only about 150 to 200 people present. And although he did speak about "white devils," no one blinked an eye or seemed to be bothered by my presence, nor did I feel any animosity. The only directly hostile behavior toward movement whites that I experienced at that time came from black nationalist writers and poets. The odd thing was that, rather than being centered in Harlem or Bedford Stuyvesant, they hung out on the Lower East Side, in the same bars and cafes frequented by the white artists, poets, and musicians. Maybe one attraction of that setting was the convenience of having the object of your derision sitting at the next table. Once, when I was meeting a black friend from school for a drink, it was impossible not to overhear the snide remarks and epithets like "race mixer" and "white bitch" being directed at us. My friend challenged them to look beyond the color of my skin as they knew nothing about me, and pointed out that if I had not been present they would have treated him as a brother instead of a traitor. Their response was as shallow as their initial comments. Later I was amused when I would run into these same "nationalists" at integrated parties, some of them with white wives or girlfriends. This was the early stages of the 1960s black nationalism, and although their antiwhite rhetoric was historically understandable, it seemed to me as confused as those who preached it.

Another aspect of the nationalist dilemma of the early sixties was the stereotypical brainwashed response of blacks against any identification with their

"African-ness." One day as I walked down a Harlem street with a HEP teenager I was stunned when black people started taunting and insulting her—even calling her a "jungle bunny"—all because she had stopped straightening her hair and let it grow "natural."

Change comes slowly, and not always in a clear path. Fortunately, there are some extraordinary people who have devoted their lives to showing the way. There is a gospel tune, "This Little Light of Mine," which was sung in the movement, and after the refrain "I'm gonna let it shine," the next verse would be filled in with movement references, like "all over Little Rock" or "in the Birmingham jail." I experienced the intensity of "that light" when I met Miss Ella Baker. She'd come to see what we were doing at HEP. In her distinctive, deep, and serious voice she asked one of the fourteen-year-old tutorial students what she wanted to do in life. The girl answered that she would like to be a doctor. Miss Baker immediately began telling her what things she needed to do and what scholarships were available in order for her to become that doctor. It was then that I saw Miss Baker's "light" as she focused her undivided energy on that child. It was as if that girl was on a darkened stage, with a spotlight shining just on her. At that moment she was as important as any person in the world; *she* was the reason for the civil rights movement. And I knew that she'd felt it too. Whether Ella Baker was shaping the direction of the civil rights movement by advising the southern student movement to remain independent of adult organizations (advice that was key to the formation of SNCC) or listening to the dream of one child, her whole being was concentrated on and dedicated to the constant struggle of eliminating the barriers and injustice of racism. Being around someone like Ella Baker put me in contact with focused purpose and true greatness. I could see that light shine and it made clear to me what is really of importance in this life.

I got another heavy dose of inspiration in the early spring of 1963 when I made my first trip south to a SNCC conference in Atlanta. We were in a hall filled with several hundred people. The energy level was intense, and the spirit expressed through the freedom songs was startling. The building vibrated from the power behind the voices and the rhythm of the music. I'd never experienced such exhilaration and immediately understood how these young people had literally awakened America, myself included. It was the first time I met many of the SNCC staff, like the legendary Charles Sherrod, Dorie Ladner, and

Penny Patch, whose work I knew about from the support network I'd belonged to for the last three years.

Stokely Carmichael was another SNCC person I met in Atlanta. He, like me, was from the Bronx, and we became friends when he came to work at HEP in 1963. During that summer racial fighting broke out in the fringe area separating our two neighborhoods, and we had a good laugh when he suggested, tongue in cheek, that since it was "my people" rioting and attacking blacks, I should go there and try to "organize" them. The mutually understood clear absurdity of such a suggestion made it funny. It was a given that people like my old neighborhood friends were as much the enemy as the Mississippi racists, yet it had been only four years since I'd left that community.

I returned to school the following fall wanting to learn more about the African American culture I'd become so involved with. But in 1964, even at a progressive school like the University of Wisconsin, there were no courses in what we know today as African American Studies. The university community reflected the rest of American culture. Although Africans were exotic enough to merit study, or be allowed into white-only hotels, scholarly works by and about Americans of African descent were absent from the curriculum. I had to create my own independent study program in African American history, literature, and sociology in order to get academic credit for reading Frederick Douglass, W. E. B. Du Bois, Booker T. Washington, Langston Hughes, James Baldwin, Ralph Ellison, and Richard Wright. I discovered that although Marcus Garvey was never mentioned in any course work, the University of Wisconsin had his papers on microfilm. I used the Garvey archives to anchor much of my studies. I created a cohesiveness between my classroom studies and my participation in the movement; each fed the other, and both were directed toward social change.

By the fall of 1963 the civil rights movement had escalated dramatically in part as a reaction to the assassination of Medgar Evers, the March on Washington, and the church bombings in Birmingham, which had killed four little girls. Civil rights news was on the front page of newspapers, in magazines, and on radio and TV every day. That fall I founded the Wisconsin Friends of SNCC. For the first meeting I reserved a university room that could hold about thirty people. When I arrived I was stunned that the room was already filled and more people were waiting in the corridor. Interest and participation continued to grow throughout the year.

During that winter/spring SNCC announced the Mississippi Summer Project, which gave a strong focus to our support work. We set up committees to publicize the drive for voter registration, lobbied the state legislature for support resolutions, kept the university and local newspapers supplied with information, and had an outreach program that sent speakers out to schools, churches, and campus and community groups. During this time I came in contact with a broad segment of the community, and I was shocked to realize that most whites had no idea that blacks could not vote in the southern states and that they risked their lives if they tried to. Once informed, however, the Wisconsin community responded with an emphatic condemnation of things as they were in Mississippi. Several Summer Project volunteers came from Wisconsin, and Friends of SNCC raised more than ten thousand dollars and truckloads of food, clothes, books, paper, and office equipment for the project.

Because of this popular support as well as the pro–civil rights stance of Governor William Proxmire and Congressman Robert Kastenmeyer, SNCC targeted the Wisconsin State Democratic Convention from which to seek a formal resolution challenging the legitimacy of the all-white Mississippi delegation to the 1964 National Democratic Nominating Convention on the grounds that blacks had not been able to participate in the electoral process. Such a challenge, part of the Democratic Party's procedural rules, could only come from a state Democratic Convention; it would then automatically be on the agenda of the party convention in August. This would put a national spotlight on the heretofore accepted practice of black disenfranchisement and in effect hold the entire Democratic Party responsible for its Mississippi component.

SNCC sent Walter Tillow from the Atlanta office, and the two of us went to the Wisconsin State Democratic Convention. This was a typical SNCC operation: two twenty-one-year-olds are sent to present the case of the ouster of the white Mississippi delegation and of its replacement instead with the Mississippi movement's Freedom Democratic Party (MFDP) delegation. So off we went, getting in touch with other movement people throughout the state, asking for their help in identifying and lobbying socially conscious delegates as well as in finding us a place to stay (hotels were never even considered). Fortunately, I knew many of the regional civil rights supporters through the Friends of SNCC outreach program, and they were often also active in their local Democratic Party. We worked with our known supporters, buttonholing delegates and gaining their votes. In retrospect I realize we were so naively confident because the injustice was so obvious. It never occurred to us that we wouldn't succeed, and we did, getting resolutions to challenge the legality of the Mississippi delegation not only from the Wisconsin Democratic Convention but from the Minnesota one as well.

That August the MFDP delegates and hundreds of black Mississippi supporters and Freedom Summer volunteers came to the National Convention of the Democratic Party in Atlantic City to demand that the MFDP be recognized as the lawful representatives of the state of Mississippi. Walter and I arrived early, along with Casey Hayden and Emmie Adams, and helped set up a lobbying office while others prepared an "educational" display for the convention delegates. SNCC rented all the spaces in a parking lot that was on the Atlantic City boardwalk next to the convention center and filled it with some of the actual fire-bombed cars of civil rights activists that they'd trucked from Mississippi. There was also a poster-size photo display of burned-out movement churches and homes, of black Mississippians being dragged off to jail as they tried to register to vote, of mob attacks on voter registration workers, of bullet holes in the homes of MFDP workers targeted in drive-by shootings. As the delegates walked along the boardwalk on their way to the convention center they had to pass this display. You could see their easygoing convention smiles visibly change as they encountered this actual representation of the brutal reality that faced some Americans when they went to vote if they were black and lived in the South. This display of the political reality of Mississippi politics, along with the one-on-one testimonials of MFDP delegates about their experiences while trying to vote, led to a grassroots upsurge of delegates who committed to voting to unseat the white Mississippi delegation.

The Mississippi Summer Project had educated and linked together a national network to bring to an end the whites-only system of southern politics. Lyndon Johnson and his minions had to delay the opening of the convention for several days until they could regain control and squash this small-*d* democratic alliance that challenged the status quo. He then made a "compromise" offer to the MFDP that would give them token representation.

The MFDP's organizational allies in the Convention Challenge consisted of the established national liberal political groups, labor unions, and church groups, as well as liberal luminaries such as Hubert Humphrey. One by one representatives of these groups came before the MFDP delegates and urged them to accept the compromise as a "first step." Later that afternoon the MFDP delegates met in a closed session, and the farmers, beauticians, domestic workers, school teachers, housewives, and janitors voted to by-pass the so-called wisdom of the liberal leadership and reject the compromise. These everyday, extraordinary people were able to cut through the pretense and recognize that the so-called compromise was nothing but flimflam. Without advanced degrees in political science, but because of their own experience and wisdom, they knew what was real.

Historians point to this vote as an example of the class divisions that were beginning to emerge in the Mississippi movement because it was the more middle-class delegates within the MFDP who supported the compromise. I agree, but also think it is important to recognize that the racial isolation of most of the MFDP members had insulated them from the manipulative, self-seeking world of regular white-style politics, enabling them to act with moral integrity.

One of the delegates who voted against the compromise was a woman named Hazel Palmer. We worked together every day in the MFDP office, and it was clear to me that when she said she was fighting for her freedom, she meant just that. Freedom, to her, was the end of things as they had been. It meant the opportunity—for her, for her children and for every other black Mississippian—to function as any other person in this country could. So it was clear that if the electoral system in Mississippi did not allow people like her to vote, then those chosen by that system had no right to be delegates. Hazel Palmer was fighting for her freedom, for her human and civil rights. The "compromise" was just another back seat in the bus.

For me, working in the civil rights movement was the beginning of seeing the world through black eyes. I learned a lesson about personal integrity and clarity of action. I was present when the announcement came that the MFDP would not be seated. In response to questions from the press Joe Rauh, the MFDP legal counsel, attempted to put a positive spin on the matter, saying something like, "It was a real success to come so far," etc., etc. Bob Moses took the microphone out his hand and called it like it was: The MFDP had lost. The racist white supremacists had been protected from expulsion from the convention so that Lyndon Johnson wouldn't risk losing any southern votes and

Hubert Humphrey would get the vice-presidential nomination. The truth was that black people's rights were bartered away, and to say anything else was to demean all that the Mississippi people had struggled and sacrificed for.

There never was a question about what I'd do after college: I was going south to work for SNCC. After the convention in Atlantic City, I went back to Wisconsin, turned in a final paper, packed up my things, and in September took the train south from Chicago to Mississippi. When I got off in Jackson I walked into the segregated station and followed the signs through the "colored" waiting room into the street where a black taxi driver took me to the Lynch Street office of the Council of Federated Organizations (COFO). For the next year I never again came in contact with the white community, except when I went to serve a subpoena on the governor. I was recently astounded to discover that many histories of the movement date the beginning of the end of SNCC to that fall of 1964, a period, according to these accounts, of unfocused and undisciplined work, with people "floating" from project to project. For me, it was a time of intense work. I was living at the "Literacy House" in Tougaloo and went into the COFO office in Jackson every morning, working in that windowless building until nine or ten at night. Later that fall I worked in the MFDP office on the main street of the black downtown; that was much more pleasant—the building at least had windows. One Sunday morning in winter, as I sat on the back steps of the Literacy House having my coffee and enjoying the sun, I had a novel idea: Maybe I should take a day off! Until then it had never occurred to me to do anything but work seven days a week.

My focus was the MFDP "Congressional Challenge," an extremely creative and complex political and legal procedure. The challenge to the seating of a congressional delegation is governed by the by-laws of Congress that set forth the procedures to be followed in order to contest elected representatives. The challenger—in this case the MFDP—had to prove the systematic denial of rights of the African American community. To accomplish this, the challenger was granted the "power of subpoena." Black Mississippians would be called to give depositions supporting their claims of disenfranchisement. The MFDP could also subpoena the testimony of state officials, from the governor right down to the local sheriffs and election board members who were accused of having violated the voting rights of black citizens. The challenger also got to name the locale where the depositions were taken, which meant that the hearings could be held in the black community. White officials would be questioned by the MFDP attorneys in front of the very people they had been attempting to intimidate and terrorize. The state officials would have to appear or face federal contempt charges. I can still remember the glee of Arthur Kinoy, MFDP's lawyer, and the ear-to-ear grin of Lawrence Guyot, the party chairman, as they described the wide latitude set forth in this congressional procedure.

The movement lawyers' approach to the law was as political activists; as a result, they, together with SNCC and the MFDP, saw the challenge not only as a way to unseat the white racist congressional delegation but also as another tool for organizing within the black community. The Lawyers Guild recruited about 150 lawyers from all over the country to come to Mississippi to work on the challenge. They volunteered their services, paid their own expenses, and sometimes brought their own court stenographers. The Jackson MFDP office worked for months coordinating the arrivals, transportation, housing, and social and legal orientations of this large legal staff. Local MFDP and SNCC field workers provided information on who should be subpoenaed, hand-delivered the subpoenas, set up the meeting halls, briefed the attorneys on the specifics for each community, recruited black citizens whose rights had been denied to come forward and testify, and helped organize strong community support and turnout.

At first we were shocked to find that the white power structure was responding en masse. Every white official, with the sole exception of the governor, answered the subpoenas, coming to the black community and submitting to questions about their part in denying the voting rights of African American citizens. There's no way to explain how radical and freeing this process was, except to contrast it to a year earlier, when white Mississippians had assumed that the idea of masses of black people voting could be dismissed as a joke. The worldwide attention to the political and social outrages in Mississippi that resulted from the Summer Project, and the murder of three civil rights workers, James Chaney, Mickey Schwerner, and Andrew Goodman, changed all that. The MFDP's near win of the Convention Challenge in Atlantic City the preceding August had shown the Democratic Party that "the times they were a changin'."

I've always believed that the national Democratic Party organization told the regular Mississippi Democrats that, given the amount of support for the MFDP nationwide and the fact that the challenge was mandated by Congress, they could not afford to ignore it. Black Mississippians, law student researchers, white and black northern volunteers, SNCC staff, and lawyers from all over the country worked together day and night, each contributing what they could. These efforts culminated in a caravan of hundreds of MFDP members and supporters going to Washington to lobby Congress when the challenge was presented on the floor of the House.

We didn't win the challenge, but that was only one battle. The movement had shown that white Mississippians of all ranks could be held accountable for their actions. Black Mississippians had confronted and broken the cycle of intimidation. In the words of Dr. L. C. Dorsey — executive director of the Delta Health Center in Mound Bayou, Mississippi, the area where she grew up as a sharecropper — from the video *Freedom on My Mind,* "The movement . . . removed people from fear. The freedom from fear of being dragged out of your house in the middle of the night for daring to want to be a part of the mainstream, from a want to dream, a want to participate, a want to have that equal justice and equal pay for equal work." The oppression that black Mississippians had been constricted by for so long was broken. "The generations since the movement have not been taught to stay in their place or to understand that there is a certain way to walk and stand and look at and relate to white people."

My involvement with the movement began as a moral reaction to the blatant injustice of segregation and the denial of basic human rights of African Americans. Along the way I got an education in the intricate patterns of racism and began to experience what I think of as the small-*c* culture of the African American community: the wisdom, dignity, strength, humor, gentleness, and creativeness of its everyday life and people. The experience of living within the black world changed forever the person I was to become and the way I lived my adult life.

Like most Americans, I'd kind of known that there was a black world that ran parallel to the white one and that the two intersected in only a superficial and ritualistic way. However, as I got involved in the movement, I came to realize that the social separation between whites and blacks which resulted from the white exclusion of blacks had ultimately left whites ignorant of the black community. In addition, this breach kept hidden one of the fundamental differences between the two communities, which was their perception of "life in America." The white version was characterized by Norman Rockwell's warm and fuzzy portraits of mom, apple pie, and a Sunday Sousa band concert. The black version, in contrast, was epitomized by the tortured voice of Billie Holiday mourning "black bodies swinging in the southern breeze, strange fruit hanging from a poplar tree," and by the joyous energy and sophisticated musical intricacies of the Duke Ellington Orchestra at the Savoy Ballroom in Harlem.

Because of white racism, African Americans had taken a defensive strategy in relation to white America. They interacted in a careful and guarded manner with whites, allowing them to know very little of the black community and especially its feelings toward whites. But the movement was happening within the African American community, and so whites who came to work in the movement lived within that world. It was a real eye-opener for me when the racial balance was turned around and, as a white, I became part of a small minority. In the movement, black folks were at home; this was their world, they could speak and act naturally. They weren't on guard, as in the white world. They didn't have to weigh their words or "hold up the image of the race," but instead spoke their minds and hearts. It allowed me to see across the racial divide and become aware that there was an intensely bitter distrust of and disdain for the white world, and a unity of vision about how this country had long operated at the expense of blacks. This view of the pervasiveness of racism throughout American culture and in the interaction between whites and blacks may sound familiar now, in the first decade of the twenty-first century, but in the early 1960s virtually the only place black people openly expressed these ideas and feelings was within the black community, out of earshot of the white majority. Being there and seeing the world from their perspective had a profound impact on me and forever altered the way I would perceive the patterns of American racism.

But the impact of and the fight against racism was only one aspect of the African American community that I came to appreciate. I realized I wasn't just experiencing involvement in a social movement; I was experiencing the substance of a definable culture, one that was present in the everyday occurrences, attitudes, habits, and styles of being that make up how a community feels to an outsider. This distinctive communal texture was expressed in nuances of warmth, gentleness, humor, intelligence, wit, and strength. In music this subtlety is called a "blue" note. It's the bending of a note so that the sound falls between the notes of the tempered European scale, which are represented by the white and black keys on a piano. It is this African tonality coupled with the African use of multiple rhythms that gives a unique and dynamic impact to black music, whether it's the funky sound of James Brown or the complex melodic patterns of John Coltrane. It's what we have come to know as "soul," or why Duke Ellington said, "It don't mean a thing if it ain't got that swing." That unique blend of African and European heritage made for a distinct way of life, a style of being that is as pronounced in the African American small-c culture as it is in its music. In the early sixties the breadth of this vibrant culture was still mostly contained within the segregated world of black America. Encountering it was a profound experience for this twenty-year-old white girl from an Italian American ghetto in New York.

I recognized this distinctiveness in the bearing and body language of African Americans, whom Maya Angelou personifies in "And Still I Rise": "'Cause I walk like I've got oil wells / Pumping in my living room . . . 'Cause I laugh like I've got gold mines / Diggin in my own backyard. . . . Does it come as a surprise / That I dance like I've got diamonds / At the meeting of my thighs." I can remember watching an attractive woman laugh and flirt while cooking an impromptu dinner, at a small wood-burning stove, in a one-room cabin, with walls that were layered with newspaper to keep out the breeze. Suddenly it hit me that this is what being a survivor means: being who you are, an attractive vibrant person, not withstanding the bullshit you have to put up with or the things you have to live without. I would abstract people from the oppressive reality they were living in and marvel at the depth and heroism of a farmer like E. W. Steptoe, a smallish, thin man, graceful in his movements and gentle in his speech, and wonder, Is it possible that this person is going to face up to a mob of threatening, vicious whites, in order to try to register to vote? But it wasn't the idea of the threatening mob that startled me; it was the gentle man.

I was always uneasy when reporters or people outside the movement asked questions about how it felt to be involved in the "struggle." I knew they expected to hear horror stories of intimidation and brutality. And although all movement activists were continually aware of the possibility of violence, knowing that at any time a fire bomb could come through your window or your car could be forced off the road and you might not be heard from again, in fact all black southerners lived with an awareness of this type of police state threat all the time. So if you were white and you chose to come south and work with the movement, you understood that you were putting yourself in harm's way; likewise, if you were black and active in the movement, your chances of that "threat" becoming a reality were greatly increased. This was part of the daily reality, but it did not dominate our lives. Therefore, without disrespecting or diminishing the suffering experienced by so many, I would try to explain to inquirers that more than anything else, the movement was about the positive spirit of community and being involved in working toward a higher ideal—as expressed in one of the freedom songs, "Woke up this mornin with my mind stayed on freedom . . . walkin and talkin with my mind stayed on freedom." It was enlightening, inspirational, thrilling, and life altering—the best it could get.

It was a remarkable and humbling opportunity to work alongside and get to know and learn from "ordinary" exceptional people like E. W. Steptoe, Fannie Lou Hamer, and Annie Devine. One night after months of work leading up to the Congressional Challenge I was in the office until about 3:00 A.M. waiting for the last signatory to the final documents that would launch this precedent-setting procedure. And after an evening-long journey, in she walked, a tiny seventy-year-old woman, dressed in her Sunday best, crowned by a small black pillbox hat. Just another everyday person, doing an extraordinary thing. There were a lot of sensational events in the South during the time I was there, 1964–65, but for me the truly outstanding were the actions of "ordinary" people dealing with one of the most fundamental questions of life: how to confront and combat tyranny. In Mississippi that is what was being talked about and acted on each day.

I remember seeing Victoria Gray, one of the MFDP congressional candidates, standing outside the Tougaloo Literacy House at the end of a very long day. She was a businesswoman, in her early thirties, who either had to accept being ground down to a fraction of her innate potential or risk everything and confront the life-and-death decisions of involvement in the movement to challenge the white domination and black exclusion of Mississippi politics. She had a beautiful face, which that day looked exhausted, but her strength and determination shone through the fatigue; she was ready to do whatever had to be done. For me, as Maya Angelou says, she was a true "shero."

I saw Mrs. Gray twenty-five years later; we were both gray-haired, and the ten or so years' difference in our ages hardly seemed to matter. We laughed together when I told her that in my twenties I knew that I wanted to be just like her when I grew up. But in fact, to me, that was no joke, because in the early sixties, when I was twenty-two years old, it was people like her who set an example and definition of values that framed my adult life.

The 1960s civil rights movement had a profound and lasting impact, not only on people like me who were directly involved in it, but on how the American people in general looked at, questioned, and acted on social and political issues. The powerful images created by the "direct action" challenges of the movement began to focus the awareness of the American public on serious issues. The 1964 Mississippi Summer Project deepened that awareness by making a direct connection between thousands of Americans from every part of the country by involving them in the Southern Freedom Movement. SNCC understood that the government would cease to ignore the disenfranchisement of and brutality against black Mississippians if that terror were also directed at whites. If the federal government wouldn't come to Mississippi, they would force the issue by bringing America to Mississippi. When the student volunteers came south from all over the country, they brought not only themselves but also the attention and concern of their families, friends, and churches, of their hometown and state, as well as of national newspapers, magazines, radio, and TV. This interracial national networking of the civil rights movement created a broad coalition of individuals and groups that united tens of thousands of everyday people providing an environment for discussion of and a vehicle for action in the fight for human rights and justice. It was a turning point in the culture of American politics.

The impact of this national awakening and activism began to spill over into other issues, especially the opposition to the Vietnam War. The impact the civil rights movement had on the sociopolitical atmosphere of the country can be measured by contrasting the pre- and post-1964 antiwar movements. Prior to 1964, anti–Vietnam War efforts were limited to a small number of organizations and individuals who identified themselves as the "New Left" and to some pacifist organizations. They had little success in spreading that protest beyond their small groups. In 1963 I took part in antiwar demonstrations at the University of Wisconsin that involved no more than three hundred protesters. By the spring of 1965 a student strike against the war was able to close down the entire university of fifty thousand students. The growth of the antiwar movement was initially fueled by a higher social and political consciousness as a direct result of the southern black Freedom Movement, and further activated by the American military's effort to draft young men. The absolutist moral values espoused by the movement were applied to a war that had no just purpose, and the Freedom Movement's activist mode was used to fight it.

It is ironic that as social activism spread throughout the country the momentum of the southern civil rights movement began to slow down. Because SNCC had played such a pivotal role during the early sixties, its diminished role after 1965 has become the focus of much attention. I simply think its time had come and gone. It had done what it could do. I believe that SNCC's accomplishments should be recognized and its limitations accepted as just one phase of the historical continuum of the black struggle against the aftermath of slavery; organizational longevity in itself has no inherent value.

Originally SNCC came into existence to coordinate the student sit-ins, and then its work changed to full-time community organizing. The staff were the messengers; they carried the torch to the most rabid racist center of the country, with the vision that if they could crack the system in Mississippi, the rest of the South would follow. The black community was ready to stand up to the white racist terror and to demand its rights, and once a previously isolated and ignored people were linked to the rest of America through the 1964 Summer Project, their audacious and heroic example took the rest of the South and the country with them. Legal segregation—the disenfranchisement of the black population and the police state mentality that enforced it—was being confronted and overcome one step at a time. Racially, Mississippi and the rest of the South were beginning to be on somewhat of a par with the rest of the

country. And although some people would say that that is a sorry state of affairs, I've never met anyone who experienced the pre-1960s South who didn't
believe that these changes were momentous steps in the freedom struggle.

Although I've always felt that SNCC was successful in its time and place,
it is undeniable that after the Summer Project and the Congressional Challenge it began to lose focus and founder as its direction became unclear
and as some first-generation activists like Bob Moses, who played such a key
role in the Mississippi movement, began to move on. Recently, I was amazed
to learn that SNCC's decline in this transitional period is often attributed
to schisms, factional fighting, blatant antiwhite sentiment, and even to the
"tongue-in-cheek" self-mocking group of people who characterized themselves as "freedom highs." To me, these "eruptions" were just the symptoms,
the open sores, of an organization dying off, an organization without a clear
programmatic vision and the ability to carry one out. At first I laughed at the
absurdity of the idea that these conflicts could be seen as having caused SNCC's
decline. Yet I later became seriously concerned when I learned that such simplistic and sensationalized accounts of the changes within SNCC were finding
their way into civil rights history. Fortunately, we now have more scholarly
research to turn to, such as Charles M. Payne's *I've Got the Light of Freedom*,
which looks at the post-1964 era of SNCC in great detail and with a subtle understanding of the complexities of that time, placing the group's demise in
historical perspective.

In fact, there were many changes within SNCC during 1964–65. One major
one was the addition of large numbers of staff, both black and white, after the
Summer Project. It follows that any time an organization goes from a small,
intimate group — in the case of the movement, from the "Beloved Community" that Casey and Penny talk of — to a much bigger, geographically scattered one, there's going to be a qualitative change in how that organization
feels, for the simple reason that you don't know people as well as you did
before. However, divisions and tensions were nothing new within SNCC. There
were regional North-South divisions, class divisions, rural-urban differences,
gender differences, differences in leadership styles, programmatic and struc-
tural differences — as well, in 1964–65, as the increasing black-white tensions
as many more whites began to work in Mississippi. But in true jingoist fashion,
the spotlight has been on racial strains alone, because it's the "juiciest" subject

and feeds America's prurient racial obsession. Therefore, it has been blown out of proportion. Once in an interview, I was questioned about the "breakup" of SNCC and how I felt about "being made to leave because I was white." I pointed out that I'd left in July 1965, several years before anyone was asked to leave "because" they were white, so the question really didn't relate to the time period I worked with SNCC. The fact that the interviewer was telescoping time in order to address this "vital" question didn't seem to bother her; that is what she was interested in, so she just rearranged the question and instead asked me to comment on "whites being asked to leave SNCC."

Certainly there were racial strains within SNCC, but so what? After three hundred years of racial separation, why should that be surprising, especially in a civil rights organization that was the youngest, most personally radical, and up front about all types of conflict. In the early sixties, the movement was the only interracial situation in which racial issues were confronted openly and blacks were matter of fact about their antagonisms, suspicions, and contradictions with whites, as well as their pride in their own culture. Therefore, it makes sense that it was where the confusing and painful dialectic of black separation from white allies would be first played out. It wasn't just a coincidence that the late-sixties "Black Power" movement grew out of a nearly all-black SNCC. The growth of racial consciousness and pride that burst into the mass media with the call for Black Power and the affirmation that "black is beautiful" did not arrive without gestation and evolution in the black community.

There's no way you can step out of history, just as there's no way you can step out of your own skin. Nonetheless, understanding that doesn't ease the personal pain and humiliation of being dumped on because you're white. Bigotry and mob behavior isn't pretty, no matter where or when it occurs. I still cringe at the memory of the jeering face and snide remarks of a black SNCC worker (now long married to a white partner) who taunted me and a gentle young black man when word got around that we were spending time together. In 1965 it began to be politically incorrect in some movement circles, especially those dominated by northern black college students, for blacks to be personally involved with whites, at least in public. Many interracial friendships and romances were cut off or went underground — another convolution of the American racial drama. The fact that movement whites had acted right-

eously couldn't shield us from the racial juggernaut set in motion three centuries earlier. We all were caught at a cultural crossroads, and the best white
movement workers could do was try to understand this new form of racial
separation in its historical context and deal with its painful exclusion with the
same dignity that African Americans had done so for so long. I was grateful
that I had encountered black nationalism during my self-created college program in African American studies and that I had been somewhat inoculated
with it in 1963 in New York City, so that when it began to surface in SNCC I
wasn't unprepared for it. And on a gut level, I was thankful to be thick skinned.

Other, less obvious gender and race issues that came to be publicly discussed
years later were also being raised within the movement community in the
sixties. At a SNCC staff meeting in Waveland, Mississippi, in November 1964
the "role of women" in the movement was raised as an issue that we needed
to begin to discuss. It's not surprising that among a group of people who were
fighting for social justice gender discrepancies would be noticed and questioned. But the folklore that has grown up around this event is totally out of
proportion to and distorts what actually happened. An example is the idea that
the "dastardly" and backward statement by Stokely Carmichael "that the position of women in the movement is prone" set off some sort of feminist revolt.
That is a funny line today, and it was then, and no one took it any other way.
Especially not Stokely, Casey, or me, several of the alleged antagonists in this
debate, who were part of a group of black and white, northern and southern
men and women partying together on the Waveland Pier. The memory of that
night was literally highlighted in my memory because soon after we left it, the
pier was fire-bombed.

It was strange being white and identifying with black people just as radical
blacks began their disassociation from whites. Being in the movement was
an immersion, a baptism, and you saw reality from a black point of view
whether you were working in the movement or not, and whether black people
were speaking to you or not. Having white skin in a Euro-centered, white-
dominated racist culture obscured who I was and the rage and pain I shared
with the black community. Many whites feel that people like me are obsessed
with race, but I believe, at best, such critics are ignorant of and oblivious to

the depth of the outrages to which African Americans are subjected. Since the sixties I've often found myself in situations where I was trying to interpret to other whites how they might better understand racism and racial conflict. One thing that I've always found is that if you're white, other white people feel free to make racist remarks to you about blacks. They seem to assume a racial bonding—or bondage, depending on your point of view—based on your white skin. When I lived in New York City in the late sixties it seemed that every cab driver had some racial ax to grind. I often had to stop a cab and get out so as not to have to listen to a harangue about how "da niggers" were trying to "get us" (by demanding such radical measures as civilian review of charges of police brutality twenty-five years before the Rodney King beating). Of course, this is an extreme example, but the depth of white racism even in "people of goodwill" is ultimately defined by the limitations of their understanding of what racism is. The fact that white Americans were so shocked to find such a divergence of opinion between whites and blacks on the O. J. Simpson case proved once again how little white people know about the distrust black folks have of the white establishment, from the media to the police, and how much rage and alienation are generated by the continual racism African Americans suffer, whether from the poor education of their children, the murder of an Amadou Diallo or the actions of L.A. "cops who routinely frame the innocent by planting ('throwing down') drugs and guns, smack around ('thump') citizens on the street for kicks and perjure themselves ('join the liars' club') to get convictions [in which] . . . public defenders predict upwards of 4,000 cases could be affected" (*Time*, March 2000).

And yet many whites, even those who supported the civil rights movement of the sixties, think that racism is a thing of the past and that black people are just whining and self-indulgent when they raise the issue. Recently, at an art gallery, an African American poet was exhibiting a sociobiographical photographic essay that mixed personal images with photos of devastated inner city streets. A white acquaintance, an artist, whispered to me in a mocking tone, "Oh, poor little black girl, look what she had to contend with." This same person would never consider herself a racist. Yet when no black person was in earshot, she betrayed hostility, insensitivity, and an absence of any understanding of the permutations of racism and how it is played out.

A sensitivity to questions of race sets you apart, defines the world you inhabit, and is one of the determining factors about people with whom you can be close. That race consciousness left many white people out in the cold as they began to migrate out of the movement. I was fortunate that when I left in the summer of 1965 I did so with my lifelong friend Emmie Adams and moved in circles with other movement people, including Elaine DeLott, Casey Hayden, and Alan Ribback.

Although I spent the next five or six years in personal pursuits, my political self was never far from the surface. In today's terms, political correctness was absolutely essential to me, especially when it came to race. This defined and limited my world. I was conscious of that and couldn't have had it any other way.

Meeting men outside the movement who understood about racism was a real problem until I met my first husband, Bob Moses. He was a young white jazz drummer, and his respect for the African American masters of that music and his understanding of and outrage about the impact of racism on the creative, social, and economic realities of the music business made him a kindred spirit. In college when I first was introduced to jazz I intuitively understood that it was kind of "beyond" me, but Mose, in an informal way, was a wonderful teacher and he helped me to bridge my musical limitations. He listened to music all the time, focusing on either an instrument or artist for days, sometimes weeks, at a time, commenting on and putting the music into a creative and developmental perspective. It was music appreciation 101 to 2001, woven into my everyday life. The highlights of that experience came when, several times a week, we'd go to hear live music. In retrospect I realized how fortunate I was to have my musical sensibilities shaped by masters of this incredibly complex and beautiful music, which was primarily an innovation of African American artists.

My exposure to jazz reinforced everything I'd learned and absorbed in the South. There was music everywhere in the black Mississippi community. The soulful blues on jukeboxes, the plaintive wail of Sam Cook proclaiming "change gonna come" that floated out of cafes and grocery stores, the driving rhythmic chants of gospel music, and the inspiring energy of Freedom Songs were always in the air. During that time I heard only black music because that's all black folks listened to. Black radio, something I'd never even known existed before living in Mississippi, flourished because of the black communities' inventiveness and distinctive "make do" attitude. Like the movement, black radio operated on a shoestring. With the barest minimum of technical facilities and a fraction of the resources available to any white college radio station, it "made do" and was an essential link in a creative musical culture that was the envy of thousands of white imitators, from Elvis Presley to the Rolling Stones. Even though American racist Euro-centrism was as brutal to the cultural genius of African Americans as it had been to Emmett Till, the indomitable spirit, intelligence, and creativity of a Fannie Lou Hamer or an Art Tatum could not be denied. Just as the civil rights movement unleashed the creative energies of a generation of American activists, the musical genius of African Americans has changed the course of twentieth-century music throughout the world.

The values and the lessons of the movement stayed with me into the seventies, when I resumed what I think of as my public self. Mose was part of an interracial jazz rock band, "Compost," that was offered a recording contract with Columbia Records. At the last moment the manager of the group dropped out of the negotiations, so the wives of the band members and other assorted friends filled in. Because of my movement experience dealing with lawyers and legalese, I took on the recording contract negotiations. I didn't know a thing about record contracts, but with typical movement-like confidence I figured it couldn't be more complicated than the Convention or the Congressional Challenge and so I set out to find out what I needed to know. I continued to learn about the music business as I went along. If I could organize a car caravan from Mississippi to Washington, D.C., how different could it be to organize a tour for a band?

By the mid-seventies my marriage to Bob Moses had ended, but I continued to work in the music business representing reggae, pop, and jazz musicians. I continually experienced the double standard of that industry when working with mainstream record companies, whose minimum recording budgets were sixty or seventy thousand dollars, while at the same time representing jazz musicians who were recording for specialty jazz labels with budgets of seven to ten thousand dollars. The disparity of monies available was almost in inverse proportion to the quality of the music involved. The major record companies mirrored American values: the simpler and more predictable the music, the more support it got. In the seventies the big labels had little interest in African American jazz, whose standard of quality was its originality. Racism and the capitalist bottom line set the industry standard. And yet jazz, the true American classical music, thrives today, as does the creative African American community that produced it.

My involvement in the music world kept me connected to African Americans and the culture of the black community during a time when black nationalism was making it difficult, if not impossible, for whites and blacks to interact. The jazz world in particular reflected the vibrant and generous spirit that I'd come to know in the movement, welcoming anyone who shared an appreciation of its creative expression.

The work pattern that I developed in the movement has remained with me ever since. It is a combination of what I was good at: organization, administration, critical thinking, planning, and the willingness to work hard for what I was committed to. In the movement, whether you were running a mimeograph machine, working in a Freedom School, or coordinating a complex legal procedure, you worked to the limits of your abilities. Even on the days when you were just answering telephones, it wasn't like a nine-to-five, ho-hum job. In the movement people were confronting a three-hundred-year-old pattern of brutality, and that telephone call could be a person's link to safety. In the movement there were no little jobs, there were only hardworking people, who sometimes did little things. The particulars of whatever someone was doing didn't matter, only the big picture. I learned an appreciation and respect for the importance of each step along the way. As a result, I have never felt diminished at being a "behind-the-scenes" person. Not everyone can be a congressional candidate, or be the one on stage, but if you're centered and doing work that you've chosen and believe in, I think you can count yourself blessed.

In SNCC I worked with Lawrence Guyot, who was chairman of the MFDP and an all-around extraordinary person. There was nothing he was cowed by, not the White Citizen Councils or smart and capable women. One night he sat quietly in the kitchen of the Tougaloo house while four or five of us women laughed, cried, and lamented the male-female question over a bottle of scotch. When someone commented on his being the only man there, he responded, in his typical theatrical style, that it had been a great privilege to just listen, that it was one of the most educational evenings of his life. And he meant it. Guyot was able to listen to and work with anyone. He treated a delta share-cropper, a New York lawyer, a minister, a barber, a high school activist, or a white volunteer with equal respect—or disdain, depending on their actions. As long as you had something to contribute you were okay with him. We worked together on the Congressional Challenge doing whatever was needed. Sometimes this would involve strategizing about the hearings, other times it would be collating documents. If you were there and doing the work, you were part of it. It felt great.

Years later I had a similar experience working with a Jamaican man named Herbie Miller, who was the personal manager of the reggae musician Peter Tosh. Tosh had just signed with the Rolling Stones' new label and was about to record an album and open for the Stones on their 1978 world tour. Herbie was based in Jamaica and needed a partner to work with him in the United States and Europe. I had experience producing records and organizing tours and, more important, I knew Jamaica, having spent time there during the past eight years visiting my SNCC sista, Emmie Adams, now a Jamaican citizen.

Representation of Peter Tosh was a high-profile situation, and there were many people vying for the position. Herbie choose me because my business experience was blended with my knowledge and appreciation of both Jamai-can and African American music and culture. I understood that the reggae scene, in its broad context, was a creative expression of a postcolonial society trying to set the "shitstem"—to use the inimitable expression of Peter Tosh—straight and proclaim the unity of all peoples of Africa and the African Dias-pora ("No matter where you come from, if you're a black man, you're an Afri-can"—Tosh lyric).

With Herbie Miller and Tosh's legal and financial advisors I was involved in all major decision making as well as organizing the day-to-day work. Jamaica is a third world country, and trying to run an international business from there, especially in 1978, without big money and with an almost nonexistent phone system, was next to impossible. Fortunately, one of the things I learned in the movement was the "make do" mode of operating, so these practical limita-tions were never insurmountable. The musical experience I'd absorbed in Mississippi and my later exposure to the varied musical sounds of the African

American experience also enabled me to know which American vocalists and musicians would be compatible with the Jamaican sound for recording and in performance.

Choosing me, a white woman, to represent a politically significant major black musician internationally was a brave thing for Herbie Miller to do, and he took plenty of heat for it. But he is an exceptionally strong-minded and moral person who wouldn't allow himself to be restricted by either black or white racial stereotypes. We shared the same values and respected each other and therefore worked well together. We will be lifelong friends, and in the music business that's saying something.

In the years from 1981 to 1998 I was married to Kenny Burrell. Kenny is a master of the jazz guitar, as well as a composer and a dedicated teacher. He has never been on a picket line or in an organized demonstration, and yet he is one of the most political people I have ever known. His public life has been focused on extending the artistic legacy of jazz, in securing acknowledgment of its creative importance and recognition of the African American artists who have been its major innovators. While sharing a life with him I had an intimate view of the impact of cultural racism. I also saw how with a conscious, movement-like determination and a supportive network Kenny maintained artistic and personal integrity and inspired generations of African American musicians to remain true to themselves and to their cultural heritage; in movement fashion he was another "soldier in the army . . . holding up freedom's banner." I was proud to be part of that network, whether I was mixing the sound for a Carnegie Hall concert, negotiating the terms of a Japanese tour, or picking up dry cleaning, I felt that I was continuing to make a contribution. In the sixties, Mississippi blacks were expected "to stay in their place," remain sharecroppers, and not dare to think of graduating from Ole Miss. Similarly, black jazz musicians were expected to play in smoky, noisy nightclubs while white European-style classical musicians performed in concert halls. But just as black Mississippians broke the social and economic bonds of the cotton field, so have jazz musicians like Dizzy Gillespie and Kenny Burrell taken their place in the concert halls of Europe, Japan, and, finally, America.

Looking at the piece of movement history that I was a part of, it strikes me that history happens in little trickles at a time, building up to a stream that will eventually knock down the dam. Scholars look for major events to footnote the historical path, but without the small advances, the change in consciousness and change in reality can't happen. SNCC was a part of the historical stream, laying the groundwork for the next phase of the struggle: the discourse about the subtler forms of racial bigotry and its impact on the economic, social, political, artistic, and personal life of the black community. The movement also initiated a pattern of social activism that has redefined the way Americans relate to local and global concerns.

I was able to see the change of consciousness within my own family. In June 1965 I got out of jail after a demonstration in Jackson and found a letter from my mother that said how ashamed my folks were of me. They felt that they had to make up stories about where I was and what I was doing, to hide from family and friends the fact that I was in Mississippi involved in "that mess." My parents were never rabid racists; they were just average first-generation working-class Americans. They accepted the American idea that all people should be treated fairly, but they never could understand why I was so concerned about what happened to black people. They always asked, why didn't I stick to my "own kind" and be concerned with "my own"?

I was finally able to answer that question for my mother thirty years later as she faced the desperation of dealing with my father as he slipped into dementia and finally death. At this point they were living in Florida, and at each setback in my father's condition I would travel there from New York and stay until a solution could be found. In addition to her shock and grief at seeing her husband of sixty years become infantile, my mother was overwhelmed by the medical bureaucracy. Each time I came, she would begin crying, repeating that she couldn't imagine what she would have done without my help. She was amazed that I was there for her as each new crisis unfolded, and admitted that she'd never realized how dependable, sympathetic, and loving I was. One night as we sat cuddled together grieving the loss of my dad, I explained that I was the same person, with the same love and sense of doing the right thing for her and my family, as the person who went to Mississippi. It had taken a long time, but she finally understood.

Beginning in the seventies my parents and I began a slow and gradual reconciliation. My parents had also evolved and grown in their own relationship and their attitudes to the world, especially their attitudes about race. They accepted the fact that I'd married an African American man. As they got to know him, his mother, and his children, they came to love him and see his family as part of our extended family, a wonderful blending of Italian Americans from the Bronx and African Americans from Detroit. In my mother's own words (from her holiday report in her retirement community newsletter), "I feel very lucky, I have a truly wonderful son-in-law." My folks had come a long way from their narrow working-class background. I see that transformation as a reflection of the changed American consciousness that was brought about by the impact of the civil rights movement of the 1960s. For people like my parents, whose main information source is television, programs about and public discussion of racism, inspired by the movement, made it possible for them to begin to accept the idea of an interracial world. Once African American people took on real-life personalities, the circle was completed. Familiarity breeds respect.

Circle of Trust

SUE THRASHER

It is popular now when talking about the sixties to view it as either the quintessential romantic revolutionary moment or a decade waylaid by personal indulgences of sex, drugs, and rock and roll. I believe that the rock and roll music was grand, that the sex was freeing but often degrading to women, and that the drugs helped destroy us. But that is not what the sixties were to me.

I believe the sixties started in 1955 when Rosa Parks refused to move from her seat on a Montgomery bus, and ended at some imprecise moment in the early 1970s, perhaps when four students were gunned down by National Guardsmen at Kent State. In the intervening years the Southern Freedom Movement, characterized by the startling courage of black southerners of all generations, marched its way into the nation's consciousness, forever changing the landscape of the South and the nation. It was what one freedom worker called "a dazzling moment of clarity," a moment when choosing between right and wrong had no blurry edges, and when choosing the future over the past was essential. For that brief historical moment, believing we could create a community based on justice and equality, we did. As the new millennium begins, and we seem farther and farther away from resolving the issues of racism that have plagued our country's history, I become ever more grateful that I was privileged to have been a participant in what Jim Forman called "the band of brothers, circle of trust."

I entered high school in 1955, the year the Montgomery Bus Boycott started, and graduated in 1959, one year before the sit-in movement began in Greensboro, North Carolina. Savannah, Tennessee, where I grew up, sits beside the Tennessee River shortly after it begins flowing north from the Muscle Shoals, Alabama, area. It is within a hundred miles of Arkansas, where Governor Orval Faubus stood in the schoolhouse door to prevent black children from entering; Mississippi is a mere ten miles to the south, and Alabama, twenty to the southeast. I distinctly remember discussions in my family and in the larger community about the Supreme Court decision of 1954. And just as vividly, I recall the attempts to integrate the public schools in Clinton, Tennessee. Local papers were filled with news about the National Guard troops that Governor Frank Clement had called out to protect the rights of the black students. But by and large the challenges made to the segregated South during those years seemed distant. No black families had come forward in Savannah to send their children to the white schools, and if there was a voting rights issue, there was no locally organized movement to challenge it — at least not one that was visible to the white community.

I was a teenager, and my attention was focused on the wonderful, slightly dangerous music being made by Sun Records in nearby Memphis, specifically that of a silver-tongued, hip-swiveling, lip-curling boy named Elvis. I practiced emulating the dance steps I saw on *American Bandstand*, and tried to hold my own in the complicated social world of Central High School. For me, 1955 was the year of the Chevrolet.

My parents came from farming families in McNairy County in West Tennessee. My mom's dad, Grandfather DeLaney, was also a cabinet and furniture maker. After my parents married, Daddy farmed and worked as a carpenter. Mama's first baby died at birth, and then she had my older sister, Mildred, and two years later, Joe Frank. There was a seven-year intermission before my brother Carl was born, and I followed two years later in 1941, slightly ahead of the boomer generation.

Like others of their generation, World War II took my parents off the farm. In 1942, Daddy moved the family to Oak Ridge, Tennessee, where there was a newly established defense plant. He got a job building houses for defense workers. I don't think my parents or anyone else at the time knew that Oak

Ridge was a key site for building components of the bombs that were later dropped on Hiroshima and Nagasaki. For them, it meant their first real paychecks. Even Mama got a job, driving a payroll truck for the army. Years later, when I did an oral history interview with her, I realized how important this time was for her. Like other Rosie the Riveters, she never really wanted to go back to being a housewife. She was never good at being a traditional homemaker — not a great cook or a model housekeeper — so, fortunately, I did not grow up with that as my female role model.

When the war was over, Mom and Dad moved to Savannah, the county seat of Hardin County, just east of McNairy. Both of them went to work for the Brown Shoe Company, the only factory in town. Mama worked there until after I graduated from high school, but it wasn't to Daddy's liking. He was a carpenter by trade, but a farmer at heart: he wanted his own piece of land. As soon as possible, therefore, he bought some land and moved us to the country.

I have very fond memories of my growing years in the little town of Savannah. I associate my childhood with always being outdoors — on the street, at the neighbors, in the nearby store where I would buy a Coca-Cola in a bottle and fill it with a bag of salted peanuts, copying the habits of my older sister and brother. Because both our parents worked, Carl and I were left in the care of Mildred. I absolutely adored Mildred; we all called her "Sister." When I was six and she was seventeen, she married one of the best-looking boys in town, a sailor recently returned from war. They set up housekeeping in a tiny house near his parents, and I remember thinking (for a while) that this was my dream also: to grow up, marry, and settle in a house in Savannah.

I started school at the age of six at Savannah Elementary. It was a very big day for me, and for my mother, who was nervous about my safety. I was put in Carl's charge. He walked me to school and to my class, and I was told to wait for him at the end of the day. I must have waited for a millisecond, decided I had missed him, and proceeded to walk home by myself. He wasn't at home, so I walked back to school to find him. Needless to say, my mother was more than a little alarmed by this turn of events, but I felt totally capable and unafraid. My independent streak had made an early showing.

By the time I was in the second grade, Daddy had scraped together enough money to buy a farm on the other side of the river. He did carpentry work in the winter when he couldn't farm, but from spring through fall he was a farmer. He loved working the land; for him, it was a way of life. Owning his own land was important to him, but in truth, I think it was always owned by the bank. I remember tense moments of "settling up" at the end of growing season every year, the two of them always wondering whether they were going to be able to pay the bank note. Mostly, we lived on Mama's weekly paycheck from the factory.

Another important thing I recall about this time is the way we shared in the work. Daddy cooked breakfast every morning, and both he and my brother helped around the house. We shared most of the work on the farm, although my brother learned early to drive the tractor and do the plowing. Later, I learned to drive the tractor, but I was never taught how to use the heavy equipment. I think as we got older, I began taking more responsibility in the house and my brother began doing more of the outside chores, like feeding the stock. But I grew up in a household where work was not narrowly defined by gender.

On the farm we grew cotton, corn, and soybeans. We had minimal equipment. I know that my dad always rented or borrowed a large harvester in the fall for the corn, and as for the cotton, we chopped and picked it by hand. The big landowners would hire black people to pick their cotton and pay them three dollars a day, but small family farmers got their kids to do it. There was really only Carl and me at home then, since Mildred was married and Joe had joined the air force. While in the service he married Nell, a waitress at the local coffee shop. Pretty soon Mildred and Joe started their own families, and by the age of seven I was an aunt for the first time.

I didn't like farming, but I loved the land. I could run free in the country, with plenty of space to explore. My favorite place was the little stream on the backside of the property. I spent hours there trying to catch tadpoles or watching crawfish climb against the current. We had a huge garden, a strawberry patch, a potato patch (for Irish potatoes), a sweet potato patch, an orchard I could lose myself in, and a barn with a wonderful hayloft. Those were the things I liked about the farm.

What I didn't like was all the hard work. In the summer, my dad and brother and I canned everything it was possible to can from the garden — green beans, okra, beet pickles, lima beans, tomatoes. And we didn't stop at the garden. When the season was right, Daddy would bring in several bushels of peaches from the orchard and we would peel and can them. We made apple sauce and then cut up apples to dry on the roof of the henhouse.

All of this wasn't so bad, but as soon as I was old enough my brother and I became the primary labor for our cotton fields. I didn't mind "chopping" the cotton — going down each row and cleaning out the grass — but I never liked picking cotton. I was not good at it, and began rebelling in rather odd ways — like sitting on my cotton sack and singing. My own version of a sit-down strike, I suppose. My Dad spanked me once, but after that I think he gave up. I'm proud to say I never ever picked a hundred pounds a day. Good cotton pickers will think me a slacker, and they are right. It was just something I didn't want to become good at. Years later, I developed the same attitude toward typing, fearing that if I ever got really good at it I would be consigned to earning a living doing it.

After we moved to the country, Carl and I continued going to school in Savannah. Even though the school system was quite small, it offered a much better education than the rural county schools, where many of the teachers had no college degrees. I never asked my mother how she figured out that this would make a difference for Carl and me, but whatever her reasons, she was determined to keep us in the best school. When we moved to the farm, she paid a personal visit to the county school superintendent and asked if she could keep us in the town school as long as she delivered us and picked us up in the afternoon. Back then, the county school superintendent was elected, and he was one of the most powerful men in the county because of the number of jobs he controlled. I don't know what her arguments were, but he agreed. So every morning we got up very early and drove to school with my mother when she went to work at the factory. She had to be at work by seven o'clock, which meant we arrived at school a little before seven. We got there an hour before anyone else arrived, and we stayed an hour later in the afternoon.

I liked the coziness of riding to school with Mama, but I was scared of the levee. A narrow two-lane highway, it seemed held together, to my childhood eyes, by concrete posts and steel cables as it stretched for two miles across prime Tennessee River bottomland. Drainage ditches cradled each side, adding to my anxiety that we would career off the levee and end up in the dark, muddy water. Even worse were the times when the entire bottomland was flooded and angry, swirling water lapped at the sides. In the early summer, when the corn and soybeans were growing, I was less afraid. But on foggy, rainy mornings I held my breath until we were safely across the river.

Every morning I looked for the Cherry Mansion. Sitting on a small bluff overlooking the Tennessee River, it came into view just as we crested the long incline of the bridge. One of Savannah's prized possessions, the mansion was both a symbol of the old South and a bitter reminder of its downfall. It had served as General Ulysses S. Grant's headquarters during the Battle of Shiloh — a mere seven or eight miles down the river. I was fascinated by its history, and envious of the people who lived there now. I often imagined Grant in the house barking alcoholic orders to his troops and waiting for his reinforcements.

Shiloh National Military Park was a very important part of our local history, but it was also very much a part of the present, a way of defining who we were as southerners. I grew up with it. Every class picnic I had in grammar school was held "on the park." Deviled eggs, macaroni salad, and Confederate flags. Like the rest of my friends, I maintained a righteous indignation that the park tour included only one monument devoted to the Confederacy. This never seemed quite fair to me. It was, after all, southern soil, and southerners as well as Yankees had died. But the monuments throughout the park were dedicated to the victors. Dead Union soldiers are buried in neat rows in the official cemetery overlooking the river. The sons of the Confederacy are buried in trenches. Even to this day, there is a melancholy quality to me about these trenches, the mass graves of the Confederate dead. How was it, I wonder, that these sons of the South, mostly poor farm boys, come to believe that fighting for an aristocratic slaveholding society was in their best interests? Years later I discovered that, like many other southerners, I had ancestors on my father's side of the family who had fought for the union. Across the park is Bloody Pond, where the water turned red from so many wounded dragging themselves there for water. Even on a lovely spring day, when the peach trees in the orchard are in bloom, there is still an overwhelming sadness about this place. It is a reminder of the brutality of war, and the uselessness of it all.

I really tried to be a good southerner. I bought Confederate flags in the park gift shop and decorated my room with them. I was outraged that "we" had only the one monument. Like everyone else around me, I succumbed to the mythological history of the South. Thankfully, I couldn't sustain it. There are some contradictions I won't embrace, and by the early 1960s a new history was working its way into my consciousness, turning the old symbols sour.

My parents were decent, good people. They neither feared nor hated black people, and they did not instill fear or hate in me. But they lived, and I lived for the first twenty years of my life, in a segregated society. There was one black family who lived in the countryside close to us. The father farmed with my father on occasion. They would do some harvesting together and share equipment. Most of the black people in the county either lived in Savannah or in a rural community farther south called Hookers Bend. Later, much later, I became aware that the students from there were bused every day to go to school in Savannah. The trip was at least an hour each way.

I remember listening in on a conversation Daddy had with a neighbor one night, about the 1954 Supreme Court decision on school desegregation. The discussion was quite heated, and I listened intently. I don't remember all the specifics, but I do remember that my father defended the decision. To the argument about interracial marriages, he simply said that if you educated black folks, they would not want to marry white people. I knew at the time that my father's position was different from that of most of the people around us. I was proud of him, but also a little afraid. It was clear from the tone of the argument that this was a very emotional issue.

My father and mother fished a lot, and they often fished side by side with black people on the riverbanks. I hated fishing because I was told you had to be quiet so as not to scare the fish away. When I think back about that time, I have no way of knowing, through the gauze of so many years, how paternalistic those relationships were or what the power dynamics were. To my innocent, youthful eyes, they seemed comfortable. I know that they weren't fearful.

I entered high school in the fall of 1955, completely happy to be a teenager and to leave elementary school behind. Central High was a consolidated, segregated school. Students—white students—were bused in, having graduated from nearby feeder elementary schools. The school had its own unique tracking system that seemed to be based in part on the personalities of the teachers.

I scored high on the placement exam when I entered and was therefore assigned to Latin class, a subject that was considered difficult. Students scoring in the medium range on the test were placed in a civics and government class, not so much because of the subject matter, but because it was taught by a slightly batty woman and therefore was not too demanding. Those who scored lowest on the test were placed in science. To understand how truly bizarre this system was, it is necessary to recall that the Russians and the United States were engaged in a race to see who could put a satellite into orbit first. In Savannah at least, the Cold War race for space was definitely overshadowed by the fact that the science class, taught by the basketball coach, was reserved for dummies and jocks.

I had virtually no science or math in high school and have spent a good part of my adult life cursing that fact. I did, however, discover words. One of the courses that enthralled me was journalism. I was chosen as editor of the school paper in my senior year, and quickly began to devote the majority of my time and energy to that job. In addition to Mrs. Sevier, who taught the class, I found a mentor in the local editor of our town weekly. He put printer's ink in my blood, teaching me more than I ever could have learned in a classroom. He was one of my first heroes, and I toyed briefly with the idea of going to work for him, but I knew I wanted to go to college instead. He was also one of my first heroes to fall when, a few years later, I opened the weekly paper and found his editorial about "Martin Luther Coon." It was a racist diatribe against King in particular, and the civil rights movement in general. I remember being angry, and I remember also a keen sense of loss and disappointment. But the tone of the editorial was such that I also remember being afraid: whatever else he thought of me, I knew that he could just as easily turn his venom against me. Less than three years had passed since he'd taught me about editing and publishing a paper. I was changing fast. I was changing fast because the events swirling around me demanded it.

I liked being in high school. I had a gang of girlfriends, and at the lunch hour we would meet in the home economics department and play rock and roll music and dance. Elvis was young and pretty then, but there was something else about Elvis, something I have never been able to define to my satisfaction. I've always thought that his music and his defiance and his overt sexuality opened the way for me and others to join up with the Freedom Movement when the time came. Because I don't quite understand it myself, this feeling is hard to defend. But in my soul, I know it is true. There was something dangerous about Elvis; and as far as I was concerned, it only added to his appeal.

I was as self-absorbed as any high school student. But quite early during those four years, I knew that I wanted to leave Savannah. Perhaps I had figured this out much earlier — when I staged my sit-down strike in the cotton field. I loved my sister dearly, but I had watched her go to work in the same shoe factory that our mother worked in. I didn't want that; I no longer dreamed of marrying and settling down in the little house. I knew the world was bigger, and I simply wanted to taste it. Going to college was my ticket out — or so I believed.

I've often thought that my involvement in the Freedom Movement was simply a matter of being in the right place at the right time — Nashville, Tennessee, in 1961.

The sit-in movement started in 1960, the year after I graduated from high school, but at that point I was still focused on how to make my dream of going to college possible. I pieced together some scholarships and went off to Lambuth, a small Methodist school in Jackson, Tennessee, about an hour away from home. My interest in journalism had taken a great leap: I now imagined myself as a religion writer. Never one to be forced into choices, I combined my interest in education, writing, and religion and decided I wanted to write educational curriculum for the church.

Growing up on the farm, the church was one of the most important institutions in my life. Mama and Daddy weren't big churchgoers, but every Sunday Carl and I would pile into the pickup truck with Mildred and her husband and go to Sunday school and church. It was a small country church, Methodist, and the preacher was there only twice a month. I became quite active in the Methodist Youth Fellowship — which, in fact, is where I first played spin-the-bottle. I loved the singing and I loved the fellowship.

The church provided a major part of my social life during this time, but more important, it taught me some of the basic values I brought to the Freedom Movement—like the fatherhood of God and the brotherhood of man. I believed in this concept, and inevitably these beliefs led me to turn away from the church later.

Lambuth wasn't much bigger than my high school, but the religion department had two professors who both took an interest in me and encouraged me in my thinking. One of them in particular, noticing that I was fast outgrowing Lambuth, encouraged me to think about going to Scarritt College in Nashville.

During my second year at Lambuth, I participated in a mock United Nations at Vanderbilt University in Nashville, sponsored by the Methodist Student Movement. There were students there who attended Lane College, a black college also located in Jackson. I was nineteen years old, and it was the very first time I had ever participated in an interracial event. Soon after I returned from Nashville, I was driving in downtown Jackson and I saw one of the Lane students I had met, picketing the local Woolworth's store. I think it was the first time I had ever seen anyone picketing outside of the news coverage on television. I didn't dare approach him or speak with him, but I was inspired by him. There was so much dignity and courage in his act, and I recognized that. But I also recognized the danger of what he was doing. There was something about that moment that made me stop and think. I felt like an outsider, an onlooker. And that's what I was. I was watching someone else make history.

I didn't have a clue how to show the solidarity that I felt. The result was an intense feeling of isolation and aloneness. I was growing ashamed of the South. Having been taught about the Fatherhood of God and the brotherhood of man, I couldn't see why anyone should have to picket in order to eat at a lunch counter.

A more defining moment happened a few weeks later. I was driving with several women friends in downtown Jackson on a Saturday afternoon. The downtown was crowded, and as we stopped for a red light a large number of people began crossing the street in front of us. The young woman driving the car was a good friend of mine. She was gregarious and knew how to make people laugh. I enjoyed her company. But that afternoon, I saw a side of her that scared me. Several young black girls were in the crosswalk directly in front of us. She slowly edged the car up, close enough that it appeared to me, and to them, that she planned to run them over, and snickered, "I'm going to get me a nigger." I do not remember the words that passed between us in the car. I remember making a feeble protest, but mostly I remember thinking that I was suffocating and that I had to get out of the car. I was angry, but I was also embarrassed and guilty. I had seen the fear in the eyes of the young black women. I was one of the people responsible for it. I knew that I didn't want to be in that situation again, and I was desperately afraid that the world of my friends was going to suck me in.

Just as I was about to finish the first semester of my second year, Mama was in a car accident, hit head on by a dump truck. For several days we didn't know whether she would live, and for several months after that we didn't know whether she would ever walk again. I left school to come home and help take care of her. I had independently assessed the situation, and I could see no other way. To this day, I appreciate the fact that I came to this decision on my own. Not one family member suggested it. But I knew that my father needed help.

It took a year and several operations before my mother recovered. Leaving school was a difficult decision. College was important to me, as was graduating in four years. I was fearful that I might not be able to return. My father had given up the farm by this time, and we were living in Savannah. My mother had continued to work at the factory while he did construction work on bridges in other parts of the state. In retrospect, I'm very happy for the time I had with my parents; it was a critical period for all of us. We got to know each other as adults. I've often felt that without that time, the support that Mama and Daddy later offered for my activism might not have been so clear. Later, when I made certain decisions, my parents trusted I had made the right ones.

Intent on returning to school, I had applied to the Methodist-run Scarritt College in Nashville, and I was accepted for that fall, with a scholarship. Although Scarritt was much smaller than even Lambuth, it had a substantial number of international students, as well as American students who had spent time working for the church overseas. It was primarily a graduate school, but if you wanted a degree in religion you could complete your last two years of undergraduate work there. The best thing about Scarritt, to my mind, was that it was a small school in the middle of a large university: it was part of the Joint

University Center, which included Vanderbilt University and Peabody College. Scarritt was also integrated, and had been for fifteen years, longer than any other predominantly white college in the area. Many older students who were missionaries working overseas returned to Scarritt for study leaves. This created an unusual college environment and a very different campus culture from typical undergraduate institutions. For example, young women had dorm curfews in those days. This had certainly been the case at Lambuth, where one of my most hair-raising experiences was sneaking in past Ma Mac, the dorm mother, one night after we had run out of gas on a country road. But at Scarritt, I was given a key to the front door of the dorm, and I could come and go as I pleased. Our individual rooms had no locks at all.

I arrived in Nashville in 1961, just at the tail end of the first wave of the sit-in movement there. Nashville had been a hotbed of activity, and many of the leaders of the sit-in movement came from Fisk University, Tennessee A&I University, and American Baptist Theological Seminary. Some of them, like James Bevel and Diane Nash Bevel, had moved on to work with the Southern Christian Leadership Conference (SCLC). But Bernard and Colia Lafayette, Lester McKinney, and John Lewis were still keeping a very active Student Nonviolent Coordinating Committee (SNCC) chapter alive.

I soon got involved in the student council at Scarritt. Although I was a good liberal and supported the civil rights movement, I was not inclined to activism — until one of the women students from the Fiji Islands was denied service at the local greasy spoon restaurant. A friend, Archie Allen, came to me and said, "What are you doing? I think that the council should pass a resolution saying how bad this is and that we support this student." And I said, "Sure." So I took some language from *The Methodist Discipline*, the book that states the basic doctrine of the Methodist Church, and began fashioning a resolution. As I recall, I just rewrote direct quotes, saying essentially that we believed in the fatherhood of God and the brotherhood of man, and therefore it was neither just nor right to deny this student service based on her skin color. I presented the resolution to the student council at our next meeting. Much to my dismay, it didn't pass! I was shocked. The result was a critical moment of understanding for me. In the first place, the resolution didn't say anything other than what we all repeated in church on any Sunday. Second, it was intended to support a member of our own community. In addition, this was a

Methodist school, and all of the students there were just like me: they planned to work for the church when they graduated.

It became quite an issue on the campus, and I, along with others who thought that we should "do something," became marginalized rather quickly. The argument, of course, was that we were getting involved in direct action, that what we were doing might lead to picketing, and that there had to be a better way to effect change. Of course, everyone agreed that it was too bad that she had been discriminated against, but everyone did not agree that something had to be done about it.

I came to understand in short order the fear that people had of "picketing" or "direct action." When I think back to my own feelings that day in Jackson, Tennessee, when I saw the young man from Lane picketing in front of Woolworth's, that fear of action makes more sense. There was something very powerful in the act of confronting segregation, in standing up and saying, "No more," with the body. It was very different than the endless talk about interracial gatherings and working behind the scenes. The action said, "Now." The reason my little resolution didn't pass is that it was thought to be too radical. Picketing was extreme. You could talk about race in the human relations councils or in the church, but to actually make demands was going too far. The statement, of course, was none of that, but it was perceived as supporting such activism.

I don't think the statement ever passed the council. If it did, we had to water it down so much that it became worthless. By the time this incident played itself out, however, there was a small nucleus of people on the campus who stood together — and who, like me, had suddenly been put in a position where our belief in the church was called into question.

Perceived by others as a radical didn't necessarily mean that I had become one. Even after that episode, I think I could have gone along and not gotten too involved, had it not been for Alice Cobb. Alice Cobb was one of those women who appeared to be totally helpless and absentminded. Later — much later, when I began to have some consciousness about the role of independent women in this society — I revised my perception of her. I believe that in order to do the things she wanted to do, she developed a nonthreatening persona as a "cover." Her tactic was quite simple: by appearing to be rather helpless, she became the kind of woman people like to take care of. The truth, of course, was that she was doing the leading. Under this guise, she traveled to the Middle East to work in Palestinian refugee camps. In her teaching, she sent her students into community situations that taught them about the real world. And she didn't flinch when the time came for white people to speak up in the South about matters of race.

Alice found me one morning at the campus mailboxes and asked me to go to a mass meeting with her that night, organized by the Nashville Christian Leadership Council (NCLC), the local affiliate of the SCLC. I remember thinking, "Why doesn't she leave me alone? Haven't I done enough?" I really did not want to go, because, I think, it was a step toward more engagement — which is exactly what all those people who wouldn't sign on to the council resolution were afraid of. When push came to shove, I, too, was reluctant to take even this tiny action step. Alice Cobb knew all this; but she was not someone I could easily say no to. After all, she seemed so harmless.

I went to the meeting with her that night, of course. I told myself it was because I didn't want to hurt her feelings, but the truth was, if I hadn't gone, she would have known it was because I was afraid, and I didn't want her to think that of me.

That evening changed me forever. I knew when the night was over that I would never go back to being who I was before. It was the first time I had ever heard black people speak for themselves. The first time I understood in even a small way the meaning of freedom and equality. The first time I got any real inkling about the costs and the pain of segregation. It was my dazzling moment of clarity. Of course, the entire Freedom Movement was that for me as well, but it all started that evening. There was no question about what was right and what was wrong, but I also understood something else: I knew then that I could stand on the side of the future, or I could stand on the side of the past. It really was that simple. And it was that simple because I could not turn away from, or deny the truth of, what I had heard that evening.

Nashville at that time was still a major center of the growing Freedom Movement. The sit-ins had started in Greensboro, North Carolina, but a significant sit-in movement had sprung up in Nashville as well, led by the Reverend James Lawson, a conscientious objector and disciple of Gandhi. The ambivalence of the institutional church on such issues was demonstrated when Vanderbilt Divinity School booted James Lawson out for his espousal of civil disobedience. In addition to Lawson, the local movement had a wealth of leadership, many of whom later became known both regionally and nationally. On that particular evening, I remember hearing the Reverend C. T. Vivian, a man with whom I would have the privilege to work more in the days to come; the Reverend J. Metz Rollins, a Presbyterian minister and advisor to the local SNCC chapter; and the Reverend Kelly Miller Smith, the local president of the NCLC. All three of these men played an important role in my increasing involvement in the movement.

While it was absolutely inconceivable that I could walk away from that meeting not knowing which side I was on, I had no clue what I was going to do about it. Slowly I, along with a few other students from Scarritt, got involved with both the local SNCC chapter and the NCLC. I started by going down to Kelly Miller Smith's church and doing support work behind the scenes. I was still reluctant to join a demonstration, because whites were always targeted by newspaper photographers and I was fearful of the repercussions at home should my picture appear in the paper. So it was not an easy step for me. Even though I thought my parents would support me in the end, I was certain they would be afraid for me. Thinking that I was shielding them, I never let on during this time about my increasing activism.

Other white students were involved in the Nashville sit-in movement earlier who were much braver. Paul LaPrad and Candie Carawan, both exchange students at Fisk University, were active participants in the lunch counter protests. The counterdemonstrators quickly developed a special venom for the whites who dared to show their solidarity, and Paul LaPrad suffered the unhappy fate of having lit cigarettes ground into his back.

Those were hectic and heady days. I was still reluctant to get involved in direct action, but the changes in my worldview were cataclysmic, and pretty soon my days were completely different. In addition to all the other things I appreciated about Scarritt, the intellectual growth and stimulation I found there were wonderful, and I loved the courses I was taking at both Scarritt and Peabody. However, it's a good thing I was as close to graduation as I was, because suddenly the movement seemed much more important than school. Although I managed to make it to my classes, almost every afternoon I showed up at Kelly Miller Smith's church to volunteer. I don't recall that I did anything useful, but I think Reverend Smith knew the education I was getting was important.

The Nashville Movement during this period had evolved into a broad-based effort, supported by the local black churches and the black political leadership. It was in a sense unique in that the local student movement, led by the local SNCC chapter, and the adult movement, led by NCLC, worked closely together. Even though many of the early sit-in leaders were now dispersed, having moved on to work at the regional level with SCLC and SNCC, the Nashville Movement remained vibrant and aggressive as it continued to push for integrated public accommodations and voting rights.

In the spring of 1963, demonstrators were using Kelly Miller Smith's church as a rallying point for marches to downtown Nashville as they continued to test public accommodations. By this time, the focus had shifted from the dime-store lunch counters to two cafeterias, and local high school students now made up the majority of the demonstrators—much as was happening in Birmingham and other places. I was at the church when they left, and there when they returned. One particular afternoon, some of the young students returned bloody, having been harassed and beaten by counterdemonstrators while the police stood by. The images of children in Nashville being beaten did not make national headlines, nor were they captured by television cameras. But those young black people, many of them hurt and bleeding as they returned to the church singing, made an indelible impression on my mind. Years later, I saw another image that reminded me of Nashville during this time: one of the Soweto uprising, with very young black students staring down a mob. That same spirit was alive and well in Nashville in the spring of 1963.

In addition to spending afternoons at Kelly Miller Smith's church, I had also begun to regularly attend local SNCC meetings. I was especially lucky in the people I met, some of whom had a lasting influence on me. John Lewis—now a member of Congress—was the head of the local chapter. John was from a rural community in Alabama and had come to Nashville to attend the American Baptist Theological Seminary. I also discovered a "homeboy," Lester McKinney. Lester wasn't really from Savannah, but he was from Bolivar, just a little to the west.

James Lawson had left Nashville by the time I arrived, so I learned about nonviolence from John Lewis, who had participated in Lawson's seminars. Being deeply religious, John, more than any other person I knew during this period, believed in the philosophy of nonviolence. While others were willing to employ it as a strategy, for John it was a deeply held belief. On yet another afternoon in Kelly Miller Smith's church, after yet another demonstration, John taught me a lesson in nonviolence, a lesson that was the beginning of my understanding about my whiteness and my class.

We were sitting in the front of the church, talking quietly. Lester was there, John, me, and a few others. Suddenly, three young white men entered the back of the church. I can't swear this is the actual truth, but the way I remember them is with tattoos on their arms and T-shirts, cigarette packs in the pockets. Not having had enough confrontation downtown, they had actually followed the demonstrators back to the church and were looking for trouble. John went and talked with them for a little while, and they went away. More than anything else in the world, I wanted to separate myself from these white southerners, to make it clear that I was not like them. I said something to the effect of "How dare those hoods come into this church." John looked me dead in the eye and said, "Don't call them hoods; they are human beings, just like you and me." He meant they were to be treated with dignity and respect. I was chastened, and I don't suspect that John ever fully knew how much, in that moment, he made me begin thinking about how important it was for white southerners to reach out to other white southerners.

Two friends at Scarritt were particularly important to me during this period. Gerry Bode was a student from Texas studying to be a director of religious education. Whereas involvement in the movement caused me to flee the church, in Gerry's case it only increased her resolve to serve. After graduating from Scarritt, she became the director of religious education at an all-white church in North Georgia, and eventually she became a Methodist minister. Archie Allen was the friend who had first insisted that I "do something." The two of us continued to work together in the local movement and, later on, were founding members of a new regional organization.

Another important person in my life during this time was the Reverend Will D. Campbell. He was a preacher without a church. He had just published a book called *Race and the Renewal of the Church*. Will wore cowboy boots, smoked a pipe, and strummed a guitar. He believed that you had to love everybody. He came from Amite County, Mississippi, and had been politely asked to leave the University of Mississippi because of his radical views on race. Will shared a small office with Metz Rollins near the Scarritt campus — an outpost, of sorts, of the church's commitment to the Freedom Movement.

I was surrounded by church folk. Everyone at Scarritt were preparing to go into full-time church work, and I was no exception. It had long been my dream to work internationally, and I had entered Scarritt believing that I would work overseas as a short-term missionary. I still had my vision of writing educational curriculum for the church, and I was beginning to think that I could write for one of the church's publications as well.

Church administrators were pointing me in the direction of working in Indonesia, but suddenly I found myself having doubts. For one thing, it just didn't make sense to me to travel halfway around the world when there was so much to do in my own backyard. Second, I was beginning to have real disagreements with the local Methodist leadership and an escalating sense of disillusionment with the institutional church. Two critical incidents that year brought me face to face with the contradictions of the church as well as southern society.

A young minister and his wife from what was then Rhodesia came to Scarritt, and I became friends with them. His name was Abel Muzorewa. He later became a bishop in the new Zimbabwe and challenged Robert Mugabe for the presidency of that country. In Nashville, however, upon their arrival, the church that had sponsored them—the second largest Methodist church in Nashville, which had recently sponsored a white missionary family in Rhodesia—found Abel's wife unworthy of membership simply because she was black. It was unbelievable, really. The church had no black members and was unwilling to change its policy. In truth, I think the church felt rather proud of itself for allowing blacks to even visit the church on Sunday.

The second incident was an encounter I had with a Vanderbilt University psychologist working for the Methodist Church. In order to become a Methodist missionary, applicants are subjected to a series of interviews, including psychological. In the course of the interview he said to me, "If you were told to do something and you didn't think it was right, you wouldn't do it, would you?" And I said, "No," thinking, of course, that was the right answer. And he said, "Well, it is very important that you learn to take orders in the mission field. There are people who know more than you do, and you have to do what they tell you." This little exchange was like another light bulb going off, another contradiction unearthed. What if the orders were wrong? In truth, I suppose part of my caution was at the prospect of being ordered about at all.

In retrospect, it's entirely possible that I have blown these incidents completely out of proportion. The truth was, I simply didn't want to leave. My involvement in the local Nashville Movement had given me a new life. And in spite of all the things I said above about the old symbols turning sour, I loved the South. I wanted the South to be different, to free itself of segregation, to usher in a new era of equality. I believed we could do it. Without knowing exactly when it happened, I realized I had made the decision to stay in the South. But it was more than a decision to simply stay; it was a decision to work to change it.

When I graduated from Scarritt in spring 1963, I took a job at the Methodist Publishing House, located in Nashville. This allowed me to continue working with the local movement. One September weekend, I drove home to Savannah to visit my family. That Sunday afternoon I was driving back to Nashville when news came on the car radio that a church bombing in Birmingham had killed four little girls. I remember pulling off the road and crying helplessly. But I was also angry. I knew that the men who planted that bomb believed they were defending the white South. Without having been asked, they were presuming to represent my views and my interests. I knew then that if I didn't speak up, such men would continue to speak for me. There on the side of the road, I made a silent vow to make my own voice heard.

Two of the most remarkable people I got to know during this period were Anne and Carl Braden. The field secretaries for the Southern Conference Educational Fund (SCEF), they worked with Jim Dombrowski, the executive director of the organization in New Orleans. SCEF was a reincarnation of an earlier civil rights organization founded in Birmingham, Alabama, in 1938 called the Southern Conference for Human Welfare. The Southern Conference had the strong support of Eleanor Roosevelt. Indeed, at the founding meeting of the organization, she stood up to a man named Bull Connor, the same Bull Connor who in the 1960s became infamous for turning dogs and water hoses on civil rights demonstrators. As the meeting was beginning, Connor strode into the auditorium and reminded those gathered that segregation reigned in Birmingham; therefore, he instructed, whites would need to sit on one side of the aisle and blacks on the other. Mrs. Roosevelt, refusing to be bullied, simply placed her chair in the center aisle.

But Bull Connor wasn't the only enemy of the Southern Conference, or the Bradens. The Cold War, the red scare tactics of McCarthy, and hearings such as that conducted by Mississippi senator James Eastland for the House Un-American Activities Committee were often used to undermine the civil rights movement. Jim Dombrowski and the Bradens were singled out for special attention in this regard, and later the Highlander Folk School came under the same kind of attack. The Bradens, for example, had sold a house to a Negro family in Louisville in the 1950s. For this they were charged with sedition, and Carl spent nearly a year in prison. Anne documented the events in her book *The Wall Between.*

The Bradens, and especially Anne, became important mentors for me. Anne, a writer and an editor, was from Anniston, Alabama. She encouraged me to write some articles for the *Southern Patriot,* SCEF's monthly newsletter, about the group of students that had emerged from the Joint University schools, Vanderbilt, Peabody, and Scarritt. The incident involving my friend from Fiji had resulted in students from the three schools picketing the small greasy spoon restaurant. From this action, an organization emerged called the Joint University Council on Human Relations. The structure of the council, and its ability to involve white students to speak out against discrimination, was a model that was simultaneously occurring at other predominantly white campuses in the South, and the *Patriot's* coverage of these local civil rights activities proved critical to the development of a southern organization of white college students — critical because it was important for these students to know they were not alone. So, even as I was writing an article about the Nashville Movement, we could read in the *Patriot* about students in Durham who were involved in similar activities. By spring 1964, we decided it was time to pull some of these groups together. Thus began the idea for what would later become the Southern Student Organizing Committee (SSOC).

Late one night at an interracial party near Fisk University talk turned to the way the Joint University Council on Human Relations had been organized, and how important it was for white southern students to find ways of becoming involved in the movement. We thought they were not likely to join SNCC; that seemed too radical a first step. Our own personal experience told us that commitment often grew from a series of small acts. Primarily we recognized the benefit of simply getting out and talking with people our age, letting them know there were other students who felt the same way they did about segregation and that they were not crazy and alone.

I was so focused on the need for white southerners to work with other white southerners that it took me years to understand why some people considered this a bad idea. While many supported the formation of ssoc, others questioned the wisdom of establishing an organization that was predominantly white — even though its main purpose was to bring more white students into the Freedom Movement. For example, Anne Braden was worried about the implications of a predominantly white organization. She also clearly saw the need to bring white students into the movement. scef funded a sncc position to do just that, originally filled by Bob Zellner, and later by Sam Shirah and Ed Hamlett.

ssoc's founding meeting was held in Nashville on April 4–5, 1964. Several of us involved in the local movement sent out a letter to activists at other southern campuses, extending an invitation to come to Nashville. The purpose of the meeting was to assess the extent of involvement in civil rights by students throughout the South, to determine what other political and social issues students were engaged in, and to see if a "structure" for such activities was needed. The person largely responsible for getting the new organization to this stage was Ed Hamlett, a graduate of Union College, also in Jackson, Tennessee. Ed was on the sncc payroll, and his special assignment was to work with white college students. He, along with Sam Shirah, who preceded him in this position, were instrumental in making sure that campus organizations across the South were represented at the ssoc founding meeting in Nashville.

Forty-five people from seventeen colleges and universities from Alabama, Florida, Kentucky, Georgia, Louisiana, Mississippi, North Carolina, South Carolina, Tennessee, and Virginia attended. The meeting was primarily white, but not entirely. Marion Barry was among those present; he was at the University of Tennessee at the time. Howard Spencer from Rust College, an all-black school in Holly Springs, Mississippi, was also there; he later became the vice-chairman of the new organization. We adopted a statement that Robb Burlage had written called "We'll Take Our Stand" and established a rudimentary structure that would allow us to continue working to form a regional organization.

When I look back now at "We'll Take Our Stand," I am amazed at both its eloquence and its ambition. Had we been able to meet only one of the goals we outlined in that founding statement, the world would today be a kinder, gentler place. Had we been able to meet all the goals, we would all be living in a utopian paradise. We began by comparing ourselves to the Fugitives, the group of Vanderbilt intellectuals who had earlier endorsed an agrarian vision of the South over the coming industrialization. I'm not sure how many of us in that room were familiar with the Fugitives, but Robb's prose became a touchstone of sorts for our assertion of building a "new" South.

> We do hereby declare, as Southern students from most of the Southern states, representing different economic, ethnic and religious backgrounds, growing from birthdays in the Depression years and the War years, that we will here take our stand in determination to build together a New South which brings democracy and justice for all its people.

The statement went on to cite Roosevelt's naming of the South as the number one domestic problem, and noted that even with a southerner currently in the White House, "our Southland is still the leading sufferer and battleground of the war against racism, poverty, injustice and autocracy." We claimed it as our intention to win that struggle in our lifetime, and therefore:

> We hereby take our stand to start with our college communities and to confront them and their surrounding communities and to move from here out through all the states of the South—and to tell the Truth that must ultimately make us free. The Freedom movement for an end to segregation inspires us all to make our voices heard for a beginning of a true democracy in the South for all people. We pledge together to work in all communities across the South to create non-violent political and direct action movements dedicated to the sort of social change throughout the South and nation which is necessary to achieve our stated goals.

We went on to outline six specific goals: ending poverty and segregation; securing a democratic society with politics that posed meaningful dialogue; and ensuring a society that provided not only meaningful work but also leisure opportunities and healthy communities for its citizens. The statement ended by saying we wanted to create a new South, "for all the world to emulate, not ridicule. We find our destiny as individuals in the South in our hopes and our work together as brothers." The "We'll Take Our Stand" statement was meant to be our manifesto, and when I reread it now, I am amazed that we stated so boldly that we expected to create a new South in our lifetime, that "tomorrow was not soon enough." But there was an air of possibility in the nation then, and we opted for the possibility rather than the cynicism. Clearly segregation had to end, and I suppose we thought that when segregation ended, racism would end as well.

We ended the Nashville meeting by appointing a Continuations Committee that would meet in Atlanta on April 18–19 to further structure the new organization and, more important, to meet with the Executive Committee of SNCC to ask for their support. At the meeting in Atlanta, our first item of business was the development of a proposed organization that included the following:

> Campus services and educational programs — based on the perception that southern white campuses were insulated from the civil rights movement and that students lacked a critical awareness of social and political issues. The intention was to offer educational programs on a very wide range of issues, but focusing in particular on civil rights and the Freedom Movement. A newsletter was also proposed.
>
> Opportunities for southern students to participate in the movement, including engaging in fundraising for SNCC, bringing SNCC speakers to campus, and conducting research. The intention here was to let students know they did not have to turn to direct action right away but could find ways of supporting more "moderate supportive activities."
>
> Resources for initiating, organizing, and sustaining community organizing projects in both black and "disinherited predominantly white communities."
>
> Promotion of employment opportunities for students in summer and full-time community organizing.
>
> Information and support for new kinds of liberal-left political coalitions and integrated issue political campaigns.

The second item of business was a meeting with the SNCC Executive Committee. We considered their support critical to the establishment of SSOC, and I do not believe we would have proceeded had it not been given. A paper prepared for the occasion noted that the students meeting in Nashville expressed a loyalty to SNCC and wished to find ways to work with, through, and for SNCC. We even went so far as to suggest some ways SNCC could help us meet this goal, such as by developing materials aimed at moderate white students and allocating supportive roles to interested white students and by cosponsoring and participating in workshops with other groups such as American Friends Service Committee (AFSC), Students for a Democratic Society (SDS), and the National Student Association (NSA). We also urged SNCC to expand the Mississippi Summer Project to include training for organizing in poor white communities and non–Deep South communities. The inclusion of this last point, organizing in non–Deep South communities, was probably included in the document by Tom Hayden from SDS, who was present at our meeting. As I recall, I and some of the other southern students deferred to Robb and to Tom, in part because they seemed to have such a full political and economic grasp of the situation, not to mention far greater intellectual skills. I know that I felt inferior intellectually, and out-of-sync with the overall political analysis. I was still just a good Christian girl trying to do something about racial inequality.

We also elected officers that weekend in Atlanta. Gene Guerrero from Emory University was voted the first chairman of the organization; Howard Spencer, from Rust College in Mississippi was elected vice-chair; and Roy Money, from Vanderbilt and the Joint University Council on Human Rights, was elected treasurer. I was elected executive secretary. I hadn't yet made a decision about what to do the next year, but I know that we did expect this to be a full-time position once the Summer Project had come to an end.

The meeting with the SNCC Executive Committee was held on Sunday afternoon. Some SNCC people were fearful that we were setting up a parallel organization that would drain off human resources as well as funds. We continued to maintain that our group aimed at reaching a different constituency and perhaps leading them toward more activism and involvement with SNCC. As I recall, one of the key people who gave us support in that meeting was Stokely Carmichael, one of the first to later articulate Black Power. I think he understood we had an important role to play as whites and was willing to recognize the difference in roles. Other key supporters for the SSOC proposal included Ella Baker, Bob Moses, Ruby Doris Robinson, and Connie Curry. At the end of the meeting, SNCC voted to support SSOC and give us $300. It was enough to get us started.

While we were holding the founding conference of SSOC in Nashville that

April, final preparations were being made in the Atlanta SNCC office and in the COFO office in Jackson, Mississippi, for the beginning of Freedom Summer 1964. Several of us were planning to join the Mississippi Summer Project, so we decided to hold our first Executive Committee meeting in conjunction with the orientation sessions for that event at Oxford, Ohio.

That is how it happened that I was in Oxford on the afternoon it was discovered that three civil rights workers—James Chaney, Michael Schwerner, and Andrew Goodman—were missing. As we were ending the Executive Committee session, we heard that a big meeting had been called for all volunteers, and it was there that Bob Moses made the announcement. Some questions were asked, and then some announcements made about logistics as the first group of volunteers prepared to leave for Mississippi on buses that were waiting. But mostly the feeling was one of overwhelming somberness. Everyone in that room had to deal with his or her fears about going into Mississippi.

Under the leadership of Ed Hamlett, SSOC had helped set up a "white folks project" as a part of the Summer Project. It was a good idea, but one whose time had not yet come. The idea was to search out sympathetic white people in Mississippi and try to get them involved at least enough to establish a moderating voice in the state. But Mississippi was so polarized that this proved an impossible task. Moderates were hiding out, often for good reason. Almost anyone who spoke up against segregation was quickly isolated. The tense atmosphere created a nearly impossible situation for us as we found ourselves calling up ministers who didn't want to talk to us and were definitely afraid to be seen meeting with us.

We had high hopes in the beginning, though. Having completed one week of training in the overcrowded town of Oxford, we were asked by COFO staff to complete the second week with Myles Horton at the Highlander Research and Education Center in Knoxville, Tennessee. Shortly after the announcement was made about the missing civil rights workers we left Oxford and drove through the night, arriving in Knoxville the following morning.

Myles and Aimee Horton met with us there, often facilitating discussions about the next steps to take. We tried to make plans and talked about contacting liberal ministers in Mississippi, though we really didn't know what to expect. About midweek, we took off for a picnic in the Great Smokey Mountains. We swam in a beautiful mountain stream and relaxed in a place that seemed far removed from the troubles in Mississippi. For that afternoon, we were able to put the uncertainties of the summer out of our mind.

As the sun began to set, we were driving through Cade's Cove, one of the most beautiful areas in the park. We were dispersed in two cars, a vw van belonging to one of the volunteers and Ed Hamlett's vw Beetle. I was riding in the van when we heard on the car radio that the burned-out shell of the car of the missing civil rights workers had been discovered near Philadelphia, Mississippi. This report confirmed our suspicions that they were already dead. We stopped to make sure that the other car had also heard the news, but what I remember mostly is the silence that descended on us.

Halfway down the mountain, we stopped to visit with Florence and Sam Reece. Sam was a former coal miner from Harlan County, Kentucky. During the height of the 1930s struggle to unionize coal miners in the eastern part of that state, Florence had grabbed a calendar off the wall and written the song "Which Side Are You On?" Somehow as we sat around their living room that night, listening to Florence sing and tell us about how she had come to write the song, and about all the good and bad times she and Sam had had helping to organize the miners in "Bloody Harlan," the iciness began to slip away. Before we left that evening, Florence and Sam had "rooted" us in our history, had helped us see ourselves as part of a much larger historical process for justice. If I'd had any sense at all, I might have begun to wonder right then about the language in the "We'll Take Our Stand" document about curing the ills of the world in our lifetime.

After the second week of orientation at Highlander, I went back to Nasvhille for two weeks to complete my work at the Methodist Publishing House. I then traveled on to Mississippi, arriving in Jackson by train in early July; I was met by Howard Romaine, a student from Louisiana who had been involved in demonstrations that spring to desegregate Memphis churches. That fall Howard entered the University of Virginia and later helped establish the Virginia Students Civil Rights Committee. Howard took me to the home of Mrs. Jane Schutt, a white Mississippi moderate who bravely came forward to support the Summer Project. She took a great deal of risk that summer by having us stay in her house. I began working right away with Mrs. Schutt and the local Unitarian minister to put together a mailing inviting people to join the Mississippi Council on Human Relations. For the rest of the summer, I bounced back and forth between Jackson and the Gulf Coast, the headquarters for the "white folks project."

Quite possibly we had one of the most bizarre "freedom houses" in the state that summer. Ed had rented a suite of rooms in a rundown clapboard hotel called the Hotel Riviera. The Riviera faced the Gulf, but it was definitely of the seedy variety. The proprietor seemed unperturbed about housing civil rights workers. Sam Shirah and a few others eventually moved to a working-class white community in Biloxi and began trying to talk with people there. But as I said earlier, it was a good idea whose time had not yet come.

We followed all the protocol that COFO projects across the state followed. When we left to drive somewhere, we phoned the Jackson office and told them what time we were leaving and what time we expected to arrive at our destination. Danger was always present, but its manifestations seemed entirely random. There was no need to dwell on it.

I was frightened once, however. Actually, frightened is not quite the word: I really thought I was going to die.

It was the week Martin Luther King Jr. came to Mississippi to speak. I was in Jackson at the time, and three of us decided to drive over to Vicksburg to hear him speak in a church that evening. We left Jackson headed toward Vicksburg on the interstate—an easy ride under normal circumstances. But that night, there were highway patrol cars at every exit and all along the highway. This should have been comforting, but no civil rights worker ever found the presence of state police comforting. The driver of the car made a quick decision to exit the interstate and take a back route to Vicksburg. It was a serious mistake. Shortly after we headed west on an isolated county road, a truck pulled up behind us and began following—began toying with us, really. The truck would come close, nearly hitting us in the rear, and then back off. We slowed for them to pass, but they never did.

We made it to Vicksburg, almost too late to hear King speak. The church was overflowing, so we stood on the lawn outside and listened. We had the good sense to drive home on the interstate. It was that incident that evening that helped me to understand the randomness of the violence in Mississippi. We had made a quick decision and put ourselves in jeopardy. We fit the profile of civil rights workers: a car with an out-of-state license plate, and we were young. We were also all white. I don't know what would have happened had we been an interracial group. Perhaps nothing more, but perhaps a lot more. That was the thing about violence and danger in Mississippi. It was best not to spend a lot of time thinking about it.

At the end of the summer, when projects were beginning to wind down, the COFO office in Jackson asked us to help out while volunteers and staff headed to Atlantic City for the Mississippi Freedom Democratic Party challenge. So I went to Palmers Crossing, near Hattiesburg, where I lived in the home of Mrs. Victoria Gray and worked in the community center. Mrs. Gray was in Atlantic City, but her children and her husband were there, and everybody under the sun was passing through. I loved working at the community center with the kids.

At the end of the summer I went home to Tennessee for a few days. I remember watching the Republicans elect Barry Goldwater as their presidential candidate and thinking that I wanted to go live in another country. I flaunted my Freedom Movement uniform around the house—a blue work shirt and a pair of jeans. When Mama asked me about it, I simply said everyone was wearing it. Later, I heard her stick up for me when someone else asked her the same question. She and Daddy had come down in the middle of the summer to visit me in Biloxi. I had told them I was working with the National Council of Churches, which was a lie. It was a little one, since the NCC was officially a part of COFO, but I thought the truth would have them beside themselves with worry. They knew what I was doing, of course. They had already met Ed Hamlett and liked him, and they seemed to like the other people on the project as well.

That fall I returned to Nashville and established the SSOC office. I was now a full-time movement worker. My pay was $25 a week.

My work with SSOC was to help build the organization, along with the other key people in the organization. Ed Hamlett continued working for both SNCC and SSOC, and Archie Allen, my friend from Scarritt, joined the organization as a campus traveler. One of my jobs was to put out our monthly newsletter, then called the *New Rebel*. One of the SNCC workers in the Boston office had designed a button for us that combined the SNCC button with the Confederate flag. I loved it: it was so indicative of what we were about. This same symbol— black and white hands crossing over the flag—was printed on the first few issues of the newsletter. Later, the symbol became highly controversial because of the use of the flag, and it was dropped. Much of the history of our organization is evident in the pages of the newsletter, which was eventually renamed the *New South Student*.

The October 1964 issue reports on ssoc's involvement in the Mississippi Summer Project. It also includes an article on the draft by Archie Allen, a quote from Albert Camus on political leaders (probably my contribution), and the lead article, called "Toward Building a New South." My rhetoric was not as eloquent as the "We'll Take Our Stand" statement, but it was no less a call to action:

> From the time the sit-in movement hit the South in 1960 and ushered in a new generation of students who were demanding equal treatment, the white South has re-acted. It has reacted in various ways — from police dogs, fire hoses, and cattle prods to interracial teas and human relations committees. Now we have had four years and we have some history-making precedents that should point us toward constructive action for the future: Little Rock, which attracted no new industry for years; Nashville, where the desegregation of department store lunch counters showed no substantial financial loss; Atlanta, where token de-segregation of schools was peacefully achieved; Birmingham, where fire hoses and police dogs stirred the conscience of the nation; and Mississippi, where death has not halted the responses from an idea whose time has come. However, our period of grace has passed. We can no longer be content to react. The time has come to put away old ideas and begin constructive action geared toward creating a New South.

I am honest in the article. While exhorting southern college students to join with us, I acknowledge that "at this point, ssoc is a poverty stricken organization with a big dream and a very small bank account. Yet two full-time staff persons and several volunteers are working hard to achieve our goals. For years the South has been shouting that it could handle its own problems — and ssoc has accepted that challenge."

It is in this article that I first link the South with international issues — a precursor for me and the organization of our growing anti–Vietnam War sentiments.

> The South, long left to glory in its own tradition and "way of life," has finally had its share of the national and international spotlight. The death of three civil

rights workers in Mississippi does not seem too far removed from soldiers dying in Vietnam. The migrant workers, the plantation sharecroppers of the Delta, and Appalachian coal miners who remember the days when the mine worked 1,800 men and now works 25, are seen in clear sharp perspective with the hungry people of Asia.

SSOC held its first full-fledged student conference in Atlanta in November 1964. It was attended by 125 white students from campuses throughout the South. Speakers for the event were Larry Goodwyn, then living in Texas and the former head of the Texas Democratic Coalition, now a professor of history at Duke University; Ed King, national committeeman for the Mississippi Freedom Democratic Party, who reported on the Convention Challenge of the Mississippi Freedom Democrats; and Don West, a poet from West Virginia. Don was a 1930s activist from rural Georgia and a cofounder of the Highlander Folk School with Myles Horton.

That fall, SSOC began planning a Christmas project in Mississippi—part of our goal to ensure that young southern white students were able to experience the growing Freedom Movement firsthand. We asked students to volunteer to come to Hattiesburg, Mississippi, at their own expense to help renovate a community center. We also asked that they raise money on their campuses to help support the project. Thirty-eight volunteers from seventeen southern colleges and universities worked in Hattiesburg and Meridian painting and remodeling community centers and participating in voter registration drives. Both projects were sponsored jointly with COFO.

The project divided into two four-day periods—before and after Christmas—with an orientation in Hattiesburg before each session. One of the volunteers summed up the experience:

> The SSOC Christmas project provided tremendous opportunity for SSOC and the individuals involved to come into direct contact with the tensions and pressures which pervade the civil rights community in Mississippi. In my opinion, the project was more meaningful to the persons who went to Mississippi than it was to the COFO projects. We very probably did little of a significant nature for the projects, but the personal contact which we had with the Negro community . . . kindles in us a new realization of the necessity for commitment on our part to the democratic tradition which is as much the heritage of these people as ourselves.

A SSOC newsletter published after the project notes that "only one incident occurred throughout the project. Ed Hamlett, a white participant from Tennessee was beaten by a Hattiesburg hardware store owner when he and two Negro students attempted to purchase supplies."

SSOC had been right in its assessment that active involvement in civil rights issues was growing on predominantly white southern college campuses. From 1964 to 1966, campus activist groups sprang up all across the South. These organizations were often defined by civil rights activism, but did not limit their activities to this arena. University reform, free speech, solidarity with labor and poor people, were all concerns. And the activities reported on in the *New South Student* reflected this rising awareness.

By the time SSOC held its second southwide conference in Atlanta in the spring of 1965, there was growing concern over issues of peace, and particularly the war in Vietnam. Stokely Carmichael was the keynote speaker for that event. Steve Weisman from the Berkeley Free Speech Movement was also present, on his way to a southern speaking tour sponsored by SSOC.

By the end of 1965 I was beginning to feel burned out. The Freedom Movement was changing rapidly, so rapidly it was hard to keep up. I left the South in the spring of 1966, and at a time when SSOC was already entering another era. The Vietnam War and the draft were fast encroaching on the Freedom Movement, demanding an analysis of U.S. society that went beyond the southern system of segregation.

I've always thought that SSOC as an organization had three lives. The organization that I helped create, based on the simple notion of getting more white people involved in the civil rights movement, lasted for about a year and a half. I think we were pretty successful, although I remain convinced that white southern students would have come forward in any case. Our work paralleled and complemented that of the National Student Association Southern Project, so there were any number of ways that students could become involved. We also developed a close working relationship with SDS. Our closest working relationship, however, at least during the early days of the organization, was always with SNCC.

I was around for a little bit of SSOC's second phase, though I had been thinking about leaving the South for a while by this time. I wanted especially to get away from the drudgery of running the SSOC office, so in the spring of 1966 I went to Mississippi and began organizing one of the first statewide interracial student conferences. I would characterize ssoc's second phase as creating a more broad-based student movement in the South, and especially in helping build an antiwar movement. Two of the best things to come from this period were the Southern Folk Culture Revival Project, organized by Anne Romaine and Bernice Johnson Reagon, and a Southern Peace Tour, led by Tom Gardner, Nancy Hodes, and Lyn Wells. The *New South Student* took on a new sophistication, with longer, more analytical articles. It was a vibrant, active period for the organization, reflecting awareness of and concern for a broad spectrum of social and economic justice issues.

I think of ssoc's third phase as the beginning of the end of the organization. By this time I was in Washington, D.C., and not fully aware of all the organizational changes, but by 1968 a trend toward southern nationalism emerged that I considered dangerous. Our founding had been based on a vision of what the South could be, not a reflexive defense of regional identity. Thus ssoc was already internally weak when some staff members, in collaboration with the current leadership of sds, moved to disband ssoc, arguing that there was no role for a predominantly white student organization.

Earlier incarnations of sds had been very supportive of ssoc, but the student movement was beginning to fragment in the late 1960s. I've often thought that what happened to ssoc was a precursor to the growing split within sds. Following the Days of Rage in Chicago in 1968, sds divided into two factions: the Weathermen and the Revolutionary Youth Movement (RYM). The Weathermen moved toward terrorism, RYM toward rigid Marxist-Leninism. The leaders of both of these factions attacked ssoc for being liberal and white. In order to understand this period, it is important to recall that ssoc, from its beginnings, had been a part of the national student movement. As the executive secretary, I worked closely with sds national office staff during our group's first year. In general, we attended sds's national meetings and had a formal fraternal relationship with that organization. Many ssoc chapters were in fact joint ssoc/sds chapters. As the antiwar movement gained momentum, and as tactics to oppose the war became more hotly debated, ssoc's role as a southern "predominantly white" organization was called increasingly into question.

A special meeting was called at the Mt. Beulah Conference Center in Edwards, Mississippi, to decide the group's fate in the summer of 1969. Thus, although ssoc remained a membership organization, the decision about its future depended solely on who could get to Mt. Beulah. After much discussion and speech making, ssoc died an ungraceful death. The ssoc staff was just as divided as the national student movement, with several concurring that an organization devoted to working with white students was politically incorrect. In retrospect, I think there was a lingering sense of inferiority about our ability to engage in political analysis and a tendency to want to support the most radical positions — that is, those positions outlined by sds. White southerners who supported the perpetuation of a predominantly white organization in the face of charges of racism were extremely vulnerable. The organization was simply not strong enough to deal with the challenge of the sds leadership, especially given internal staff divisions. I don't recall who proposed the final resolution to disband, but it was clear to me, watching the events from the back of the room with Ed Hamlett and Gene Guerrero, that the organization would not survive.

I found it especially poignant that the meeting took place at Mt. Beulah, the gathering place for the Mississippi Movement. How ironic that in that place in particular, with its grand legacy of black and white people struggling together for freedom and equality, the RYM faction of sds should resurrect the tired old Communist Party doctrine of the 1930s of a separate Black Belt nation in the South. I suppose that if such a call had come from black Mississippians, I would have supported it — because I would have trusted it. But there was something terribly arrogant in young white revolutionaries telling Mississippi black folks to separate themselves from the citizenship they had fought so hard to win. Unfortunately, ssoc's ending was not so much about ssoc as it was about the state of the student movement.

ssoc had a short life, but since I have always felt that its primary mission was to provide an avenue for white southern students to enter the Freedom Movement, I believe it was successful. I fully believed that if we offered white southern students a means to act on their principles, they would do so, and having acted, they would become more and more involved. The organization's founding document outlined a critique of American society and a vision for changing it that began on our home turf. "We Take Our Stand" was an eloquent statement with an impossible agenda. It was, however, from the heart. Underlying the words was a rejection of the current definition of what a white southerner stood for, and a pledge to actively work against that stereotype. Most important, we believed there were others out there who, like us, did not share a vision of a southern society divided by race. ssoc provided a mechanism to bring those southerners together.

Although I was tremendously saddened and disheartened by the demise of the organization, especially given the way it ended, the work that I had originally envisioned it accomplishing was effectively over. In many ways, history had overtaken us. We had formed for the purpose of bringing white southerners into the Freedom Movement. By 1968, the Freedom Movement had progressed from being a southern movement to end segregation to a national movement that also opposed the war in Vietnam.

I had been toying with the notion of graduate school and was interested in studying sociology. I wrote to several schools and dutifully tried to complete the application forms. It was a painful process. Not only did I have no money, but I invariably felt stymied by the questions regarding long-term career goals. Inevitably, the application wound up in the wastebasket. My heart was still in the daily work of the movement, and I didn't have a clue about how a professional career plan might fit into my increasing political involvement. Finally a form came from the New School for Social Research. The application for admission was one page; the financial assistance form was one page. I filled them out and was accepted for the fall of 1966.

I decided to join Robb and Dorothy Burlage in Washington for the summer before relocating to New York and enrolling at the New School. Robb was a fellow at the Institute for Policy Studies (IPS), and Dorothy had settled into a community organizing job. I became a short-term student in the Institute's nondegree program that gave young people the opportunity to work with Institute Fellows for a year. Robb was undertaking a study of the New York City hospital system, but my assignment was to help run a seminar for congressional assistants—which essentially meant ordering sandwiches and making sure participants knew when and where to come. The truth was, it didn't matter what my duties were. Being at the Institute was one of the most exciting and productive times of my life, in large part because of the appreciation I gained there for the power of ideas and political analysis and dialogue.

I've often been critical of the student movement for its arrogance. As a feminist, I came to locate most of this phenomenon in the male left—not an entirely erroneous perception. However, I arrived at the Institute with more than my own share of arrogance, perhaps fueled by the prevailing winds that full-time movement work and all that implied—voluntary poverty, constant work and travel, often dangerous situations—was what was demanded of anyone who wanted to change the world. It took a while for me to understand just how much I had to learn.

Located in a three-story townhouse on Florida Avenue, the Institute's offices and seminar room provided a salon of sorts for Washington's liberal/radical community of policymakers, journalists, and intellectuals. Richard Barnet was then writing the first of several books on American imperialism and transnational corporations. *Intervention and Revolution*, originally intended as a chapter, was later followed by *Global Reach*. Marcus Raskin was finishing his second book, *Being and Doing*. Robb's work on the New York City hospitals would eventually lead to the formation of the Health Policy Advisory Council. Never had I been in the kind of heady atmosphere where ideas were debated so furiously and where national and foreign policy issues were held up to such critical examination. By the end of the summer I had made the decision to stay at IPS rather than enrolling in the New School, and that fall I became a full-time student.

In retrospect, I've often marveled at how intuitively I made decisions about my life during this time. Two years earlier, I had made the decision to stay in the South and work to build SSOC—fully aware that I was choosing a path that had no safety net. Going to work for the Methodist Church was a professional path, but it was not the one that beckoned. In that case, heart was more operative than head. Deciding against graduate school, however, was a combination of instinct and a sure knowledge that I would learn more at the Institute for Policy Studies.

By the spring of 1967, the escalating war in Vietnam—now being played out on the evening news and in the increasing number of young men resisting the draft—was beginning to crowd out other political agendas. A group of intellectuals based in Cambridge, Massachusetts, including Samuel Bowles, Michael Walzer, Martin Peretz, and Gar Alperovitz, organized a national project to educate the public on the war. Borrowing from the experience of the Freedom Movement and the Mississippi Summer Project in particular, they conceived of Vietnam Summer as a first step toward a community-based, grassroots effort to stop the war. Lee Webb, a former member of SDS and one of my fellow students at IPS, was asked to direct the project, and he drafted me and several others to follow him to Cambridge in the late spring to set up a national office.

My job, of course, was to coordinate the southern effort. Given that SNCC and SSOC had an existing infrastructure of local organizational contacts, it was not difficult to establish a southern network fairly quickly. I did not see this work as a turning away from the Freedom Movement, but rather as a way of expanding it. The Freedom Movement had been played out primarily in the South. To some, it was viewed only as a problem of southern segregation. The riots in northern cities in the summer of 1965, however, began to challenge the view that race was strictly a southern problem, and the Vietnam War raised further troubling questions about systemic issues of U.S. racism.

The Vietnam Summer project and the time I spent at the Institute were very important for me in that they moved me away from a narrow, regional frame and identity to a growing consciousness about national and international issues. However, my earlier decision to stay in the United States in order to work to change the South remained intact, and already I was looking homeward.

Part of my agenda at the Institute for Policy Studies was to explore with Robb and others the possibility of establishing an institute in the South. Sometime in 1965 or early 1966, Julian Bond, Howard Romaine, and I had a discussion in the SNCC office in Atlanta about the need for a southern institute that would conduct research on policy issues central to the Southern Freedom Movement. That was our beginning point. We saw it as an integral part of continuing to build a southern freedom movement. As I recall, we talked about two issues in particular: the militarization of the South, which meant that a disproportionate part of the southern economy was based on military dollars; and racial and social equity. The two were not unrelated. Powerful southern senators such as Strom Thurmond of South Carolina, Richard Russell of Georgia, and James Eastland and John Stennis of Mississippi fought for military dollars with the same intensity they fought against equal rights for blacks.

The sudden death of the Institute's administrator in the fall of 1967 left IPS in the lurch, and I was asked to become the Administrative Fellow. *Administrative* meant that I was responsible for running the place; *Fellow* meant I had the independence to begin laying the groundwork for a southern institute.

In the fall of 1969, I resigned from my duties at IPS and returned south to found the Institute for Southern Studies with Julian and Howard. Howard had persuaded Jerold Cohen, an attorney in one of Atlanta's largest and best-known law firms, to help us charter the Institute and gain tax exemption. Angels come in various guises, and Jerry was ours. He became the fourth member of our board, and for years did pro bono work for the Institute, getting us established as a 501C3 organization and thereafter making sure that we remained within our operating boundaries.

We were one of three new institutes receiving support from the IPS. Around the same time we launched the Institute for Southern Studies, the public policy–oriented Cambridge Institute was established by Gar Alperovitz and others in Cambridge, Massachusetts, and the Bay Area Institute was born in San Francisco, primarily to tackle issues of the environment and Pacific rim policy matters. These regionally based institutes would set their own agendas, rather than becoming satellite institutes of IPS. The Institute for Southern Studies is still going strong at the age of thirty, and recently celebrated the twenty-fifth anniversary of its award-winning journal, *Southern Exposure*.

That fall of 1969, we moved into a one-room office next door to the southern regional headquarters of the American Civil Liberties Union in downtown Atlanta and began figuring out what to do next. The first order of business was to reexamine our original intention of servicing an active southern movement. By 1969, the Freedom Movement as we had known it in 1965 was in tatters. The war had done its share, as had the government's COINTELPRO policy (a counterintelligence program against domestic organizations), and internal differences and conflicting political agendas had taken their toll as well. There was also a new movement on the horizon, a burgeoning counterculture, made up of an uneven mix of communalism, politics, hallucinogens, and attitude.

I was the only full-time staff person, since the Institute for Policy Studies was continuing to pay me a minimal salary until we could raise our own budget. Julian was now a representative in the Georgia legislature. He had been seated only after a protracted legal battle and a Supreme Court decision because his fellow legislators considered his opposition to the war in Vietnam sufficient grounds for overturning his election by his constituents. Howard, always the creative visionary, was working for *The Great Speckled Bird,* an underground newspaper he had helped found which blended counterculture and new left politics.

We reconsidered our mission. If the movement had disassembled, then we would help rebuild it. I don't know if my fellow founders had this simple a notion of what we were doing, but we all had a doggedness about us that meant we simply had to keep trying things. Shortly after we opened our offices, Gunnar Myrdal, the great Swedish sociologist and author of *The American Dilemma,* came to town. I still don't know how he did it, but Howard arranged for him to give the Institute's opening seminar. Later we hosted Daniel Ellsburg, author of *The Pentagon Papers.* These public events helped us maintain some momentum as we went about the daily grind of developing projects and raising money.

Critical to the success of the Institute was the addition of three new members, Bob Hall, Leah Wise, and Chip Hughes. Bob had the idea that we should start a southern journal; since we had no outlet to publish the results of our research, he reasoned, we should create our own. In the first year of the new journal, which was called *Southern Exposure,* we put out three theme issues, each one reflecting a major research project of the Institute. "The Military and the South," published in the fall of 1973, documented our long-term work deconstructing the regional dependency on military dollars. The second focused on the energy crisis and the corporate structure of the region's powerful utility companies. The third, delayed for so long that it turned into a double issue, showcased our work in the area of southern oral history.

My life at the Institute was made happier with the addition of female colleagues. Leah Wise joined the staff full time, and Jacquelyn Hall began working with us as an unpaid volunteer while completing her doctoral studies. The three of us set about defining a project to "recapture" southern progressive history. My own interest had been piqued by Anne Braden, who told me one time in no uncertain terms that my generation was not the first actively to oppose segregation and that I owed it to myself to find out more about the radicals of the 1930s. We wrote a grand proposal that did not get funded, and then we simply set about doing it.

"No More Moanin': Voices of Southern Struggle" was published in the winter of 1974. I remember that it took forever to assemble; when it was finally done it contained more than 220 pages of interviews, stories, articles, and book reviews about southern activist history. The introduction to the issue stated our philosophy: "This issue . . . represents a search for that part of southern history that is usually ignored or distorted, the history of people fighting for the right to lead productive and decent lives. It is not our intent to romanticize the past, but rather to place our own work and lives within an historical context." I have always thought of "No More Moanin'" as an excellent collection that was rough around the edges. We had massive amounts of information, too few really good editors, and too many space and money constraints. But to this day it remains one of the projects of which I am proudest. It allowed Leah and me to publish research we did together on the history of the Southern Tenant Farmers Union, an interracial union of sharecroppers that originated in the Arkansas River delta. It also included one of my favorite interviews, a group interview I conducted with five retirees of an Atlanta United Automobile Workers (UAW) local. In November 1936—two months prior to the historic Flint sit-down strike of 1937—these workers launched a sit-down strike of their own, shutting down the Atlanta plant and generating wide community support for their cause. Labor historian Neill Herring noted in his introduction to our piece that "the labor movement, perhaps more than any other institution in our society, is a thing of flesh and bones, demanding a history of people, not individual leaders. This is particularly true in . . . that period when solidarity is not just a curious word."

I remember well the day I went to do the interview. I was scared that I wouldn't do a good job, afraid I wouldn't ask the right questions, afraid they would give short answers. I had never interviewed more than one person at a time, and that day I was trying out my new top-of-the-line tape recorder, not at all sure I knew how to make it work. It worked, though, and that was really all that mattered. The very fact that I was there and cared about their story unleashed a torrent of memories. They played off of one another's stories, filling in and adding details. Thus, from a tentative retelling of unfolding events, came a story about pride and solidarity. Neill and I did a follow-up interview with the man who had been president of the local in 1936, a man who spent the rest of his lifetime working as a union organizer. Photos of the sit-down strike emerged from personal collections and were loaned to us for publication with their stories. The story of the 1936 Atlanta sit-down strike had been recaptured.

Leah and I worked intuitively. Our research methods consisted of taking a tape recorder and going out to capture stories. If we knew of primary sources, we tried to sift through them in advance and prepare as best we could. The results of our work were quite different from the hard corporate research that characterized the two first issues of *Southern Exposure*. Other special issues followed, and over time the journal became a combination of southern culture and politics.

For my part, I loved working with Leah and thought we made a good team. Gender dynamics finally became an overt part of our everyday working environment, as did race. Although all of us considered ourselves nonracist, and in fact were rather prideful about our stance on behalf of racial justice, it was from my work with Leah that I began to appreciate the value of ongoing consciousness raising. My heart may have been in the right place, but I clearly had a lot to learn about the deep roots of racism. While neither of us considered it Leah's job to be my teacher, she did help keep me honest. More than any other person I encountered in the Freedom Movement, Leah lovingly taught me that struggling against both personal and institutional racism is a lifelong affair.

In retrospect, I think my primary contributions to the Institute were to help get it started and to collect a substantial body of oral history interviews on the progressive southern movements of the 1930s and 1940s. During my eight years there, I reconnected with Myles Horton and the staff at the Highlander Research and Education Center in East Tennessee. By the time it celebrated its fortieth anniversary in 1972, Highlander had relocated to a beautiful mountaintop in Jefferson County with spectacular views of the Great Smokey Mountains. Shortly thereafter, I was asked to join Highlander's Resource Committee, and eventually its board of directors. In 1978, Highlander applied for and received a grant from the National Historic Publications and Records Commission of the National Archives to establish an archive of its historical papers. They wanted someone who understood the history of the South, and in particular the history of Highlander. I was asked to join the staff and build the archive.

Going to Highlander felt like going home, and its location in East Tennessee was only part of the reason. Myles Horton, the founder of Highlander, was from my hometown of Savannah. In 1961, I had read about the closing of his "communist training school" in the local weekly paper. It was not difficult to read between the lines enough to know that the school was called communist because it was interracial. I was definitely intrigued. In subsequent years, Highlander, and Myles and Aimee Horton in particular, had been very supportive of ssoc. We'd held a number of meetings there, and they had met with us several times during the 1964 Summer Project.

Highlander's long history of active involvement had started in 1932 when it opened its doors as the Highlander Folk School. For nearly fifty years it had been an integral part of the southern progressive movement. Throughout the 1930s and 1940s it was primarily a labor school; in the early 1950s and throughout the 1960s, Highlander became one of the primary gathering places for the civil rights movement; and in the 1970s it turned its attention to the poverty of Appalachia. In 1961, the folk school was seized by the state of Tennessee and its charter revoked. Among the seven charges brought against it were its operation as an integrated school and the fact that it sold beer without a license. Highlander was guilty of both charges; at workshops, a hat was sometimes passed and beer bought cooperatively. Somehow, Highlander managed to outlive and outwit its segregationist enemies. It established a new charter and relocated to Knoxville as the Highlander Research and Education Center in 1961.

I spent the better part of two years organizing the Highlander archives, an incredible collection of documents, photographs, and recordings. I also began working with the educational program, helping to plan and facilitate weekend workshops. I spent a lot of time with Myles, trying to figure out exactly what he meant when he talked about Highlander as a school for social change. My work in the papers, my talks with Myles, and most of all my observation of Highlander workshops were an intense learning laboratory. I became totally immersed in figuring out exactly what happened at Highlander, and how it differed from other progressive organizations. Highlander was a school, not an organization. It did education, not organizing. Its mission was based on the simple philosophy that people learn from each other by discussing their own efforts to solve problems in their communities and workplaces. People came to Highlander, talked with other people in similar situations, and went back to their communities to do phenomenal things.

The eight years I spent at Highlander were an intensive internship for me in popular education. I spent hours talking with Myles, visited folk high schools in Scandinavia (the model on which Highlander was based), traveled and worked with popular educators in Central and South America, and, most important, planned and conducted numerous workshops with community leaders from the South and Appalachia.

In 1983 Highlander collaborated with the International Council on Adult Education in Toronto, Canada, and the Council for Adult Education in Latin America to sponsor an exchange between North and South American adult educators. The meetings took place in Managua, Nicaragua, two years after the historic literacy crusades sponsored by the new Sandinista government. Managua in 1983 felt like Mississippi in 1964. The energy that had been unleashed by the revolution was still very much in evidence; hope, intense energy, creativity, and international solidarity were all alive and well throughout the countryside. Even though I watched Nicaragua change over the next few years, that moment was a critical one of reinspiration for me. It was there I met Paulo Freire for the first time, author of *Pedagogy of the Oppressed*, and I began to read as much as I could about adult and popular education in Latin America. Freire outlined an approach to education that was reminiscent of what I had seen in the Freedom Movement—education that begins with ordinary people beginning to challenge and change the status quo, acting to shape the world rather than simply negotiate it.

Sometimes it seemed to me that magic happened in Highlander workshops. My own need to understand that magic, the unfolding of critical consciousness, led me finally to say that I needed some time—at least a year—to read, write, and think. So, after twenty-two years of working for social-change organizations, I decided to take a break. This time I knew how to fill out the graduate school applications, and in my mid-forties I entered the School of Education at the University of Massachusetts.

As I reflect back on the Freedom Movement of the early 1960s, it seems to me that we found ourselves in a historical moment that was quite remarkable—our dazzling moment of clarity. And yet, I don't particularly see that time in my life as something apart; I see it, rather, as the beginning of who I am and what I do now, the foundation of values and beliefs that have determined the shape of my life. So while I recognize and appreciate the uniqueness and the intensity of that moment, the gift of the Freedom Movement was the vision it gave me of a world that was possible to create.

My own vision of the "Beloved Community" has broadened since the early 1960s. It took me a while to discover the women's movement. I read *The Feminine Mystique* when I was working for SSOC, desperately looking for something that would tell me I wasn't crazy for feeling angry at times. But Betty Friedan's words weren't for me; they did not speak to a farm girl who grew up working the land and whose mother labored in a factory. Nor did they speak to the situation at hand. Finally, in Atlanta in the early 1970s, I became a part of Atlanta women's liberation and a member of the Women's Caucus of *The Great Speckled Bird*. Since that time, a feminist consciousness has shaped my view of the world.

I remain perplexed, however, by the tenacity of racism in our society. While I embrace to a degree the splintered identities of postmodernism, I fear for our ability to fight within those identities for a community that recognizes difference but is also able to transcend it. The Freedom Movement offered us the vision, a glimpse of what we could be, "a Beloved Community" that transcended difference. Perhaps we didn't know how to make it happen, but I doubt that any of us have lost the power of that vision. It is still something I hold on to.

In the spring of 1994, the Southern Student Organizing Committee had a reunion at the University of Virginia. I couldn't attend, but I sent a long message that ended with the following words. I send it out again to all those who created and sustained the Freedom Movement.

> All of you are a very important part of my life. My circle of friends and compañeros now includes people from around the world. But of all the hands I have held in the circle, yours were the ones that held mine at the most important time. Your circle is the one that gave me strength, confidence, commitment, and joy.

They Sent Us This White Girl

ELAINE DeLOTT BAKER

"We've been calling down to Jackson and asking for someone to help with starting a co-op up here in Batesville, but they've been real busy down there with voter registration and all, so in the meantime, they sent us this white girl." That's how I remember being introduced by the Reverend Middleton, an independent black farmer, during our many visits together at farmhouses and community meetings during my first few months in Panola County, Mississippi.

It was late winter in 1964–65, and the black civil rights workers who had led the Mississippi Summer Project were spread too thin to respond to all of the requests for help from invigorated black populations, like the farmers and sharecroppers of Panola County. Exhausted civil rights workers, black and white, were still trying to sort out the lessons of Freedom Summer. When hundreds of volunteers had left the state in September, there had been no sense of victory, no reason to believe that the events of the last few years would end in anything other than a hardened segregationist response, bringing more violence and more dislocation of sharecroppers.

The federal government and the American conscience, once the targets of movement efforts, had not delivered on their promises for justice. Standing up to segregation had changed the lives of local people, but it wasn't clear what those changes would mean, or what could be done to continue the momentum for change that had begun over the summer. The costs of the freedom struggle were high. Churches had been burned, people beaten, lives lost, scores of families thrown out of their jobs and off the land where they had lived and worked for generations as sharecroppers.

While many civil rights workers questioned what had been achieved, and at what cost, many of those with the most to lose did not waver. Panola County, Mississippi, was one of those communities where local people continued to put their personal and economic lives on the line. In the county seat of Bates-ville, the white agent who bought the okra crop from black farmers lowered his price from seven to six cents a pound. The farmers objected. The agent refused to negotiate. The farmers decided to try and market their crops themselves.

What prompted a community of black farmers to challenge the social and economic order of their day? How did they arrive at the decision to stake their economic lives on principles of fairness that traditionally did not apply to commerce between white and black? And why were they willing to listen to the counsel of a twenty-two-year-old white woman, who didn't know a trac-tor from a combine, in their efforts to organize an okra marketing coopera-tive? The answers to those questions are in the times, electrifying times charged with the determination and courage of people who refused to allow injustice to continue as a matter of course. In these extraordinary circum-stances, unusual alliances were forged, and race and gender were sometimes suspended — not forgotten, but momentarily subsumed in the passionate pur-suit of a common goal.

In retrospect, when I reflect on my involvement with the civil rights move-ment it seems more like an accident than a conscious decision, but as I move further back into my own life, the strange confluence of events that brought me into the movement loses its mystery and emerges not as an accident of fate, but as a spiritual path along which I was privileged to travel.

My connection to the South began at the turn of the century, when my maternal great-grandfather left Russia for rural Georgia after his ten-year-old son was kidnapped and conscripted into the Cossack army. Fifty years later, in 1947, my grandparents moved from Georgia to the outskirts of Boston to be closer to my mother and her brothers and sister, who had moved north during the war. The two families shared a house, my grandparents living in the down-stairs apartment and our family living in the upstairs apartment. From my mother's family I would often hear stories of the "colored people." I could sense the disdain in my grandfather's voice as he talked about the customers in his dry goods store, stories of how he outsmarted them, sold a suit that didn't fit or a hat that was two sizes too large. They were mean-spirited stories of a small-town merchant who was host to a captive market of the poor, whites and blacks who paid on credit.

Stories of the South were a feature of the dinner table at family holidays, reminiscences of the days when my grandfather was a white man in a culture where the mere fact of being a white man brought stature and privilege. I had been south at the age of two, but my images of the South derived not from that visit, but from the black-and-white photographs and old home movies shot in the pecan orchard outside of Grandpa's house in Sparta, Georgia. There is Grandpa, standing in the front yard, dressed in a white linen jacket. In the distance black men and women move up and down the rows of trees, harvesting pecans in baskets, the women's hair tied up in cloth like the picture of Aunt Jemima that adorned the bottle of pancake syrup on our kitchen table. In the South they called my grandfather "Boss," and years later the men in our family still called him "Boss." "Boss, do you want some more coffee?" or "Boss, how's business?" It was an echo of a time and place when Grandpa was at the top of the social order, a white man in a racist society.

"But they sure did love your grandmother," my aunts and uncles would say to me. "They" were the "colored people," the quiet, hardworking, courteous men and women who came into my grandparents' country store to shop. I was told that the customers asked for my grandmother and often left if she wasn't there. "No thank you, Mr. Cohen, I'll wait till Miss Esther comes back," my uncle would mimic, laughing at how the black men and women made every effort to avoid dealing with my grandfather. "But they sure did love your grandmother," he would say.

How does a child detect the tones of injustice in the words of her elders? I always knew, could always feel the terrible wrongness. It was in their voices, in their nervous laughter, in the looks on their faces, in the way my aunt and mother looked down at the tablecloth when my uncle began talking about "darkies" and telling his stories of the old South. Grandma was never a party to those stories, never commented during their telling. Sometimes my uncle or grandfather would ask for her corroboration, saying, "Do you remember that, Miss Esther?" Grandma would look down and nod slightly, refusing to dignify the stories with her voice, her silence an implicit rebuke.

The images of the South communicated by my father, a northerner who had lived in the South briefly following his marriage to my mother, were very different. In my father's stories, the "colored woman" was the embodiment of warmth and love. When my father spoke of Miss Dollie, the family cook, and how much she loved my sisters, his voice took on a joyous lilt. For my father, whose mother had once left him and his brother in an orphanage during a time when food was scarce, Dollie's love for his children had great meaning. I think in some way it soothed an unloved and abandoned place inside him.

Our family had left Georgia in 1942, the year I was born, so Daddy could join the war effort as a pipefitter in the Boston shipyard. Dollie remained an important figure in the family mythology, the loving black woman who cared for the white woman's children as her own. I must have yearned for that kind of love as well. When I was twelve, I wrote a letter to Miss Dollie, a woman whom I had never met. In a letter dated October 1954, Miss Dollie replied in a round, firm scroll:

> Dear Sweet,
>
> I rec your sweet letter along time ago and how glad I was to here from you and to no that you all is well. I was sorry that I was so long write you back. I lost your letter and did not has address to write you. But then other day I fine your letter. How glad I was to fine it. So I hope when this letter rech your lovely hand, I do hope it will fine you enjoy your happy life. To hope that you love me as I do you all. I did not no you, I love just like I do the other children. Please tell me about all the children. . . . Tell all to write me for I just want to See you all so bad. If you all is white child, I am you all black Ma. Write and tell me how your grandma and all is get along . . . I think you is so sweet are you to write me . . . don't know me. But I know you is sweet, for all the DeLotts is So Sweet. So please don't forget the pictur and if you can please send all you all pictur and please write me a long letter and I no I enjoy read a letter from one. I always love you all.
>
> A Cook,
> Dollie B. Gordon

I have no memory of what transpired next, of whether or not I sent pictures, or if Dollie and I continued to correspond, but I am certain that Dollie's loving response remained with me, deep in my heart.

My family lived in Winthrop, a bedroom community outside of Boston, one square mile of land bound by water on three sides, population 25,000. There were probably about four hundred Jewish families in Winthrop, not enough to be a substantial minority. We were a small, working-class Jewish community in the midst of a predominantly Catholic town.

I've sometimes wondered if every individual who has experienced discrimination remembers the first time it surfaced in their lives. I was in the second grade when one of my classmates pushed me off the swing, taunting me for being Jewish. There were other lessons that let me know that being Jewish meant being different. From the Christian world I heard that Jews were smart, that they were preoccupied with money, and that they would endure eternal damnation for killing Christ.

From my parents' generation I heard that there were two groups of people in the world, the Jews and the "goyim," or "non-Jews," as we called them. They were the "other," the ones you had to watch out for, the ones who would never really accept you, who would always think of you as a Jew. "Goyim" captured the complex feeling our parents had toward the "other," fear sometimes mixed with disdain, along with an almost desperate desire to be accepted.

My maternal grandmother, Grandma Esther, took her religion seriously, keeping its traditions, observing the Sabbath, and practicing the "mitzvahs," the good deeds commanded by Jewish law. Grandma never spoke ill of anyone. She read a chapter of the Old Testament each day and did her best to follow its teachings. I loved and respected my grandmother, but her world felt like the world of the "old country." At the same time, the conformity and materialism that characterized our small Jewish community frightened me. When I was thirteen, I railed in my journal against a life I feared: "'My surroundings.' What are they? The date-crazy, social conscious, shallow, giggly, happy-go-lucky stereotype of the Jewish teenager, later to become the rich, mature, social-status-conscious, self-centered stereotyped married person living in suburbia. I will not be one of these stereotypes!"

My education was a peculiar mix. My father, who dropped out of school after the eighth grade, was uncomfortable around books, but my mother was an avid reader. In narrow, dusty eaves off the upstairs hallway, stacks of books lined the shelves in a series of bookcases. This was my library during the winter, when childhood asthma kept me at home for weeks at a time. My torso propped up against a stack of pillows to help me breathe more easily, I read voraciously from a diverse mix of socialist writers, history, fiction, and the classics: Emile Zola, Upton Sinclair, Lincoln Steffans, Somerset Maugham, Chekhov, Dostoyevsky, Charlotte Brontë, and my mother's favorite, Margaret Mitchell, author of *Gone with the Wind*.

In addition to public school, I attended sixteen hours a week of Jewish studies, from the seventh to the tenth grade. The texts—Bible, Talmud, Jewish history, and Hebrew language and literature—were taught by an assortment of mostly kind male teachers with clear, powerful minds. One of my teachers, Arnie Band, a brilliant and iconoclastic young scholar completing his doctorate at Harvard, was my first real mentor. It was Arnie who sat the class down and showed slides of concentration camp survivors in 1954, when I was twelve years old. Later, it was Arnie who first suggested I apply to Radcliffe.

The logic of the Talmud and the mystery of the Bible delighted me, but it was the world of the great Yiddish storytellers that captured and transported me. It has been forty years since I last read these stories, but I can still envision the Hebrew letters on the pages of my books.

The story that moved me most deeply was the tale of the "Lamed Vov," which in Hebrew stands for the number thirty-six. This is how I remember the story: Throughout the ages there have always been thirty-six righteous men on the face of the earth, living their lives in piety. It is because of their righteousness, so the story goes, that God spares the world. Although the weight of humanity is on their shoulders, these extraordinary individuals never know they are among the Lamed Vov, or that it is their pure actions that maintain the fabric of life. The image of the Lamed Vov, their humility, simple virtue, and righteousness for its own sake, was the image of goodness that I carried inside me. It was the image that foreshadowed the goodness and courage of the Mississippians I would meet in my journey south.

In 1960 I accepted a scholarship to Radcliffe, while requesting a year's leave of absence to work and study in Israel. Israel provided me with the adventure I was seeking, but it did not resolve my issues around identity. I loved the vibrant society and the equality of men and women on kibbutz, with their matter-of-fact attitude toward sexuality. The social sacrifice and commitment that I felt from Israelis moved me deeply and drew me toward them, but it was clear to me that Israel was not my country. As wonderful as it felt to be in a world where being Jewish did not mean being an outsider, and where being a woman did not necessarily dictate a host of compromising behaviors and roles, I couldn't get past the discomfort I felt with Israeli nationalism.

During the last month I was in Israel, May 1961, I taught swimming at a public pool in Haifa. On one particularly hot and cloudless day I noticed several young Arab boys, about nine or ten years old, splashing and playing at the shallow end of the pool alongside the usual group of small children. I was fairly certain from their behavior that the boys didn't know how to swim. "Arabs are sinkers," the lifeguard told me when I asked if I could invite them to join our lessons, a reference to the fact that certain body types lack a layer of fat that make them more buoyant in the water. He shrugged his shoulders. His message was clear: These kids were not part of the new Israel. They were outside of the group. They were "the other."

The notion of "the other" has cast long shadows over my life. One morning, when I was about nine or ten, I was sitting at the kitchen table with my mother and my father's mother. Grandma Alice spoke only Yiddish and could not read or write English. Mama was reading aloud from a newspaper account of a plane crash the night before, shaking her head with sadness at the loss of life. "Any Jews killed?" Grandma Alice asked. This was the familiar refrain: "Any Jews?" If there were no Jews, it was a non-event, something of no concern. I was confused. It made no sense to me that a segment of humanity would be excluded from concern because they were not part of our membership group. It was my first awareness of culture as a system of belonging, of insiders and outsiders.

My year in Israel did not resolve my personal search for a cultural identity, but it gave me something else I had yearned for: the experience of living among people who were ready to lay their lives on the line for their beliefs. It was one of the topics I wrote about in my letter to Radcliffe formalizing my admission in the spring of 1961:

> There is another phenomena of this country that has influenced me greatly. It is the great regard that its citizens have for life, and the childlike eagerness they have to live. People that have often gone through so much seem to come out of it all, not with pessimism or apathy, but with a stronger sense of the meaning of life. These are people who will never let the world die "with a whimper." I am proud to be among them, even if only by spirit.

The Harvard/Radcliffe milieu of 1961 was far different from that of today. There were four Harvard men to every Radcliffe woman, and the reputation of Radcliffe women among Harvard men was forbidding. Many Harvard men publicly announced that they did not date Radcliffe women. No one had to ask why. It was commonly understood that even among Harvard's intellectual elite, smart women were less desirable.

Sexuality, once a forbidden topic for proper young ladies, was beginning to surface around the fringes of campus life. There was a story that made the rounds of Radcliffe women during my freshman year. Looking back, I wonder whether it was true or whether it was an urban college myth, passed down from class to class. The story was set in a Harvard lecture hall, one of those immense, dark, paneled rooms with high ceilings, where hundreds of college freshmen would sit quietly, taking notes, dozing, doodling, or doing the many things that students do to occupy their minds during the fifty-minute lecture. The popular professor (in the story I heard, it was my humanities professor) was said to have interrupted his morning lecture and addressed a female student who was knitting in class. The professor, apparently annoyed by the sound of her knitting needles clacking together, called out, "Miss Jones, do you know that knitting is a form of masturbation?" Miss Jones, so the story goes, called back, "Professor, when I knit, I knit, and when I masturbate, I masturbate." True story or urban myth, unapologetic sexuality was breaking through the veneer of the prim and proper Radcliffe student body.

It often felt to me that the Radcliffe freshman class of five hundred was little more than an annoyance to the Harvard faculty. In the classroom it was not unusual for Harvard professors to make sexist remarks or convey sexist messages in nonverbal ways. One fall afternoon, I entered a room where the breakout session for Social Relations 110 was meeting. It didn't take long for me to realize I was the only female of about ten students. The instructor, Martin Peretz, gestured to a couch with his tightly sheathed umbrella and with no hint of humor said to me, "Why don't you lie down on the coach over there, Miss DeLott, and just be our sex symbol." Rattled by his remark but unwilling to acknowledge it, I draped myself seductively on the sofa, feigning indifference. For the remainder of the class, Mr. Peretz paced back and forth behind the sofa, punctuating his remarks with a slap of his umbrella along the side of the sofa as he walked past me. The next day I switched sections. The

Harvard community was more than a bastion of male privilege. To me, it was a hostile environment.

And then there was the issue of class. I had never been around rich people before and I was confused and intimidated by the social elitism that permeated the Harvard sense of privilege. It would have been difficult for me under any circumstances to enter into the elite world of Harvard and Radcliffe, but my status as a commuter during my freshman year made the experience almost surreal. Every day I boarded the transit system in Winthrop, emerging an hour later at the Harvard Square subway station, light-years away in cultural time. I imagined how I appeared to others, a provincial, lower-middle-class Jewish girl from the outskirts of Boston. I didn't feel a particular kinship with the affluent women of privilege who studied hard, and whom I generally liked; still, I really didn't want to be that little girl from Winthrop. Drawing from my year in Israel and from the two months I had spent in Europe before returning to the States, I constructed an image for myself, something akin to "beatnik chic" or "ethno-trash." Its core characteristics were no makeup or accessories, black turtle necks, black pants, boots, and Gauloise cigarettes — a tough, sultry look, part challenge, part seduction, that worked well with my physical appearance. It was an image constructed of sheer bravado, separating me from the person I was afraid was me.

In my sophomore year, Radcliffe awarded me a larger scholarship, which allowed me to move into campus housing. I had already begun to spend more and more of my time in the apartments of upperclassmen, friends with whom I shared both a marginality to the Harvard world and a love of ideas. There were those wondrous philosophical discussions of Sartre and Camus, Kant and Wittgenstein, politics and sexual mores, love and despair, accompanied by the mournful strains of Edith Piaf and Miles Davis — late-night confidences shared in rooms lit by candles protruding from the necks of squat, straw-covered Chianti bottles encased in wax drippings. My cultural heroes were Jean-Paul Sartre and Simone de Beauvoir. In my mind, they had broken through the hypocrisy of society to live as philosophers and lovers in their separate but equal lives.

Academic studies were never very difficult for me, but neither did they engage me. On a recent visit to the Radcliffe archives, I stumbled across my college tutorial reports, which shed some light on how faculty viewed me:

> She is by far the most intelligent of my students this year. . . . She is capable of
> very clear and complex thought. Her problems as a student are: 1. Erratic work
> habits, 2. Failure to work on courses in which she is not interested, 3. Failure to
> consistently work up to capacity even when she is interested. She is independent
> and somewhat bohemian; definitely not grade oriented. She seems to antagonize
> instructors who value neat appearances and promptness.

In polite terms, I was a renegade.

I was still struggling to find my place in the academy when a bizarre event
altered not only my college career but the course of my life. It was just after
dawn, in December 1963, when the Cambridge police entered an off-campus
apartment where I was staying during Christmas break with a Harvard classmate, Rick Fields, who would become my lifelong friend. The two of us were
arrested and charged with violating sections of what were known as the Massachusetts blue laws: fornication, lewd and lascivious behavior, and corrupting
the morals of a minor — two felonies and a misdemeanor. Our "crime" was
being found in the same bed in a room adjoining that of a sixteen-year-old girl
named Terry, who had been staying at the apartment (hence the third charge).
Terry was a Cambridge girl, from the ethnic Irish community, whose mother
was unable to control her. She was also the niece of a captain in the Cambridge police force.

The plan, as the police later relayed to our lawyer, was to arrest and charge
Terry as a "willful child," a crime under Massachusetts law, to place her in
solitary confinement for twenty-four hours, to send in a priest, and, finally, to
parole her to the custody of her mother, thereby putting an end to her rebellion. It was a well-crafted family intervention, executed with full cooperation
of the Cambridge police.

Rick and I were not part of the police strategy, but we instantly became part
of a different drama: the ongoing saga of town and gown. Lieutenant Joyce
Darling, a member of the police team, was outraged by our presence. With
the kind of perverse glee and determination reminiscent of Lotte Lenya in
From Russia with Love or Eileen Brennan in Private Benjamin, Lieutenant
Darling barged into our bedroom, announcing to the other officers, "Look
what we have here!" Rick and I were arrested and taken down to City Hall,
where Lieutenant Darling confiscated my birth control pills (illegal in Massachusetts), bellowing at me, "Don't you have any respect for your body?"

A Radcliffe dean contacted me at Henry House, my off-campus residence, informed me that I was not fit to live in Radcliffe housing, and ordered me to pack my bags and leave immediately. About a week into the scandal, the Harvard dean of students requested that I come in to talk with him. He had no formal jurisdiction over me, he explained, he just wanted to meet me. As I sat across from him at the broad mahogany desk in his dark, paneled office, the dean began telling me the story of his own daughter, whom he said "some might have thought of as wild," and how she had finally found someone willing to overlook her past indiscretions. He concluded by assuring me that my life was not ruined, and that someday I too would meet a man who would be willing to forgive my past. I left the dean's office in a state of disbelief, stunned by his presumption and his patronizing attitude.

Soon after, Radcliffe's new president, Mary Bunting, asked me to her office. I was apprehensive. The Radcliffe dean who was managing the incident for the school could never quite look me in the eye, but President Bunting's voice and demeanor held no reproach, only curiosity. "I want to know about the morals of the girls," she said. "I want to know what the girls are thinking." It was 1964, a critical juncture in Radcliffe's history. Heated discussions raged over the pros and cons of abolishing "parietal hours," the rules that governed co-ed visits in dormitories. The policy of the time restricted visits from members of the opposite sex to between four and seven in the evening, and even then the door had to remain ajar six inches. It was a hotly debated issue, as men and women, students and administrators, staked out their positions on morality, propriety, and college life.

President Bunting and I talked freely about parietal hours, about changing attitudes toward sexuality, and about the Radcliffe community. At the end of our conversation she warmly encouraged me to attend the open houses she hosted each Sunday at her home. When I left the office I felt I had met an unusual and wonderful person. A week before finals I was informed that I was no longer suspended and could return to Henry House, pending the outcome of my trial. Although no one confirmed it, I was sure that President Bunting had intervened for me.

The trial was a travesty, a collusion of town and gown. Using some flimsy pretense, the judge ordered us all into his chambers, thus skillfully removing the possibility that the local press would pick up the story and create a public embarrassment for the university. The deans were asked to speak first. "What does Harvard have to say about this?" and then, "What does Radcliffe have to say about this?" When Rick's turn came, he stood up defiantly and delivered a short treatise on changing morals. The statement I remember went something like this: "In our generation, we don't have to consume a bottle of wine before sleeping together." My turn never came. I was never asked to speak. No one even looked at me.

It was over in half an hour. Rick and I were given deferred prosecution and placed under the supervision of our college deans. Immediately afterward, a police squad car delivered me from the courthouse to a Harvard classroom to sit for my final exam in political sociology. The exam had been given earlier, at the same time as my trial, and Harvard had insisted that I be escorted directly to the make-up exam to preclude the possibility that someone might pass me an advance copy of the exam. It was a disturbing inference. I had breached the prevailing code of morals, creating a public embarrassment for the college and was now suspect on all moral grounds. I would be tolerated, but it was clear that I would no longer be treated with the respect accorded to the Ivy League elite. A week or so after the trial I received a letter from President Bunting:

> Dear Elayne,
>
> This is to confirm in writing the action of the Radcliffe administration which I reported to you orally.
>
> In our opinion the behavior leading to your arrest was reprehensible, showed poor judgement and certainly did not reflect creditably on you, your family or the college. We have seriously considered requiring you to withdraw from the college, but in view of the recommendations of the court and our evidence of your growing sense of responsibility we have chosen to put you on probation until the end of this academic year. . . .
>
> I wish to make it quite clear that if the terms of your probation are broken you may be asked to leave the College immediately and that any misrepresentation of the seriousness with which we view your past conduct or other willful expression of attitudes that we believe harmful to the Radcliffe community will also be reason for severance. If you do not feel you can or wish to comply with these conditions I recommend that you voluntarily withdraw from the College for at least a semester.

President Bunting's letter was the last assault, catching me off guard after what I thought had been a clear communication about the changing social mores of the college community. I had no way of knowing about any battles President Bunting might have fought with her Harvard counterparts or with the conservative Radcliffe board of trustees. The only issue I understood was my own sense of betrayal. It was the winter of 1964 and I had just completed my first course in institutional hypocrisy and the politics of gender—graduating with honors.

That spring I took a sociology course in race and social structure from Professor Tom Pettigrew. Still bristling at the way I had been treated by the Harvard/Radcliffe establishment, I was ready for a change. In April, a classmate of mine named Johnny Mudd invited me to join a group of Harvard graduates headed to Tougaloo College, a private black college in Jackson, Mississippi. The project, which was funded by an extraordinary individual named Charles Merrill, provided summer tuition and expenses for black Tougaloo faculty to work toward advanced degrees in northern colleges while Harvard graduate students took over summer faculty assignments on a volunteer basis. I had only completed my junior year, but that didn't appear to be an obstacle. I set off on a Greyhound bus to Jackson. It was May 1964.

My journey to the South was not political, nor was it a principled stand based on a critique of racist society. What I responded to was more of an unconscious pull. There were no real black people in my life. There were only bits and pieces of other people's experiences and memories lodged deep inside of me, alongside an ethical foundation that had been established during my early years and an adventurous nature that has been part of me for as long as I can remember.

When I first arrived at Tougaloo I was fairly removed from the turmoil outside of the campus. An early letter I sent to my parents reflects both my innocence and my distance from the events of the day:

> The kids are just lovely. They've had pretty bad schooling, but they are real bright and quite willing to work. . . . As far as Jackson itself, I imagine there will be a lot of trouble this summer, but don't worry, because I won't be involved. There will be demonstrations, but I won't be taking part, so please don't be alarmed when

you hear about trouble down here. . . . I'm sure I'll be safe and sound and have a nice quiet summer.

I was teaching sociology, writing, and art history at Tougaloo when Student Nonviolent Coordinating Committee (SNCC) staff member Jesse Morris came to see me. Jesse was the first movement person I had met. I remember thinking how somber he looked, how subdued and thoughtful, with his stately composure and wry smile. I can see him now, walking slowly up the dirt road to the main hall of Tougaloo College. He was not much older than I was, but there was a seriousness about him that placed him beyond time.

It was May 1964, about two weeks before the Freedom Summer orientation in Oxford, Ohio. Jesse had heard I had been involved in Professor Pettigrew's study of the African American community in Boston, and approached me about designing a survey that Freedom Summer volunteers could administer across the state. Pettigrew sent me materials from the Boston study, and Jesse and I began working on the design. The day before staff was scheduled to leave for Ohio, the survey was still not complete.

I don't remember making a conscious decision to join the Freedom Movement. I just got on a bus headed for the Oxford orientation. Unaware of the significance of my action, I entered the vortex of energy that was the movement, fulfilling my childhood dreams of adventure and my longing for a world of meaning.

At the Oxford orientation I operated as staff, working on the survey in the day and filling in on the WATS (wide area telephone service) line at night. At the time, staff status was more a function of the work people did rather than whether they were on a payroll or whose payroll they were on. Still, someone had to pay for food and essentials. During the time I taught at Tougaloo I lived on money I had saved from teaching Hebrew school during the year. After the first six-week summer session was over I began working at the Jackson COFO (Council of Federated Organizations) office. Once my savings were gone in early August, I headed to the Catskills to work as a waitress.

When I returned south with my small savings after Labor Day, SNCC had just added a large number of summer volunteers to the payroll, a controversial action that strained the racial balance of staff and led to a temporary freeze on additional SNCC staff. Jesse took me to meet with Dick Jewitt from the Congress of Racial Equality (CORE), who graciously agreed to place me on the CORE payroll—where I remained, at $15.00 a week, for the rest of my stay in Mississippi.

Working as a white woman in the midst of the freedom struggle was a tremendous privilege, but it was also a source of enormous tension for me. I completely identified with the SNCC principles of local leadership, respect for the common man, consensus, and participatory democracy, but I was always aware of my status as a newcomer in a very deep and lengthy struggle. My arrival in Jackson a month before Freedom Summer as part of the Harvard-Tougaloo exchange had placed me in a peculiar position. I was not grouped with the legion of summer volunteers who, it seemed to me, were often viewed as a kind of disposable labor and public relations source, but neither did I share a personal history with the pre–Freedom Summer civil rights community.

I had arrived too late to be incorporated into the culture of trust that was the hallmark of what movement people often called the "Beloved Community." I participated in tortuous policy deliberations and attended countless SNCC staff meetings and retreats; I even submitted a position paper at the SNCC staff retreat at Waveland in 1964, writing from the perspective of staff. But I never felt myself to be a member of the Beloved Community. My skills as an organizer gave me the ability to work and move freely in the field, but my membership in the civil rights community was always marginal.

In the fall of 1964 Jesse Morris, who headed the Mississippi Federal Programs effort, handed me an advance copy of the Poverty Bill and asked me to come up with a proposal to implement in nearby Madison County. Skeptical about designing a strategy that would rely on the cooperation of local Mississippi agencies, I proposed a different approach:

> October 11, 1964
>
> After a review of these types of programs it is my personal feeling that little can be done directly through the community and the federal agencies sponsoring these programs. . . . Our job is to put pressure on local agencies to cooperate with federal men. . . . As to how to apply this pressure, I have a few ideas. One is to organize a large scale welfare type organization, staffed by local people and administered through the political organization of the Freedom Democratic Party (FDP). Using the blocks as units, I would like to train about ten people in the

basics of the Social Security Act, disability provisions, plus unemployment laws, plus welfare programs like Aid to Dependent Children and Old Age Assistance. They could get around to all the families in the Negro communities and . . . advise the people [on] what programs they are eligible for, and help them apply and appeal denials. If we do not win our just appeals, we have a legal leverage in Washington.

The organizing strategy I outlined was one of the early versions of welfare rights. I saw it as an attempt to force the white community to play by the rules and, at the same time, as a way to dramatize the institutionalization of racism in federally funded state programs.

The initiative took me to the State House in Jackson, where I obtained copies of state regulations for various federal programs. During the fall and early winter I visited projects around the state, answering questions on eligibility and documenting incidents where black Mississippians were denied access to programs. It was an eerie feeling, traveling alone, operating primarily as an independent, borrowing vehicles from other civil rights workers. During the summer, when discipline was tight, it would have been unthinkable for a white woman to travel alone, for fear of accidentally provoking the insane rage that accompanied white supremacists' fears of "race-mixing." But the sense of discipline that prohibited solitary action had been worn down in the events of the past summer.

My experiences in the field didn't fit with how I had been trained at Harvard to decode the world. The more I worked with local people, the more I became immersed in the way they viewed the world, and the more difficult it became for me to communicate with people outside the movement. This struggle to communicate comes through clearly in a letter I wrote to a Marxist classmate during this period:

I really can't talk too much analytically anymore about the movement or what we or anyone is doing here or why or what it means. But I can tell stories of things that have happened. . . .

Mrs. Ruffin, from Laurel Mississippi, a fifty-year-old woman on welfare who runs the freedom library in Laurel, came into the office the other day after reading some magazines and books. She said to me, "Honey, you know . . . that war in Vietnam, well I'm not even sure we should be there, or if we are, which side we should be on." Mrs. Ruffin sat down with another woman from the Jackson

FDP (Freedom Democratic Party), who also had less than six years of school, and wrote a letter to the FDP chairmen in each county, asking them what they thought about Vietnam, and about 300 kids getting kicked out of school in one county for wearing SNCC buttons. I don't know the response to Vietnam. I do know we've had school boycotts since then.

Let me redo Marx a little. A man is not really a slave to the objective conditions of his life. By that it means that a man is a slave to the past and present. How I would change it would be to say that a man is only a slave to the extent that he is a slave to the future. To the extent that he could not perceive alternatives and choices in his future, to that extent he is not free. To the extent that he could not effect these, perhaps he would also be not free.

I was becoming radicalized. I no longer trusted the *New York Times* to bring me the news or the FBI to protect me. When I read *New York Times* accounts of events in which I had participated, or listened to SNCC staff plead with Justice Department officials to send in agents to observe situations that were almost certain to become violent, I realized I had entered a different America from the one in which I had been raised. Liberal politicians talked about reason and compromise, but what we were up against lay outside these categories. The enemy was the preservation of a way of life built on the subjugation of one part of the population by another part, based on convention and law, and enforced by violence and intimidation. Reason and compromise held no sway against that power.

In the fall of 1964, several women huddled in a conspiratorial press around a mimeograph machine in the middle of the night at a SNCC staff meeting in Waveland, Mississippi. My friends and I were responding to a call for position papers on issues confronting the movement. Our paper, titled "The Position of Women in the Movement," one of over thirty papers presented at the November SNCC retreat, addressed the issue of sexism. We wrote as movement women, objecting to the "assumption of male superiority," to women being called "girls," to women being left out of key decisions, to women's talents and skills being underutilized, and to a host of gender-based situations that were emblematic of sexism. No individual was listed as author. Instead, "Name withheld by request" was typed in the upper corner, the same notation of anonymity that marked "Semi-Introspective," the position paper that I submitted as an individual. Both as an individual author and as a member of a group, I struggled with the conflict between the desire to speak my mind and the discomfort of speaking in a public forum. But it was a discomfort tinged with a mischievous quality. I remember how I felt, like a naughty schoolgirl, sneaking up to the second floor of the main building with one or two co-conspirators late in the evening, quickly placing the copies of "The Position of Women in the Movement" on a table alongside the other stacks of position papers, and then turning, laughing, and running hurriedly down the staircase to avoid discovery.

In my travels across the state working in Federal Programs I had collected examples of sexism (we labeled it "discrimination"), which were incorporated into the text of the memo. In the analysis section, I remember my voice as one of the more strident, the voice of an outsider with little to lose. I had been in the state less than six months, a relative newcomer free of the considerations that came from long-standing loyalties, and quick to challenge what I saw as inconsistent intellectual positions.

Despite the camaraderie and periods of intense reflection that character-ized my experiences at the Waveland retreat, it was a deeply unsettling time for me. In the position paper, "Semi-Introspective," that I submitted to the collective deliberations, I wrote, "As an organization we have never decided whether or not to be: (1) agitators (2) demonstrators or (3) organizers." I had hoped to find clear direction in Waveland, but I left in sadness and confusion, with no clear sense of direction or of renewal.

After Waveland I became more focused on day-to-day work. It was the only thing I trusted. By late fall 1964 I had collected considerable evidence of the systematic denial of black Mississippians' rights to participate in federal pro-grams. With no leverage at the local level, I looked to Washington, arranging prospective meetings between Mississippians and sympathetic contacts in the federal agencies that oversaw Mississippi's federally funded programs. The meetings would take place during the MFDP's upcoming trip to Washington. Staging these kinds of meetings was classic movement strategy — orchestrating situations where ordinary people could confront the people and institutions that, until that moment, had operated as the unchallenged arbiters of power in their lives. It was a powerful tool that only sometimes changed the imme-diate course of events but almost always affected the dynamics of traditional power relationships.

In early October, as a poll watcher for the Agricultural Stabilization and Conservation Services (ASCS) election, I had witnessed one such confrontation — a series of faces, the weathered faces of black farmers as they stepped up with determination to place an X or sign their names on a ballot that would decide who would serve on the powerful Madison County ASCS board, the body that determined how many acres of cotton each farmer was permitted to grow. In 1964, cotton was still king, and cotton allotments, with their accompanying price supports, were the mechanism that determined which farmers would prosper in this marginal agrarian economy.

The black farmers, who had come to vote in the ASCS election for the first time, moved slowly and resolutely toward the ballot box, hats in hand, eyes lowered, steady in their gait, refusing to be turned back by the hostile stares of local whites who crowded into the designated polling place, the A&W Root Beer Stand. Many who cast their votes that day were arrested, along with several poll watchers, including myself, but jail could not curtail the momentum of protest. It was one more in a long line of incidents, a series of confrontations between authority and legitimacy, between the racist practices of society and the law. No matter what the immediate outcome, each of these confrontations served to unravel the fear woven into the fabric of segregation.

In January 1965, along with several busloads of MFDP members, I headed to Washington for the Congressional Challenge. Picket lines of black Mississippians moved up and down the avenues in front of the White House and Capitol, calling attention to the voting violations and segregationist practices of the all-white Mississippi Democratic Party and questioning the right of the white congressmen from Mississippi to take seats in the House and Senate. Before leaving Mississippi I had scheduled several meetings between local people and officials from key federal agencies. With the drama and pain of the summer fresh in public memory, there were still many open doors in Washington. On a cold January afternoon, groups of six to twenty Mississippians, accompanied by SNCC staff, filed through some of those doors into the offices of highly placed officials in agencies like Health, Education, and Welfare; Veteran Affairs; and the Department of Agriculture.

I was the escort for a small group of quiet and determined World War II veterans whose benefits had been denied. At the Bureau of Veteran Affairs, one by one, they told their stories. The bureaucrats sitting across the room, brows furrowed in distress, furiously took notes on a truth not heard before in those halls.

The Cooperative Division of the Department of Agriculture was in a small office tucked away along a sterile corridor in a cold, sprawling, stone building. I had contacted its single staff person during an earlier visit in November. This time, after a brief conversation and an exchange of addresses with a man in a brown suit, I felt ready to provide assistance to fledgling farm co-ops. This was how the movement worked: if you cared deeply about something, could make a strong case for it, and were ready to put your own energies into it, you were generally allowed to do whatever it was you wanted to do. My personal experiences with the Israeli collective, kibbutz and moshav, had given me a confidence in cooperatives as economically and socially viable vehicles for change. Back in Mississippi, Jesse Morris was receiving increasingly adamant requests from the town of Batesville in Panola County for help in organizing a co-op. No black staff were available to go, and I don't recall if any white men were interested in going. In retrospect, I believe it was probably Jesse's confidence in my ability to move the project forward that sent me that March into the hill country of northwestern Mississippi.

Part of my decision to work in Batesville was an attempt to avoid what I felt was an escalating negativity in black-white relationships. The meetings I had set up during the Congressional Challenge between local people and Washington bureaucrats were exhilarating, but the interpersonal difficulties I faced during the trip to Washington troubled me. I can still remember the look of disdain on the face of the black male staff member who greeted me as I walked through the doors of the Washington SNCC office. "What are you doing here?" were his first words. "Why did you take up a seat on the bus that could have gone to a local Mississippi person?" It wasn't an unreasonable question, and I had a reasonable answer, having traveled to Washington in a private car specifically to avoid occupying a seat on the bus. What hurt was the anger that accompanied his challenge and the never-ending requirement that I justify my work. It unsettled me, forcing me to look at myself as veteran staff might see me: as one more white person trying to get in on the action.

The next day, when I tried to finalize the list of SNCC staff that would act as escorts for the agency meetings, I found that some who had previously committed to the project were vacillating. I didn't take it as a rejection of this particular effort. Staff were heavily involved in the daily protests and political maneuvers, and with so much going on, I didn't have the status to facilitate a parallel event, even one sanctioned and supported by the MFDP. Eventually, I was able to pair a staff member with each group, but my memory of that day is of desperately pleading with people to participate in something I had mistakenly assumed was a shared priority. It was a lesson I took to heart, leading me to conclude that I needed to concentrate my efforts on a single project, outside the maelstrom of movement politics.

In the field, tensions were less marked. If a person was an effective field worker, whether black or white, male or female, he or she was likely to be respected. In the annals of the movement, working in Federal Programs was not very glamorous. But out in the field, the federal programs initiative proved a powerful organizing tool, and as a result it had a place at the project level as long as the person in charge was seen as competent.

When I arrived in Batesville in early March 1965, the groundwork for the co op had been laid and resolve was strong. I was given the front bedroom in a farmhouse owned by Robert Miles, a courageous and outspoken independent farmer. Mr. Miles, his wife, Mona, and their two children slept on the floor in a room at the back of the house, where they had moved months earlier after local whites shot into the front bedroom. There were always several civil rights workers living at the Miles home. The strength, dignity, and graciousness of Mr. and Mrs. Miles, along with the sweet devotion of their family life, provided the bedrock for my daily work.

The bullet holes in the pane-glass window and in the headboard of my bed were reminders of just how real and serious a threat we were to the white power structure, and conversely, just how serious a threat they were to our personal safety. Once, in the dead of night, on the way to the kitchen, I unexpectedly came across one of the neighbors who rotated watches in the dawn-to-dusk rooftop patrol. We all knew the men were there but seldom saw them. For the most part, they came and went wordlessly in the darkness. That evening, the neighbor on watch was taking a break, warming his hands around a cup of coffee, shotgun at his side. When I passed by, he looked down toward the floor and nodded his head silently. It was not the first shotgun I had seen in Mississippi. Months earlier, I had walked into the house of another farmer, Mr. Steptoe, late at night, only to find SNCC field secretary Rap Brown asleep in a rocking chair, a shotgun across his arms. We didn't talk much about the guns. Nonviolence was still the credo; in the trenches, however, self-defense was becoming the reality.

Local leadership was in place. Indeed, the community was way ahead of the civil rights workers on this one, so far ahead that they didn't seem to be bothered by the fact that their main resource during this pivotal time was a very young white woman. I began visiting different farms, often accompanied by Chris Williams, a white civil rights worker who had done some of the groundwork before my arrival. Sometimes the Reverend traveled with us and sometimes I called on farmers by myself. House by house, we talked about our plans. Sunday was church meeting day. I loved the meetings, the starched dresses of the children, the slow rhythm of the day—moving from song to sermon, to call and response, the spirit-filled cadence of faith, and back to song, to passing the collection plate, to song again, bodies swaying, hand-held cardboard fans adorned with images of Jesus fluttering in the still air thick with moisture. Sunday was a day of renewal, of personal faith and collective courage.

When I went to individual farms I would always try to get the woman of the household to commit to come to meetings. "We know who chops the cotton," I would say—referring to the difficult job of weeding the cotton rows—to which I would receive a nod of agreement. But most of the women never appeared at the general meetings. Sometimes they would promise to come, perhaps to please me, or perhaps because they didn't know how to speak honestly to me, but I learned not to expect them to appear.

The farmers formed an organization, elected officers, and pooled resources to purchase seed. The meetings were getting larger and larger. Momentum was growing. The co-op was becoming real. The members adopted by-laws, bought and distributed seed, and planted crops. The man in the brown suit from the Department of Agriculture in Washington helped us secure a $78,000 War on Poverty program loan to purchase farm equipment.

By that time I had become relatively isolated from most staff, except for co-op visits with Chris Williams and late-night talks with my friend Penny Patch. In my spare time I began experimenting with the new organizational tool of photography. I had never thought of a camera as anything more than a way to capture memories, but in the field photography had become a way to democratize what got documented. Instead of waiting for the few overworked SNCC photographers to come and take pictures, anyone could become part of documenting the movement. I sent for my camera. Emmie Schrader, a friend from my Jackson office days, taught me to develop film in the darkroom of the SNCC Atlanta office. I shot rolls of film of co-op meetings, Mr. Miles's farm, the community center, the streets, and the plantation shacks that still housed families of struggling sharecroppers.

One of my favorite subjects was Mr. Miles's mammoth sow. I was fascinated by her massive white-pink body and was fond of following her movements from the other side of the fence. I found a certain tranquillity in watching and photographing her. It must have looked odd to the household, this young white woman photographing the family pig. I was making a print of Mr. Miles's pig when Jim Forman, SNCC's executive secretary, walked into the Atlanta darkroom where I was working. Jim was indignant at this blatant waste of SNCC resources. What possible value could there be in an 8″ × 11″ photograph of a pig? He railed on and on, while I slunk away, properly chastised. I had been uncovered in a middle-class pose, developing photographs of a pig while the revolution was raging around me. In the political climate of the time, when whites were being accused of "bourgeois sentimentality," I was caught.

Back in Batesville, I continued to photograph the different stages of the co-op. I invited Maria Varela, a SNCC staff person who was also working with photography, to visit the project. When I left the state a few months later, I gave my photos and negatives to Maria, who made other trips to Batesville and eventually created a slide show called "How to Organize a Farm Co-op." Other co-ops followed, other people continued Federal Programs work, and Mr. Miles was instrumental in organizing the Federation of Southern Cooperatives, where he served as the first elected vice-president. The Batesville co-op itself lasted more than fifteen years.

My time in Mississippi was nearing its end. No local person had ever made me feel unwelcome, but the shift in staff attitudes toward the participation of whites made it increasingly difficult for me to continue. I believed passionately that the civil rights struggle, as a human rights struggle, was mine to share. At the same time, I was painfully aware of the tensions emanating from the differences in background, beliefs, and communication styles between blacks and whites, educated and uneducated, northern and southern, veteran and newcomer. The constants of external violence, financial crisis, policy gridlock, and the growing support for an all-black movement pushed tensions even higher. My journal entries from that spring reveal the dark demons of frustration and despair.

March 16, 1965

Coming into a new project is very painful. People are full of pain, guarded, unhappy, depressed, bored, mostly hurt. It is the same everywhere. . . . They are pessimistic, or realistic about the extent of the change that they are producing. Mostly they are caught up in the recognition of the faction fighting. . . . Things never seem to get done. No one seems to believe in their ability to affect change. And then they are all exhausted by the tensions of movement life. We are the hardest wearing on each other. We destroy each other, but mostly offer each other no comfort.

As long as I was totally consumed by the work, I was able to maintain a manageable distance from staff strife, but as the co-op moved from the organizational to the operational stage, my role became less clear and my doubts about working as a white female in a black movement harder to dispel. I was an organizer, but I knew little about farming or marketing crops. I no longer felt that local farmers were peering anxiously down the road waiting for a male, preferably a black male, to appear, but at the same time I felt less connected to the daily work.

In May 1965 my Harvard colleague Johnny Mudd arrived in Batesville to pick up a car he had loaned me during one of his trips north. Johnny offered to stay in Batesville and keep things moving while I went north to scout outlets for the co-op's okra. It was there that I met the remarkable man whom I would marry two years later. When I returned south, it was clear to me that Johnny was much better suited than I to move the co-op into its next phase. Johnny was a master of detail, a relentless intellect, a totally committed individual — and a male. The Panola County co-op finally had their "man." In May 1965 I left Mississippi.

What I learned in Mississippi about people, about political and social change, about race and class, about politics, about right action, and about my identity as a woman have stayed with me to this day. But I never thought of my own actions as having historical significance. The drama itself was too great, the stage too large, and the characters too brilliant for me to see myself even as part of the play.

Being a white woman in that time and in that context was incredibly challenging for me. The movement gave me the opportunity to work and the opportunity to assume considerable responsibility, but despite the civil rights community's focus on social justice, the society of the early sixties was still a heavily sexist one. There were times when I felt that neither gender nor race interfered with my work, but there were many more times when I was acutely aware of just how much race and gender impacted my effectiveness.

Nevertheless, my work in the movement, even within situations that I would later identify as sexist, radically altered my personal expectations of what I could accomplish as a woman. The power created by individuals acting from commitment and principle was incredible, and being swept up in that power was a freeing experience that transcended gender. I worked and I read and I talked with my women friends. In a milieu of challenge, where all social mores were suspect and all actions subject to scrutiny, I sifted through the powerful ideas of Anaïs Nin, Doris Lessing, Betty Friedan, and Simone de Beauvoir and considered the world around me.

It was this vibrant context, the collective influence of highly charged events and wonderful minds, that led me to new perspectives and realizations. On balance, I attribute the fundamental shift in awareness of myself as a woman to the juxtaposition of my experiences with gender equality in the progressive atmosphere of the kibbutz, where it was a given, and the presence of gender discrimination in a civil rights community that declared itself to be egalitarian. This was the ground upon which all else stood. Added to this was the intellectual stimulation of a remarkable group of women, both black and white; the SNCC tradition of constant questioning and challenge; and the works of feminist writers, viewed through the lens of an outsider, a white woman in an environment that was becoming increasingly intolerant of whites. The result was a shift in my awareness of what it meant to be a woman in American society.

I have been asked by feminist historians why more of us who are considered to be "early feminists" did not go on to leadership positions in the women's movement. My response is that despite the personal anger that I sometimes felt when confronted with sexist situations, and despite my yearning for equality between the sexes, it was always the freedom struggle that held me. To shift my identity, commitment, and energy from the freedom struggle to the women's struggle was not something I could do, especially at a time when I was still grieving over my separation from the movement. The freedom struggle was the flame; all else was shadow.

I left the South with two powerful realizations. The first was a deep appreciation for ordinary people and the ways in which they understand the world. My teachers were the people whose faith, intelligence, and willingness to risk everything were the heart of the black freedom struggle. The second realization was a terrifying, gut-level understanding of racism, a terrible awareness of its corrosive and pervasive legacy. As an outsider, I had underestimated the power of racism as a social phenomenon and the lengths to which our society would go to preserve its privilege.

Somewhere, in the midst of the struggle, I felt that my fellow civil rights workers and I lost whatever ability we once had to move beyond race in our own lives. There were moments when race and gender did not separate us. I know that to be true. The feeling of being one mind and one body is so profound that its memory is palpable. I think of Mississippi as a sacrament. It was in that communion that I experienced a grace whose memory has sustained me as I have moved along in my life and in my work.

When I left the South I was devastated, dazed, displaced. I hadn't even noticed that my Mississippi experiences had pushed me quietly but completely out of the American mainstream. My values, my frame of reference, my understanding of society, my identity as a young adult, had all been realigned in the reality of the struggle. When I left that reality I was lost. To have returned to Radcliffe and finished my senior year would have gone against everything I had experienced in Mississippi. After Mississippi, I was unable to be part of any system of privilege. To have bowed my head to receive the final "credential" of society, a Harvard diploma, was absolutely unthinkable.

Instead of returning to school, I drifted into the turbulent and heady counterculture that was emerging in New York City. In some ways it was an easy transition. The counterculture lacked the political focus of the Freedom

Movement, but it suited my deepening alienation from mainstream institutions. In a letter to a friend that I wrote right before I left the South, I talked about the struggle to break through the conventions of society, personally and politically:

> Mostly what is going on is the unstructuring of the old ways of dealing with things to as great an extent as possible. It is difficult to drop the old categories and structures, difficult to recognize them, to get others to see them. Probably the hardest things are getting people to see that things don't have to be done the way things are [always] done. People seem only to accept this provisionally. Even extending things back from society to the individual to say that we must free ourselves if we ever hope to "free society" is something whose understanding is an ever deepening involvement, bringing you further and further somewhere, though the words themselves are operationally meaningless to bring you there.

My sojourn in New York City began in the Tompkins Square apartment of Alan Ribback, who was editing the record "Movement Soul," a compilation of music recorded in southern black churches. Emmie Schrader was living with Alan and making a filmstrip on the Vietnam War. It was at Alan's apartment, during my okra-scouting trip, that I met my husband, Chip, a folk singer from Macon, Georgia, whose stand on segregation had separated him from his Georgia roots. Chip was a poet and musician totally immersed in his own artistic expression and the "happenings" of the Lower East Side. His apolitical stance toward life was appealing to me at a time when I felt particularly vulnerable to the aggressive emotions that I associated with political life. Chip was antiracist, he understood in broad terms what I had gone through, and he gave me a lot of room. He was also many other things, but at that time I could not see much further than the moment.

During the days, I worked with minority kids in the ghettos of the city. At night I rejoined my new community, the Lower East Side. Chip played in an avant-garde jazz-rock band called the Free Spirits, the first jazz fusion band. The band performed at the center of the explosive counterculture music scene — the Balloon Farm, Fillmore East, Ondine's, and the Scene — opposite bands like Warhol's Velvet Underground and the Doors. The night Dr. Martin Luther King Jr. was assassinated, the Free Spirits were playing Fillmore East opposite the Who. The band lobbied rock impresario Bill Graham to acknowledge the event in a more than superficial way. Graham, who appeared nervous and angry at being asked to make a political statement, responded by calling the band "a bunch of unruly musicians." It was a sad and lonely evening for me. I had moved from the austerity of political correctness to the psychedelic laissez-faire of the counterculture, but I had not succeeded in quieting the persistent voices that still spoke to me from that clear place inside my heart.

I loved the freewheeling feeling of being in the midst of people who were disconnected from mainstream society, but in a more fundamental way I was in hiding, grieving for what had been lost. Occasionally I would run into local political activists. I remember looking at Jeff Jones and Mark Rudd, two student leaders of the Columbia uprising, as they urged me, afire with excitement, to come uptown with them and join the struggle. They seemed so young and so immature. It reminded me of the way I'd felt at the end of my year in Mississippi when new volunteers would show up in Jackson — old and tired. The gulf between us was too wide. I was glad that students were challenging their institutions, but I didn't share the same political focus as these young college folks, and I had exhausted my interest in politics as personal adventure. Students' concerns just didn't seem all that important.

In 1968, Chip's band moved to San Francisco after one of their songs, "Witchi-Tai-To," rose to the top of the national charts. We soon left San Francisco for the hills of Sonoma County, where our son was born, then in early 1969 to Colorado, where, a year and a half later, our daughter was born. We settled in Huerfano County, a rural Hispanic region of southern Colorado in the foothills of the Sangre de Cristo range, where we lived with our friends in a commune called the Anonymous Artists of America, or Triple A (AAA). The commune centered on the nuclear families of the AAA band members. In the beginning we lived in a tepee. I tended the garden, canned and preserved food, picked piñon nuts, basked in the sun, and sat meditation in the midst of the aspens, the junipers, the cedars, the sun, the snow, and the silence. Within a few years our small group of families had built houses, a water system, a barn and a bathhouse, and had begun grappling with the tougher issues of communal life — fairness, compromise, consensus, character, individual freedom, and collective responsibility.

The local community was poor and accepting, despite their reservations about our lifestyle. Eventually we became friends with our neighbors, sharing the concerns and the work of the community—the school, the politics, the roads, the environment, and the future. I loved the gentility of the Hispanic culture, its devotion to family, and its deep connection to the land. As a community we did wonderful things together.

I organized parents to petition the school board for a kindergarten. I linked up with the community college a hundred miles away to open a community school. I worked on grants for a playground that was designed and constructed by the community and a bilingual multicultural preschool. I wrote grants and directed a series of oral history projects that culminated in a play sponsored by the National Endowment for the Humanities that toured southern Colorado, celebrating the area's history and culture. Huerfano County was home. I loved living there with my husband as we raised our family, I loved the rough and beautiful land we lived on, and I cherished the opportunity to work and contribute to the timeless life around me.

Our last project in southern Colorado was constructing, launching, and operating a regional FM radio station financed through a socially conscious investment group committed to employee-owned businesses. Chip had always maintained his musical connection to the world. The radio station was his vision of linking the community through music and honest communication. Chip was general manager, sales manager, production manager, and program director; I was business manager and news director. Our slogan was "Community Radio Makes a Difference," and it really did. The ordinary people in the communities we served viewed the station as their own. We did original radio plays and provocative news series. High school kids put together shows, the football coach did sports, and on Sundays local people brought in their own collections of records and did specialty shows: bluegrass, classical, old time rock and roll, jazz, contemporary and traditional Spanish music. We were totally entwined in the life of the community.

Before the end of our first year of operation, the station had the highest Arbitron rating of any FM station in the state, and before the end of the 1980s it had won more than thirty-five statewide awards in broadcasting, including two consecutive awards for best editorial from the Colorado Society of Professional Journalists. But the station's popular success had a hidden cost: we had become a clear threat to the local power structure. Our politics were simple: "Tell it like it is." Our news and public affairs coverage challenged the control of city councils, county commissioners, and virtually every established political and economic institution in the community.

One day, a friend of ours inside the police department came into the station, his face drawn with concern. He warned us that rumors were being spread that we were big cocaine traffickers and that we were about to be set up and busted by the Colorado Bureau of Investigation. Hearing this slander was almost a relief. We had been feeling the animosity of the old guard toward us, an ominous sense of danger, but couldn't figure out what form the assault would take. When I walked past the plate-glass window in the front office I had an uneasy feeling, reminiscent of the way I felt walking past the shattered pane of glass in the front bedroom of Mr. and Mrs. Miles's farm house in Panola County. I suppose you could call it post-traumatic stress. It felt like instinct to me.

It never came to that. A week after Chip completed the installation of two translators, increasing our market coverage and bringing us into a viable economic position, the Jeep he was driving was broadsided by a vehicle running a red light. With Chip unable to walk or travel because of his injuries, there was no way we could meet our financial projections for the new markets. We frantically looked for local investors, but after strong initial interest, potential backers mysteriously disappeared. In early 1989 we sold the station and moved to Denver.

In many ways, leaving Huerfano County after twenty years was like leaving the South, filling me with a sense of loss. We had believed we would live out our lives in this community that we loved, and suddenly it was over. Chip didn't spend any time in regrets. Within a year he taught himself a new art form and entered a new profession, video and television production. The transition was more difficult for me. I knew I would never be part of another community in the way that I had been part of southern Colorado. I was back in the city. It was time to look around and see what there was to do.

I had always loved the city, but after twenty years in rural Colorado I had no credentials, no city friends to "network" with, and no experience that would translate into a career. I did have a college degree in alternative education, something I had managed to complete in 1974 through the University of Massachusetts University without Walls program, but education meant social action to me, and teaching in a school was not what I'd had in mind when I got my degree. I didn't know enough about the Denver community to write grants, and I had nothing to commend me to employers. I was forty-seven years old and I was starting over again. While I was figuring out how to reenter city life, I worked as a waitress in a local restaurant. My sisters were upset and worried, but I remembered what our father used to tell us: "A man never has to apologize for making a living." For me, being among working people was a way to get back to my center.

Before long I had found a forum where I could work, at the intersection of education and community. I was drawn to family literacy, first as an adult education teacher in a family literacy program, and later as curriculum coordinator of an adult education agency. The power of family was something I understood, and the idea of working toward social change by working with the family unit made sense to me. As part of my professional development I started taking courses at the University of Colorado at Denver, where I met several wonderful professors who shared my views on education and social change. At their invitation, I worked as a co-principal investigator in a federally funded research project focusing on high-achieving classrooms for minority students in Denver's public schools. My role was to explore the connection between home, community, and school.

The study brought up a new set of questions for me, and without really considering the implications, I enrolled in a doctoral program in Educational Leadership and Innovation. I still haven't committed to writing a dissertation, but what I've learned about applying formal analysis to problems of practice has given me a way to contribute to the public dialogue on education and social change.

Adult education led me to workforce education at the Community College of Denver (CCD), where I focused on skill development for entry-level workers. From workplace education it was a natural shift to my present focus, preparing women to move successfully from welfare to work. In many ways, my work in welfare reform is a return to the work that I did in the South. The circumstances of people's lives are different, but the work that engages me is the same: working with individuals to remove the barriers that prevent them from participating fully in society.

In March 1990, the U.S. Department of Labor and the American Association of Community Colleges named the CCD welfare-to-work project an exemplary program. The experts who approach the program, trying to decipher its unexpected success, tend to describe what we do in terms of "best practices." What they see is a blend of vocational training, case management, and workplace internships that lead into full-time jobs with career advancement. Those of us who work with the program on a day-to-day basis understand how much more is involved. For me, it is the sum of everything I've learned about working with people, about what it means to be marginalized, about poverty, about racism, about family, about community, about education, about goodness, about respect, about trust, about strength, about hope.

One of the unanticipated consequences of relocating to Denver was entering a community with a strong black presence. Being around black people again reminded me of the way I felt when I walked into JFK International after a year abroad and heard the sounds of English being spoken, or how I feel when I return to the town where I was born and walk in the salt air along the beach where I first learned to swim. It is a physical experience, a sense of homecoming. It was, and is, a bittersweet experience. In February 1995, I went to hear African American philosopher, professor, and author Cornel West speak at a black church in Denver. That night I wrote in my journal:

> The speech was beautiful, The speech was beautiful, partially from the experience of being in a black church, surrounded by a large number of black people of faith, and partially because of Cornel and his message. It has been so long since I have been there and so good to feel part of the black community again. It is the easiest thing in the world for me to do, to sink back into the congregation. All that has to happen is for a black person to look me in the eye and say, "It's still your struggle" and I'm there.
>
> We had believed it was our struggle, and then we were told it was not, left to struggle on our own with what it means to be separated from the black community and still feel a part of it. We partook of the sacrament, the struggle for freedom, and we understood that our humanity would be judged by how well we incorporated the knowledge of what that meant into our actions. But the space that we occupy is a lonely one. We miss our black brothers and sisters, and they are seldom available to us, seldom speak to us as white brothers and sisters. They are sometimes our colleagues, sometimes our students, sometimes our clients,

but seldom our brothers and sisters. That was the gift of hearing Cornel speak. His words to me were simple: "It is still your struggle."

For thirty years I rarely thought about my experiences in the South. When I occasionally saw friends from those days, we never really talked about the movement. The South lay shrouded in shadowy memories and in pain. At one point, I got a call from Casey Hayden, saying that a woman named Sara Evans would be contacting me to ask me about the Waveland position paper on women for a book she was writing. I remember asking if Sara Evans was black or white, and being stunned by the idea of a white female venturing into the history of the black movement. Sara Evans didn't contact me, but from my perspective it is just as well. At that time, there was not enough distance between me and the past for me to see clearly.

I listened eagerly to accounts of SNCC reunions. I longed to go, but was confused about it all and didn't really feel invited. When I heard about the upcoming thirty-year reunion of Freedom Summer in 1994 in Jackson, I was determined to attend. In the month before the reunion, something else moved me closer to the past. In the somber activity following my mother's death that winter, boxes of journals, letters, materials, and memorabilia that I had stored in my parents' basement made their way to Colorado, via my sweet sister Renee, who painstakingly sorted through the remnants of our family's life. In the weeks preceding Jackson I reread the contents of my boxes, the position papers, minutes of meetings, letters, and journals. Those reflections of a passionate, idealistic young woman, struggling to make sense of the world in the midst of extraordinary events, were my gateway into the turbulent emotions of the past, the beginnings of recapturing the wealth of memories stored deep within, and the beginnings of *this* work, the task of reflecting on the past and telling our stories to our children.

We were wide-eyed children, acting on dreams of equality and social justice, fighting the good fight, unwilling to accept the brutality and degradation of segregation, convinced that if we could only find a way to demonstrate the truth, justice would prevail.

From Africa to Mississippi

EMMIE SCHRADER ADAMS

I lived in Jamaica for twenty years and was never interviewed or contacted for any of the books about the Freedom Movement. So this is my one chance to say things I've always wanted to say, to tell stories I've always told but never written.

I came to Mississippi after two years living and working in the aftermath of two wars of liberation: in Kenya and in Algeria. The FBI had torn my family apart with their insinuations that I was part of a "Negro communist spy ring" in Africa. All members of my family were placed under a security clearance block because of me. My father was suicidally depressed by the FBI's revelations, my mother emotionally battered by his continual attacks on her, her church, and her alma mater for having caused my "ruin." I didn't discover the real world of injustice, brutality, and racism in Mississippi. That world had been with me since I stepped off the plane in Kenya in 1961. What I did find in Mississippi was a new America, or the seeds of it, in the community of the freedom struggle.

I was born in St. Paul, Minnesota, at the end of 1941, twelve days before Pearl Harbor. I was the youngest of four children born to Ernst-Joseph Schrader, eighth child of German immigrants, a lawyer, and Lydia Augusta Cutler, of old New England WASP ancestry, a devoted member of the Swedenborgian church. My father was born in 1895, the only one of his siblings to be born in this country. My grandparents may have emigrated because of family and social pressure over their "intertribal" marriage: she was Low German Protestant, he was High German Catholic. In Germany these two tribes had been shedding blood for centuries. The newly arrived Schrader family continued to speak German in the home. During World War I they suffered from the wave of anti-German feeling that swept the country: my father was kicked down the stairs at his high school; the family was no longer welcome at the Episcopal church they had been attending. When my father enlisted in the army, he discovered that as a German American he was not considered trustworthy to fight in Europe. He spent his life hoping to be accepted as a real American and never once traveled outside the country. This insecurity led him to espouse conservative political positions. In the McCarthy era he was convinced that there were twenty thousand communists at the University of Minnesota.

St. Paul was majority Catholic. My mother struggled against the Catholic power structure that controlled the city government and had made birth control, even condoms, illegal. In the 1950s she worked as part of a Planned Parenthood–led coalition of Protestant and Jewish forces to get those laws repealed. My father, with his warped outlook, thought that Margaret Sanger, the founder of Planned Parenthood, was a communist. There was a major social cleavage in St. Paul between Protestant and Catholic kids, the latter attending their own parochial school system. My dating Catholic boys in high school sent my father into paroxysms of distress, foreshadowing his later crucifixion over my loving across the color bar.

When my mother was confronted with my interracial path through life, she took it like a good Christian. She also understood that my fighting against segregation and the war in Vietnam was consistent with the Christianity she had taught me. She may have been fairly aware of the racial evils of the world she inhabited, and perhaps even felt guilty about not having done more to fight them, but the sexual freedom and my years of pot smoking were much harder for her to deal with. Still, she never cut me off and always treated me with motherly love. I have always thought that both Judaism and Christianity, in their root forms, are the revolution, not the status quo. Those who have perverted both of them over the centuries cannot stamp out the message of struggle and liberation that is at the core of both religions.

In a modern sense I would say that my mother was not liberated: she suffered through a relatively unhappy marriage. But in the world of her church, she escaped my father, so on Sunday they went their separate ways; he was an Episcopalian. My mother's father had agreed to their marriage only on condition they sign an agreement that the children would be brought up as Swedenborgians. Our church was ill attended, a shrinking congregation in a church of no social status, located on the edge of an expanding ghetto.

As a child I used to hear that our church had branches in West and South Africa. From pictures in the national church paper I gathered that our fellow Swedenborgians were black, not white South Africans. I never understood why this little church should have taken root in Africa, for we were too tiny to sponsor missionaries. Some thirty years later, in Jamaica, when I started to read Swedenborg's eighteenth-century writings for myself, I stumbled on the answer: this famous Swedish scholarly genius turned mystic had regularly gone into long comas, during which he visited the world of spirits, or the after-death world. On his return to terrestrial consciousness he wrote of his spiritual education there in many volumes. At one point he marvels at the number of Africans who people the highest of the heavens, and he is told by his angelic guide that the African culture is the most open to the direct absorption of spiritual truths. This struck me as an eighteenth-century variation on the ancient Greek report that, of all peoples, the Ethiopians were the most beloved by the gods and had been the first to be taught the proper rites of divine worship. But I cannot blame my lifelong journey through black worlds on my Swedenborgianism, for no one ever taught me as a child about these obscure Afrophile passages in Swedenborg's writings. I found them by accident when I was already a mother of black children and a citizen of a black nation — Jamaica.

I think as a child I got the impression that I wasn't too needed in my world, because I very early began trying to peck my way out of it. I started running away at age four, then tried again at age nine and age ten, the last two times with co-conspirators. We never got far. We were busted by a combination of police and parents. I was usually the one who was perceived as the ringleader, a pattern that followed me through high school. Interesting that the last two times I ran away my escape route was to have been the Mississippi, by river raft straight south to the Gulf of Mexico. Jamaicans have a folk belief that the Mississippi flows all the way to Jamaica, following a bed underneath the sea.

The fact that before reaching my final home in Jamaica in 1971 I first became caught up in the war against segregation and terrorism in Mississippi doesn't surprise me. One thinks strange thoughts when reviewing one's life in reverse order.

What did I know about the Old South? Nothing — except for one memory from my childhood: Sometime around 1950 my mother's college friend moved with her family to Minnesota from St. Louis, Missouri. They told a story that stuck in my mind about Negroes, long, long lines of them, trying to integrate a white swimming pool. I had this image of these scary long lines of Negroes stretching across wide fields, all walking to the swimming pool, and somehow made the connection that this was what had caused this family, with their three little daughters, to emigrate to the North. It was the mid-1950s. About St. Paul African Americans I knew nothing. There was a black community somewhere beyond our little old church, but I was not allowed to go there. Nor were we allowed to go to certain movie theaters because, I later learned, they were near the black neighborhood.

In the sixth grade my parents moved me to an all-girls private school, a college-prep school that remained unofficially segregated for the whole of my seven years there. As senior year approached and our class, the class of 1959, was preparing to take over the student government, we turned our energy to trying to reform the school. We voiced our discontent with the authoritarianism in school administration, the lack of real student and teacher participation in significant decision-making, and the depressive effects these had on school life. Protesting the lily-white complexion of our student body never occurred to me. I had still never met a black person.

After graduation I spent the summer in France with the Experiment in International Living. I lived with a French family and tried to speak French all day long, until I started to think and even dream in it. This summer brought me my eventual college roommate and lifelong friend, Dorothy Stoneman, as well as a penchant for learning about other cultures through trying to learn their languages. Crossing back through the Strait of Gibraltar on the ship home, I was captivated by the mountains of Africa looming in the distance. Something reverberated inside me, as if I was seeing my future.

The next summer, 1960, after my freshman year at Harvard-Radcliffe, I got a scholarship to American University in Washington, D.C., to take a graduate seminar called "Introduction to Africa." Back at Harvard I took all two of the available courses on Africa and began sophomore tutorial with Harvard's only Marxist, Barrington Moore, and Robert P. Wolff, who later became one. I applied to go to Africa the next summer with Operation Crossroads Africa. I got two jobs to pay for it, delivering papers in the predawn hours and working in Radcliffe Library at night. I petitioned Harvard to grant me independent credit to study Swahili on my own, since no African languages were taught there.

I guess it was a natural development that after the Experiment I discovered Operation Crossroads Africa. Crossroads was founded and run by an African American minister from Harlem, Dr. James Robinson. It resembled the Experiment minus the language emphasis, with work camps instead of homestays. The fact that the sponsoring organization and the country to be visited were now black instead of white was almost incidental to me. I craved more travel. Still, images of Africa and Africans had haunted me since my later childhood when I had waded through the original nineteenth-century edition of Henry M. Stanley's book on his expedition to East Africa to find Dr. David Livingstone. The book contained dozens of etchings of the worlds he passed through, including some shocking ones of the Arab slave trade. Yet I did not apply to go to Africa out of any sense of political or moral involvement in anyone's liberation struggle. I was still very unconscious.

My parents had their doubts: one of their neighbors said, "I certainly would not let *my* daughter go to Africa!" My father feared the worst, but my mother prevailed. He never forgave her, nor did he ever stop reminding her that he had been right.

The first Operation Crossroads group ever to go to East Africa would be going to Kenya. It was the first time Crossroads had sent a group to a country with a race problem — in other words, a country with a white settler population. Not only that, it was 1961, and Kenya was just emerging from a ten-year-long race war: the so-called Mau Mau rebellion was really a war of liberation waged by the Kikuyu nation, spearheaded by the Land Freedom Army. At the time we arrived in Kenya, thousands of freedom fighters were still in detention, including Jomo Kenyatta, president of the Kenyan African Union (KAU), the political wing of the struggle. Kenyatta was the Nelson Mandela of his day, and the world was full of rumors of his imminent release. KAU had tried in the early 1950s to mobilize the other African ethnic groups in Kenya, but to little avail. "Join the Kikuyu and fight a war against England? Were they crazy?" I remember being told by a Taita man, who lived hundreds of miles to the south, near Mt. Kilimanjaro—where I ended up teaching high school after the other Crossroaders went back to the U.S.

Our group was led by an African American professor of sociology from Atlanta University, Dr. Timothy Cochran, whom we all called "Coach." There were three other African Americans, two women and a man, in our group, along with about twelve whites. That first night in Washington, on the eve of our flight to Africa, the three blacks had a meeting alone with Coach and Dr. Robinson, the head of Operation Crossroads. They said they had special problems they needed to talk about without whites being there. I must have wondered what they talked about, but I don't remember having my feelings hurt by being excluded. What did I know about African Americans? Next to nothing. Rumor had it there were more Africans at Harvard in those days than African Americans. I was on my way to Africa without ever having stepped into a black neighborhood in America.

Somewhere in our orientation we learned that Operation Crossroads had a principle that, if possible, all groups were led by African Americans. This was not only to facilitate communication with the leader of the African group, our counterparts in the work camp, but also a conscious policy, the wisdom of which has only grown on me with the passage of time. Dr. Robinson believed that in this period of history, while Africans and African Americans were struggling to be free, blacks and whites could best work together under black leadership. I think when we have an African American president for the first time, the whole nation may learn why this is so.

Dr. Robinson and Operation Crossroads were maligned during a certain period in the late sixties when anyone who was not an overt Black Power revolutionary was liable to be called a sellout or an Uncle Tom. Apparently the CIA had utilized Crossroaders as sources of intelligence about various African countries, and I gathered Dr. Robinson was being accused of knowing about it and tolerating it. Yet here was a man who went to visit Kenyatta long before his release from detention, when he was still regarded by the world press as a dangerous demagogue who had engendered an "atavistic" uprising. When African Americans were taking up African names and styles in the late

1960s, it seemed as if all this African identification had just emerged full-blown from the Black Power movement. But Operation Crossroads had laid a foundation for this cultural revolution by taking hundreds of young Americans, both black and white, to Africa during the fifties and sixties, each of whom was committed to giving speeches about Africa for a year after his or her return. The total spin-off from all this contributed to the growth of the nationwide civil rights support network of the early sixties. Dr. Robinson may have been naive about the CIA, but that is not surprising; it was typical of his generation. But his contribution to the awakening of American consciousness about Africa had both cultural and ultimately political results, which far outweigh any shortcomings he may have had in the eyes of a later generation.

In a way what we were doing in Kenya was like a tiny Mississippi Summer Project. Black and white together, under black leadership, we came to a racially divided country just pulling out of a bloody race war. Some 200 whites and some 20,000 Africans had been killed, while 80,000 others spent ten years in concentration camps. We came to live and work with a group of African students, almost all of whom were Kikuyu. Their entire childhood had been scarred by this war — which was a military defeat for the Kikuyu, but a political defeat for the British. It was as if, on the eve of Kenyatta's release to become the first African prime minister of Kenya, both sides were just coming to the full realization of these two facts. The country was boiling over with freedom fever, only it was called Uhuru Sasa! — Freedom Now! We thought we knew all this, but we couldn't really know it until we literally dropped from the sky into the boiling pot.

We were an enemy flag waving in the face of the colonialist whites, a provocation, a glob of spit on their faces. Not only were we camping in an integrated group, but all our leaders were black. We lived on the African side of the racial fence. The only whites whom we officially met were those rare few who had reached out in some liberal way during the Emergency and accepted the inevitability of African self-rule. Our first project was building a road in a rural area near Nairobi, a driveway to the clinic of Dr. Njoroge Mungai.

One weekend our host, Keriuki Njiri, M.P., invited us to visit his father, Chief Njiri, the British-appointed paramount chief of Kikuyuland, a man who had thirty wives. His being able to afford thirty wives was a distortion introduced by the British, who paid him a fat salary that enabled him to acquire many cows to pay the bride-prices. We learned that in the old days no one could afford more than two or three wives in a lifetime, adding a new wife every twenty years or so, as each wife reached her childbearing limit. The Kikuyu on their own, before the British takeover, were such zealous and extreme democrats that they had no chiefs: each elder or man over forty had an equal vote in tribal affairs. Eurocentric anthropologists used to describe these acephalous, or "headless," societies as less evolved than those nations, such as the Baganda, that had kings. But we learned that that was not the case. It was the Kikuyu who were the more evolved. Centuries ago, they had lived under the dominion of a wicked tyrant. They had a revolution, and then set up a democratic constitution based on the council of elders—a sort of "loose structure" constitution. One might say they were "freedom high"—to use the insulting epithet later applied to proponents of decentralized structure in SNCC!

It is interesting that it was this "freedom high" nation, the Kikuyu, whose uprising finally cracked off the shackles of British rule. Many of the more centralized tribes with paramount rulers, those with more "structure," were more enmeshed in the colonial hierarchy. Thousands of Kikuyu sacrificed their lives for *wiyathi* (Kikuyu for freedom), and from then on the days of the British dominion over Africa and the Caribbean were numbered. The British learned from the specter of Mau Mau what the Americans didn't learn until Vietnam. They committed genocide in the name of military victory, but they lost the political war, and as a consequence, they lost their empire.

Up in the beautiful cool mountains we all joined hands in a huge circle with Chief Njiri's family while a sheep was sacrificially smothered. We were thus taking personal responsibility for the sacrifice, which was to provide our dinner. I wanted to break out of the circle and rescue the sheep. It was shocking to have to experience the killing of this cuddly-looking sheep just to fill our bellies. We had been eating meat all our lives, but had never taken moral responsibility for what we were doing. The profundity of the traditional African culture, its fundamental spiritual meanings permeating every aspect of daily life, was starting to sink in to us.

At this feast at Chief Njiri's a journalist took a picture of Dr. Mungai and me chewing on a large leg—the same leg—of the roasted sheep. It was a striking "black and white together" black-and-white picture, and it made the front page of the Kenyan *Daily Nation*. Nowadays it would be called soft-core pornography! I had made an early start at being the white woman in the black community who shocked and provoked racist whites.

After we finished working on the road to Mungai's clinic in Riruta, we began to excavate a cellar for a new Kenya Federation of Labour building being built by Tom Mboya. This site was in downtown Nairobi, and people used to gather at the fences and watch us working with our picks and wheelbarrows down in the hole. An old man, impressed with my size and labor power, offered Coach sixteen cows for me, which provoked a lot of jokes in languages I could not understand.

Throughout the summer a few of us had been talking about not going home. We had come half way round the world, and our tickets had been very expensive. How could we possibly go home so soon? Just as Uhuru was coming! Day by day the rumors of Kenyatta's imminent release escalated. There were several false alarms. Meanwhile, I heard about a school down by Mt. Kilimanjaro, in the Taita Hills, that needed teachers. I hitchhiked down there and fell in love with Wusi High School. The schoolyard looked over an expanse of pink hills and plains fading away in the direction of the Indian Ocean. The equator ran nearby, marked by a yellow sign on the road. Amazingly, my parents gave me permission to stay and teach, probably because it was an Anglican mission school. I was told that since I did not have a college degree, I would be paid on the African pay scale, the only "European" in the country to be so low paid, a fact of which I was quite proud.

Coming back from this trip to the Taita Hills, I found Nairobi in an uproar. Kenyatta was definitely being released the next day. Jayne Craddock and Dorothy Butler, the two African American women from our Crossroads group, were also in Nairobi, waiting at Dr. Mungai's house. We decided we did not have time to travel back to our Crossroads camp in Naivasha to ask permission from Coach to go to Kenyatta's homecoming celebration. Our group would be mad at us, but we were not going to miss this moment in history. We spent the night at Mungai's and set off in the predawn hours the next morning for Gatundu, Kenyatta's home village in Kikuyuland, where his people had built a modern home for his return.

Several miles away from the village the people were already so thick on the road that it became impossible to drive. The sound of women ululating filled the air. It was said that the women passed the joyful news of Kenyatta's release from Nairobi to the Indian Ocean and Lake Victoria within hours, by ululating from ridge to ridge. Ten years in detention, and finally Mzee, the Old Man, the Mkongwe wa Siasa, the Rock of Politics, was coming home. We walked the last mile or so, and then were blocked by the security guards at the gate around the house. He had not arrived yet. A reporter from a London paper, whom we had met several times before, recognized us and let us in.

Twenty years later Dorothy Butler Gilliam wrote her column in the *Washington Post* about this day. She says we helped Kenyatta's wives unpack the dishes the people had bought for him. I only remember dancing with his female relatives, circle dances to celebrate his freedom. A picture of this hit the Western press, and my parents started to worry that I was getting in over my head. They were right, though I didn't know it yet. After Kenyatta arrived and addressed the crowd from the top of a truck with a megaphone, he came down to enjoy his house and all his friends. We were introduced to him. He knew Dr. Robinson already and was very friendly to us. He was seventy-something, but to me he looked fifty.

After the other Crossroaders flew back home, I was the only white woman in the whole country living on the African side of the fence. I hardly knew any whites. At age nineteen I was in African hands — in a totally segregated society that had just passed through a barbaric race war. If I was high on freedom, this is when it began, not in Mississippi. The whole world was black and beautiful and warm and green and sun-drenched, and if I did not see my reflection in a store window, I could forget that I was white. I felt like I had been reborn. But by the time I reached Mississippi more than two years later, I had got caught in the antagonistic contradiction between the races and incited the hostility of the powers that be. Like the zone between two mutually repelling magnetic poles, the interracial communication-breakdown zone in the middle was where I ended up spending the rest of my life — less by choice than by the pressure of forces beyond my control.

But I have jumped ahead of my tale. I have strayed. All this storytelling. I am beating around the bush to avoid grappling with the overwhelming realities we faced that year in Kenya, the three Crossroaders who chose to stay on and work after the summer: me; John Briscoe, a Harvard graduate student; and Jayne Craddock, who had once danced professionally with Lena Horne.

We lived in the aftermath of the ten-year-long State of Emergency, the military rule imposed by the British to suppress the Mau Mau rebellion and the freedom struggle, including all its political and cultural manifestations. On all sides we heard of the terror and violence the everyday Kikuyu had suffered. Most people that we met had suffered at the hands of the British. Some, whose voices were more muted by 1961, had suffered at the hands of the guerillas. The plight of civilians in such civil wars is now very familiar, now that we have seen *The Battle of Algiers* and lived through the war in Vietnam. It was not familiar at all in 1961. We had not been prepared for it.

It was a relief to discover that the "savage atavistic Mau Mau" as portrayed in the Western press and British propaganda had been only a tiny minority who had committed excesses. The majority of the eighty thousand detainees and twenty thousand martyrs were either politically and morally committed freedom fighters or else innocent civilians who had been trapped in the crossfire. Many of them were the principals, teachers, students, and pastors of the Kikuyu Independent Schools and Churches, folks who had worked for years founding African-run parallel institutions to separate themselves from the colonialist institutions imposed on them by the whites.

On my trips to and from my school in Taitaland, I often passed by one of these abandoned concentration camps. Located near Tsavo, in the arid tract inhabited by man-eating lions who had once brought the construction of the railroad in that area to a total halt, the dozens of low zinc barracks glinting in the glaring sun looked more like chicken coops than human prisons. But the high barbed-wire fences with telltale corner guard towers made one's heart stop—unimaginable the heat and misery inside those zinc ovens, not to speak of the barbarous acts that must have been perpetrated on its prisoners, none of whom had had a lawyer or a trial. They were gathered up and thrown in trucks just like their later counterparts in America—only many had not returned until just before Kenyatta himself was released, ten years after his and their arrest.

Later in the year, after I had fallen in love with one of the freed detainees, Achieng Oneko, I made a pilgrimage to try to visit the island of Manda, off the Kenya coast near Lamu, where he had spent ten years in detention. Most of the party activists had been sent to Manda, to isolate them from the less political innocents who filled up the other detention camps. I still remember the stories I heard. On Manda they sometimes got copies of books from one of the guards. The more educated prisoners organized classes in history and reading and writing for all those whose generation had not included primary school. Pio Pinto, a Kenyan Indian who was a former high school track star, had read *Cry the Beloved Country* by Alan Paton to hundreds of detainees.

Pio had gone into detention voluntarily. He had known about twelve hours in advance that he was going to be arrested for funneling arms and money from the Indian community to the freedom fighters in the forest. He had enough time to flee the country but decided he could do more good inside the camps than outside. I had never known anyone like Pio before. He was a Marxist by faith, but in practice he was an activist organizer in the freedom struggle. He had been born a Catholic, not a Hindu, for his ancestors were from Goa, at the time still a Portuguese colony on the west coast of India. Of the eighty thousand detainees, only two were Indians — both Marxist labor organizers. In 1965 Pio was machine-gunned down in his driveway as he drove his year-old daughter to meet her day nurse. Amazingly, the baby was not hit. He was buried on the day Malcolm X was killed, which may not be a coincidence. I was in Mississippi at the time. I thought then that the CIA probably was involved in instigating his assassination. But that is another story. The Kikuyu honored him by naming the year after him: the Year the Indian Communist Was Killed.

By 1962 I had transferred to Kahuhia High School in the heart of Kikuyuland. I was supposed to teach my students East African history, but their history had not yet been written. They were carrying it in their own heads. My attempts to get them to elucidate their recent history inspired the Australian headmistress to spy on my classes by hiding in the little concrete storeroom behind my teacher's desk.

The young women and teenagers who had grown up in the terror all showed the telltale symptoms of shellshock that I later reencountered in Algiers. If I burned the midnight lamp oil correcting my school papers (we used kerosene lamps), my fellow teachers, Mary Muthoni, Mary Wakuraya, and Naomi Gakoi, would hang blankets over the windows in alarm — one should never present a lighted silhouette at night. If I walked back alone after dark from the school dormitories to my house, they would scold me. Even the dogs were hyperparanoid, barking at any little sound in the night, sometimes all night long.

I recently gained access to the file on me at Radcliffe College and found therein a letter I had written to Dean Williston, dated January 25, 1962, offering an explanation for my failure to return for my junior year. Even in a business letter I couldn't refrain from trying to convey to her the truths I was learning:

> Since then I have had a six weeks Xmas vacation, and am now installed in my new home, literally *Facing Mt. Kenya*. . . . Without the language it is difficult for me to break the ice here as I did at Taita, and I don't yet know how to cope with the icy stares which I receive whenever I wander through the fields outside the school compound. They do not regard me as the new teacher, but only as a *nyakeru*, a white, for it was only a few years ago that undisciplined white men were roaming through these villages with Sten-guns with the law in their own hands, rounding up swarms of Kikuyu suspected of supporting Mau Mau and doing away with them en masse at the edge of the forest. Even the two young Kikuyu teachers I live with had to file past the man with the bag over his head, whose nod was fatal.

The overwhelming impression I got from the oral history that was coming at me from all sides was that the vast majority of the ordinary people were caught in the middle, trapped in a lethal double bind. They had not taken principled, thought-out positions either for or against the freedom struggle. They were caught between the Land Freedom Army and the English, both of which had descended to levels of barbarism that appear only in times of war, each demonizing the other. Both sides inflicted on the common people the maxim "If you help my enemy, you are my enemy." Yet both sides demanded help — food or money or intelligence — at gunpoint. The British may have called their demands "taxation" or "cooperation with the law," but to the average person the two sides were behaving identically. Caught in between, thousands were summarily executed or scooped up and sent into detention for the rest of the decade.

In many cases those who returned from detention found that those who had avoided arrest had not survived; wives and children were often dead, or had been taken over by other men. They also found on their return that their houses and lands had been confiscated and given to those who had sided with the colonial government. Thus the freed detainees became a volatile mass of "floaters." The Western press at the time usually focused on the younger, Western-educated, "been-to" generation of African nationalists, never on the older, wiser, generally poverty-stricken ex-detainees. These men and women had been the architects of the original Kenyan African Union, the Kikuyu Independent Churches and Schools Association, as well as the organizers of the armed struggle. They returned home to a world where they did not seem to have a place. Theirs was a bitter lot. These were the people whose struggle inspired me.

I decided to spend my last three months in Kenya doing field research for a paper I would write on my return to Harvard, about the Kikuyu Independent Churches and Schools and the more fundamentalist, traditionalist Kikuyu Karing'a Education Association. Though lumped together by the colonial District Commissioners, the "Bwanas" who wielded power on the local level, these two organizations were often engaged in bitter ideological disputes, somewhat like the various civil rights organizations in the later sixties. When these warriors of the book and the cloth, the teachers and pastors of Kikuyu-run schools and churches, returned from their years in detention, they often tried to resurrect their schools. I traveled through many remote Kikuyu villages in my last months interviewing these old men and hearing about their suffering.

By midsummer of 1962, it was time to head back to Harvard. I said farewell to my friends, who advised me to go south on my return to America to join the struggle there. My fellow Crossroader, John Briscoe, and I decided to hitchhike home down the Nile. This involved walking fourteen miles across the no-man's land between the last town in Uganda and the Sudanese border. The Sudanese war between the Islamic north and the Nilotic south was already under way, as we immediately learned. Beyond the Sudanese border we were picked up by a tourist bus on its way to Juba; we were given the ride for free in exchange for unloading luggage when we reached the Nile. After we crossed the Nile by ferry, the Sudanese luggage handlers at the wharf invited John and me home to spend the night with them.

We were comfortably installed on mats around the fire when we were summarily arrested by northern Sudanese Arab military officers. After bringing us back to their district headquarters, a sort of old stone fortress with huge rooms, they explained that we had endangered ourselves by staying with "the Blacks." Imagine what they might have done to us, they said, casting suggestive glances in my direction. They then placed us in separate rooms for the night. In the middle of the night a sound awoke me, and I saw the white-robed figure of the commandant sweeping through the moonlight that streamed into my room. He came to my bed and started to argue and beg for my favors. We argued all right, and I think I threatened to scream for John. In the end, he accepted my rejection and retreated without a physical struggle. The next morning, as John and I boarded the ferry that would carry us through the hundreds of miles of papyrus swamps separating us from Khartoum, I blurted out my story. John laughed. The same thing had happened to him — only it was the deputy commandant! I wondered if they had flipped coins for us. Such a thing could never have happened in East Africa. We both knew that we had crossed a major cultural frontier.

We spent about a week traversing the papyrus ocean, known as the Sudd. The Nile winds in interminable hairpin curves through this swamp, where there is very little gradient. From horizon to horizon one sees only an ocean of green, which undulates in waves when stirred by the wind. Our ferry consisted of six or eight barges, tied together in twos. The only way this awkward craft could negotiate the tight turns was to crash into the banks. The whistle would blow just before each crash. For food during the long journey, people had brought live chickens and goats onboard and cooked them over fires in coal pots. When the whistle blew, someone had to steady the cooking pots. About once a day we stopped at a village, situated on what must have been islands in the papyrus sea. We all rushed out to buy any food or livestock we could get.

After a few days in Khartoum we crossed the Nubian desert by train. We rode fourth class, so there was no glass in the windows. Sand blew into our faces and got into every fold of our skin. At each stop along the way you could jump out on the platform and pay a man to pour a big pitcher of cold water over your head, clothes and all.

On that trip I was reading Sekou Toure's *Le Pan-Africanisme*. Years later when I opened the book there was still sand between the pages.

Back in the U.S. at the end of August 1962, I went home to Minnesota for a couple of weeks before classes started at Harvard. While I was in St. Paul I met some Kenyan college students and brought them home with me. My father behaved civilly. I did not fully realize how deeply freaked out he was by my

escape from his white world. When I got back to Harvard, one professor offered me his tape recorder so I could record my memories. I took it to my
room, but only looked at it. I thought somehow the CIA would get hold of
anything I said and that I might betray someone. I couldn't have guessed that
one day in the future my father would turn over all my letters from Africa to
the FBI, at their behest. After he died I got back those letters, all underlined
with red magic markers. I have since lost them again, to my utter frustration.

A friend at Harvard, Bob Johnson, had been in Mississippi that summer of
1962 as a law student volunteer. He had met Bob Moses there. So when Moses
came to Cambridge that fall, after having his head smashed in McComb, Bob
met him for dinner in Harvard Square and invited me along. Many Kenyans
had asked about the repression going on in the South and had chided me for
my ignorance. I wanted to go down to Mississippi to find out for myself—if I
could be of any use. Bob Moses's head was partially shaven, exposing a big
bandage over some fresh stitches. He looked at me wearily and explained that
the presence of white women often endangered other workers. He told of their
sometimes having to hide under towels in cars. I got the message, and I made
up my mind to go back to Africa instead. After all, it was all part of the same
struggle.

That winter of 1962–63 I began canvassing in my free time in Roxbury for
the Boston Action Group, led by Noel Day. We were organizing a boycott of
Wonder Bread, whose bakery, though located in the heart of the black community, employed no blacks. About this time I also started going out with a
Ghanaian student, A. K. Armah. On the fringes of the Harvard African scene
were some Muslims from the Boston temple led by Louis X (now Farrakhan),
who had made a record called "White Man's Heaven Is Black Man's Hell."
Every week Roy X brought us copies of *Mohammed Speaks*, and we were reading *Negroes with Guns* by Robert Williams, about what had happened in Monroe, North Carolina. By this time I was practically living in Armah's room in
Adams House, Harvard's "hotbed of radicalism." One day he confided to me
that after he graduated that spring he was going to join the Angolan war of
liberation. The Portuguese had already slaughtered nearly a million Angolans;
tens of thousands had flooded into the Congo, where they were living in refugee camps. He heard that the Cubans were offering guerrilla training to Af-

rican freedom fighters. He scoffed at the idea that I would abandon my degree and go with him, but in the end he relented.

We were encouraged to believe we could get a visa to Cuba through the auspices of a well-known attorney from the Lawyer's Guild. We surrendered our passports, which we were to recover from the Cuban embassy in Mexico City. That summer we took the money Armah had won in a Harvard short story contest and hitchhiked to Mexico, via Denver, traveling almost the whole distance cross-country with a white trucker who let us sleep in his bed in the cab. This was about a month before the March on Washington. I had not told my family where I was going. How could I tell them I was going to go get killed by the Portuguese in Angola? Consciously or unconsciously, we both believed that is what would happen to us, given the brutality of the repression taking place there.

In Mexico City we realized we were being followed on our return trips from the Cuban embassy. We were waiting for our passports, which were still in Havana. A Mexican man would follow us back to the hotel, darting into doorways, peeking around corners and such. Finally we got our passports back, but without the visas. Rejected. I cannot remember what the reason was, though probably we assumed it was me. I was a liability to Armah. They couldn't take a chance on an American. After all, how many times had the CIA already tried to kill Castro?

We then moved to Vera Cruz and holed up in an old hotel waiting for the next ship to North Africa. We had heard that the southern African guerrillas were all getting military training in Algiers, now run by a socialist army in the wake of the victory over France. We were reading Maoist tracts in Spanish, which we had picked up in Mexico City. I didn't like living in a Latin country any more than I ended up liking North Africa. We were both the object of all sorts of sexual harassment when we went out on the streets separately. Together, people didn't know what to make of us and pretty much left us alone. This was a real difference from the U.S., where we were fine alone but harassed when together.

It was during this Mexican period that the FBI first contacted my father about "my activities." Apparently the possibility that two highly visible and successful Harvard students might be about to go to Cuba for guerrilla training had pushed their red button. In a folder entitled "Emmie: To Be Read After My Death," my father recorded the following entries:

August 21, 1963: Office of FBI: consultation with Agent Herb Doll. I left a seven page letter from Emmie with him at his request. Subject has been referred to another agent which will call me. They have contacted Radcliffe college through their Boston office. He urged me to inform all of my children of the probable consequences to Em. Because of this they can expect to receive a *non-clearance* in Security Matters in a civilian government job, including myself. . . . That Bill [my brother] should contact his superior officers before they did, that he could not get clearance for any corporation that had a government contract. That I should contact him at once if I received any money demands.

Sept. 19: Office of FBI Herb Doll, Agent in Charge. Case is being developed by Agent Hollingsworth who is working on the assignment. He wants to consult with me about government file. Doll instructed me to contact Boston office of FBI next October. . . . I am not to contact Radcliffe College or have any discussions with them about Em. The Boston office will instruct me as to procedures. This is an *active* file and prosecution is contemplated and much publicity is expected.

I note that the FBI did not want him to talk to Radcliffe, which would have meant to President Mary Bunting. She pooh-poohed the FBI's idea that my "activities were inimical to U.S. interests," and clearly they did not want him to hear that. Also in my father's file was the following letter to my brother:

September 12, 1963

Dear Bill, RE: EMILIE SCHRADER

I find it extremely distasteful to have to send the within enclosed Photostatic letter, which is a copy of a letter now on file in the offices of the Federal Bureau of Investigation, to any son of mine—least of all you.

This letter speaks for itself. You can make your own reasonable inferences, draw your own conclusions, and weep.

Because of my illness the F.B.I. did not contact me last spring although they said they had been watching her activities prior to, and while she was running loose in Africa. They inform me that while in Africa, she was consorting and living with another Negro Communist. I saw their local office file—nearly two inches thick. A similar one is on file in their Washington D.C. office as well as in Boston and New York City. It is not completed nor have I been informed as to what specific action is contemplated by them.

I can confidently assert that we shall hear more about her activities in the future — very likely in published newspaper notices.

Because of her record all alleged members of her family will have this block to contend with in the future when any Federal Security clearance might be required. . . .

As you may suspect from her letter, your new brother-in-law is a Negro as well as a member of the Communist spy ring. This is official and is part of the F.B.I. and C.I.A. files.

It should not be necessary to add that Mother is heart broken, Radcliffe College and Harvard has let her down and I am just plain God Damned mad.

Affectionately,

Father

Thirty-four years later, in 1997, I finally got my Freedom of Information packet, which I had applied for two years earlier through the Center for Constitutional Rights. Of course 95 percent of the pages from the FBI were blacked out. But one significant story slipped through the censor: it was my father who informed the FBI that Armah and I were "card-carrying Communists," not vice versa. When repeated inquiries in New York, Washington, and Boston failed to turn up any evidence of this, the Minneapolis FBI office was instructed to recontact my father. Had he ever seen our cards? Sheepishly he admitted that he had made it up because he was upset that I was going back to Africa "to devote myself to the Communist cause."

Armah and I sailed to Spain on a freighter and then hitchhiked to Morocco, where we got our visas for Algeria. I remember the first night we spent in Algeria. We were taken to a farm that had formerly belonged to one of the "pieds noirs," the French settlers, in defense of whose privileged lives under the old colonialist status quo the French army had attempted to crush the Algerian people's struggle for independence. More than one million Algerians lost their lives. The farm was now controlled by militants of the Algerian FLN (Front de la Libération Nationale): it had become a communal farm. Prints of eighteenth-century French paintings of corpulent naked white women and babies had been slashed diagonally near the four corners, and posters of Prime Minister Ben Bella, "Le Militant," had been inserted over the ruined art. The brethren proudly showed us the bullet holes in the walls all over the house and the heavily armored metal doors, clear indications of the state of siege the French farmers had lived under before they caved in and fled the country.

That night during dinner we discoursed on international revolutionary topics while seated on pillows on the floor in traditional manner. At some point we started to talk about the status of women, and they spoke about how the revolution was going to change things for women. Then one of them asked if we would like to see how the couscous was prepared. He led us into a very large and poorly lit kitchen, where a number of women were squatting on the ground shaking huge round flat baskets — I guess they were threshing the grain. Others were cooking at low fires on the ground. The whole place seemed like a sweatshop. I hadn't really taken notice of the fact that I was the only woman at dinner. I felt ashamed.

Later that year, after much controversy, the FLN government abolished the wearing of the veil, a sign of women's inferior status. But many women, especially the older ones who had worn it all their lives, put up a lot of resistance to this change. Our landlady, who was in her forties, would take off the veil when she left the house, but whip it out and put it on again as soon as she entered one of the shops where she had done business all her life — from under a veil.

We rented a little two-room apartment in Algiers, dug into a cliff at the top of a steep street. Here we worked translating articles from the newspaper *Revolution Africaine*, helping to produce a monthly English edition for distribution to English-speaking African countries. My French was better than Armah's, but his English was better than mine. I wrote a rough first draft in English, then he turned it into good English. How did we get this job? We were working under the supervision of two Portuguese communists, refugees from the fascist Salazar regime. Algiers was full of communist exiles: exiles from Franco's Spain, Perón's Argentina, Tito's Yugoslavia. It was also full of African exiles from South Africa, Rhodesia/Zimbabwe, Southwest Africa/Namibia, Mozambique, Angola, and Portuguese Guinea Bissau.

Meanwhile, our real purpose for being in Algiers, to volunteer for the Angolan war, was meeting with pure frustration. We checked out both Angolan organizations, the FLN and the MPLA (Movimento Popular da Liberação de Angola). I think Armah sometimes visited them without me because I don't remember being there when the following incident happened at the offices of the FLN (which later was revealed to be financed in part by the CIA). When Armah explained that he wanted to get guerilla training, they told him he had a Harvard education, this was not how he should serve. One man confided, "Ce sont les illettrés qui meurent" (It is the illiterates who die). He came home totally crushed. The scales were definitely dropping off of our eyes. We kept repeating at odd hours of the day, "Ce sont les illettrés qui meurent!"

Feeling disillusioned and alienated, we met a tall, middle-aged African American man who described himself as an ex-Trotskyite. He told us many tales of his life's adventures and disillusionment, but, having lost all my journals, I remember only the punch line: "If I had to do it all again, brother, I'd go for the money! Yeah, man, this time I'd go for the money!" We wandered around the streets of Algiers repeating this too. I guessed what he meant was that although it may be cynical to go for the money, at least in the end you have something—a comfortable life? something to pass on to your kids? But if you go for the revolution, you also become cynical and disillusioned, but now you have nothing at all except a poverty-stricken old age. Now that I think of it, he was probably an FBI agent!

What happened next? I caught hepatitis—after a while Armah got it too. He went to the hospital with his. We may have gotten it from donating blood in a crowd scene at a school gymnasium during the short Algerian-Moroccan border war. Somewhere around the time Armah was in the hospital with hepatitis, I discovered that I was pregnant. We argued about what to do. If he had wanted to get married, I would have had the baby, but our relationship was already disintegrating. Our mission had been a failure, so now our relationship was going to be a failure too. He wanted me to have the baby and give it to his mother to raise. I had never even met her. She was in Ghana. This was not a cultural idea that was familiar to me.

Somehow we decided that I should get an abortion. Or I decided, and he accepted that he couldn't stop me. I visited several Algerian doctors, who threw me out of their offices like I was a corrupt infidel turd, which I guess I was: I was trying to destroy the greatest gift God had given me. I had come expecting death, and got life by accident, so now I was going to destroy that life because I wasn't allowed to let my own be destroyed. Peculiar logic by which we shatter our innocence. Finally I met a doctor who informed me I could go to Switzerland, where abortion was legal.

Armah walked me to the ship that was to carry me to Switzerland. There was no question of his coming: we were too short of money and he was still not fully recovered from the hepatitis. It was a migrant labor ship, carrying Algerians to France to work. I spent the whole voyage down in the hold filling out immigration forms for people who couldn't read or write French. The unisex lavatories were awash with vomit. I took a train from Marseilles to Geneva. I thought about my one other passage through Switzerland, four years earlier, on a train from Italy to France with my group from the Experiment in International Living. We hung out open windows in the train practically picking flowers from alpine meadows and I thought I was in heaven. Now I was in hell. It was winter—gray, windy, and cold. I was alone. I knew no one. I was on a hellish mission. I never thought about the little brown-skinned child who might have been. I only thought about myself. "I" got pregnant. "I" do not want to be pregnant. "I" am going to get fixed.

The Swiss woman abortionist had her own little hospital, in a Gothic house which seemed right out of a Charles Addams cartoon. When they asked why I was doing this, I told them that my African boyfriend and I wanted to go to Angola to fight against the Portuguese. It wasn't the right time in our lives, to put it mildly. When they asked me medical questions, I mentioned that I had just had hepatitis, that in fact this child was conceived during the hepatitis. "Well, for the hepatitis we will do this," she said, "pas pour tout ce truc-là"— "not for all that other jive."

When I got back home to Algiers, Armah was in bed upstairs. He seemed different, sort of chaotically confused. We argued about the abortion. He said I had murdered the baby. I said, "You could have stopped me, you walked me to the boat. You are also responsible. You wanted to shuffle off responsibility to your mother!" We could never be one again after the abortion, because I now had a wall surrounding me of refusing to admit I had sinned or committed a crime. I was angry that this was his only reaction. From here on, I became an angry, rebellious woman. I started to read Simone de Beauvoir. The combination of Armah and the Islamic society and their attitudes toward women drove me into a rage. It took me eight years and a job as a doctor's assistant in a New York abortion clinic before I could admit to myself that, in spite of gender injustice, what I had done was wrong.

Along about this time we got the news of Kennedy's assassination. Everyone thought the CIA was behind it. No one, not even the European papers we read, like *Le Monde* and the *Economist,* no one thought Oswald had acted alone, or that crazy leftists were responsible. Everyone was *au courant* with recent CIA attempts to assassinate Kwame Nkrumah in Ghana and Fidel Castro in Cuba.

By this time we had begun to argue a lot. Clearly we were at a dead end. Did we fly back from Morocco? I think so — from Rabat. I guess the Algerian-Moroccan border war was over. I don't remember one thing about the trip. Neither one of us could bear the thought of going back to the United States. I remember the feeling of a huge black drape dropping behind us as we reentered the American information system. Americans think they know so much about the rest of the world, but everything is filtered through American eyes, American correspondents. I had also felt this keenly when I returned from my fourteen months in Kenya a couple of years earlier. I could see that the news Americans got from Kenya was superficial and warped and full of distortions. Yet I would read the news from all the other distant countries and believe it, because it was all I had.

Once back in Cambridge, Armah and I finally decided that we should separate. He would be returning to Ghana, and I needed to follow my own life path. Just as the first time I returned from Africa, I saw nothing in America for me except joining the struggle against racism. College had become irrelevant. I was beyond the pale.

In Cambridge we had reunited with Armah's good friend Peter de Lissovoy. Pete had just returned for a respite from a year in Albany, Georgia. While we were in Algiers he had sent us copies of articles he had written for the *Harvard Crimson* about events in Albany. His articles and later his book, *Dr. Feelgood,* put the black men of the Albany pool hall crowd on center stage; the larger organized struggle of C. B. King, the Albany Movement, Charles Sherrod, and SNCC was the backdrop rather than the focus of his stories. Pete was going to hitchhike back to Albany soon. He told me that they were now taking in white workers in Mississippi and that I should write Mendy Samstein. I did and I waited. But Pete was soon itching to get back, so I decided to go with him. I had no idea when I went south in April 1964 that I was just in advance of a flood of white volunteers. *Après moi le déluge!*

At the SNCC office in Atlanta I met Larry Rubin, who was also on his way to

Mississippi. We drove down together in his car. Soon after we arrived at the Jackson COFO office on Lynch Street, we were offered a job distributing books that had been donated by SNCC supporters for Freedom Libraries. My first letter informing my parents I was in Mississippi, photocopied by my father and recovered by me after his death, mentions Larry Rubin and the books. My father has circled his name, as he did the names of any males in my letters ("Are they her consorts?") or the names of any Jews ("You see, all her associates are either Negroes, Jews, or communists!"):

Dear Mom:

Someone told me it was mother's day, so I thought I might break my privacy strike and tell you I was down here. I don't think the address will be much good for long, because I am supposed to be going to live up near the Tennessee border in a few days. I will be living at a Negro college up there, doing what I did in Kenya for a while — sorting out some 50,000 books which are going to go to 13 new libraries all around the state, as Negroes can't use the public libraries down here. I am in charge of this with a boy named Larry Rubin from Antioch College, but things are getting bogged down right from the start. He took the first U Haul load of books up there a few days ago and the cops had a roadblock out for him. He is in jail on charges of carrying subversive literature instigating the people to revolt or some other such claptrap. A trailer load of children's books! I am not so much worried about him, as everyone seems to be in and out of jail down here, but am worried that they may destroy the books.

I don't give you any specifics because I guess I don't trust you not to give my letters over to father with his FBI mania. If he sets the FBI on me down here, it could be more than a little unpleasant. Hope you are having a nice spring, it is already hot down here.

your recalcitrant daughter,
emmie

With Larry in jail, no one was going to send me out driving the book truck, so I was put to work in the Jackson Office doing clerical work preparing for the upcoming Mississippi Summer Project, working with Penny Patch and Casey Hayden, both veteran SNCC staff. I hadn't been working long at the COFO office before I was arrested. They tried to pick up each new person in order to get your name and check out your record with the FBI. I had gone to the restaurant next door to have a beer with some folks from the office. The police walked in when I was still in the middle of my first beer. I was singled out and arrested for public drunkenness, the only evidence of which, apparently, was my being a white girl in a black establishment. I was put in a cell in Jackson, but bailed out that same night by a movement lawyer. This arrest probably alerted the FBI to my presence in Jackson, if they didn't already know. I don't remember at what point I learned from the president of Radcliffe College that an FBI agent named Sullivan used to call her once a month for information on my whereabouts. He had to fill out some kind of card on me, because I was considered a "security risk."

One strange afternoon in May we emptied out the office and went for a picnic at a swimming hole somewhere in rural Hinds County, outside Jackson. I say "strange" because I don't remember such a thing happening for the whole of the next year: that we should actually stop working on a beautiful day and take time off to have a good time together. Some went swimming, some sat on the shore singing freedom songs to the accompaniment of a guitar. All of a sudden we heard Alma Bosley shouting and waving her hands while waist deep in the water. "Jimmy! Where is Jimmy! He was in here with us, and now he's not here!" Somebody on shore remembered having seen someone in the water waving his hands, but had not realized anything was wrong. Jimmy Bolton was our hardworking office manager, but did he know how to swim? No one was sure. Some started calling and beating the bushes on land, the rest of us rushed into the water and began to dive.

The water was dark and muddy, quite deep in the middle. You could not see anything, and Jimmy was very dark-skinned. On his third dive Bill Light, a gentle-spirited COFO worker from California, touched something with his foot that felt like a body. He dove again, and came back up with an unconscious Jimmy. Bill was gasping for breath. I was the nearest swimmer, so I took Jimmy in a cross-chest carry. As soon as my feet touched bottom I began to give him mouth-to-mouth resuscitation. With my first blast into his lungs there was an immediate response: he retched. Could he still be alive? A couple more blasts, and we had him on the shore. We turned him on his side — water was running out of his mouth. Then Bill began the old kind of artificial respiration, pressing on the back and raising the elbows. Jimmy began to breathe and then to regain consciousness! We cheered and loaded him into a car to go to a hospital.

I didn't go in that car, but Casey reminds me that they were stopped by a trooper for speeding. Surprisingly, he gave them an escort to the nearest hospital, which happened to be the white hospital. When they brought Jimmy into the emergency room, the authorities would not admit him. They were directed to the colored hospital, some miles away. To make matters worse, one of the nurses asked Bill, "Why did you save this nigger's life?" Jimmy was treated at the colored hospital and released.

Thirty years later at a reunion in Jackson, Bill and I and our families went out to dinner together. "Jimmy isn't here," Bill said. "I wondered if he would come." "Me too," I said. I didn't mention the last time I had seen Jimmy, at a private SNCC party in New York in late 1965 or 1966. He brushed right by me when I greeted him. He must not have recognized me out of context. But that's what time it was: someone was muttering, "Who invited the gray broads?"

In late May 1964 someone decided that I should join the communications department, which consisted of Bob Weil, Bill Light, and Francis Mitchell. Mary King was going to come over from Atlanta in June to head up COFO communications for the Summer Project, while Julian Bond remained in charge of SNCC communications in Atlanta. Our job was communicating with the press, FBI, and the general public, both orally when they appeared in the office or called on the phone, and in writing—press releases, background information, etc. Sometimes I got to go to Freedom Democratic Party (FDP) precinct meetings around Jackson at night. I remember always Mrs. Hazel Palmer, local Jackson FDP organizer par excellence, tall and wiry, strong and outspoken, funny and friendly and brave. I missed her in Jackson in 1994 at the thirtieth reunion. I asked for her. Everyone else knew she had died. I'd been in Jamaica for twenty years. I missed a lot.

In the late eighties, while I was still living in Jamaica, I had gotten a letter, together with clippings from the Memphis and Jackson papers, from Jan Hillegas, a COFO worker who never left Jackson and later founded the Freedom Archives. My name had come out in the movement's lawsuit to gain access to the secret files of the White Citizens' Council archives: "Emmie Schrader says she is a communist, reports Agent 79 in his report dated April 23, 1964." She asked if I wanted to respond to these articles, ostensibly to clear my name. I pondered: after the FBI/CIA had smeared my name at home and in Africa, how could I possibly clear it with a letter twenty-five years later? I tried to write Jan an answer. You see, I felt fairly sure I knew who Agent 79 was. I never knew he was a spy when he worked for COFO and befriended me, but when he disappeared soon after a nighttime break-in at the COFO office and the theft of some of our files, the thought did occur to some of us. I tried to write her everything I remembered about X: he was a dark-skinned African American from Alabama who had been in the Marines and was recently returned from Vietnam. But in the end I tore up the letter.

Now that I have the actual reports involving me, courtesy of the Mississippi State Archives, I have no doubt that X was indeed Agent 79. Furthermore, David Garrow, in a *Newsweek* article from March 30, 1998, entitled "Mississippi's Spy Secrets," calls him "'Agent X,' the Sovereignty Commission's most productive African-American spy." In his report of May 14, 1964, Agent 79/X states that "I met Emmy Schrader a w/f. . . . Right off we were very good friends." My interest in X was obviously that he had been through a war so similar to the ones in whose wake I had worked. We had long discussions over beer about Vietnam. His report that I said I was a communist needs to be understood in its proper context. I had never been to a Communist Party meeting in my life, though I had read some Maoist literature. Still, whatever else X may have distorted, he was clear about one thing: I was on the side of the Vietnamese National Liberation Front. It was their country and we had no right to be over there slaughtering them to keep the country divided. Ergo, I was a communist.

If you take everything Agent 79 says with quite a few grains of salt, his spy reports are actually an interesting glimpse from that pre–Summer Project period, supplying details that we have all forgotten and sending us into peals of laughter. For my part, though I was given the chance in 1997 by the State of Mississippi, I could not bear to censor any but the most egregious of his creations. But even this minimal attempt to protect myself was later denied by the ACLU, who pointed out that Agent 79's reports about me had been in the public record since the original trial — so in effect my rights as a "victim" were already irreversibly violated.

Since X was black and confident and had his own car, he found COFO a very easy organization to infiltrate. "My investigations of CORE and SNCC led me to the COFO office at 1017 Lynch St.," he wrote in his report of April 23, 1964. "This place is a haven for both white and black people who are engaged in

'Freedom' activities. The mixed groups walk the streets together and eat in Smackover's and other local cafes together. It was easy to mix in with them. After a few interviews, I was offered a position with COFO. They are in critical need of willing and able staff personnel."

By May 18, Agent 79 had made great progress: "To retain my importance as area captain of the 26th Precinct, I did some door-to-door canvassing before going to the office. I was successful in that I found many people who wanted to offer themselves as block captains. At the office this was accepted as very good news by Jessie Myers [Morris] and xxx. . . . All of the girls were glad to see me and I received many hugs and kisses from both Negro and White."

Had I been more experienced in the ways of the Mississippi police, the following incident should have tipped me off: One May night we needed some scotch tape and glue for the office. It was after dark, about 8:00 P.M. For some reason X and I volunteered to go, using his car. I don't remember anyone forbidding us to go out together looking like an interracial couple. On the way to the store we were stopped by police. They made X get out of the car, and left me inside. He said something to them that I couldn't hear. Instead of spread-eagling him on the car or talking rudely to him, they took him back to their squad car. Looking back through the rearview mirror by the light of their headlights, I could see him producing what I assumed was his driver's license, and then more cards—his military ID's? He was back there a good while, then they let us go. I don't think I realized how totally this incident deviated from the usual pattern of police harassment of interracial cars—let alone a black man and a white woman at night—or if I did, I figured his being a vet had trumped his being black. Now I suspect he must have told them he was Agent 79.

In June 1964 I went to Oxford College in Ohio to the Summer Project orientation. But first I'd gone to be in my sister's wedding in Denmark township in rural Minnesota. I arrived by bus in my combat fatigues. No one had seen me since my disappearance from Harvard a year earlier, before my escapade to Mexico and Algeria. Mississippi was a much easier pill for them to swallow. Friends of my own generation were eager to hear about events in the South. Some of my friends' parents looked at me like someone visiting from the realm of the dead, a duppy: having crossed the most forbidden interracial boundary, the sexual one, I was no longer qualified to belong to their society;

put bluntly, I was no longer white. They didn't insult me, but I could see it in their eyes. When they had last seen me, the valedictorian and student council president in my long white dress at my high school graduation, I had an armful of awards and honors. Now they stole morbid looks at me, probably thinking, "What a fall!"

At the end of the first orientation session in Ohio it was agreed that Frances Mitchell, Bill Light, Bob Weil, and I—the Jackson Communications Department—would leave the day before the first buses to go back and manage the phones until the volunteers arrived. We must have left Oxford at approximately the same time as Mickey Schwerner, James Chaney, and Andrew Goodman, who also left a day early to investigate a church burning in Neshoba County. We hadn't been back in Jackson for long before the calls from Meridian began coming in. For the next month, this is what we did: handle the press and FBI, call police stations—almost all about the disappearance of our three brethren. A pall of horror hung over us the entire time, yet we could not officially speak of lynchings or assassinations until their bodies were finally found six weeks later. Meanwhile, the mainstream Mississippi press had continued to insist that the disappearance of the three workers was a hoax.

At some point I became aware that several of the FBI men seemed to be singling me out, as if our knowing each other's names meant that we now knew each other. Now that I have Agent 79's reports, I see the big picture. I became very uncomfortable. I told Mary King I did not want to deal with the Feds anymore. It was making me even more paranoid than I already was. Meanwhile my father was continuing his contacts with the FBI in the wake of threats received after articles with pictures of me in the Jackson office appeared in the St. Paul Dispatch and the Minneapolis Tribune. He also reported to Agent Hollingsworth of the Minneapolis FBI office on July 6: "We received a telephone call from Mrs. Shippee, asking for a substantial donation to a defense fund of $13,000.00, which she reported was the amount to be raised in Minnesota. She was not very gracious to learn that I did not approve of my daughter's activities and I doubt if I will hear from her again—at least not for a cash contribution."

In mid-July someone suggested I help work on Mississippi Freedom Democratic Party materials being prepared for the upcoming challenge at the Democratic Convention in Atlantic City. Just doing writing jobs with other movement people was much better than working with the press and the FBI. About this time I got put on staff (which meant collecting a $10 weekly pay-check) — probably because I had spent my subsistence money buying a much-needed used car.

For some reason I was sent on the buses to Atlantic city — maybe because I came from Minnesota, land of Hubert Humphrey, Walter Mondale, and Eugene McCarthy, all of whom were going to be key players in the drama of the MFDP Challenge. In fact, the most important person I met in Atlantic City was Theresa Del Pozzo, then head of Wisconsin Friends of SNCC, who became my lifelong sister, buddy, and friend. The slimy story of the lessons we learned at the Democratic convention, this gruesome eyeful of white liberal politics stripped naked, exposing their intimate involvement with white southern rac-ists and their manipulation of "acceptable" black leaders, has been told and retold. I have nothing new to add.

Atlantic City was a watershed for COFO and SNCC and the FDP. Personally it was also a watershed for me. While there, I decided to try to work in the white community in rural Mississippi, if indeed I could still pass myself off as white in their eyes. That remained to be seen. It seemed as if certain SNCC people were asking for whites to do this because of the distressing specter of white volunteers threatening to swell the ranks of the staff. It would be a way to divert us whites, and possibly some good might come of it. That the rumblings on the horizon meant that the day would inevitably come when whites would no longer be welcome in the movement was unthinkable to most of the white staff at that point. I didn't like to think about it either, but I couldn't avoid *feeling* it.

I have written elsewhere on my very tentative White Folks Project, so will just skim over it here. Inspired by Sue Thrasher and Ed Hamlett, who had worked in a pilot white community project in Biloxi during the Summer Pro-ject, I began to work in Ittawamba County in the northeast corner of Missis-sippi, an area that is not only poor and rural but also 95 percent white. I used the issue of remaining loyal to the Democrats in the upcoming presidential election as a means of canvassing among the white small farmers, but really I always tried to broach the subject of race. But race was not a major issue with them; their concerns were economic. When word spread that I was actually a "freedom rider" — that is, that I worked for COFO — doors started closing in my face. A few went for their guns while I beat a hasty retreat. Nobody wanted "trouble" (from the dominant whites in town), and "freedom riders" or "nigger lovers" were by definition "outside troublemakers."

After the election, my heart was no longer in this seemingly hopeless task. My being a Yankee and my living in the Freedom House in Tupelo, from where I commuted to Ittawamba each day, had proved to be insuperable obstacles. As Anne Braden remarked to me thirty odd years later, "You were trying to organize in a police state." This fact was less of a psychological obstacle in black community organizing, because blacks naturally perceived the state as the enemy. But very few rural whites had such a perception, so the atmosphere of rigid group conformity and intimidation made it nearly impossible for people to step out of line with their own community for very certain risks and very uncertain benefits.

I began to go to meetings in the black community in Tupelo with Ike Coleman, the COFO project director; Stu Ewen, a summer volunteer who had stayed on; Harold Roby, an active local FDP supporter; and James Harris, who led the Tupelo Freedom Singers. Ike, an African American college student from Tennessee, had come down for the summer and soon headed up the new project in Tupelo. He was cool and rarely ruffled by problems, his easygoing good nature appreciated by everyone who worked with him. Stu was a Jewish New Yorker, smart, funny, and energetic. The bond between the two of them typified the lack of racial tension I remember that fall in those struggling new projects in the First Congressional District: Starkville, Tupelo, West Point, Aberdeen. It took a certain number of white workers in a project to create racial stress, and that crucial level was never reached. I was the only white female on board in Tupelo, and I was "on strike" as part of coming to terms with my feelings of female oppression. Ike and Stu were hardly male chauvinists. I never tried to work in the black community (as opposed to observing and helping), but I did have an old VW bug, so I was of some use.

Looking back thirty years later, I am struck by the thought that what was happening in the First District, or northeastern Mississippi, COFO projects in the fall of 1964 was just what should have been happening: slow quiet work trying to lay some foundations of the FDP and new groups like the Mississippi Students Union, collecting local activists, feeling out relations with existing community groups. The budgets were a fraction of those of the larger projects.

This was a period of prolonged lull, but what is wrong with that? When I read the histories of the movement, what strikes me are the lulls. The focus shifts from place to place: Southwest Georgia and Danville, Virginia, in 1962, Birmingham in 1963, Mississippi in 1964, Selma in 1965. But no one writes much about what was happening in the lulls when the focus moved elsewhere.

I have very few memories of this time. Doug McAdam, in *Freedom Summer* (1988), says this is typical of most volunteers. I wrote often in a journal and kept a lot of movement memos and stuff, but unfortunately this all ended up in a box with the residues of my two years in Africa—a box that disappeared during my twenty years of exile in Jamaica. As I belong to an Alzheimer's family, my gray matter is leaking out at an alarming rate, along with my memories. One story remains clear in my mind, because it was my only brush with a potential lynch mob. Maybe it is worth telling, as it epitomizes "the white woman problem."

During the Freedom Vote at the time of the 1964 presidential election I was enlisted in the Tupelo project's Freedom Ballot collection drive. Ike did not have a driver's license, and for some reason I had been chosen to drive a volunteer's car, an old beat-up Oldsmobile with Michigan plates. Five of us had gone all the way up by the Tennessee border to Corinth to pick up the Freedom Ballots: Ike and I; Nedra Winans, who had come to work with the White Folks Project; Liz Blum, a Bennington College student who had come south for the Freedom Vote; and the car owner, a white male Freedom Vote volunteer whose name escapes me. (In our normal comings and goings in Tupelo we regularly traveled in mixed cars, though not out of familiar territory at night.) That afternoon we were returning from Corinth with several thousand marked Freedom Ballots locked in the trunk.

Halfway between Corinth and Tupelo is the little town of Booneville. At a Booneville stop sign I stopped to pick up a hitchhiker, a white college student—a thoughtless impulse, stemming from my own years as a hitchhiker. Unfortunately, a policeman a few cars back, whom we had not noticed, spotted us. We were pulled over and arrested. It was sometime in the late afternoon.

We were put in two cells, men in one and women in the other, and held for several hours. After a while, the hitchhiker was able to separate himself from us, make his phone call, and be released. I have often wondered if this experience had any kind of radicalizing effect on him, either at the time or later in life. It seems strange that he hadn't immediately disassociated himself from us. Perhaps he felt guilty, knowing that it was my kind impulse to help him that had gotten us into trouble.

There must have been early calls to the Jackson office, but I don't remember them. It was dark by the time I remember talking to Mary King in Jackson. An ugly mob of excited white men had gathered outside the jail and were standing in front of the window by the telephone waving a rope with a hangman's noose. Ike was sweating heavily.

I told Mary we could not be released without a police escort for protection. This was looking like Neshoba County, the lynchings so fresh in our minds. She was unable to reach John Doar at the Justice Department in Washington, so instead she called Earl Warren, chief justice of the Supreme Court. He called someone at the Justice Department, who called the chief of police in Booneville. The police chief was informed that some troopers from the State Highway Patrol had been "federalized" and would be coming to escort us back to Tupelo, some twenty miles away.

When the troopers finally arrived, two of them in one car, we were escorted to our car and told to follow them. We proceeded out of town and onto the highway. By the time we remembered to look behind us, we saw a whole line of cars following us out of town — the mob from in front of the jail. Just about then the troopers stepped on their revved-up gas pedals and flew away from us at eighty miles an hour. I floored the gas on the old Oldsmobile, but there was no way it could keep up. Behind us the lights snaked back into the night.

We conferred hurriedly on what to do, feeling totally trapped. What fools we had been to trust the so-called federalized state troopers, who were still the same racist Mississippi cops they were before they were federalized! About this time someone noticed that a couple of huge semi trucks had become entangled in the line of cars behind us. A ray of hope — at least they weren't part of the mob! They might even be from out of state. We decided to go very slowly, so as to entrap as many non-mob cars and trucks as possible in the crawling motorcade. It took forever to reach Tupelo at thirty-five miles an hour, stressing the whole way.

On the way we came up with a plan. There was a dirt road a mile or two long that entered the highway on our left, which would lead us into the black community of Tupelo by a back route. When we got near this road we would speed up, switch off our lights, and hope that we could make the left turn without them seeing us. We did just that—and of course they saw us. Now we had to speed; we knew the road and hoped they didn't. We made it into Tupelo just as a Saturday night dance at the Negro high school was letting out. A lot of people were on the streets. The thugs chasing us started shouting racial taunts at the people on the streets, and some responded by throwing stones and bricks. Harold Roby saw us and went for his gun, as did another local man.

By now the mob had forgotten about us—they only wanted to get out of the black community alive. They roared on through to white Tupelo. We had been protected by the force of numbers. We drove to the Freedom House, called Jackson, and told them we were back. Unfortunately, the next morning we had to call again and tell them that Harold and another man had been arrested for carrying guns. Ike bailed them out, and eventually they got off with fines, perhaps because "moderate" Tupelo didn't want any adverse publicity. I have felt guilty about this incident for thirty-five years. Of course, maybe we would still have been spotted even if I hadn't picked up the hitchhiker. But I did, and we were. Amazingly, it did not affect Ike's and my friendship.

I left the First District after the November 1964 election. Mississippi—meaning white Mississippians—had indeed voted for Goldwater, even though there were few Republicans in the state. Johnson, in the end, was abandoned by the Dixiecrats—the ones for whom he had sold us out at Atlantic City, humiliating and rejecting the Freedom Democrats, the only loyal Democrats in Mississippi.

I returned to Tougaloo to the Literacy House and wrote a report for the upcoming Waveland staff meeting on my abortive White Folks Project, later published by the Southern Student Organizing Committee (ssoc) as "Poor Whites and the Movement: A Working Paper." Admitting my failure to do anything more than talk with the rural white folk of Ittawamba County, I then passed on what I had learned from them. Bob Williams and Dove Green, two working-class white southerners who had joined me in my last week or two in Ittawamba, decided to go back and try to work in Tishomingo County, across the Alabama border.

When I read the history books I deduce that I was considered part of a faction at Waveland, the "antistructure" people. That's interesting. I thought we had a big discussion on structure after reading various position papers on the subject. We divided up into groups and were supposed to come up with suggestions for new structures. The point wasn't whether we were pro- or antistructure, but rather what kind of structure we needed. To reread the minutes from Waveland is inspiring; we were all so young and trying hard to solve the perceived problems. Too bad that in the history books so much retrospective focus has been placed on factional divisions at Waveland. Most of that happened *after* Waveland. The end of Waveland may have been the beginning of the breakdown of trust, though I wouldn't have thought to put it this way at the time. The conference ended with a tired and frustrated whimper, no agreement having been reached on a new structure to replace the old.

The only "faction" I do remember being a part of at Waveland was a group of women huddled around a mimeograph machine putting the final touches on the now famous "Waveland women's memo." In the preceding months many people had contributed to the discussion about women's issues — we didn't have the term "women's liberation — not just we white women on whom it got blamed. Among the black women in those early conversations during the spring and summer I remember especially Dona Richards Moses, Margaret Burnham, and Jean Wheeler. All of that sharing, which would later be called "consciousness raising" by the women's movement, underlay this initial written effort, this attempt to force some attention to an issue that had never been seriously addressed in a staff meeting. To make our memo relevant to a SNCC staff meeting, we listed examples from the daily life of female SNCC workers. This has led to a distorted slant by later commentators, as if the problem was "sexism in the movement." In the last year alone I have heard two male speakers, one black and one white, ostensibly out of their support for the women's movement, criticize SNCC for its male chauvinism. The real question is: Which organization in the world before 1965 did not manifest male chauvinism? No one ever said SNCC was in any way worse than the world at large. Indeed, it was quite a bit better.

Thirty years later Casey received a note in the mail from Calvin "Bud" Trillin, a *New Yorker* reporter who had been on the scene in those days. He passed on a quotation that must have leaked out during the movement lawsuit to gain access to the White Citizens Council secret archives. Agent 79 reported from Jackson on July 3, 1964, that "the 'strong' females on the permanent office staff have told me earlier of a revolution among females, 'the women's fight for equality with men.' To the students, this is a deeply serious matter. I have watched it gain momentum over the past months. There are many male supporters of this new 'thing.'" Well, at least it's good dated evidence that the discussions didn't begin in November with the Waveland memo! As Agent 79 confirms, this wasn't just a women's change in consciousness. There were quite a few men into it too, not initiating the discussion, but supporting it and looking at themselves and each other. Obviously there were lots of jokes, both open and good-natured, and (by the macho "commando" types) covert and poisonous. But there definitely was a gentle wing of the male staff; indeed, one reason a caucus of women's liberation thinking developed around Jackson COFO was because here was a group of men who had real power but did not attribute that power to their male prowess. Their power was due to their spiritual, mental, and emotional qualities, as is the power of women. And they surrounded themselves with strong, hardworking women, both black and white. In Bob Marley's words, "Emancipate yourselves from mental slavery!" The thinking of the freedom struggle gave us the tools to analyze all kinds of oppression.

After Waveland I decided to go learn basic photography in New Orleans from Matt Herron, an independent photographer who had covered the Summer Project for *Black Star.* I wanted to join Casey and Mary King in their new photo project. Nobody in Atlanta gave me permission to join them, but then no one had given me "permission" to do the white folks thing either, even though they knew I was doing it. It's just that that one was supported in Atlanta by Jim Forman and Ruby Doris Robinson, so no one quarreled. We first produced a filmstrip about the MFDP, followed by one about black and white poverty, with words by Jane Stembridge, called "The Peoples Wants Freedom." We took some flack for our use of rural black dialect, which was considered to be "bourgeois sentimentalism." (Stokely Carmichael later gave an excellent seminar to a group of young girls on language as a tool of oppression, a record of which, written by Jane, is preserved in the SNCC microfilm archives.)

In February there were a lot of rumors and tensions about the big upcoming staff meeting at Gammon Seminary in Atlanta, as if it was going to be a show-down — ostensibly still over the problem of structure versus program, what-ever. Everybody was supposed to try to attend. By this time the specter of decentralized fundraising as a way of getting money to the field, and allega-tions that one or two people had once mentioned doing away with the position of chairman or executive secretary, had produced new levels of hysteria in the "structure debate." By this point, "structure" had become a euphemism for centralism. Money had always been centralized in Atlanta, but now personnel decisions and program supervision would follow suit, with the promise that the tightening up at headquarters would result in more resources reaching the field projects. This is what "hard line" meant, with all its phallic appeal and connotations.

The question was often asked in meetings: Are we trying to build the SNCC machine or to build local movements that can stand on their own feet? By this time, some Mississippi projects had begun informal fundraising on their own, utilizing the northern connections of their summer volunteers. A more decen-tralized SNCC would have been a many-headed creature, much less easy to behead than the centralized Atlanta SNCC operation, which failed to live out the decade.

Perhaps FBI infiltrators were spreading many of the rumors of factions, con-spiracies, and power struggles. In retrospect, I must admit, it all feels like pure FBI modus operandi. It has been said that FBI agents in the late 1960s were instructed to discover any potential splits in an organization and support one side — it didn't matter which side. The organization would soon be paralyzed. (On this subject, see Kenneth O'Reilly's excellent "Racial Matters": The FBI's Secret File on Black America, 1960–1972 [1989].)

I moved to New York in the summer of 1965 to work on a filmstrip about the war in Vietnam. It was distributed through the National Guardian, some two hundred copies to the antiwar movement in the U.S. and Canada. It was also shown in Mississippi, and I got much positive feedback. It was called "This Filmstrip Has No Name: It Is About The War."

In 1967 I moved from New York to a mountainside in southwestern Vermont, where I lived in a rural commune called the Huggs Family for three years. We grew organic vegetables and sold them in New York and Boston. In my mind, our sole political accomplishment was the conversion of one local disabled Vietnam veteran to oppose the war. He eventually flung down his Purple Heart on the steps of the Pentagon and left it there. Eventually our benefactor, the landowner, died, and another local Vietnam veteran burned down our house with a flamethrower. By then, we had already scattered to the four winds.

What was happening in SNCC in 1967? I had only the grapevine and the *New York Times* for news, which were about comparable for accuracy. One thing was clear: there was change at the top. According to Clayborne Carson's 1981 account, *In Struggle*, Jim Forman had resigned as executive secretary and John Lewis's reelection as chairman was undone in the middle of the night in a highly suspect manner by a rump of nightowl staff. At the bottom, few programs survived. The field was dying of hunger and neglect, the staff now clustered around the urban offices north and south. The bones of the golden goose, with its $800,000 annual budget, lay in dusty file cabinets, and the dream of a nationwide protest movement of both races, now disowned, lay buried in guarded hearts. With the earlier causes for division now cleared off the table, attention had finally turned to the race question. The vote to expel whites in December 1966 passed by one vote: 19 to 18, with 24 abstaining, including all 9 whites still left in the organization. The majority of the staff had gone to bed — it was 2 A.M.

What about Mississippi? By 1967, the situation is best described by John Dittmer in his excellent 1994 history *Local People*. SNCC has almost vanished, but the FDP still holds on, vying with the new coalition of moderates, trying to hold on to a piece of the action:

> Resisting demands by nationalists, the Freedom Democratic party remained open to white participation and continued to work with the integrated staff of the Delta Ministry. . . . At a time when northern cities were erupting in violence and black militants were calling for revolution, the Mississippi Freedom Democratic party continued to work within the political system. Becoming more militant in its rhetoric, and now running only black candidates on its tickets, FDP nonetheless continued to welcome support from all people who identified with its program of black empowerment." (p. 411)

Why couldn't this have been SNCC? Mrs. Fannie Lou Hamer said it all, with her characteristic bluntness, when Emily Stoper interviewed her for her 1968 book *The Student Non-Violent Co-ordinating Committee:*

> Q. What was the effect of the summer on white workers in SNCC?
> A. They got on very well. They did pretty good work organizing.
> Q. What did SNCC set out to accomplish and not accomplish?
> A. To get a coalition between whites and Negroes.

There were plenty of other possible answers to that very open-ended second question. Mrs. Hamer's answer is not just an accident, because elsewhere in the same interview she gives primacy to the same issue again: "The big thing about the summer of '64 was the people learned white folks were human." Did Mrs. Hamer really believe this is true? Would she say it if she didn't believe it? Not the Mrs. Hamer we knew! So if in her opinion local people had their first opportunity in the summer of 1964 to rub shoulders with nonracist whites, why is it that the same experience caused the staff not only to resent and dislike the new whites, but even to turn on their old white comrades-in-arms? The local people discovered that some whites are different, just as some staff discovered that all whites are fundamentally alike?

Clearly, it was a matter of staggered timetables. SNCC staff had learned in 1961–62 that there were nonracist whites who would stand and be beaten and jailed with them. For them the summer of 1964 was primarily the shock of numbers: there are tens of thousands of these white volunteers, from all walks of life, eager to come and join the movement, and it could not contain them. The folks who fought so long for inclusion would have to learn quickly to exclude, which would hurt people's feelings, in order to preserve the Beloved Community and the movement. If not, their days were numbered. Unfortunately, this realization did not come in time, though many, like Hollis Watkins, had predicted it before the summer. And when the reaction did hit, in late 1966 and 1967, it ran to excess, expunging even the original white veterans rather than simply drawing lines against the new ones.

If SNCC had never put new whites on staff, if it had remained with small numbers of token key whites, it might have avoided its early disintegration, in spite of all the political power struggles and ideological polarities. These can be found in any organization, many of which manage to hold together for decades. A "token" is the little white spot in the black half of the tao, or yin-yang symbol, and the little black spot in the white half. Alan Ribback (who later became Moses Moon and produced an LP of SNCC singing and preaching called *Movement Soul*) had a huge tao on the wall of his New York City apartment. Those little dots, he said, hold the whole thing together. Without them it would break in half.

The main problem with whites in the movement was that there were suddenly too many of them, and their hosts, who had asked of them the ultimate sacrifice if necessary, felt reluctant to ask them to leave against their will, so soon after they had made a commitment and disrupted their own lives. Had the number of whites remained at about ten to twenty, spread thinly over the project areas and not concentrated in the seats of power, they would have been no contradiction to the agenda of Black Power. COFO and SNCC had proved to me what I had already learned from Operation Crossroads Africa: that in this period of history, whites and blacks needed to work together under black leadership. Whites working under black leadership — something that had not happened since the days of Egypt — was liberating for both blacks and whites. Were there any white allies in Nat Turner's rebellion? Why should having valuable white servants not be a part of Black Power? If even three whites had remained as full members of the organization, SNCC might still be alive today.

Once infighting began over the issue of getting rid of every last white, even to Bob Zellner, any doctor would have realized that the patient had succumbed to a paranoid-obsessive disease. Witch-hunting really. A black person's position on the "white question" simply became one more weapon or weak spot in the power struggles over the leadership and direction of the organization. According to Clayborne Carson (*In Struggle*, p. 238 and chap. 13), the separatist Atlanta Project seems to have borne a good degree of responsibility for continually pushing the leadership on this matter, as if racial purity was more important than organizational survival. Both Stokely and Jim seemed to have held reasonable positions on this issue during the Peg Leg Bates meeting: if whites work in the white community, they maintained, the problem will take care of itself. It took Bob Zellner to run the test case on even this limited option.

The FBI couldn't have planted a better virus designed to tear apart the heart and soul of SNCC than this insistence by the Atlanta Project that every last white be expelled from the organization. (The FBI always hated black and white together, especially interracial marriage or sex. Hoover was with the segregationists in his heart.) The resulting traumatic racial rift among leftists during this period threatened to close that integrated opening in the walls of the status quo through which the decade of the sixties had erupted. The new virus was triumphant. Now they were singing, "Black and white apart, Black and white apart," and the FBI was exultantly closing with "We have overcome today-ay-ay-ay-ay . . . !"

The power structure thrives on division, not unity. Letting everyday black folks talk to everyday white folks, letting them live at close quarters, is too dangerous. Interracial communication is a matter for leaders, for expert negotiators, not for local people. They might decide that more unites them as human beings than divides them. They might want to go on forever holding hands and singing together and changing the world . . .

Postscript: I moved to Jamaica in late 1971, married Dada Adams, had two children, Paloma and Kwao, and ultimately became a Jamaican citizen. I stayed for twenty years, living in a one-room bamboo hut, washing clothes in a tin tub with a wooden brush, cooking over a wood fire, growing my own food, and building and renting African-style thatched huts to tourists. I also raised two stepchildren, Kedela and Kwamen. The children attended the one-room schoolhouse in the fishing village of Robin's Bay. In 1991 my book on the Jamaican language was published in Kingston: *Understanding Jamaican Patois: An Introduction to Afro-Jamaican Grammar.* It was an immediate best-seller and is now in its ninth printing. I returned to the U.S. with my family in 1992 to earn some hard currency while our children pursued their education.

Fields of Blue

CASEY HAYDEN

WHEN I was little my mother and I lived with my grandparents and my Aunt Merle in Victoria, Texas. Mom was a secretary for Frels' Theaters, and Merle was the bookkeeper for Conti's Ironworks. Papoo was sick and Mamoo kept house. I was fourth generation in this town. Papoo's parents came in covered wagons from Tennessee, and their parents before them from Kentucky, and on back to Virginia, always moving west.

My grandparents' house was solid, and it sat in an old part of town, where the South Texas plain of longhorns and mesquite had long been tamed, right on the edge of the rich people's neighborhood. Before raising me, Mamoo had raised her own five kids in that house, while Papoo was sheriff. It was a South Texas version of lace curtain Irish, with dark, carved furniture and over-stuffed chairs, wooden floors with worn rugs, crannies and closets, and a big back porch dappled with lovely light, where we ate in the summertime, wetting down the screens with the hose to cut the heat. Walnut and pecan trees towered over the house, and Merle raised ferns and poinsettias and pomegranates and figs and roses and irises and sweet peas. She carefully placed gifts from her male admirers around the house, relieving the plainness of our poverty. Mamoo kept house as she had for generations: ice in the icebox from the ice wagon, laundry boiled up in the big iron pot in the backyard, chickens she fattened up and killed with her bare hands. The house was filled with her crafts, fine crochet and quilts in the wedding ring pattern. She didn't have many things — a first-edition *Ben Hur* (*To Mama from Dad, Christmas 1900*), some bound sets of the classics, her button basket, a shell that had been her mother's, and a wooden hand mirror. Mom and I shared a room and a big double bed. No one talked much.

In the afternoons, while taking my obligatory southern nap, I listened to the radio soaps, *Grand Central Station* and *Ma Perkins* and *Stella Dallas*, and I played outdoors on the big lawn and in the puddles in the gravel streets when it rained. My favorite game was dress-up, in the gowns of silk chiffon from the trunk in the back bedroom closet, the wardrobe remnants of my mother and her sisters, the beautiful Weisiger girls. I played cowboy, in the remnants of Papoo's professional life, from the closet at the end of the hall: boots and Stetson, blackjack and empty pistol. And house, with dolls and tea sets. We went on family picnics down at Coletto Creek, meandering out of nowhere across the flat grasslands; or in Riverside Park by the Guadalupe River, muddy and surrounded by wild pecan trees, with little sandy spits where I could wade; or at Matagorda Bay, with its backwater shell beaches, on the gulf, twenty-five miles away, where we'd catch crabs that Mamoo would boil up by the washtub. Mommy took me every Saturday to the Royston Nave Memorial Library, where I read all the children's classics and looked at old collections of stereographs of faraway and vanished peoples and places, imprinting forever a connection between reading and the exotic. I attended Sunday school starched and clean in my homemade dresses every week to march around the room while singing "Onward Christian Soldiers," dropping my nickel in the collection basket and my penny in the missionary basket. Birthday parties. Dancing classes. Big Christmas trees, and Easter nests made from bluebonnets, gathered from the fields and fields of blue, wildflowers stretching as far as you could see. That's the most beautiful memory. Those wildflower fields are much smaller now.

Victoria, Texas, was a rural, semitropical small town of about ten thousand. By slogan it was the City of Roses, and by reputation it was the town with more millionaires per capita than any other in the country — oil and cattle money. A railroad ran through. Seasonally the smell of the cotton gin thickened the sultry air. Frame houses with halls down the middle sat on brick supports at the corners, under live oaks hung with Spanish moss. I played with the children of the families in the mansions, as my mother had before me. I went to primary school where I was taught by the first-grade teacher who'd taught my mother, in the public school with the big marble Jesus in the loggia, arms open and hands outstretched.

When I was about nine Mom moved out of my grandmother's house into a mean little apartment, where I cried myself to sleep on a cot in the kitchen. She soon married a dashing ex–World War II pilot, an oil rig roughneck in the civilian world. We moved across town, out among horse pastures and fields of corn and cotton, to a new little house in a new little subdivision. Zinnias scrabbled up out of the treeless bare dirt along the front walk in a setting considerably less civilized in every way than the one I'd left. Here my mom birthed my half-sister and went through some bad times and her second divorce.

In one way, the rest of my life is just a commentary on my childhood. Since having children of my own, I've often thought of my life this way. Elements of my childhood were causes of my involvement in the movement. Among them was my mother's independent and unbigoted turn of mind. She commented in a liberal vein on Texas politics over the *Victoria Advocate* at breakfast. Befriending Eddie Reyna, a colleague at the chain of small movie theaters along the coast where they were employed, she broke the color barrier of her day. She supported me and my sister on a secretary's pay and put us both through college. Her status as the only divorced woman in town caused me to identify with outsiders. I learned that schools were segregated by law as a junior in high school, when I read of the *Brown* decision in my journalism class. I took the system of segregation as a personal affront, viewing it as a restriction on my freedom.

I'd have to count, too, as a childhood influence leading me to the movement, the simple human decency and love I absorbed from the women who raised me. Perhaps the strongest influence, however, was Mom's move and remarriage, which left me forever trying to return to Mamoo's house, that safe home of lush and breathless innocence, without betraying my mother. I made huge leaps in my life — in location, identity, lifestyle, and companions — repeating Mom's move while at the same time looking for home, journeying ever toward it. On a deeper level, as part of this same pattern, I was moved to reconcile contradictions, to search for an underlying harmony within disparate elements, to take the high road for its view. I wanted encompassing truth, in which apparent opposites are unified. This was the promise of the Southern Freedom Movement. That reconciling promise abided in nonviolence, extrapolated into a political identity. This is the interior, the fire in the belly of the early sixties.

The unfolding of my childhood toward the Southern Freedom Movement commences at the University of Texas in Austin, which I entered as a junior in 1957. When I visited Jerusalem recently, it reminded me of Austin in my memory of this time: white limestone walls and red tile roofs, timelessness and learning. The University YWCA, an old building sitting on "The Drag," with its beamed ceilings, tile floor, and cool, dark interiors, recalled The University as it was when Mom and Dad were students there. I found the Y early on, looking for community in this big, urban university setting. Here I met black students and entered campus politics, becoming a regional and national Y officer, chairing a large study group on "Peace and Disarmament" at the Y's national meeting in 1959. The other study groups were "The World of Work," "Race Relations," and "The Changing Roles of Men and Women." Here I learned the term "Student Christian Movement," sometimes shortened to "student movement," long before there was one. Perhaps for this reason I considered the movement later as a national phenomenon, of which the Southern Freedom Movement in the South and the New Left in the North were both aspects. Through the Y, I was grounded in a democratic manner of work, exposed to and educated about race, and a participant in direct action — though not in civil disobedience — by the time the sit-ins exploded the racial status quo of the country in 1960. The staff person at the Y, Rosalie Oakes, was my role model then, the first of the many women of the Y who inspired me in the years that followed. She was smart, well informed, understanding, gentle, tough, and skillful, as were they all.

Through the YWCA I went to New York City the summer of 1959, after my senior year, to teach vacation Bible school at the East Harlem Protestant Parish (EHPP), the second of the institutions that funneled me into radical politics. This parish, meeting in a collection of storefronts and an old church building, was formed by middle-class ministers moving into a community of color and poverty. Letty Russell, one of the ministers there, was the first female I'd known in that position. Preaching on Sundays, she enlarged my sense of possibilities. I lived on East 103rd Street, reputedly the worst block in the city, where I waded through broken glass over the tops of my shoes, a blonde in pastel ruffled cotton frocks. Rats in the walls kept me awake at night. The EHPP was my introduction to voluntary poverty.

When the sit-ins broke out across the South in the spring of 1960, I was back in Austin in graduate school. The national president of the student YWCA was a black student at Bishop College in Marshall, Texas, where police had used tear gas to break up a march. We brought her to speak at the Y just after she had been released from jail. She was a small person, and as she talked she was very quiet and dark. I remember sweating and crying in the packed little auditorium. After that I went to the meetings of the Austin Movement with the black women who lived across the hall from me in the only integrated housing on campus, the Christian Faith and Life Community (CF&LC), known by us simply as "the Community"—the third of the life-changing religious organizations of my college years. Here I roomed with Dorothy Dawson, my oldest friend.

Calling itself a lay training center, the Community was established and staffed by ministers who had been through World War II, an event that, speaking conservatively, had challenged their beliefs. I learned at the Community to reject the absolute constructs and abstractions of civilization, following the lead of the existentialists. I learned to believe my own experience and join others to create meaning through intentional living. Intentional living was supported by honesty and, through covenant, a promise to be present and accountable to each other. At the CF&LC I experienced the creation of empowering community, and within it an image of myself, in terms of which I then lived. Later, I understood the movement on this model. Our image of ourselves in the Southern Freedom Movement was that of the Beloved Community, created by the activity, the experience, of nonviolent direct action against injustice.

In the Community, as in the Y, all leadership slots were dual, co-chaired by a man and a woman. My politics and expectations were shaped by nonsexist institutions, where I met the black students who now came forward to claim their own lives and destiny. It was critical to my future that I had a few black friends and was loyal to them. I read Thoreau on civil disobedience during this time, read it deeply. My clearest memory of this spring of 1960 is picketing on Congress Avenue in a yellow dress and high-heeled white pumps.

Later I came to the movement's center, the Student Nonviolent Coordinating Committee (SNCC), which was composed of representatives of each local sit-in group. I reached SNCC through the Southern Student Human Relations Seminar, sponsored by the United States National Student Association (NSA). Connie Curry came through Austin recruiting for her seminar and telling the story of the Nashville sit-ins. When we sat together in a little restaurant on the Drag and allowed that story to open our hearts, a new life began for me.

Chuck McDew, a sit-in leader from Orangeburg, South Carolina, also attended Connie's seminar. Chuck said that before he could do what he did, he had to be willing to die. He said a bit later that in the movement we were many minds, but one heart. He was the first of the many new charismatic friends who would guide my life in the years to come. It was at Connie's seminar that I understood our movement as southern, a radical response to our region's failings.

At the NSA congress I came to the attention of the incipient student left, black and white both, as a white southerner supporting the sit-ins. I delivered a speech to a plenary quoting Thoreau in a drawled whisper, and the student leaders loved it. They delivered NSA to the movement. I was immediately scooped up by the left student caucus, called the Liberal Study Group. Through the study group I first met the folks who would later become Students for a Democratic Society (SDS). SDS supported the southern movement and honored me as a participant there. SDS friends became a community of support, generous and kind. I loved the excitement and edginess and detailed political thinking in the Liberal Study Group, and the guys were sexier, sharper, and more verbose than the Y fellows had been. I met Tom Hayden here, the man I would later marry. When he interviewed me for his campus newspaper he told me how he'd been to California and demonstrated against the execution of Caryl Chessman. He started crying, because he was so angry remembering that he could not stop the legal murder. I was captivated by his intensity and his funny face with its very sad eyes.

I returned to Austin aflame from these experiences. In a letter to my fellow seminarians in November I describe meeting with the president of the university regarding housing integration; coordinating a meeting of the various campus human relations groups, which decided to merge and take up direct action (forming Students for Direct Action, SDA); meeting with a committee of the University Religious Council, which was passing out cards to restaurant owners urging integration; working with "Negro" students toward being heard by the regents; and a supportive reaction to a talk I gave to a new faculty committee on minority affairs. Soon SDA had hundreds of students "standing-in" at movie theaters. During this time Tom won me over with his correspondence, sending mammoth letters and whole boxes of books he'd read and loved, including Herman Hesse's *Siddhartha*. The scene at the river where Siddhartha, the Buddha, ferries everyone to the other side was madly underlined.

Tom and I met again at the second SNCC conference, in Atlanta in October 1960, at which SNCC became a permanent organization. I attended the conference by invitation, to lead a workshop on school integration. Connie, Ella Baker, and Jane Stembridge, a white native Georgian serving as SNCC's first executive secretary, were at the registration desk when I arrived. The southern white women were my base community inside the movement in these early days. I lost touch with them when I moved to the blackside in the Deep South later, all except Jane, who also made that move.

At this conference Jim Lawson, the minister who served as adult advisor to the Nashville Movement, had everyone on their feet and in tears as he preached about nonviolence. He was extrapolating on SNCC's founding statement from the spring 1960 conference in Raleigh, which began, "We affirm the philosophical or religious ideal of nonviolence as the foundation of our purpose, the presupposition of our belief, and the manner of our action."

Nonviolence, as I experienced it, was at heart a presentation or demonstration of oneself. It was the acting out of a self-understanding of oneself as essentially free — existentialism carried to the streets. Diane Nash was a leader of the Nashville sit-ins. Of my female African American peers, she most influenced me. In my notes of her talk at the 1988 Trinity College Conference on "The Life and Times of the Student Nonviolent Coordinating Committee," she cuts to the core of nonviolence:

> Nonviolence is both the creation and the activity of the redemptive community.
>> To redeem means to rehabilitate, to heal, to reconcile rather than gain power.
>> Truth and love are both ends and means. There is no separation of ends and means. Everything is just a series of means.
>> The enemy is never personal. The enemy is always systems, attitudes, as in racism, sexism.
>> The oppression of these systems always depends on the cooperation of the oppressed. The activity of nonviolent direct action is withdrawal of cooperation with injustice, the refusal to support oppression.

Nonviolence took one out of the role of victim and put her in total command of her life. By acting in this clear, pure way, in which the act itself was of equal value to its outcome, and by risking all for it, we were broken open, released from old and lesser definitions of ourselves in terms of race, sex, class, into the larger self of the Beloved Community. This was freedom as an inside job, not as external to myself, but as created, on the spot and in the moment, by our actions. This was ideology turned inside out.

This conference in Atlanta in October 1960, powerful far beyond my expectations, was held in a spotlessly clean black college so poor that the iron bedsteads in which we slept were almost completed peeled of paint, the sheets and blankets threadbare.

On my first visit to Tom at Christmas that winter of 1960, we attended a conference about the new idea of the Peace Corps and organized a national drive to raise food for sharecroppers evicted for registering to vote in western Tennessee. In February I dashed to Atlanta for a SNCC meeting. These were swift trips, the first of many. The poet Gary Snyder has said, "In the political and spiritual loneliness of American in the fifties, you'd hitch a thousand miles to meet a friend." This was true for me. My life in the sixties was strewn with crowded overnight car trips and red-eye airplane flights, so many I have never tried to enumerate them. I and others like me moved fast and improvised, carrying ideas and names and contacts, connecting folks to each other, welding, one by one by one, those crucial linkages. We moved so fast the dross burned off. We burned down to our essential selves, and our relationships were intense. I was part of a small group who were the tip of the wedge of change, carrying the weight of opening space for all who came after us. The brevity of this memoir correctly mirrors this pace. I'm not sure I have done as well in presenting our awkward youthful tenderness toward each other, the medium of our acknowledgment of that weight.

In what proved to be a decisive change, at the end of the term in 1961 I dropped out of grad school, where I'd been working toward an M.A. in English and philosophy, to take a position as program director at the University of Illinois YWCA — closer to full-time movement work and closer to Ann Arbor, where Tom was a college senior. I thought "the North" was liberal and was surprised by the conservatism of this midwestern campus. In a letter to Connie describing a range of activities in Champaign-Urbana, and the activities of the black community specifically, I said, "I got called before the exec. committee of the YWCA corporation board for picketing the local [J. C.] Penney's store on job discrimination. They didn't think it was dignified. I finally said . . . that we just differed in our understanding of what constituted the dignity of man [sic] and gave one of my eloquent little speeches and they came out of the meeting with a recommendation that we send a delegation to Penney's to talk to the manager."

I took a creative writing course, and wrote a short story based on an interracial relationship at the NSA seminar. The woman says, looking at their bodies, "Isn't skin beautiful?" I sent long letters to Tom, describing all aspects of political and social life in Champaign-Urbana. We traveled to each other on weekends. In the spring we drove down to Fayette and Heywood Counties in Tennessee to deliver the food we had gathered. This was my first entry into a community under siege. We were chased by a carful of whites, out of the tent city where the evicted sharecroppers were living in the snow. We fled to Memphis.

The following summer I first worked with the still-germinal SDS in New York City in that little national office near Gramercy Park. Tom and I crashed where we could, on couches all around town. It was terribly hot. We went to Philadelphia, relating to the National Student Association on behalf of SDS, and went to the congress at the end of the summer. I wrote a paper on civil rights in the North for SDS (which was raising funds for SNCC and supporting local efforts elsewhere) and spent my summer days in a donated basement on the Lower East Side, running off mimeographed leaflets for a reform Democrat challenging the machine. The FDR Club, a local high school affiliate, distributed the leaflets. The basement was low ceilinged, dark, and dirty. After work my nails were black from the mimeo ink, which never quite washed out, my hands like a coal miner's hands. We were working toward reform and realignment in the Democratic Party, which SDS viewed as a potential vehicle for national radical social change. We would drive the Dixiecrats out and capture the party.

I married Tom that fall, even though I thought he was too young and too blind to himself to carry out the promises of marriage. I married at his insistence, too crazy about him to refuse. Despite my doubts, the vows represented a serious commitment on my part. I had been raised in a Texas family where keeping one's word was a primal teaching and had been drilled in the meaning of covenant at the CF&LC. The ceremony, which took place in the Community's roofless chapel, was beautiful, a ritual in a ruin. After the ceremony Tom and I drove headlong through the night and day to Atlanta, where we slept on Connie Curry's couch. I'd been hired on a southwide project by the YWCA, a project Ella Baker would be directing. I had come to be near the black students who were setting us all on fire. Our marriage vows and SNCC's vow to be there on the edge even at the risk of death now merged in my life.

In the fall of 1961 I was married and working in the movement in the Deep South for a National Student YWCA project called the Special Project in Human Relations. It was designed to create small, integrated race relations workshops for students across the Southeast. I was called a "campus traveler." I flew around in little one- and two-prop puddle jumpers to black and white campuses, often in remote locations. On the white campuses the Student Christian Association or Y staff person would quietly, sometimes secretly, organize a small meeting of white students. On black campuses I was often asked to speak to the student body, and always publicly welcomed, as a white visitor. This deference was embarrassing. In both instances I recruited students to our integrated workshops, which were technically illegal because we broke segregation laws while busily deconstructing race. In my travels I met many young white people trapped in the cage of race for whom these workshops were a way out. SNCC's work overlapped with these workshops, as many black campus leaders who attended were also local movement leaders. Human relations projects continued parallel to the movement (or as an integral part of it, depending on your perspective) right on through the sixties: real meetings of people across racial barriers, fostering healing and relationships that transcended race. This work undermined and defeated segregation on the personal level, just as bringing down the legal barriers would defeat it politically.

I worked for Ella Baker, who is often called the mother of SNCC. I think of Ella now when I pin my hair above my face, as she did hers, a flattering style for an older woman. I think of her when I hold my chin high. She's in me this way, a role model for the age I have achieved. Until I reached this age I didn't know how deeply I had incorporated her into myself. Ella was an elegant woman, elegant and homey and warm. Her diction was elegant, and her mind. I remember her beginning our meetings when I got back from a trip by saying, "Let's see. Now what are we doing here?" She really meant it. She always said what she meant. It was as though she'd thought of everything, and she'd show her thoughts polished and smooth from all her years of mulling them over. She never pulled punches, and after accurately nailing someone's foibles, she'd chuckle. Although capable of righteous indignation, Ella usually found humanity humorous and her approach to people was always fresh. She was interested in everyone and always asked where they were from and about their family. She was deeply, consciously rooted in her family.

Ella was, politically, above all pragmatic. She seemed to know that however much we think and talk, and however important that is, it is action that makes social change happen. She was always directed toward action, thoughtful action. Her notion of the need to raise up new leaders, and to rotate leaders, for example, was pragmatic, based on years of experience in seeing folks, when they became leaders, join the leaders' club and leave their constituents behind. Her broad vision saved SNCC from numerous potential splits, her "both / and" replacing the tendency toward "either/or."

Personally, Ella was perhaps the most secure, rooted, and self-knowledgeable woman I've known. I never saw her flustered or without complete aplomb and self-possession. When things were rough for me later, after the movement, it was Ella to whom I turned with late-night phone calls, and she was always there for me. I really loved her. It was a great privilege to have worked with her so closely during this period, the fall and winter of 1961–62.

The fall of 1961 was one of the momentous periods in SNCC's history. Bob Moses had been organizing in southern Mississippi, and the situation there was exploding, with student marches and arrests and beatings and murder. We arrived in Atlanta in time for nonstop meetings of the new, small SNCC staff around this crisis. It was a fearful time, my first experience of being, at a distance, the contact with the outside world for people in situations of immense danger.

Charles Jones chaired and I acted as recorder for the SNCC meetings at B. B. Beamon's restaurant on Sweet Auburn Avenue at this time. I don't think we ever read and approved these or any other minutes in SNCC. The discussions were rambling and it took real effort to find the line of thinking and make it clear without distorting anything. If I could do that, I could assist in the development of consensus. Assisting in the development of consensus is a leadership task. Consensus was important in nonviolence, because the final arbiter of one's behavior was one's conscience. Thus majority rule was quite problematic, as the losing side, by following its conscience, might have to leave the group. Unity came first—holding together. In basic ways, because of its nonviolent thrust, SNCC redefined leadership.

Leadership was an important aspect of one of our main organizing tools: workshops. We held workshops with local people and among ourselves, and I led these small groups at Y and SNCC and SDS conferences. Workshops carved out public space for people to be in by creating parameters, lining out the discussion. Skills involved were simply clarifying, questioning, recruiting, and watching people emerge. Finding new leaders is a leadership task.

Leadership was important in networking. Our mailings were about networking: SNCC mailings for money, mailings later about the challenge to the seating of the Mississippi Democratic delegation at the Democratic National Convention in 1964, the second memo about women. This was labor-intensive work: writing and typing and proofing and putting the mailing in envelopes and telling recipients who else was getting it. We had the expression "hook people up." This meant create linkages, connect people with similar interests, organize them. Get out of the middle position. Give information. Sharing information in order to create networks was a leadership task. Knowledge is power. To share it shares power.

These notions of leadership were among my emerging ideals, in the smoky back room of that little dive of a restaurant on Sweet Auburn Avenue in the fall of 1961.

Southwest Georgia was another significant locus of SNCC activity at this time. Charles Sherrod was pioneering there. Sherrod was the wild man of nonviolence — dramatic, devout, and daring. His integrated project was designed to demonstrate the new world we were building. I went to southwest Georgia on the Albany Freedom Ride, incognito, undercover, because I was the specified observer. I remember with chills to this day the mass meeting in the Old Mount Zion Church, just before the local people began to fill the jails. The music washed over us as we walked up to seats of honor at the front, the Riders fresh out of jail, the crowd singing "Guide My Feet, While I Run This Race" and rising as one body in an ovation for us.

Tom and I went back to Albany later for the trial, the Riders having been arrested at the train station for trespass. At that time, Sherrod, alone and without planning, entered the courtroom and sat in the white section. It was a heated, slow-motion moment. I knew I was seeing the caste system challenged in that setting for the very first time. He went limp when the police pulled him from his seat and dragged him out of the courtroom. Tom and I, following his lead, sat on the "colored" side. Don Hollowell, our lawyer there, reminded me recently that when the police came to get us, I hooked my legs under the bench so that they had to pry me out sideways. Ever the young lady, I wore white gloves.

Tom and I held together as a couple well in the South, both of us traveling, our relationship limited and simple. We were close to SNCC; at SNCC's March 1962 leadership conference I led a workshop with Bob Zellner on the role of white students in the movement. The Port Huron convention launched SDS later that spring. We went north, both of us preparing for it, constantly discussing a statement Tom was drafting for the meeting to adopt. My only clear memory of Port Huron is an argument with Tom regarding a sentence in the introduction that said we believed in the "infinite perfectibility of man." I wasn't objecting to the sexist language, but rather to the idea. I wasn't at all sure things were getting better, headed toward perfection. I think I finally acquiesced to Tom's explanation that being infinitely perfectible didn't mean we'd ever actually be perfect. We were all so earnest.

During that summer I typed the SDS mailing list onto addressograph stencils. Sometime that summer the core of the emerging organization met for days on end, sleepless and stressed, defiantly united against the parent organization, which objected to the Port Huron Statement as being soft on the U.S.S.R. Anticommunism and the residue of the internal struggles on the left during the 1930s were everywhere. These were dead issues as far as I could tell. I didn't know any communists, only their children, who were just part of our gang. Both SNCC and SDS worked with whoever would unite around our programs. The need was great, and we were few. Privately, and somewhat simplistically, I believed left sectarians considered ideas or goals more important than process, that ends took precedence over means. In nonviolent politics, by contrast, the community was the embodiment of its ideas, ends and means were one. One could say, in other words, that the organization or movement prefigured (or should prefigure) the society it envisioned. Diane Nash's 1988 talk presents the basis for this idea.

In the fall of 1962 we went to Ann Arbor, where Tom entered graduate school. Ann Arbor was cold. I held secretarial jobs to pay the rent and we housed a social action center in our basement. The C. Wright Mills Study Group met there, along with many others. Sometimes when the study group's analysis of the objective world was not meaningful to me, I'd invite the women upstairs to talk about our lives, in an early version of a consciousness-raising group. I joined and loved Women Strike for Peace, so like SNCC operationally, and was arrested with them in D.C. Elise Boulding was a leader, a role model for me. Dick and Micki Flacks were in Ann Arbor, and Paul Potter, of SDS. I was close to the developing national SDS and, through it, to the bright, energetic people in the organizations springing up everywhere, such as the Northern Student Movement, which tutored kids in ghettos, and the Student Peace Union, which spearheaded the anti-nuke movement.

I continued to interpret SNCC and support the work in the South with food and clothes and money drives. Martha Prescod, a University of Michigan student during this time, was important to me. I met and worked with Ivanhoe Donaldson, a student at Michigan State, who was delivering truckloads of food to Mississippi, where sharecroppers were being cut off welfare rolls for attempting to register to vote. He was intense, in a hurry. I was planning a booklet on voting rights for SDS to publish. Or was this earlier? I strategized via correspondence with Robb Burlage and Dorothy Dawson about how to create SDS in the South. I followed with interest the charismatic swath Tom was cutting through the world of student politics, but I was homesick for the South, and for my strong sense of myself there. Despite all my activities, only my marriage, which I had entered as the central covenant community of my life, engaged my passion. I wanted a child. The same was not true for Tom. When he took a lover on the East Coast and started spending weekends there, I went back to Atlanta. I was very sad. Even though I thought I had entered my marriage without illusions, I was brokenhearted when it ended.

Upon returning to Atlanta in the early spring of 1963, I worked in the SNCC office in a little old house on Nelson Street, near the Atlanta University complex. My desk almost filled the room, where I sat at an old manual typewriter with keys that stuck no matter how much I cleaned them. The handful of us working there heated the place with the small, open-flame gas heaters I'd grown up with in Texas. Dottie Miller and Julian Bond had the front room as a press office, and Jim Forman, our executive secretary, had the back one. I was wedged in between. I loved my coworkers: Dottie, the first northern white woman I worked with in SNCC, was friendly and funny and hardworking. We grew close. I came to admire Julian as much as anyone I knew, and I still do. Jim and I worked closely day in and day out; we were a good team. I had to love the guy, always working too hard, staggering around drinking Maalox and telling everyone what to do.

In a new position of Northern Coordinator, I threw myself into my work, developing Friends of SNCC groups on campuses and in cities. Initially, SNCC was kept alive largely through spontaneous donations. Now we were looking for sustaining support. This position was a good fit for me. I was trained to organize and administer programs, had been on a northern campus and knew what was needed to sustain support there, and had an enormous number of contacts by now through the Y, NSA, SDS, the Northern Student Movement, and all the traveling I'd done. I sent out field reports and instructions on how to organize, created mailing lists and key supporter lists, answered piles of correspondence and endless phone calls, responded to emergencies in the field, and laid the groundwork for Dinky Romilly and Betty Garman, white women I knew from other organizations, who followed me in this position. I left two file drawers full of badly typed carbons in tidy file folders, carefully organized by a system I'd developed for the Y project. I was sad to learn years later that these documents did not make it into the archives, sorry to see the historical record of all that work lost. SNCC's crucial accounting files, which could answer many questions, didn't make it either. I did all my own work in SNCC. At this point, bringing into being a program and a network, I did the head work and the hands-on work. I thought we turned hierarchy upside down by throwing out that division of labor. This was true for me throughout my years with the organization. I was never a secretary in SNCC and never had one. I worked long hours with no days off, feeling responsible for the staff in the field whose lives were daily at risk. I visited the field, including Greenwood, where I attended the First Greenwood Mississippi Freedom Folk Festival. Traveling in an integrated car, we took turns hiding under blankets on the floor in the back. Once there, we sat with local people on planks in an open field to listen to local talent, and Pete Seeger and Bob Dylan. Whites in pick-ups circled the field, rifles on display in racks on the rear windows.

Although considerably sobered by the failure of my marriage, I felt powerful and at home in SNCC. I recall some lines I taped above my desk. I don't know whose they were. "And tenderly I pledged my heart to the grave and suffering land, and often in the consecrated night I promised to love her faithfully until death, unafraid, and never to despise a single of her enigmas."

I remember our staff meetings, the air thick with smoke, all of us just going on and on about whatever it was at the moment. And the parties afterward, with the singing and beer and dancing, and all of us young and beautiful and brave. Oh, God, I loved us all so much!

Staff meetings were where we got down, put all our cards on the table, bonded and secured trust, and worked it out. Project directors reported on what was happening and what the problems were and what they wanted to do next and what they needed. We'd take it from there. These tedious meetings were our chance to process what had happened, share information, analyze our work, chart a course, be there together.

In meetings and out, I saw our first task as creating relationship among ourselves, holding our community together. A style, an ethic, was implied. I stuck around endlessly, we all did, until some level of understanding was reached, at which point we could act. This was called coming to consensus. Once this broad consensus was reached, I didn't argue with people about what they should do. There was more than enough to do, and plenty of room for experimentation. If folks were willing to risk their lives, that was enough. They should be able to choose how they would die. I did try to do what I said I'd do. That was accountability, synonymous with self-discipline. To my recollection everyone operated like this, for quite some time.

Integration worked both ways. I was breaking the barrier between people with my own body, integrating the black community. I thought I was getting the better side of the deal. By now I referred to myself as a radical. Radical meant the root, as in math. That root truth was revealed in struggle. Our struggle was to break down the system, the walls, of segregation. This implied no barriers in our relations with each other. Once we broke down the barriers between ourselves, we were in a new space together, in community. This was our radical truth. Our radical truth was an experience, not an idea. That was SNCC's great genius.

My experience in SNCC was nurturing, warm, familial. I think of it now as womanist, a term I've borrowed from my black women friends. "Womanist" is the side of me that honors my grandmother and the value of her traditional role.

During the time in Atlanta I shared a place with Mary King, who had replaced me as white campus traveler at the Y job. We lived in a cheap cinder block apartment complex far out in the black world, on a bus line on which the buses never ran on time. I had the east bedroom, hot when I woke in the mornings as summer approached, the sun beating through a rust-colored cotton curtain I'd made. In the white-walled room there was only this curtain, a single mattress on the floor with a blue spread, a small oak bureau. But it was clean and private. I owned only the clothes from a small suitcase. The furnishings belonged to SNCC, which paid the rent. I made $10 a week, $9.64 after taxes. I took my meals at Paschal's Restaurant, across from the SNCC office. They fed us all free.

I read the emerging women's literature in my small white room. De Beauvoir was impressive, but I loved Doris Lessing's *The Golden Notebook*. It was enormously affirming to see a woman of the left view her life in the same compartments as I viewed mine, speak of all aspects of her life frankly, acknowledge her own needs, and empower her perspective by making it public. Lessing's revelations provided a new level of honesty to strive for with other women, at a time when I was trying to sort out what had happened between Tom and me and how that experience related to my politics. Mary read the book too. On the basis of our shared Y experiences and this book we engaged men and women in conversations about gender, much as I had engaged SDS women in Ann Arbor earlier. These conversations must have been extensive. Andy Young remembers that I gave him the book to read during this time, turning him on to feminism.

In the fall of 1963 I went to work in Mississippi, one of the first white female SNCC staff members to do so. I wanted to work with Bob Moses and responded to his invitation. Bob was a key person in SNCC for me, comparable to Ella Baker in his capacity to unlock people and situations into action. As one of the numerous spin-offs of SNCC's work in Mississippi, Bob had facilitated the establishment of a large, foundation-funded project designed to create a pro-grammed instruction method for adult illiterates. We weren't teaching people to read, but trying to develop a way for them to teach themselves. The project was based at Tougaloo, Mississippi, an all-black community surrounding the college of the same name just outside Jackson, of which Tougaloo is now a suburb. Tougaloo College was a church-affiliated private school, which had long maintained an integrated faculty. There were also a few white students. Thus it was ordinary for occasional whites to be seen in this otherwise all black setting. The police tended to stay away.

Doris Derby went over ahead of us and persuaded Mr. Robert Coles, a local black farmer, to fix up and rent a house — later dubbed the Literacy House — to the three women on the project staff. Doris, Helen O'Neill, and I settled in, buying used furniture and a new white plastic couch at a black store in Jackson. I still remember that sticky white couch and how it would become glued to the back of my legs with sweat. We put a kitchen together and kept a clean house. We were congenial, all with academic backgrounds in the field of education and rather quiet, and I remember our time together as simple and easy. Doris was an artist, and Helen was a young Mississippi native and school-teacher. Doris and I still see each other from time to time. I crossed paths with Helen in the 1980s in Atlanta and we sat and hugged and cried. Jane Stembridge was around, and all of us often went to the home of the Tougaloo chaplain, Ed King, and his wife, Jeanette, both white Mississippians. Doris, Jane, and I somehow got a car and took a trip along the Natchez Trace. We entered whites-only stores without hesitation, and the locals asked Doris, who was wearing her hair in braids, if she were an Indian. We went to the ghost towns on the Mississippi, to Van Cleve, which Jane later wrote about in her long poem "The Peoples Wants Freedom." I liked the quiet rural life. My grandmother's house and the Literacy House at Tougaloo merged in my dreams for years to come.

Helen, Doris, and I also worked in Jackson at the office of the Council of Federated Organizations (COFO), a coalition of civil rights groups in the state. COFO was sponsoring Freedom Registration. This was a major statewide campaign to register all persons who wanted to vote. It ran parallel to the state political structure, from which blacks were excluded, and would demonstrate how many people would register if only they could. Freedom Votes were held also. The first was for Aaron Henry for governor, held in November 1963. I remember counting ballots at a wooden table in the cold, cement-floored storefront that served as our office, under overhead fluorescent lights. The ballots—smudged slips of mimeograph paper, usually marked with pencil—arrived in shoe boxes and brown cardboard boxes with slits in the top, from black churches and businesses across the state. Eighty-eight thousand votes were cast! There were twenty thousand blacks registered to vote in the entire state. These votes were beautiful things to see. Each vote was someone's vote for a life. Violence accelerated as the movement became more visible. I invited my friend Ronnie Dugger of the Texas Observer over to observe and write. During a high-speed chase following a mass meeting in Greenwood, our car was repeatedly rammed from behind by a car full of hostile whites. We barely avoided capsizing into the deep drainage ditch on the side of the high way. We celebrated the election with a dance at the Masonic Temple, decorated with crepe paper, festive. Local people from across the state and SNCC folks from all over came to celebrate.

I met the Mississippi SNCC staff during this time and in the year that followed, all local people Bob had recruited: Curtis Hayes, Hollis Watkins, Jesse Harris, Charles McLaurin, Freddie and George Greene, Joyce and Dorie Ladner, Lawrence Guyot, MacArthur Cotton, Willie Peacock, Emma

Bell, and so many more, all such fine people, breakthrough people. People from outside the state were with us too, among them my dear friend Mendy Samstein.

Bob had been working on voter registration in Mississippi for some time. It was in his work, like this Freedom Vote, that I saw nonviolence moving forward into political organizing. The folks who were strong nonviolent activists had a problem with the move toward voting rights some years earlier. Voter registration is at the center of the political system. Nonviolent radicals saw themselves as standing outside that system, speaking truth to it. Ella had brokered a compromise, in which both tracks would be taken. This issue was never clearly resolved, and the two modes of political work were never clearly separated. This ambiguity was reflected in our notion that voter registration amounted to nonviolent direct action in the Deep South anyway. The vote as a white institution was protected by guns and law as surely as were segregated public accommodations. One of the results of this merger of voter registration (representing entrance into and action within the political process) and nonviolent direct action (representing outsiders speaking to the process from outside and from conscience) appeared in 1964: the challenge to the seating of the all-white Mississippi delegation to the Democratic National Convention.

It seemed to me Bob's work was beginning to issue forth with a more coherent organizing methodology in which these two positions, and their orientations toward power, were actually reconciled, an extrapolation of nonviolence as politics. As we went into communities as SNCC staff, some of us became organizers. Our task as organizers (our strategy, if you will, or our theory of social change) was, I believed, to open space so people could come into their own radical power. It was only to their own power that people could in the long run be true. Creating political or social power was about building mass, which meant many of these groups, all self-owning, distinct from the technocratic state, distinct from established power hierarchies, distinct from SNCC, acting in alliance with each other. To the organizer, successful organizing was both the goal and the means. Success meant that the group held together, were loyal to one another. To the group, success entailed moving toward their goals, toward power. The organizer positioned herself outside power, empowering others. She needed her own community, of which she was the insider, and within which she was empowered and powerful. SNCC was this community.

I was more comfortable working in this framework in the Jackson office than on the literacy project. To disclose their illiteracy was a source of shame to these local folks. I felt my being white compounded their discomfort and probably perpetuated visions of white superiority. Their obeisance toward me was unsettling. I was also conscious, and had been since I first arrived in Atlanta in 1960, of the danger I spread around me as a highly visible blonde white woman. It was fine with me if other white women wanted to work in SNCC projects in these killer little towns, but in good conscience I couldn't endanger my black companions, especially the guys, in this way. The literacy project was my only excursion into field organizing in the South. When the project left to go to Harlem in the spring of 1964 to field-test the work, I stayed behind, back on SNCC staff, assisting in the development of the Mississippi Freedom Summer Project, which brought almost eight hundred mostly white students into Mississippi to work in Freedom Schools and voter registration.

Mississippi had been considered too dangerous for an integrated project. There had been quite a bit of discussion about the Summer Project inside the state, and many staff there were opposed to having so many white people come down. I, however, liked the leverage white students would provide. Press and northern politicians would pay attention. We had so few resources, and I knew there were many white students who yearned to join us. I also thought that if we couldn't integrate the white community, we'd integrate the black community instead. If Mrs. Fannie Lou Hamer and other local Mississippians are to be believed, this was what mattered to them about the summer. For the first time in Mississippi, black and white met as equals. So many profound changes were wrought at this time that this change sometimes goes unremarked. In its own way it is grave and beautiful.

Despite these values of the project, however, I found the decision about the summer a tough call. I was oriented toward process and human relations concerns. The development of local leadership and sensitivity to blacks' feelings about race were my main concerns. But, I decided, it was just a short-term event, and then we would get back to normal. At a meeting in Hattiesburg in January, I spoke in favor of a small project, suggesting that we could handle one hundred people, definitely no more than five hundred. I was appointed to the six-person committee to plan for the summer. Ella was on that committee, too. It seems it didn't occur to us to suggest human relations workshops as part of the Summer Project, to allow us all to process the deep feelings about race it was bound to release and the misunderstandings that were bound to occur.

I volunteered for a summer staff assignment, which I shared with Dick Jewitt, a white CORE staff member. The Mississippi Freedom Democratic Party (MFDP) was challenging the seating of the all-white state Democratic delegation at the Democratic National Convention in Atlantic City in August 1964. We were summer program coordinators for the challenge. The MFDP was the integrated and loyal Democratic Party in the state, operating parallel to the all-white party regulars. It had been organized over the spring, growing organically from COFO's Freedom Registration and Freedom Votes.

Most accounts of the challenge at the 1964 Democratic convention focus on the events at Atlantic City. Few detail the mammoth statewide organizing that took place in Mississippi. Our work in the Jackson office as coordinators indicates the scope of that effort and our serious intent toward legitimacy. We researched through the spring, writing to the national party for information, using the library in between the endless administrative tasks involved in pulling off the Summer Project. We put out a dense four-page paper, complete with a chart, describing the structure of the state Democratic Party and the meetings that were held to elect delegates. A memo to staff and community leaders outlined the tasks at hand: staff study to learn the state structure; time in all community meetings for education on political programs; investigating in local areas to determine precinct boundaries; talking in terms of supervisors' districts as fundamental political subdivisions; locating halls for precinct meetings and county conventions. And finally, "Try to gather enough registered voters in a precinct . . . to make a meaningful challenge to the regular Democratic precinct convention."

This was the first step: to find people who would attempt to enter the all-white precinct meetings, held on April 16—a very dangerous proposition. The meetings were often in obscure locations, more dangerous even than the county courthouses, where voter registration occurred. We told staff: Hold a workshop on basic parliamentary procedure, create a slate, and discuss in full "various alternatives depending on the reactions of the other people attending the convention." (That meant how to handle violence, how to hold a meeting if they were turned away, how to participate if they weren't.)

On April 16, as staff called in to report on attempts to enter precinct meetings, I took the notes over the WATS line, the Wide Area Telephone Service, a flat-rate long-distance line at the heart of our communications system. Handfuls of people had gone to the meetings. Sometimes our people were simply blocked from the room where the whites-only precinct meeting was being held, and sometimes they were struck, knocked down. We will probably never know all the reprisals suffered. As we said in a later document, this group of people, as well as all those who attended MFDP precinct meetings later, "were literally gambling their lives against the right of being seated in Atlantic City."

When summer was upon us, I returned with the first buses from the orientation we ran for volunteers in Ohio. Immediately we faced the disappearance of Mickey Schwerner, James Chaney, and Andrew Goodman, two CORE staff people and a summer volunteer. I knew right away our three fellow workers had been lynched. A handful of us manned the phones twenty-four hours a day for the next two weeks, chain-smoking cigarettes and grabbing naps on desks. I remember saying to Bob long distance in Ohio, "Tell everyone to be careful." I thought as I said it that this was such a silly thing to say. Did it really matter how careful we were? I felt a long way from my voice.

It is amazing to me now that we kept right on working. Having completed the first phase of the challenge by attempting to enter white precinct meetings, the MFDP now called their own meetings. Staff and summer volunteers organized on MFDP's behalf.

More organizing material was produced. First, there was a paper explaining the basis of the challenge: exclusion of Negroes from voting and all phases of party activity; disloyalty to the national party; intransigence so deep the national political community needed to bring the state party into line. The paper described the formation of the MFDP, Freedom Registration, Freedom Candidates, the Convention Challenge. Dona Richards put together information for organizers on how to get the precinct and county meetings together, what to do at them (including a loyalty pledge), and what information we needed from them. We offered materials for canvassing, speakers for meetings, information on what was happening elsewhere. Bob and Dick and Dona and I put out an "emergency memorandum" on July 19, instructing staff and voter registration volunteers to focus all attention on convention challenge organizing. Amazing: we listed every county, the status of organizing (*Meeting date set? Place secured?*), the number of freedom registrations in, the number needed, and specific suggestions for weak areas and for getting people to meetings, for keeping records, for feeding us individual contacts in any areas we had not been able to organize. We said what we could offer: sound truck, radio spots, announcements at meetings, a TV show for selected areas.

We continued correspondence with delegates to the convention from northern states who might support our challenge, took phone calls, explained the project to anyone who needed information, and stayed in touch with our support office in Washington. We put out a last-minute rushed mailing to northern contacts, Bob, Dona, Emmie Schrader, and I collating and stuffing.

The summer was long and hot and brutal. The daily violence throughout the state seems incredible in retrospect. I can hardly believe we went through it day after day. I helped with the WATS line, hearing daily reports from the field of violence, the voices on the other end strained, asking for help we couldn't supply. The office was always crowded and terribly hot, a storefront with no ventilation. Often I handled whatever crises or details or logistics or arguments fell to me as an "old hand," getting people fed, finding gas money, or cigarettes, or places to sleep, or toilet paper. There were so many people. I felt overrun. I missed the intimacy and security of knowing everyone and being known. It was weird to be among so many whites. I felt exposed, like I'd been passing before and now was found out.

I continued to live at the Literacy House. I don't know whether SNCC paid Mr. Coles rent or if he just let us live there free. A succession of residents arrived, always in flux, and other staff crashed constantly, sharing beds and the floor and pillows and the couch. I spent increasing amounts of time supporting this desperately needed R & R scene, probably influenced by the fact that I had no car in which to get to Jackson, and often no money for gas even if a car were available. I cleaned and cooked, creating social space in which we could all relax, talk, plan, think, and generally cool out. We always had rice, beans, corn meal, and flour, from local people's sharing of their "commodities"—Department of Agriculture surplus food. I think we grew some greens behind the Literacy House. We always seemed to have greens.

Meanwhile, organizing toward the challenge progressed. We completed the selection and ratification of delegates to Atlantic City at a festive statewide

Mississippi Freedom Democratic Party Convention in Jackson. Dona and I registered local people and organizers as they gathered from around the state, jamming in at the Masonic Temple, spirits high. We had banners, and placards for the counties, and flags. Ella had been heading up the MFDP Washington office supporting the challenge, and she was the keynote speaker at our convention.

Then it was August, and I went on the long bus ride to New Jersey. It rained en route. We were moving so fast the rain on the window was blown backward and looked like tears. In Atlantic City at the Gem Motel there weren't enough beds. I slept on the floor, and many delegates slept three or four to a bed. I remember going out to eat bad meals in equally crowded and uncomfortable situations, feeling responsible for these people who had risked their lives and come all this way to be treated so poorly, feeling ashamed we couldn't offer anything better than this and angry that the Democrats treated them even worse. I wasn't ever in the convention hall. I just waited with the delegation at our demonstration on the boardwalk, singing in the rain to keep our spirits up, or answered phones over at the Gem Motel. I shared with the delegates their exclusion, which was the real story of the convention. These good people, patient and exhausted, sat three and four in a row on the bed they shared, in their Sunday clothes, eating cheese and crackers from a paper bag, watching TV to see if they were getting permission to take their legal and righteous place — permission that never came.

I believe we were the legitimate delegation to this convention, both legally and morally. Despite my faith in our legitimacy, I had little hope the MFDP would be seated. I was from Texas, and Texans knew LBJ was ruthless. As it turned out, only the interference of Hubert Humphrey, direct from the White House, prevented the votes for a minority report from the Credentials Committee, which would have led to a floor fight. Prospects for winning on the floor were very good. The delegation was offered, instead, a compromise of two seats and a promise of reform in the future. It was as though they were sit-inners, and the party was a lunch counter owner, who chose the only two who were acceptable, one of whom was white. The delegation rejected this compromise. Mrs. Hamer said, "We didn't come for no two seats, cause all of us is tired."

Undaunted, despite this scandalous reception, the MFDP immediately went home and organized a challenge to the seating of the Mississippi congressional delegation. The players from SNCC were more alienated from the Democratic Party, especially its liberals, who had betrayed us.

The convention was at the end of the summer. In retrospect, there is much evidence to suggest that the Civil Rights Acts of 1964 and 1965, which destroyed segregation as a legal system forever, were the result of our hard work during this time. But the explosive Mississippi Summer Project left a lot of debris, and propelled us into a situation for which we were unprepared. Mississippi was like a nation after a war. Staff had no marching orders; volunteers were everywhere, like refugees; projects were operating without funds, in essence outposts whose supply lines had been cut. Violence, fear, and tension had taken their toll. We were all really tired. We never did return to "normal."

A memo at the time of the Atlantic City convention mentions staff and volunteers who were "staying in the state." Did we ever decide they could stay in Mississippi, or did it just happen? The remaining whites changed the racial ratio. Many new African American college students, who had been recruited as summer staff, remained also. We had not processed these staff in. We hadn't really even all been introduced. The summer's interracial experiences had sometimes been tough. We were now a whole college generation away from the sit-ins and the healing power of nonviolence that they embodied. Race became uncomfortable as an issue and was seldom mentioned anymore, in stark contrast to the previous easy references.

Money became a problem. SNCC had some now as a result of the summer publicity, but where was it? Not in Mississippi. Rumors circulated that in Atlanta SNCC was purchasing a big building. I didn't believe it. I viewed the breakdown of staff morale around the issues of cash flow and strategic direction as our most critical problem. We were at the end of all our current programs. We had no plans for after the summer. At the same time, our relationship to electoral politics, as well as our alliance with liberals, was in question as a result of the Convention Challenge.

None of these issues were discrete. Nor were they clearly defined. Nor were they ever discussed through to consensus. Nor was there necessarily agreement that they even existed. These were just my observations, but based on them, I thought we needed to relax, look around, and assess what was happening. We needed to process what had happened in Mississippi, allowing issues and feelings and analysis to emerge. We needed to share across the South and decide what to do next. That is what we had done as long as I had been around, and it had worked so far. In order to continue as grassroots organizers, we would address our work, look hard at our organizing, with project directors' reports as the core of the discussion. That organizing leadership would come to the front of the organization at a staff meeting, assessing progress and problems and strategy and goals. Within this format real issues could be raised and handled.

We didn't do this, though. In October a staff meeting was called in Atlanta (Atlanta I). I found that SNCC really was buying a building. Jim took the lead at the meeting, presenting a big Black Belt summer project for 1965. I was astonished. We were still reeling from the last summer project. Ella and Bob were strong about the need to regroup, to go slowly. I spoke about the low morale of organizing staff, about promised moneys not arriving, about lack of direction. Internal democracy emerged as an issue. Staff alienation and non-involvement in decision making was one aspect of this issue. The fact that SNCC's operations were not in conformity with our constitution was another aspect. The latter evidently arose as an issue when questions were raised regarding who was deciding what. It is not clear what else happened at this meeting. Only one day's minutes survive, although the meeting lasted several days. What is clear is that there was discontentment and confusion.

In response to this confusion and discontent, a large rethinking SNCC conference was organized for November at Waveland, Mississippi. Topics were circulated before the meeting, for staff to address in writing—a very SDS sort of move. I didn't know who had developed and circulated that list, which included such questions as: What is the importance of racial considerations among the staff? What is SNCC? What should it be to accomplish its goals? What is the Student Voice? Friends of SNCC groups   What do they do? Whom do we organize, where do we organize, what do we do with what we organize, and what is the relationship of these questions to structure and decision making? Sherrod's paper was reminiscent of our beginnings. It starts, "First of all, let us thank God for the wisdom of the pinched toe and the empty belly." Bob Moses's paper was the only one to discuss staff involvement in decision making. It's a good paper, which describes the way we worked in Mississippi. Bob begins with warnings about the traps involved in the questions that had been circulated. He suggests that we view SNCC as a tool and agree to talk about what we want to do and how the tool can help us do it. Then he talks about the need for a commitment to circulate ideas and draw everyone in to SNCC's ongoing work. Since organizing staff can't sit in session continually, ideas can be circulated, with groups coming together to work on the larger problems, then disbanding when the work is done.

I thought we would have a "real" staff meeting at Waveland, but we didn't. This was a big gathering. I wasn't sure exactly who all these people were. Jim opened with a speech centered on the history of SNCC's structure. He urged us to immediately adopt a proposal for structure that he introduced. His proposal had one administrative position whose function was to support staff: program coordinator. The rest of the sizable administration would be selected by and responsible to the executive secretary. The coordinating committee would meet three times a year. The current meeting was declared the coordinating committee. A call committee would decide who would come to coordinating committee meetings in the future. An executive committee and other committees would carry out the coordinating committee's will. Jim was addressing the issue of constitutional legitimacy in decision making.

Starting things off with a big speech by the executive secretary seemed unlike us, more like the Urban League. I understood that the meeting had been called partly in response to field staff's feelings that we weren't being consulted, didn't know what was going on, were receiving word of decisions that had already been made. At issue was our process as an organization. In this light, the suggestion that we adopt a proposal that centralized and delegated power was disconcerting. After Jim's talk, agenda emerged as an issue. Many people wanted to discuss program, not structure. Should we set up a way to delegate decisions, or should we talk about what we wanted to do, with structure following later? This stalemate regarding agenda was quite lengthy.

While I agreed with the "form follows function" thinking, I believed it would benefit us to have a clear outline of how we'd operate. I had thought since the Community back in Austin, and still do, that trust is secured by clear agreements and accountability. I believed we could create a structure in which decisions we made at meetings were carried out by an administration designed to support us as organizers.

I wrote a paper that dialogs with Jim's proposal. (It is unsigned. I must have passed it out personally after the meeting began, perhaps to my structure workshop, where it was discussed.) I suggested that each area of our work be represented by a person on the administrative staff who would ensure that staff had what they needed to continue work in that program area. These program administrators would control funds. They would be selected at coordinating committee meetings from work groups and be responsible to those work groups. The program secretary would troubleshoot if there were glitches or administrative breakdowns. I questioned leaving the membership of the coordinating committee to a call committee and had a few other comments, but program folks as administration was the core of my paper.

While representing different perspectives regarding our needs, the two proposals were structurally parallel. Both provided a strong framework for the organization. Proposals for SNCC structure at this time are usually described as "tight" and "loose." As regards these two proposals, that is inaccurate. Both are tight. I've always thought of them as the centralist proposal and the organizer proposal. It seemed important to clarify the issues facing us. Once we were clear, I thought that we could compromise, easily amending one or the other, and then move on to substantive discussion. I was sure we all wanted to remain united and continue organizing. I made my proposal primarily for practical reasons. I wanted those of us who were organizing to have access to the means to do it.

I don't recall that compromise was ever discussed, however. In retrospect, this lack of annealing probably reflects commitments to conflicting visions of SNCC and thus conflicting views of where power should be located. Jim has said subsequently that he was trying to develop a strong, centralized organization during this time, to expand power and move toward becoming a mass organization. I assume that means mass membership. This is quite a different model from SNCC as a band of organizers. We were, additionally, hampered by the absence of Ella Baker, who had brokered our compromises in the past.

The work-based format for staff meetings that had led toward consensus was in the past, and we had no new agreement for how to operate. So although we went into structure workshops and reported back, we didn't have a way to make a decision. We also met in small groups to discuss programs (freedom schools, MFDP, etc.). That was educational for new staff, but it didn't deal with the real issues. Random pronouncements, of which there were plenty, attained the power of strategies through repetition, for example the saying that "whites should work with whites." The meeting was frustrating for us all, and it seemed insubstantial or empty to me, like a charade. Nothing was resolved.

We would have done better to use the approach Bob suggested in his paper. We would have had to fight for that, continuing that agenda debate until all agreed to talk about our work and to view SNCC as our tool in doing that work. Maybe I made a mistake by talking structure first. Not that my participation was that significant. I appear in some accounts of this meeting and the period following, perhaps because I introduced that paper and was so visible. This was a good time to keep quiet; I knew that, but I spoke anyway, reckless. In fact, I was not a player for long. I dropped back after being jeered from the floor while presenting my proposal. So much for clarifying the issues.

It's interesting to me now how divorced the various aspects of these events are from each other and from what the organization was actually doing in its core work. The papers were not related to the real issues of the field. The real issues of the field were not related to the discussion at the Waveland staff meeting. The papers were not related to the discussions of the Waveland staff meeting. The various viewpoints on a given issue in the papers had no forum where they could relate to each other. And so on. It was a mess.

The fallout from this meeting was heavy. A short linguistic story hints at some later effects. Jim was listing things that he thought were wrong with SNCC. He said, "And there are too many people high on freedom, just going off and doing what they want. Like Casey. She deserted her post as northern coordinator and went off to work in Mississippi because that was where the action was." Jim never forgave me for leaving that job. I think he really liked the work I did. He had convinced me to go to Chicago for him the previous winter, after I'd moved to Mississippi, to handle a faction fight in the Friends of SNCC group there. Jim's comment was the only time I heard the term "high on freedom." Later, as the central staff struggled to get a grip and create order, in the absence of programs, assignments, and strategy, unruly organizing staff were called "freedom highs." The term also seems to have become an epithet for staff at odds with SNCC's new direction and any others deemed politically incorrect. I never heard the term "freedom high" at the time, but learned of it only years afterward from books I read.

I participated in some action on the sidelines at Waveland too, as part of a group writing another paper, entitled "SNCC Position Paper: Women in the Movement." Of the actual writing of this paper I retain only two snapshot images. The first is Mary knocking on my door at Waveland after I'd gone to bed, saying, "Casey, you have to get up. We are going to write about women now." In the second, I see myself typing the document, I think directly onto a mimeograph stencil, at night, under a single naked light bulb. I was in the room at Waveland where the papers were mimeographed, surrounded by perhaps five women. I recall the group as white and related to Literacy House conversations about women, which in turn traced back to Atlanta, Ann Arbor, and Austin. I pulled the commentary together as I typed, from written scraps and things the women were saying to me.

This was an internal educational document. The conference was full of them. Everyone was educating everyone else about their pet concerns. The paper aimed to bring forward the fact that sexism was comparable to racism, a novel idea at the time — so novel, in fact, that the word *sexism* didn't exist in our lexicon. It's almost as hard to believe that, and the associated implications, as it is to believe that at this time it was illegal across the South for black and white to eat together. Our writing is simple, patchy, and erratic. But its goal is noble: to discern the effects of a system — stereotyping, labeling, and discrimination, wasted talent, separation.

My concern, in all the changes we were going through, was with maintaining the radical nonviolent core of SNCC, our old womanist, integrationist way, in which leaders and power politics were disarmed. I perceived this as the true locus of the feminist issue at this event. The paper and its topic seemed an aside. Indeed, they were. I was anxious about its reception, but our writing was generally attributed to a SNCC longtimer, the driven, stalwart Ruby Doris Smith Robinson. She did not disown it. No one was going to tangle with Ruby Doris, or with the other strong black women of SNCC. The paper caused hardly a ripple.

However, as the paper has entered the literature of feminism over the years, some historians have wondered if it exposed a struggle for power or leadership. Nonsense. We were all white. None of us were after leadership. That was for blacks. I believe we were speaking not for our private self-interest, but for all women, to share what we saw: that gender is a social construct, as is race. There was no written feminist critique on the left in our generation. We were the first. It is a good critique, in many ways, and brave, a fine example of how the tools developed in analyzing racism were translated, inside SNCC itself, into an analysis of gender. We had pierced the racist bubble and were seeing clearly. All things were open to question. As Bernice Reagon has said, "SNCC was where it could happen."

I'll end this Waveland discussion with a bittersweet memory. It was usual for us to get together after a day of meetings. We laughed a lot then. We needed it. Stokely Carmichael had the most wicked wit. He had perfected the self-deprecating self-parody of the minstrel tradition, and, like that tradition, he was utterly irreverent. He named our community's feared and hidden truths, and disempowered them by unifying us in laughter around their acknowledgment.

This night a group of us were gathered on the pier, the rancor of the meetings put to rest. It was warm, the lights on the water sparkly, our voices mellow and carrying across it. We were all stretched out, heads in laps, looking up at stars and out at silvery water, joking around and singing southern Protestant church hymns. The position paper "Women in the Movement" came up. Stokely quipped that "the proper position of women in the movement is prone." It was really funny.

Stokely sounds like a sexist, pure and simple, to any outsider. But he was quite the opposite. Our laughter represents our release and relief at the exposure of sexuality, sexist attitudes, and the paper's pomposity. Stokely was a friend of mine. We crossed paths in many settings, and talked often about many subjects. After he went to Africa, he sent me long letters on Marxism and feminism.

That night on the pier was my final experience after a SNCC meeting of black and white joining together to laugh, to touch, to bond, and to comfort each other.

Still, there was the work. I had by now sunk deeply into the vibrant culture of the African American Deep South. Ordinary language there was poetry. I longed to see it writ large. Among the many possibilities, I envisioned hanging broadsides of local people's words written as free verse, and the same material printed as posters, or as books for use in freedom schools. My friendships with

SNCC photographers Danny Lyon and Francis Mitchell had sparked an interest in that medium. I wanted to democratize their technical expertise by building a darkroom at Tougaloo and training young blacks as photographers. These photographs would accompany the poetry and find many other uses. In this way community people could be supported to interpret and shape their movement, creating their own myths and language, heroes and heroines. Over the summer I began to solicit cameras and initiated conversations about a poetry workshop for staff and local folks. The Atlantic City experience had left me uninterested in electoral politics and tired of offices, which were by now considered locations of power in which whites were overrepresented. In the fall I turned toward cultural work full time. Mary King and Emmie Schrader joined in and we made trips to New Orleans, where Matt Herron, a black star, taught us darkroom technique.

My way of handling Waveland and the entire bad scene that was emerging in SNCC was to develop acute appendicitis in New Orleans on one of these trips and barely survive. I never knew if the excruciatingly bad hospital treatment was because of the nurses' ineptness or because black SNCC staff came to see me in the hospital and the white hospital staff figured out I was a "freedom rider."

I went to my mother's house in Texas to recuperate. She was raising my half-sister, Karen, in that small southern town. Mom was independent, but cautious, and very alone. I think my radical lifestyle frightened her, or perhaps her hopes for me were disappointed. She never turned me away, but the unspoken distance between us didn't heal for many years. On this visit, she didn't think I was well enough to travel when I left. She was probably right, as I was weak and thin through the winter. I was on a schedule, though, trying to make it to the meeting of the SDS National Executive Committee, which for some reason was paying for me to attend, over Christmas vacation in New York City. We met in a dingy second-floor loft. After the SDS meeting I stayed north, visiting Tom at the Newark Community Union Project, hoping for a reconciliation, perhaps as shelter from the storm of changes in the southern movement. But that was not to be. I moved on, responding to invitations to projects and events, building bridges to and support for SNCC. I went to D.C. both for the first SDS-sponsored rally against the war and for the Congressional Challenge. At the latter I was arrested, tossed into a paddy wagon in front of the Justice Department. I remember Mendy helping me sit up, asking me if I was hurt. I was in Cleveland for a conference of poor folks, in Ann Arbor for some reason that seemed crucial at the time, and in many other places that today I don't recall being. I was thinking and talking about "working with whites," which by now seemed the clear message. I had started my interracial work in that arena. What could it mean today? Where was its cutting edge? Where could I locate? It was unthinkable to me to go back to the white community of the segregated South; I would have to go north. I met other SNCC staff as I traveled, who were similarly at loose ends.

Meanwhile, Mary and Emmie were developing the photo project. They had learned to create filmstrips and were producing them for SNCC's use in political education. I wasn't taken with this notion, but I joined them in New York, where they were fundraising.

I can barely recall the next SNCC gathering, held in February 1965 in Atlanta (Atlanta II). I retain an image of a sort of thrashing about, with occasional impassioned and sometimes incomprehensible speeches relieving an otherwise cold experience. Our irresolution regarding strategy and procedures continued. Perhaps it was at this meeting that Jim's structure proposal was adopted. It seemed irrelevant to me now. I recall being very lonely.

A funny note in Mary's cramped handwriting sits among the minutes of this meeting in the SNCC archives at the Martin Luther King Center in Atlanta. Mary describes lunch one day at Atlanta II. I'm sitting with John Lewis, our brave longtime chairman, and Jim Forman. I suggest to them that they might step down, move things along by rotating leadership. Maybe it would dislodge the logjam. Mary notes that after lunch John made a speech indicating a need for strong, militant, experienced black leadership because SNCC was the group that would liberate black people. There it is, the old and the new.

This was the period of SNCC's transition out of our nonviolent, interracial culture. I watched, conflicted and depressed, as that fabric unraveled, empathizing with the feelings expressed and sure that the public implications were tragic. The movement's promise was great, but so was its cost. Our community enabled us to pay that cost. Eventually we all lost our community. Each of us had to go through that loss alone. Even now when I give talks about the move-

ment I weep, sometimes breaking down completely. My tears are for that loss and for the innocent girl I was.

Back in Mississippi that spring of 1965, the Literacy House was full of people, none of whom I knew. Meanwhile, Stokely and other staff I respected, Courtland Cox, Ruth Howard, and Bob Mants among them, were moving into Alabama, still organizing. Partly in response, I decided to join SDS's Economic Research and Action Project (ERAP) for the summer. ERAP was an emerging national effort to create the white side of a national interracial movement of the poor. I wanted to organize white welfare women. Organizing women represented a return to my roots in the YWCA. I was also trying to follow the new line in SNCC, viewing my move as an experimental effort to find ways for whites to leave SNCC and work on the white side. I hoped for alliance now between black and white, even though we were working in separate communities. I wrote to Jim and to Ruby Doris Robinson, SNCC Personnel Committee chair, telling them my plan. They seemed to like it; I kept right on getting my paycheck, $9.64 a week.

I drove north from Mississippi in an old Ford someone from SDS gave me. I went first to the ERAP project in Cleveland, already working on welfare organizing. Then I went on up to Chicago, where the car collapsed. As SNCC staff on loan, I loosely affiliated with Chicago ERAP's Jobs or Income Now project in Uptown, a neighborhood of Appalachian migrants. Rennie Davis and some other SDS heavies were trying to organize unemployed youth. One other woman, also from SDS, worked with me. We chose the biggest, worst building and knocked on doors, locating welfare mothers. Over the course of the summer I was arrested sitting in with one of our local women at a welfare office. I recall vividly the deafening cacophony in our filthy holding tank, packed with prostitutes rounded up by the police. I found three other women who I thought would go the distance. I spent my time in their slum apartment kitchens. The project was full of conflicts between the two groups we were organizing. One of the women I was organizing dated one of the guys Rennie was organizing, and the guy regularly beat her up. The remainder of the unemployed youth seemed to be sociopaths. The welfare women were terrified of them; not only that, but they were afraid that associating with me might bring

them around. The whole youth gang showed up one night at the apartment where I was living with my traveling companion at the time, a white guy who'd been thrown out of Kappa Alpha at Ole Miss for something to do with James Meredith. The gang forced him against a wall and then backed up and threw a case of empty beer bottles at him as he hopped, barefoot, dodging the broken glass. They left, finally, taking my grandmother's wedding ring. My friend disappeared the next day and returned with a longshoreman's hook to get the gang. He had to be hustled out of the neighborhood. He took my dear Rollei camera with him when he left and went on to become a photographer for the *New York Times*.

I figured it would take five years to create a solid organization. I hadn't the heart for it. I realized, working in Chicago, how difficult it was to organize women within a setting that lacked feminist consciousness. The first step, therefore, was to create that consciousness. That fall of 1965 I wrote another, longer paper for and about women in the movement. The stated purpose of the paper was to create for myself and others a community of support, so that we could keep working for radical change. This was my issue, of course: I couldn't figure out how to keep working.

At Mary King's family's cabin in Virginia, she and I refined the paper, which we called "Sex and Caste: A Kind of Memo." It is centered on the idea of women organizing themselves, and the suggested basis and style of that organizing reflects what went on at the YWCA. We go on to talk about common themes that had arisen in our conversations with women. The paper compares sex roles to caste, and comments on how that operates in work, personal relations with men, and institutions. In this regard, we follow and expand on the Waveland paper. We suggest that the intimacy and unity this discussion provides would sustain us in our movement careers. We end by arguing that the personal is political. This notion came from SDS, as its members struggled to find the radical alternatives in their own lives. And we raise SDS's ever-present question, of how to radicalize the people:

> We've talked in the movement about trying to build a society which would see basic human problems (which are now seen as private troubles), as public problems and would try to shape institutions to meet human needs rather than shaping people to meet the needs of those with power. To raise questions like those

[in the paper] illustrates very directly that society hasn't dealt with some of its deepest problems and opens discussion of why that is so. In one sense, it is a radicalizing question that can take people . . . into areas of personal and institutional change.

I still like this piece today. It reveals the sources, strengths, and weaknesses of our understanding at the time. It's a white woman's view, but the tone is tentative and conversational, open and inviting, rather than argumentative. It doesn't blame anyone, but suggests women organize themselves toward ownership of this issue and their lives. It reflects both a realization of the gendered self as a political reality and a struggle against the tendency to see everything through the lens of that realization.

Mary and I sent the memo to a number of women, black and white. Black women in SNCC, struggling for racial equality, did not respond. In the past, if black men stood up publicly against segregation, they were often murdered, and they almost always suffered reprisals. Now they were standing up anyway. Perhaps this was not the right time for these black women to organize separately. Also, black SNCC women have said ever since the Waveland paper became public that they did not view themselves as disempowered.

The SDS women, however, had, for the most part, never found their way into the fierce intellectual contests that formed the core of the organization's group activities. In community projects, their relational skills had empowered them, already awakening a spark. The memo spoke to them directly. They took it to their next national meeting and organized around it.

This response by the women of SDS is widely credited with being the root of the women's liberation movement, the radical wing of white feminism. It was too little and too late for me. I had not been in SDS proper for years, my student days long past. I saw women's lib, when it later emerged, as emulating black nationalism. I found it unattractive. I was by then in a different life.

I had moved farther and farther out, onto the margins of the culture, into the center of the movement, leaving everything behind. I was standing on the ground of the Beloved Community, but that ground eroded. Spun out into the world at large by the accelerating force of a social revolution I had helped create, I crashed and burned. There was no going home again. I lost everything. With no place left to go after Mary's, I arrived in New York City by bus in the bitter-cold winter of 1965–66, no coat, no suitcase, no money. Some of the women I knew in Mississippi were there, on the Lower East Side. They took me in.

For the next couple of years I worked for the New York Department of Welfare and Mobilization for Youth, continued photographing and built a darkroom, and joined the youth rebellion even though I was overage for it, an émigré in a bohemian world. With others from Mississippi I moved to Vermont and created one of those rural communes to which so many of us retreated as our organizations collapsed. All my papers and photographs were destroyed in a fire there. I became an environmentalist. I read Gandhi again, and through him other Eastern thinkers, first the Vedas, and later the Buddhists. I entered into community with people who were transplanting that world to the West. Although it was inappropriate as a white to say so, I believed, in the recent words of Charles Johnson, author of *The Middle Passage*, that "through the Dharma, the black American quest for 'freedom' realizes its profoundest, truest, and most revolutionary meaning."

Back in the city I met the man who was to be my children's father, the wild and beautiful yogi-carpenter Donald Campbell Boyce III, well known in a rather small circle as the finest exemplar of that new worldview and lifestyle. We attempted to build a life and a family on the shifting sands of the counterculture. Together we helped organize the Integral Yoga Institute in San Francisco, still there today on Dolores Street, and pioneered the urban wilderness in SOHO. I wanted simplicity, to be a local person myself, building on family, from the ground up. Even as it gave me my children, the most profound experience of my life, family failed. With that collapse, I was devastated, driven to reassess and rebuild.

I was lost for a while. I supported myself and my kids in a series of low-paying jobs for good causes: an independent newspaper, a regional planning firm assisting communities impacted by oil development, a preschool for abused children, an oral history project in rural southern Colorado. I continued to consider myself an organizer, chose marginality, and lived without credentials, loyal to the movement as I understood it, not sure if I'd kept the faith or failed to do so. I felt, and largely was, invisible.

When they reached their teen years, my children chose to move from Colorado to New York to live with their dad. At the same time Connie Curry and Julian Bond recommended me for a job in Atlanta, with the Southern Regional Council (SRC). The day I arrived to interview, John Lewis and Julian came by and we sat on Connie's front porch to have a drink. I found myself breathing shallowly, feeling panicked. When I left the South we could not have appeared together publicly in a white neighborhood in this way. The next day Connie and I went to City Hall. When I left Atlanta, the only nonwhites in City Hall would have been a janitor, the kitchen help. Now almost everyone, both elected officials and employees, was black. These two events showed me that we had in fact defeated segregation. I didn't believe it until I saw it with my own eyes.

So I returned south in 1981. Atlanta was very grounding for me. I researched at the Legislature for SRC and handled administration when Connie's office took on the Department of Agriculture's free summer lunch program, a huge operation. Then I went to work as administrative aide for the Department of Parks, Recreation, and Cultural Affairs. I was with black folks again, in Mayor Andy Young's administration.

I had frequent opportunities to review and rethink my experiences of the sixties. Mary King and Tom wrote books, sending me manuscripts to read, many versions. I was part of several conferences as history began to discover women in the movement, and I started reading about SNCC. I reluctantly missed Ella Baker's funeral during this time, unable to part with the airfare, since every spare penny was committed to maintaining contact with my children. Finally, with the Trinity Conference on the Life and Times of the Student Nonviolent Coordinating Committee in 1988, there came the beginning of a great healing. I was moved to be on a panel with other SNCC women; I cried all the way through my speech. When we called the names of our martyrs, as we sang for them and wept for them, they were both black and white.

Integration reemerged as a potent symbol for me, and I struggled to make it a reality in my life. I integrated the parts of myself, getting some very good therapy and postponing my Buddhist studies in favor of twelve-step work. AA seemed strangely familiar, with many elements reminiscent of the early movement: unity and a spiritual Way as foundation for life-and-death struggle, antiauthoritarian structure, identity within community.

In 1989 I moved to Arizona, a third and finally successful attempt to return to the Southwest of my childhood. In 1993 His Holiness the Dalai Lama came to Tucson to teach for a week. Several thousand people attended, at a resort in the desert. I volunteered to help and became friendly with the woman coordinating volunteers. She introduced me to the man to whom I'm now happily married, Paul Buckwalter, an Episcopal priest and community organizer. I tell people we met through the Dalai Lama. We live in the remains of the ghetto, near the barrio, in an old house my son, Don Boyce, helped us restore, on a little piece of earth we are revegetating, inching toward permaculture. Our home is full of furniture from Mamoo's house, inherited from my mother when she died in 1993. Donnie lives four blocks from us with his dog, Natasha, and a houseful of roommates and friends. My daughter, Rosemary Boyce, is an actress in Los Angeles. My children, along with Paul's from previous marriages, form our large family. I have found a Zen community here. Zen, a path to the nondual experience of self, is what I was looking for. My childhood needs are realized. I am at home, where my mother and my grandmother both live in my heart, reconciled. If I haven't achieved firm footing on the high road, I have at least had a glimpse of the view. I can hardly believe the grace of my life now.

When I began work on this book project, my daughter Rosie said to me, "My question about the movement is how all these people got so empowered to do all these things. It's about the inside." I've tried to speak to that question with my story. That story, which has come full circle, ends in apparent separation from my brothers and sisters in struggle, my movement family. On the inside, however, that separation does not obtain. On the inside, in my bones, I am still with them all. This isn't fluffy or sentimental. It's a visceral thing, earned by doing what was common to us all. What we did was pretty simple, as we knew at the time. What we did was, we put our bodies on the line.

We embodied, not as an abstraction, but actually, the struggle and the stress, the ambiguities and the paradoxes, of creating new social realities. Giving ourselves completely, we were as lambs. The unity we achieved transcends any political differences we might have had in the past as well as the distance between us now in space and time. We were many minds but one heart. It is my own heart, and nothing can separate me from all it contains: the triumphs and the tragedies, the exhaustion and the camaraderie, the laughter and the freedom and the love and the anger, our courage and anguish, our arrogance and humility, the splendor and tears and youth . . .

Suddenly and unbidden, as I wrote the words above, the bluebonnet fields of my Texas childhood appeared with perfect clarity in my mind's eye. Blanketing the low hills, spread among the live oak trees, as far as I can see they gently lie, beautiful and vanished, the fields of blue.

Acknowledgments

As expected in a collaborative effort, many people in myriad ways have contributed to our work. Our deepest gratitude:

To the people who read our book in draft form and offered invaluable comments and insights: Victoria Jackson Gray Adams, Mary Frances Berry, Wini Brienes, Blanche Wiesen Cook, Sara M. Evans, Doug McAdam, Charles McDew, Greg Michel, Charles Payne, Francesca Poletta, Beverly Guy-Sheftall, and Alex Willingham.

To the following friends, family members, and scholars, who supported and assisted us individually; without you we could never have done it: Joyce Browning Ashley; Catherine O. Badura; Chip, Mavis, and Ruben Baker; Deborah Barndt; Paula C. Barnes; John Bell; Ancilla R. Bickley; Adrienne B. Biesmeyer; Beth Bingman; Mary Frances Bodemuller; Beverly G. Bond; Julian Bond; Nancy Boyill; Donald C. Boyce IV; Rosemary Lotus Boyce; Bobby, Bruce, and Wayne Browning; Paul Buckwalter; Randall K. Burkett; Robb Burlage; Kenny Burrell; Pam and Reggie Chapple; Jack Chatfield; Ronnie Chency; Mark A. Clarke; Cita Cook; Catherine Cooke; Dorothy Cotton; McArthur Cotton; Anne Coulter; Matthew Countryman; Jim and Patty Critchlow; Eileen and Ann Curry; Mary Ellen Curtin; Pete Daniel; Joseph M. Dawson; Dion Diamond; Theodore C. DeLaney; Peter De Lissovoy; Frances DeLott; Marie Del Pozzo; John Dittmer; Ivanhoe Donaldson; William M. Drennen Jr.; Joanne Edgar; Amy Ehrlich; Art Ellison; Diana

Asher Ellison; Sonia Erlich; Adam Fairclough; Bill Fibben; Five College Women's Studies Center; Cynthia Griggs Fleming; Lee W. Formwalt; Ann P. and Kyle F. Fort; Cate Fosl; Mary Lou Fragile; Renee DeLott Fullerton; Paul and Mary Gaston; Irene Gendzier; Todd Gitlin; M. Rose Gladney; Kenneth Goings; Sidney Goldfarb; Joanne Grant; Winifred Green; Deborah Greenwald; Don Grierson; J. Eugene Guerrero; Joan R. Gunderson; Alan Haber; Maureen Hackett; Alice Hageman; Ed Hamlett; Ruth Hamori; Vincent Harding; Robin O. Harris; Debra J. Hart; Pat Hawk; Enoch, Walker, and Coran Hendry; Morton Herskowitz; Joan Hoff; Chayanne DeLaney Hontz; Pamela Horowitz; Julian Houston; Barbara J. Howe; Cecil, Sandy, and Marc Hudson; Donald Jackson; Polly Jerome; Daniel Joensen; Julia B. Johnson; Rheta Grimsley Johnson; Ben Keppel; George King; Mary E. King; Tracy K'Meyer; Clifford M. Kuhn; Amy Lang; Chana Kai Lee; Sharon Lehrer; Susan Levine; Robert Liebman; Airie Lindsey; Helen Browning Livingston; Pharnal Longus; Frances Lovingood; Johnie and Tammy Lucas; Alice and Staughton Lynd; Susan Lynn; Danny Lyon; John Makhoul; Hermine Makman; Kathy Manns; David, Elizabeth, and Martha Martin; Zora Martin; Lana Martindale; Amy Thompson McCandless; Ann McCleary; Trixie Merkin; Gwen Miles; Laura H. Miller; Valerie Miller; Jim Monsonis; Polly Browning Montford; Emma and Ron Morgan; Nan, Mary Noel, and James G. Morgan Sr.; Susan Moon; Helen Browning Moore; Susan Morgan; Jesse Morris; John Mudd; Gail S. Murray; David Mussatt; Paul Nall; Kathryn L. Nasstrom; Alvin Neely; Kimberly E. Nichols; Sallie H. Noonkester; Martha Prescod Norman; Mary Lee Nunn; Carl Oglesby; Lynne Olson; Marna and Tovis Page; Eliza, Isaac IV, Isaac V, Nabby, and Nick Patch; Suzanne Pharr; Sheila R. Phipps; Christie Farnham Pope; Faye Powell; Chea Prince; Lynn Principe; John C. Raines; Barbara Ransby; Lucie T. Refsland; Susan Reverby; Nancy Richey; Nene Riley; Betty Garman Robinson; Reginald Robinson; Lisa Rogers; Howard Romaine; Debbie Roth-Howe; Jacqueline Rouse; Penny Russell; Lucinda Roy; Jeffrey Sachs; Cathey Sawyer; Mike Sayer; Ernst Schrader; Jeff Schweinfest; Carolynn L. Segers; Donna M. Selle; Mary Lee Settle; Jannann R. Sherman; Dorothy Huntwork Shields; Gene Singletary; JoAnn Rabun Smith; Nancy L. T. Sorrells; Harmony Soubra; Martha Sowerwine; Jane Spicer; Joe Spieler; Roger Stacey; Barbara J. Steinson; Louise Stoker; Dorothy Stoneman; Jane Streek; Patricia Sullivan; Marcia G. Synnott; Robert Talbert;

Jerry Thornberry; Sam Todd; Joe Treasure; Timothy Tyson; Carole Vogel; Karen Vuranch; Frankie Alred Walfield; A. Paige Weaver; Penny Weaver; Rebecca Weaver; Marilyn Wellons; Anna and Lynwood Wells; Robert Wendlinger; Wallace Westfeldt; Jean Wheeler; Linda Whitcomb; Heidi White; Angela Whitmal; Leni Wildflower; Gladys N. Williams; John "Ike" Williams; Seth Williams; Kathy Wisnowskis; Margaret Witecki; Robert P. Wolff; John Worsham; Richard W. Yeo; Smith Young; Eli Zaretsky; Bob Zellner; and Dorothy M. Zellner.

To the people who provided us places to meet and plan the book: Constance Curry for her cottage on Hunting Island; Rob and Cathie Holcombe for their condo on Wrightsville Beach; the Patches for their lodge in Vermont; Mame Warren, Ted DeLaney, and Sharon Nicely for the Guest House at Washington & Lee University.

To the people who helped fund our meetings and our presentations at historical organizations: Gloria Steinem and MS Foundation, the Southern Regional Council, and Jim Huston of Oklahoma State University.

And finally, to Karen Orchard and the staff at the University of Georgia Press for their support in working with us through the intricacies of this collaboration.

The Authors

EMMIE SCHRADER ADAMS grew up in St. Paul, Minnesota. After five years alternately attending Harvard/Radcliffe, teaching high school in Kenya, and working for *Revolution Africaine*, an Algerian newspaper, she went to Mississippi in April 1964 to work for the Council of Federated Organizations, which was prepar-

ing for the Summer Project. Later, as a SNCC staff member in northeast Mississippi, she explored possibilities for drawing poor rural whites into the movement. In 1965 she moved north to produce a filmstrip about the Vietnam War. She lived in southern Vermont with an organic-vegetable-growing commune and then worked as a doctor's assistant in a New York abortion clinic. Emmie emigrated to Jamaica in 1971, where she married, became a Jamaican citizen, and reared four children. She and her husband, Dada Adams, farmed captured land in a squatter's community near Robin's Bay, where she served on the school board, was locally active in the People's National Party, and built and rented African-style huts to tourists. She is the author of *Understanding Jamaican Patois: An Introduction to Afro-Jamaican Grammar*. In 1992 she returned to Vermont's Northeast Kingdom, where she worked at odd jobs while the children pursued their education. She currently serves on the board of Northern Counties Health Care. *(Kwao Adams holding Malik Hastings, Agape Looper Adams, Paloma Adams, Richard Hastings behind Kedela Adams Hastings, Emmie Schrader Adams, and Dada Adams. Photograph by Travis Allen.)*

ELAINE DELOTT BAKER grew up on the outskirts of Boston in a second-generation Jewish working-class family. She spent the year between high school and college in Israel and entered Harvard/Radcliffe in 1961. In 1964 she went south to teach summer school at Tougaloo College and remained in Mississippi for a year, working with the Council of Federated Organizations. Elaine was instrumental in developing movement strategies related to welfare rights and worked with Panola County farmers to organize and  finance an okra cooperative that became a model for rural cooperatives in the black South. She was one of several movement women who authored the Waveland position paper on women, a seminal document in the emergence of second-wave feminism. After leaving Mississippi, she spent several years in the New York counterculture, where she married Columbus Baker, her lifelong companion. For the next twenty years she wrote grant applications and implemented community education projects in the Hispanic communities of rural Colorado. Elaine and her husband live in Denver near their two children and four grandchildren. She directs workforce initiatives for the Community College of Denver and continues to reflect, write, and lecture on education and social change. *(Photograph by Larry Laszlo.)*

JOAN C. BROWNING grew up on a small farm in rural Georgia. She went from picking two hundred pounds of cotton a day to volunteering with SNCC. The first in her immediate family to attend college, she was asked to leave Georgia State College for Women in Milledgeville in 1961 because she had worshiped at a black church. Thirty years later she completed her B.A. degree at West Virginia State College, a historically black institution. An Albany Freedom Rider, she worked in human relations  and antipoverty programs through the 1970s and was an organizer of the Federation of Southern Cooperatives. Now a freelance writer, lecturer, and development consultant living in the mountains of Greenbrier County, West Virginia, Joan actively supports public schools and libraries and programs for children and youth. She serves on the West Virginia Supreme Court of Appeals' Fatality Review Committee and the Governor's Race Initiative. *(Photograph by Bob Brown.)*

DOROTHY DAWSON BURLAGE was born into a family that had
lived in the South since the early 1700s. She attended the Univer-
sity of Texas, where she was part of the struggle against segregation
in the 1950s. As a graduate student at Harvard in the early 1960s,
she helped create Students for a Democratic Society and the
Northern Student Movement and led efforts in Boston to raise
money for SNCC. In 1962 she went to Atlanta to work for the
National Student Association Southern Project, where she coordinated race relations education programs on southern campuses and directed a voter
registration project in Raleigh, North Carolina. In 1964 she helped organize the
Southern Student Organizing Committee to work with southern whites on civil rights
and worked as a community organizer in the Anacostia area of Washington, D.C., from
1965 through 1968. She returned to Harvard in 1970, where she held a Woodrow Wilson Fellowship in women's studies and received a Ph.D. in psychology. She lives in
Newton, Massachusetts, where she practices child psychology privately and at the Harvard University Health Services.

CONSTANCE CURRY, whose parents came
from Ireland, grew up in Greensboro, North
Carolina. She graduated from Agnes Scott College, where she was president of the student
body and a member of Phi Beta Kappa. During her college years in the 1950s, she became
involved in the U.S. National Student Associa-
tion and its work for integration. After studying abroad as a Fulbright scholar and doing
graduate work at Columbia University, in 1959 she returned to Atlanta to work for NSA
in human relations and was the first white woman appointed to the executive committee of SNCC. From 1964 to 1975, as southern field representative for the American
Friends Service Committee, she organized in the white community toward peaceful
school desegregation in Mississippi and worked with black families who enrolled their
children in previously white schools. She was director of human services for the city of
Atlanta from 1975 to 1990 and earned a law degree in 1984. She is the author of *Silver
Rights* (Algonquin Books, 1995), which won the Lillian Smith Award, and coauthor
with Aaron Henry of *The Fire Ever Burning* (University Press of Mississippi, 2000). She
lives in Atlanta, Georgia. *(Constance Curry and Mae Bertha Carter of Silver Rights.
Photograph by Ann Curry.)*

THERESA DEL POZZO, the child of second-generation Italian immigrants, grew up
in the northeast Bronx. In 1960, while at the
University of Wisconsin, she participated in
demonstrations in support of the southern
student sit-ins. She was an active member of
the anti-HUAC and pro–civil rights Liberal
Study Group of the National Student Asso-

ciation and attended the Port Huron organizing meeting of Students for a Democratic
Society. In the summer of 1963, she worked in the Harlem Education Project as part
of the Northern Student Movement. At Wisconsin she took part in the early anti–
Vietnam War demonstrations and set up a Friends of SNCC chapter, coordinating educational and fund-raising activities in support of the 1964 Democratic Convention.
During late 1964 and 1965, she worked for SNCC in Mississippi on MFDP's congressional
challenge to the seating of the Mississippi representatives. After leaving the South,
Theresa became a record producer and tour organizer representing jazz, reggae, and
pop musicians. She now lives in Vermont, where she works on her twenty-five-year-old
perennial flower garden and is an initiator of the Catamount Jazz Society. She is active
in the Vermont Progressive Party and on the organizing committee for the 2001 Peoples
Convention of the Independent Progressive Political Network. *(Theresa Del Pozzo and
her mother, Marie Del Pozzo.)*

CASEY HAYDEN is a fourth-generation Texan from
a southern family rooted in pre-Revolutionary Virginia. She combated segregation at the University
of Texas in Austin in the 1950s and joined the sit-
in movement there in 1960. Working with SNCC
through 1965, she organized political insurgency as
well as support, literacy, and black cultural pro-

gramming. Casey created race relations workshops across the South for the National
Student YWCA and helped create SDS. Since 1971 she has staffed grassroots social justice
and countercultural institutions ranging from an alternative weekly newspaper in New
York City to the Integral Yoga Institute in San Francisco. She is married to Episcopal
priest and community organizer Paul Buckwalter and is the mother of two. She currently lectures, writes, and builds a permaculture landscape in Tucson, Arizona. Her
writing was published most recently in *Being Bodies: Buddhist Women on the Paradox
of Embodiment* (Shambhala, 1997). *(Photograph by Rosie Boyce.)*

PENNY PATCH, who was born in New York City in 1943, spent most of her childhood in Manchuria, Czechoslovakia, and Germany and was raised by parents who had a deep commitment to social justice. She attended Swarthmore College for a year before dropping out, at the age of eighteen, to join the civil rights movement. She worked for SNCC from 1962 to 1965 in Georgia and Mississippi and was the first white woman to work in a SNCC field project. Holding a degree from the Frontier School of Midwifery in Kentucky, she works as a nurse-midwife in central Vermont and has long been active in maternal-child health. She works with "One by One," an organization dedicated to fostering dialogue between children of Holocaust survivors and children of German perpetrators and bystanders. She also speaks in area schools on her experiences in the southern freedom movement. She and her family make their home in Lyndonville, Vermont. *(Penny Patch, David Martin, Seth Williams, and Elizabeth Martin. Photograph by Jane Critchlow.)*

SUE THRASHER grew up on a small family farm in West Tennessee. Her father was a farmer and a carpenter and her mother worked in a shoe factory. She was drawn into the movement through the local chapter of SNCC while attending college in Nashville, Tennessee, in the early 1960s. She was a founder of the Southern Student Organizing Committee, an organization devoted to working with white college students on issues of civil rights, and a founder and co-director of the Institute for Southern Studies, which publishes *Southern Exposure*. While at the institute she collected oral histories of southern progressive movements and served as a special editor of *No More Moanin': Voices of Southern Struggle*. In 1978 Sue joined the staff of the Highlander Research and Education Center in Knoxville, Tennessee, and subsequently traveled in Scandinavia and Latin America to study international adult education. She earned a doctorate in education at the University of Massachusetts Amherst and continues to work in Amherst with the Five College Consortium. *(Photograph by Joan Browning.)*

Index